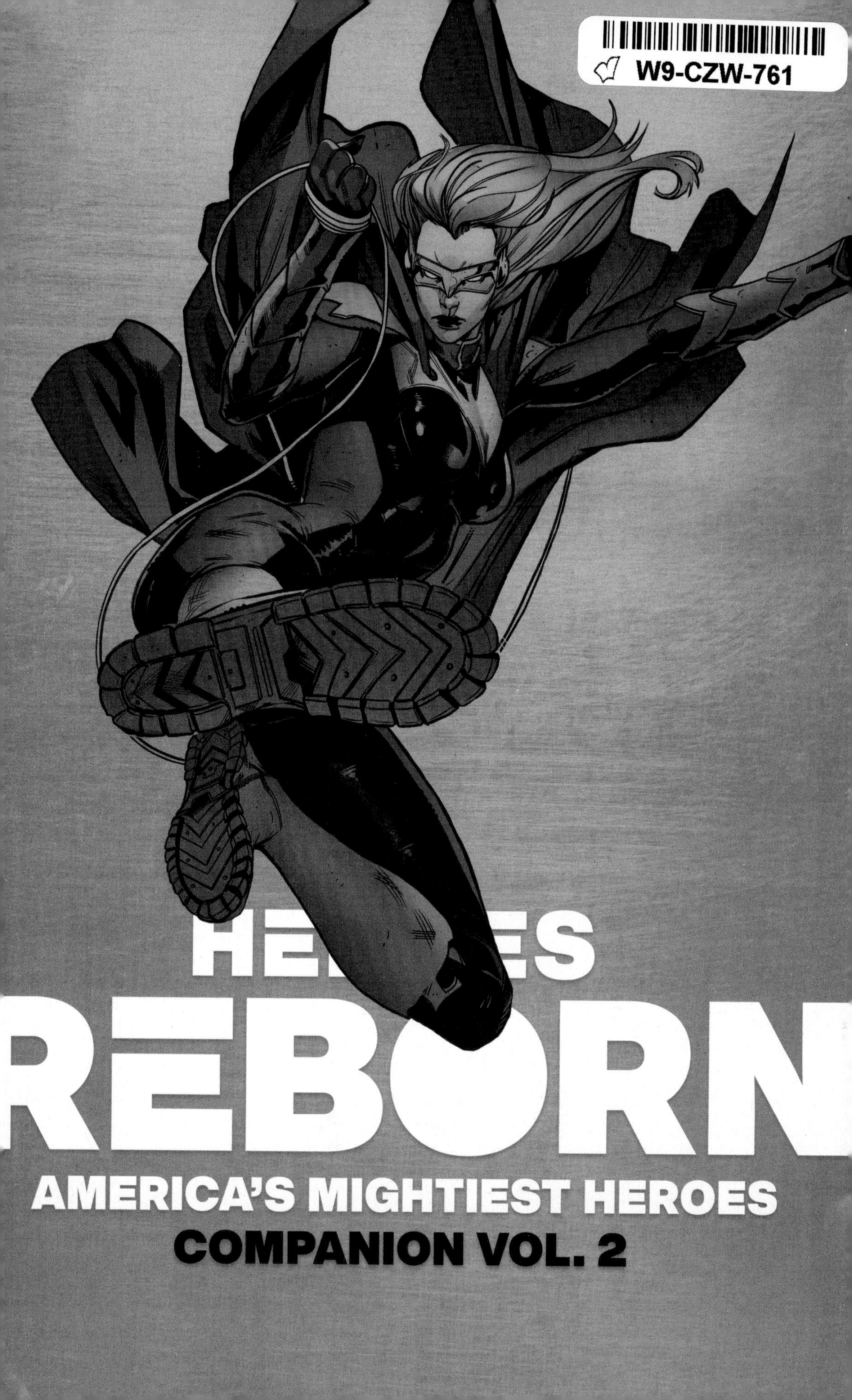

HEROES REBORN

AMERICA'S MIGHTIEST HEROES

COMPANION VOL. 2

HEROES

AMERICA'S MIGHTIEST HEROES

COMPANION VOL. 2

HEROES REBORN: SQUADRON SAVAGE

ETHAN **SACKS** WRITER

LUCA **PIZZARI** PENCILER

CARLOS **LOPEZ** COLOR ARTIST

VC's TRAVIS **LANHAM** LETTERER

STEPHEN **SEGOVIA**
& ESPEN **GRUNDETJERN** COVER ART

**HEROES REBORN:
MARVEL DOUBLE ACTION**

TIM **SEELEY** WRITER

DAN **JURGENS** PENCILER

SCOTT **HANNA** INKER

CHRIS **SOTOMAYOR**
COLOR ARTIST

VC's CORY **PETIT** LETTERER

DAVE **JOHNSON** COVER ART

JENNIFER **GRÜNWALD** COLLECTION EDITOR
DANIEL **KIRCHHOFFER** ASSISTANT EDITOR
MAIA **LOY** ASSISTANT MANAGING EDITOR
LISA **MONTALBANO** ASSISTANT MANAGING EDITOR
JEFF **YOUNGQUIST** VP PRODUCTION & SPECIAL PROJECTS
JAY **BOWEN** BOOK DESIGNER
DAVID **GABRIEL** SVP PRINT, SALES & MARKETING
C.B. **CEBULSKI** EDITOR IN CHIEF

HEROES REBORN: AMERICA'S MIGHTIEST HEROES COMPANION VOL. 2. Contains material originally published in magazine form as HEROES REBORN: SQUADRON SAVAGE (2021) #1, HEROES REBORN: MARVEL DOUBLE ACTION (2021) #1, HEROES REBORN: AMERICAN KNIGHTS (2021) #1, HEROES REBORN: NIGHT-GWEN (2021) #1 and HEROES REBORN: WEAPON X & FINAL FLIGHT (2021) #1. First printing 2021. ISBN 978-1-302-93114-8. Published by MARVEL WORLDWIDE, INC., a subsidiary of MARVEL ENTERTAINMENT, LLC. OFFICE OF PUBLICATION: 1290 Avenue of the Americas, New York, NY 10104. © 2021 MARVEL No similarity between any of the names, characters, persons, and/or institutions in this magazine with those of any living or dead person or institution is intended, and any such similarity which may exist is purely coincidental. **Printed in Canada.** KEVIN FEIGE, Chief Creative Officer; DAN BUCKLEY, President, Marvel Entertainment; JOE QUESADA, EVP & Creative Director; DAVID BOGART, Associate Publisher & SVP of Talent Affairs; TOM BREVOORT, VP, Executive Editor; NICK LOWE, Executive Editor, VP of Content, Digital Publishing; DAVID GABRIEL, VP of Print & Digital Publishing; JEFF YOUNGQUIST, VP of Production & Special Projects; ALEX MORALES, Director of Publishing Operations; DAN EDINGTON, Managing Editor; RICKEY PURDIN, Director of Talent Relations; JENNIFER GRÜNWALD, Senior Editor, Special Projects; SUSAN CRESPI, Production Manager; STAN LEE, Chairman Emeritus. For information regarding advertising in Marvel Comics or on Marvel.com, please contact Vit DeBellis, Custom Solutions & Integrated Advertising Manager, at vdebellis@marvel.com. For Marvel subscription inquiries, please call 888-511-5480. **Manufactured between 7/2/2021 and 8/3/2021 by SOLISCO PRINTERS, SCOTT, QC, CANADA.**

10 9 8 7 6 5 4 3 2 1

IN MEPHISTO WE TRUST

REBORN

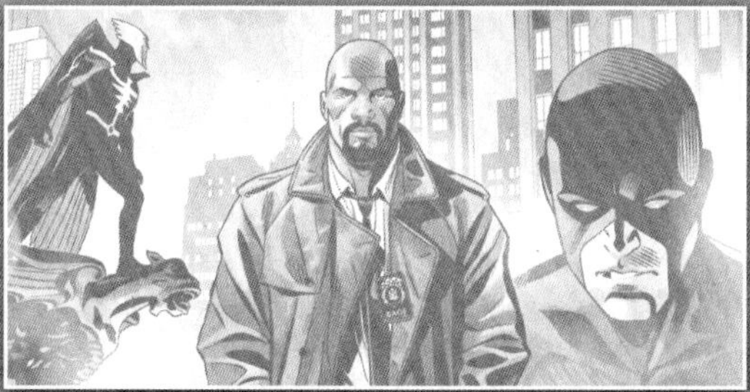

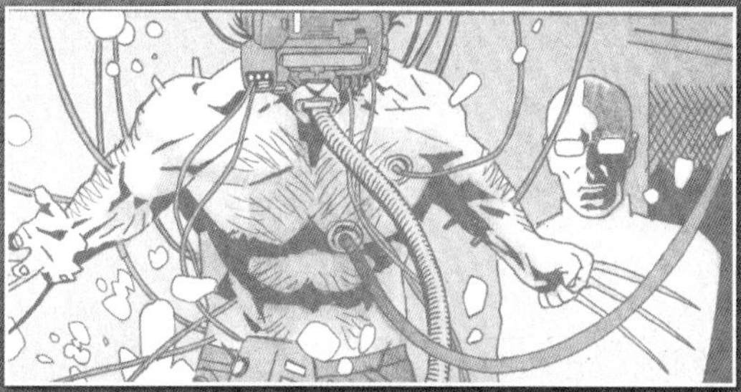

HEROES REBORN: AMERICAN KNIGHTS

PAUL **GRIST** WRITER

CHRIS **ALLEN** PENCILER

CHRIS **ALLEN**
WITH MARC **DEERING** INKERS

GURU-eFX COLOR ARTIST

VC's CORY **PETIT** LETTERER

CHRIS **SPROUSE**, KARL **STORY**
& NEERAJ **MENON** COVER ART

**HEROES REBORN:
WEAPON X & FINAL FLIGHT**

ED **BRISSON** WRITER

ROLAND **BOSCHI** ARTIST

CHRIS **O'HALLORAN**
COLOR ARTIST

VC's CORY **PETIT** LETTERER

TONY **DANIEL** & MARCELO **MAIOLO**
COVER ART

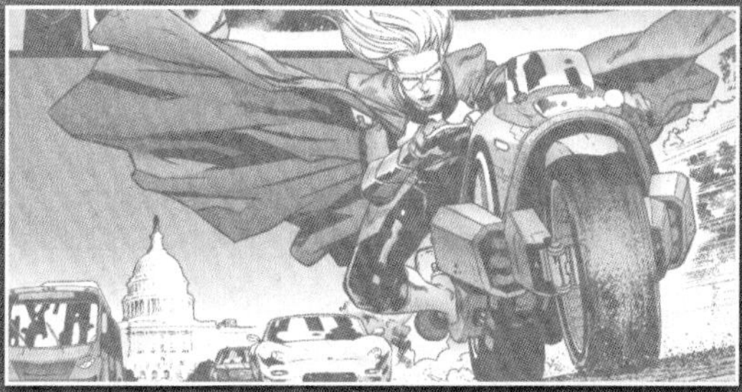

HEROES REBORN: NIGHT-GWEN

VITA **AYALA** WRITER

FARID **KARAMI** ARTIST

ERICK **ARCINIEGA**
COLOR ARTIST

VC's CORY **PETIT** LETTERER

DAVID **NAKAYAMA** COVER ART

MARTIN **BIRO**, DARREN **SHAN**
& SARAH **BRUNSTAD** EDITORS

TOM **BREVOORT** EXECUTIVE EDITOR

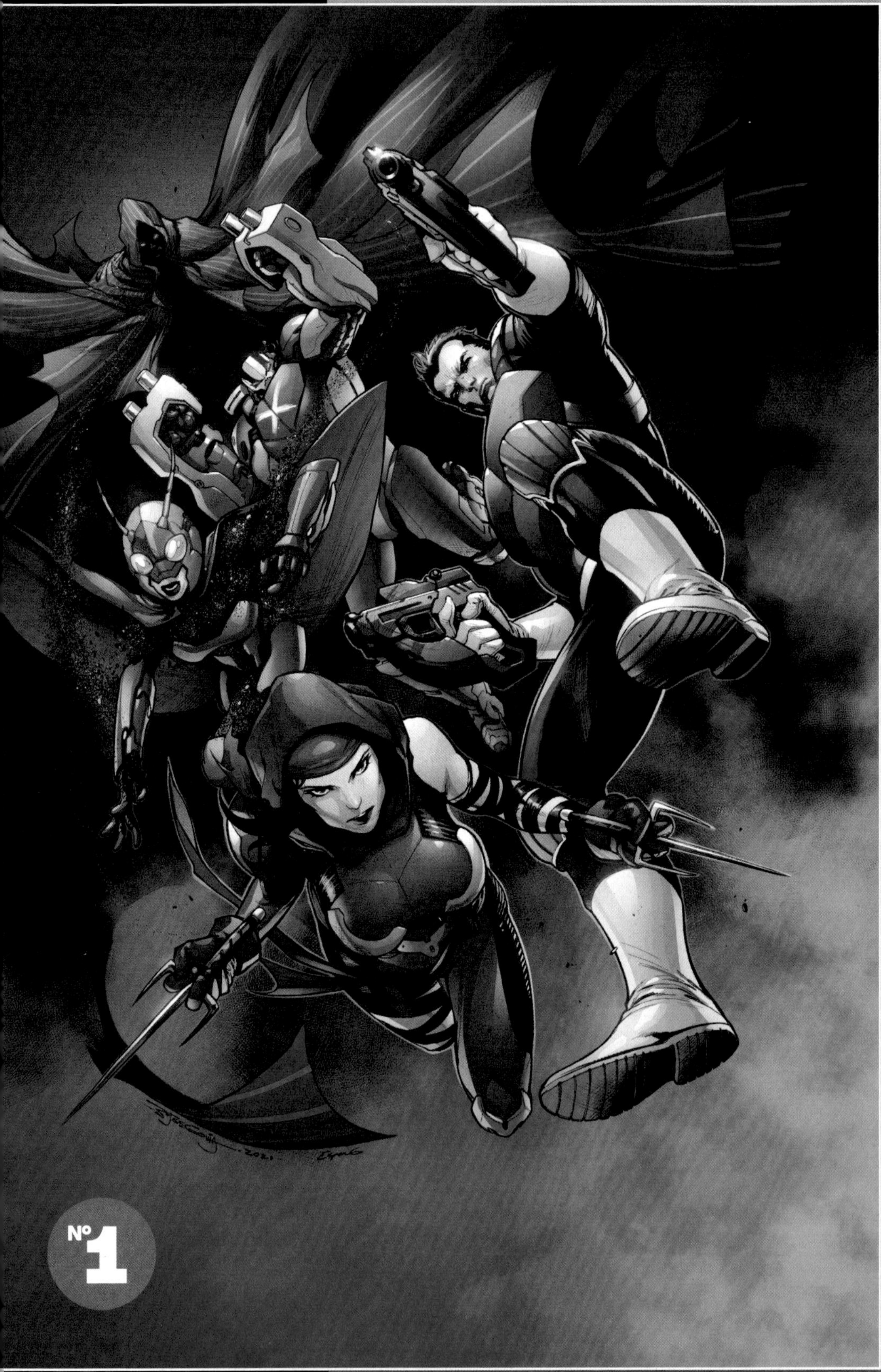
Nº 1

SQUADRON SAVAGE

"THE QUEEN'S SACRIFICE"

In a world in which the Avengers never existed, the Squadron Supreme
of America are and have always been Earth's Mightiest Heroes!

SQUADRON
SAVAGE

"THE QUEEN'S SACRIFICE"

ETHAN **SACKS** WRITER

LUCA **PIZZARI** ARTIST

CARLOS **LOPEZ** COLOR ARTIST

VC's TRAVIS **LANHAM** LETTERER

STEPHEN **SEGOVIA** & ESPEN **GRUNDETJERN** COVER ARTISTS

DAVID **BLATT** VARIANT COVER ARTIST

JAY **BOWEN** GRAPHIC DESIGN

MARTIN **BIRO** EDITOR

TOM **BREVOORT** EXECUTIVE EDITOR

C.B. **CEBULSKI** EDITOR IN CHIEF

HEROES
REBORN

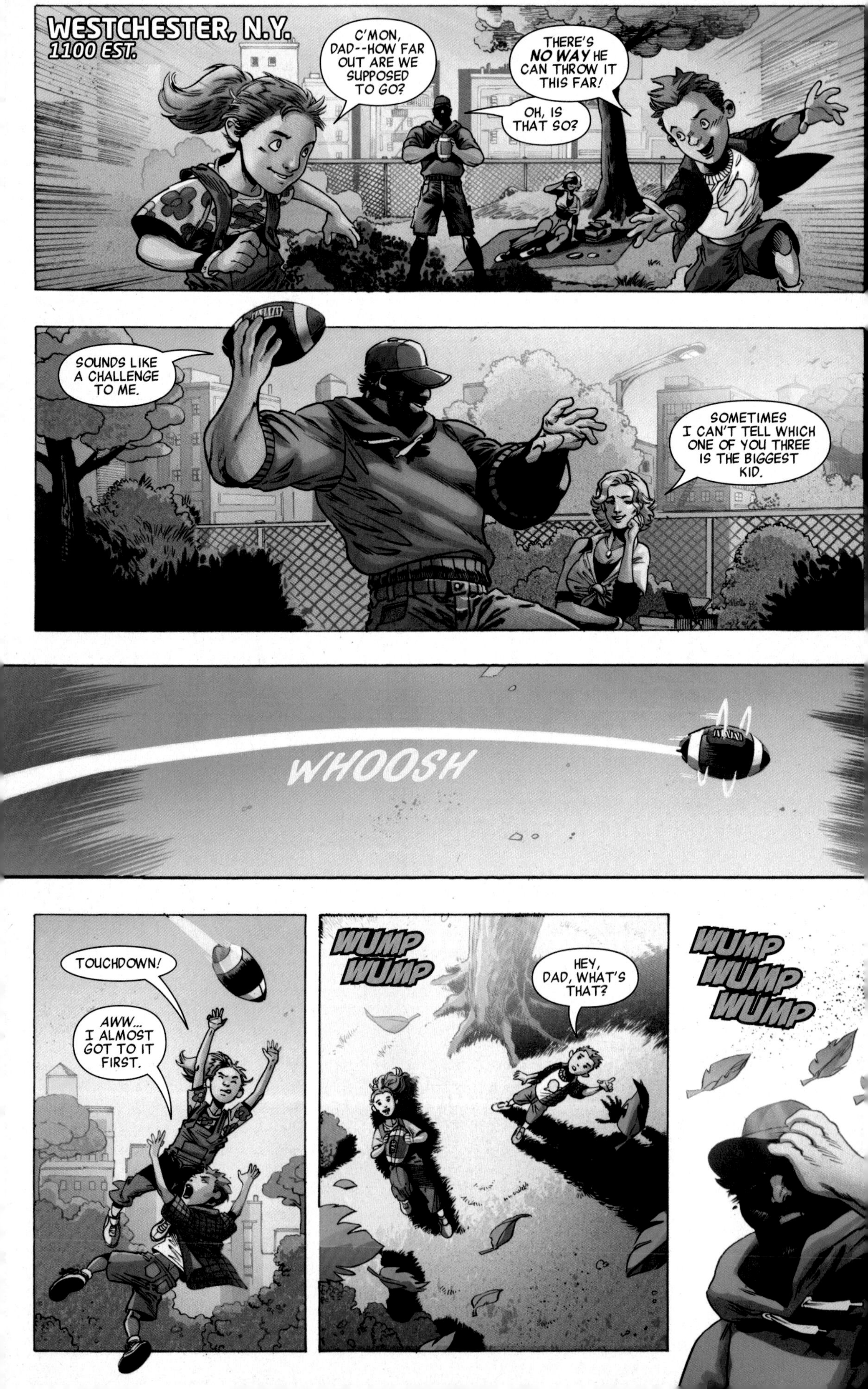
WESTCHESTER, N.Y.
1100 EST.
C'MON, DAD--HOW FAR OUT ARE WE SUPPOSED TO GO?
THERE'S NO WAY HE CAN THROW IT THIS FAR!
OH, IS THAT SO?
SOUNDS LIKE A CHALLENGE TO ME.
SOMETIMES I CAN'T TELL WHICH ONE OF YOU THREE IS THE BIGGEST KID.
WHOOSH
TOUCHDOWN!
AWW... I ALMOST GOT TO IT FIRST.
WUMP WUMP
HEY, DAD, WHAT'S THAT?
WUMP WUMP WUMP

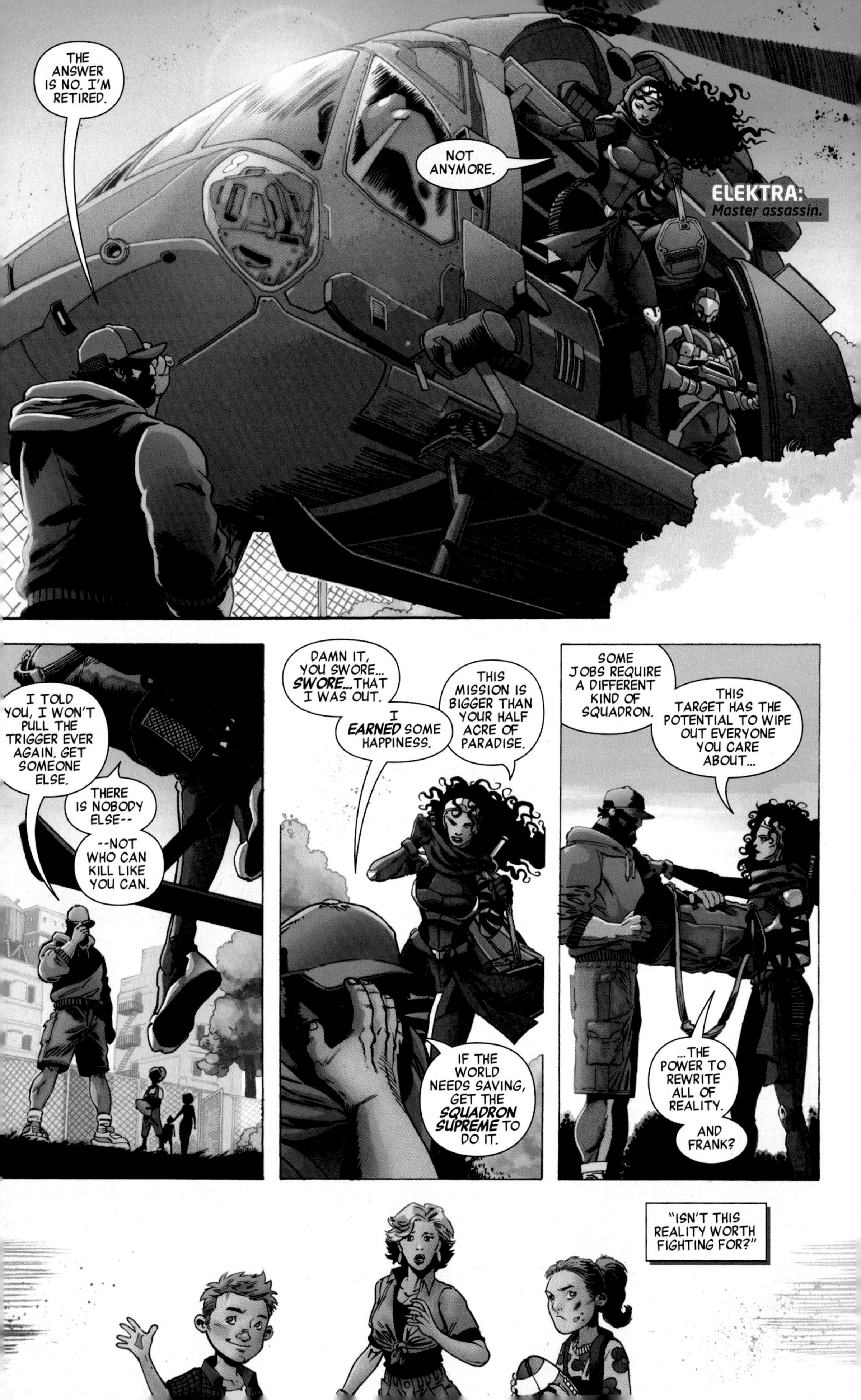
THE ANSWER IS NO. I'M RETIRED.
NOT ANYMORE.
ELEKTRA: Master assassin.
I TOLD YOU, I WON'T PULL THE TRIGGER EVER AGAIN. GET SOMEONE ELSE.
THERE IS NOBODY ELSE--
--NOT WHO CAN KILL LIKE YOU CAN.
DAMN IT, YOU SWORE... SWORE...THAT I WAS OUT.
I EARNED SOME HAPPINESS.
THIS MISSION IS BIGGER THAN YOUR HALF ACRE OF PARADISE.
IF THE WORLD NEEDS SAVING, GET THE SQUADRON SUPREME TO DO IT.
SOME JOBS REQUIRE A DIFFERENT KIND OF SQUADRON.
THIS TARGET HAS THE POTENTIAL TO WIPE OUT EVERYONE YOU CARE ABOUT...
...THE POWER TO REWRITE ALL OF REALITY.
AND FRANK?
"ISN'T THIS REALITY WORTH FIGHTING FOR?"

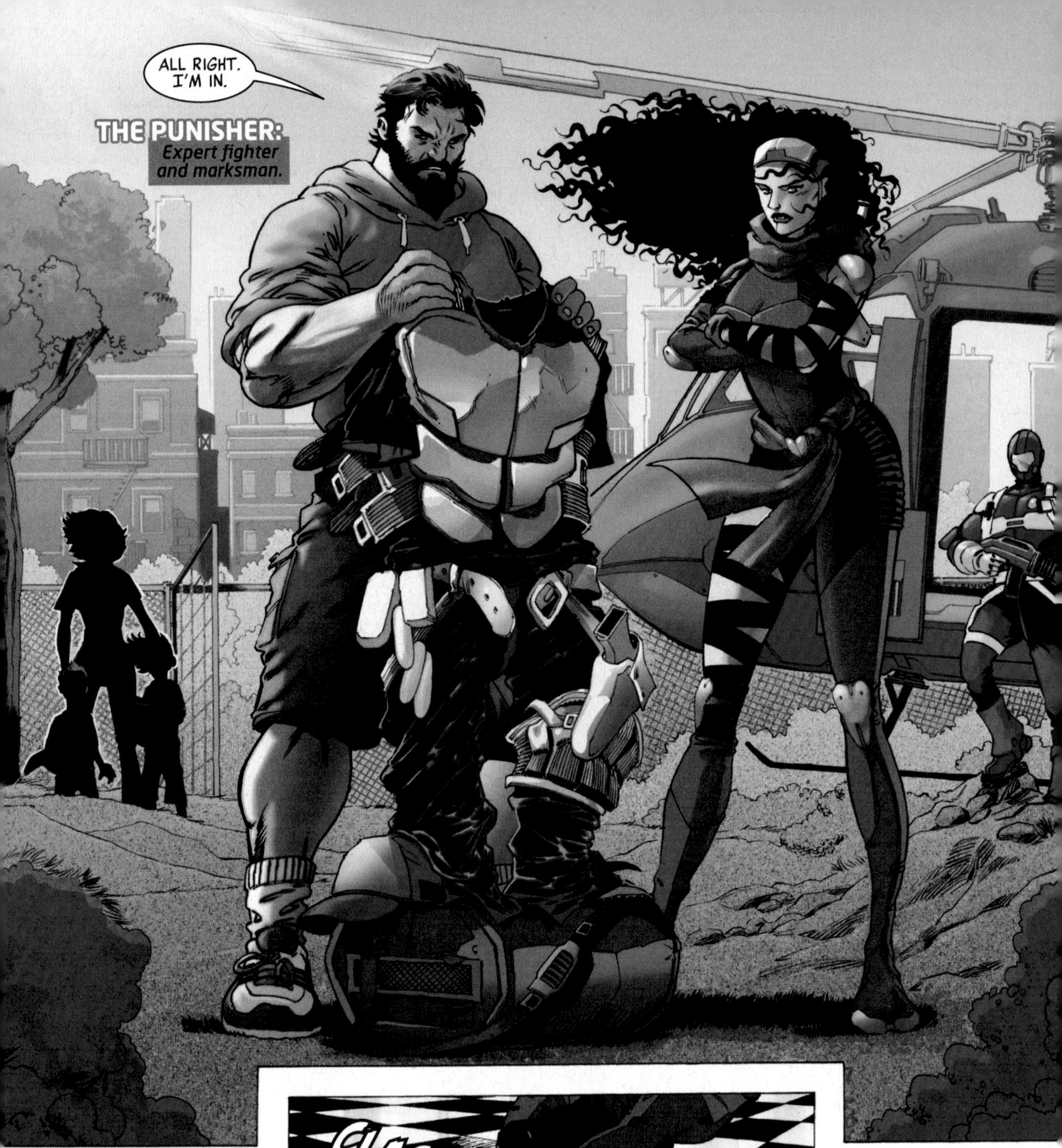
ALL RIGHT. I'M IN.
THE PUNISHER:
Expert fighter and marksman.

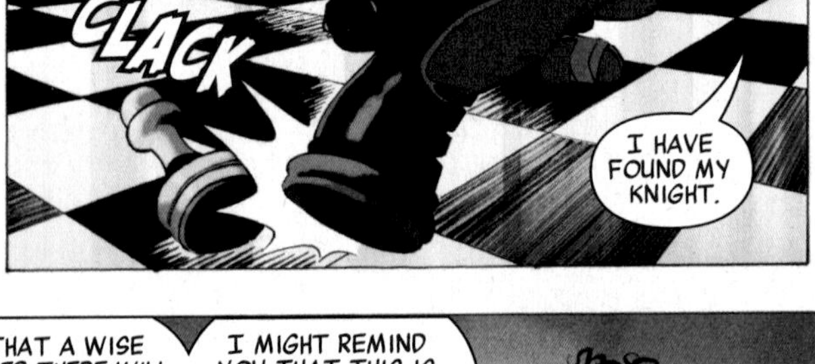
CLACK
I HAVE FOUND MY KNIGHT.

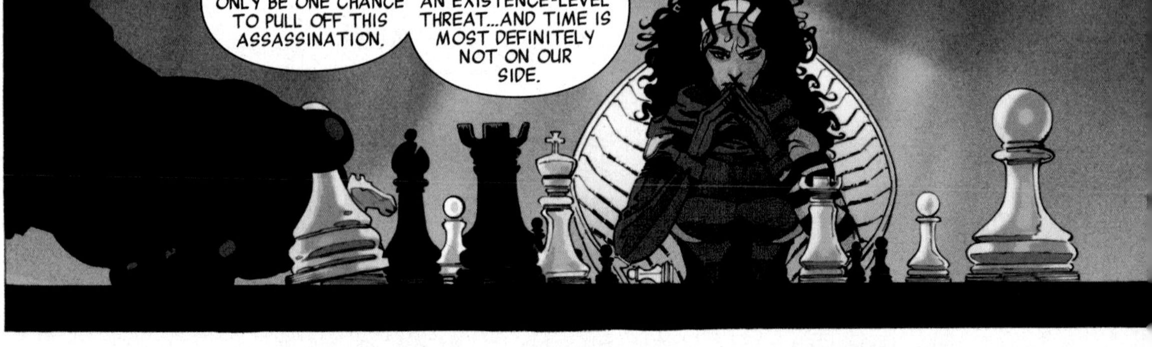
IS THAT A WISE CHOICE? THERE WILL ONLY BE ONE CHANCE TO PULL OFF THIS ASSASSINATION.
I MIGHT REMIND YOU THAT THIS IS AN EXISTENCE-LEVEL THREAT...AND TIME IS MOST DEFINITELY NOT ON OUR SIDE.

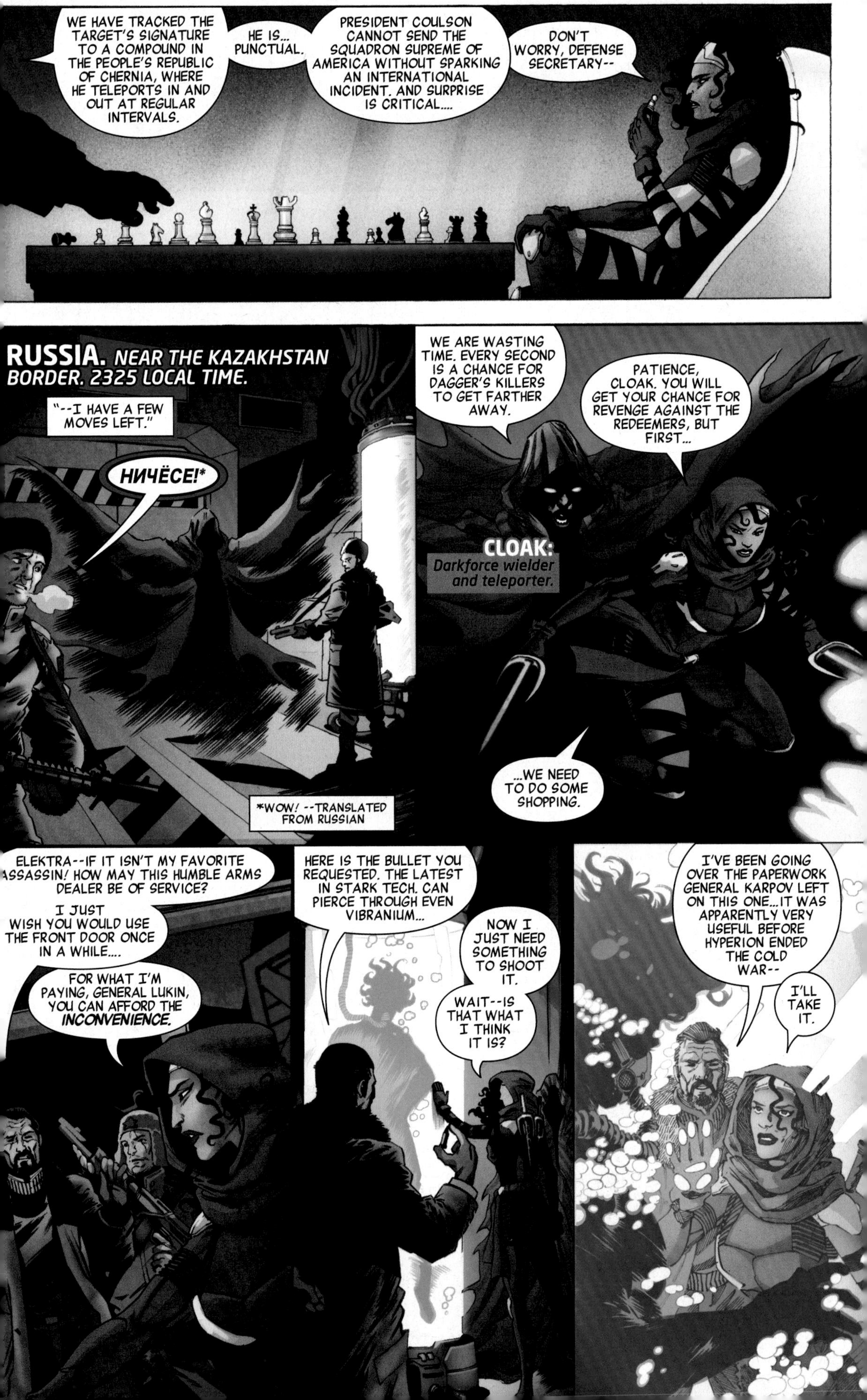
WE HAVE TRACKED THE TARGET'S SIGNATURE TO A COMPOUND IN THE PEOPLE'S REPUBLIC OF CHERNIA, WHERE HE TELEPORTS IN AND OUT AT REGULAR INTERVALS.
HE IS... PUNCTUAL.
PRESIDENT COULSON CANNOT SEND THE SQUADRON SUPREME OF AMERICA WITHOUT SPARKING AN INTERNATIONAL INCIDENT. AND SURPRISE IS CRITICAL....
DON'T WORRY, DEFENSE SECRETARY--
RUSSIA. NEAR THE KAZAKHSTAN BORDER. 2325 LOCAL TIME.
"--I HAVE A FEW MOVES LEFT."
НИЧЁСЕ!*
*WOW! --TRANSLATED FROM RUSSIAN
WE ARE WASTING TIME. EVERY SECOND IS A CHANCE FOR DAGGER'S KILLERS TO GET FARTHER AWAY.
PATIENCE, CLOAK. YOU WILL GET YOUR CHANCE FOR REVENGE AGAINST THE REDEEMERS, BUT FIRST...
CLOAK: Darkforce wielder and teleporter.
...WE NEED TO DO SOME SHOPPING.
ELEKTRA--IF IT ISN'T MY FAVORITE ASSASSIN! HOW MAY THIS HUMBLE ARMS DEALER BE OF SERVICE?
I JUST WISH YOU WOULD USE THE FRONT DOOR ONCE IN A WHILE....
FOR WHAT I'M PAYING, GENERAL LUKIN, YOU CAN AFFORD THE INCONVENIENCE.
HERE IS THE BULLET YOU REQUESTED. THE LATEST IN STARK TECH. CAN PIERCE THROUGH EVEN VIBRANIUM...
NOW I JUST NEED SOMETHING TO SHOOT IT.
WAIT--IS THAT WHAT I THINK IT IS?
I'VE BEEN GOING OVER THE PAPERWORK GENERAL KARPOV LEFT ON THIS ONE...IT WAS APPARENTLY VERY USEFUL BEFORE HYPERION ENDED THE COLD WAR--
I'LL TAKE IT.

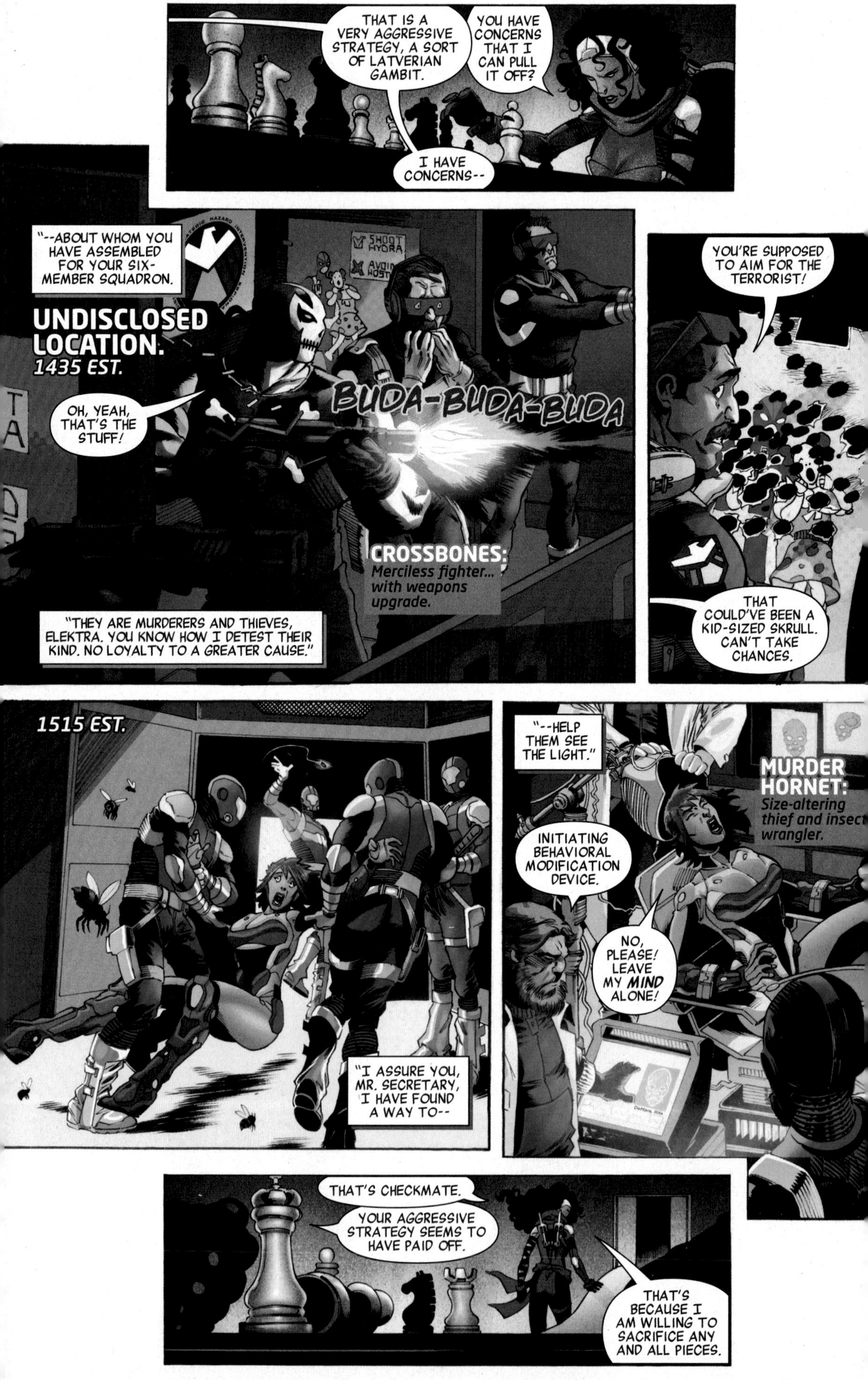
THAT IS A VERY AGGRESSIVE STRATEGY, A SORT OF LATVERIAN GAMBIT.
YOU HAVE CONCERNS THAT I CAN PULL IT OFF?
I HAVE CONCERNS--
"--ABOUT WHOM YOU HAVE ASSEMBLED FOR YOUR SIX-MEMBER SQUADRON.
UNDISCLOSED LOCATION.
1435 EST.
SHOOT HYDRA
AVOID HOST
OH, YEAH, THAT'S THE STUFF!
BUDA-BUDA-BUDA
CROSSBONES:
Merciless fighter... with weapons upgrade.
"THEY ARE MURDERERS AND THIEVES, ELEKTRA. YOU KNOW HOW I DETEST THEIR KIND. NO LOYALTY TO A GREATER CAUSE."
YOU'RE SUPPOSED TO AIM FOR THE TERRORIST!
THAT COULD'VE BEEN A KID-SIZED SKRULL. CAN'T TAKE CHANCES.
1515 EST.
"I ASSURE YOU, MR. SECRETARY, I HAVE FOUND A WAY TO--
"--HELP THEM SEE THE LIGHT."
MURDER HORNET:
Size-altering thief and insect wrangler.
INITIATING BEHAVIORAL MODIFICATION DEVICE.
NO, PLEASE! LEAVE MY MIND ALONE!
THAT'S CHECKMATE.
YOUR AGGRESSIVE STRATEGY SEEMS TO HAVE PAID OFF.
THAT'S BECAUSE I AM WILLING TO SACRIFICE ANY AND ALL PIECES.

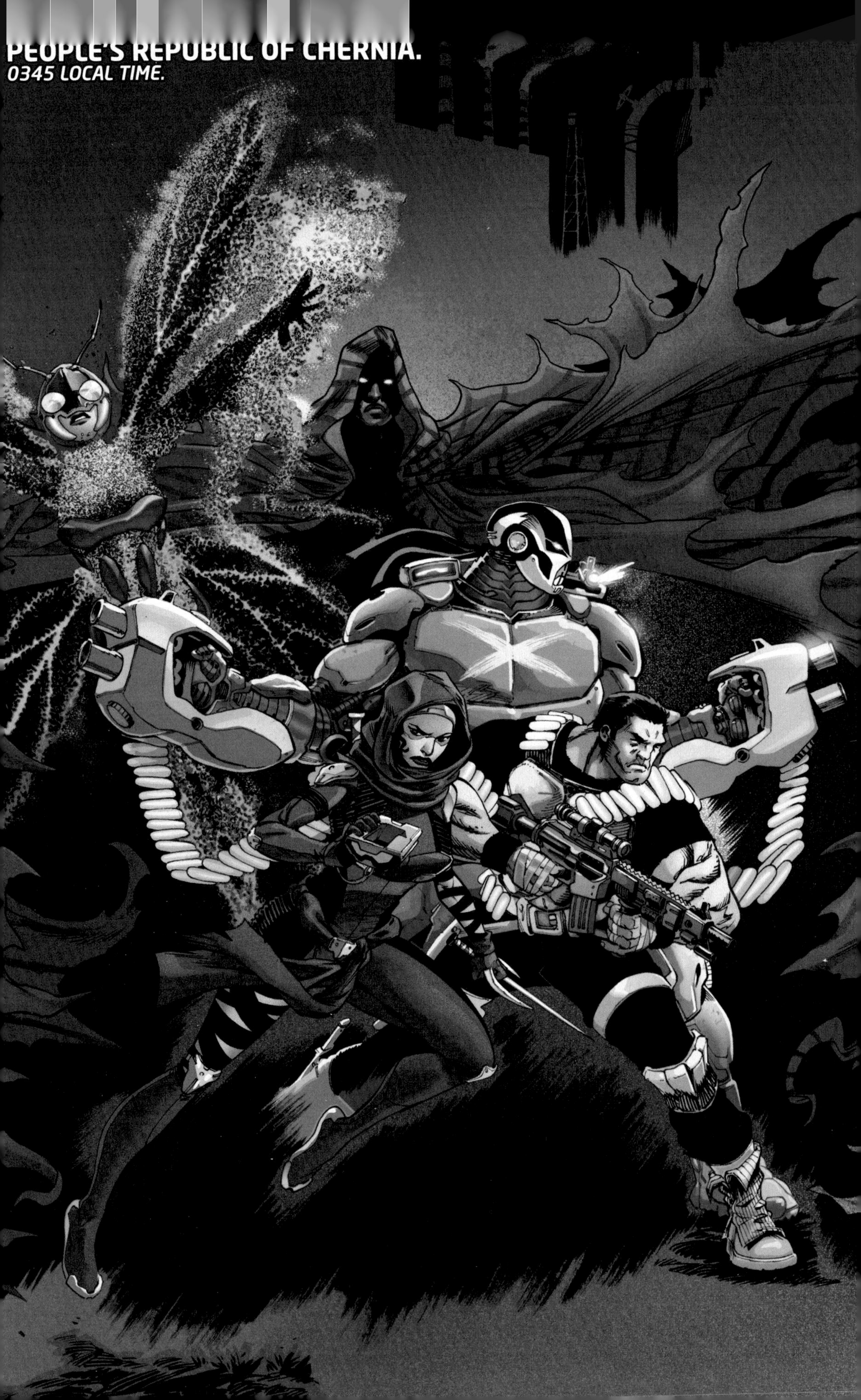
PEOPLE'S REPUBLIC OF CHERNIA.
0345 LOCAL TIME.

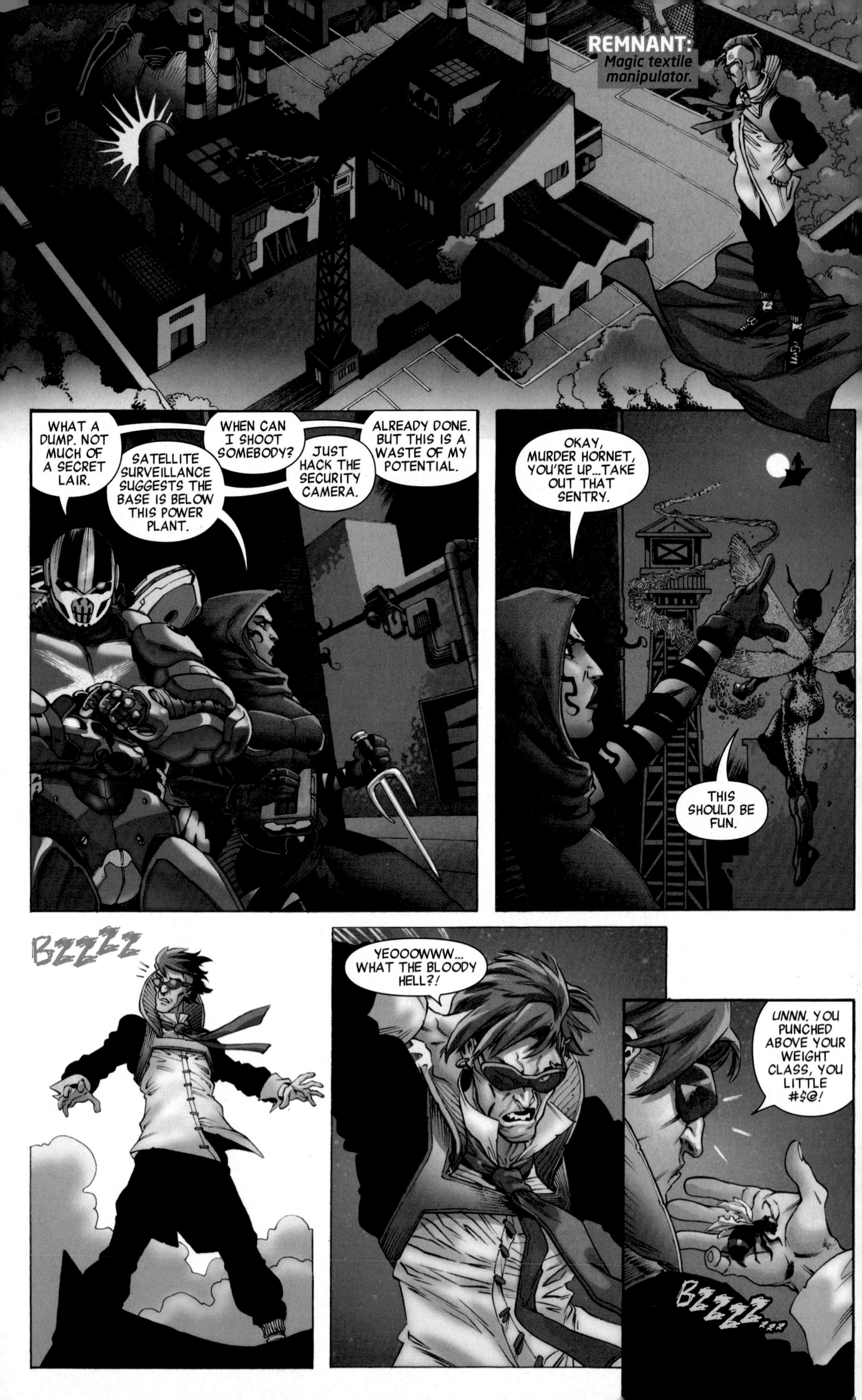
REMNANT:
Magic textile manipulator.
WHAT A DUMP. NOT MUCH OF A SECRET LAIR.
SATELLITE SURVEILLANCE SUGGESTS THE BASE IS BELOW THIS POWER PLANT.
WHEN CAN I SHOOT SOMEBODY?
JUST HACK THE SECURITY CAMERA.
ALREADY DONE. BUT THIS IS A WASTE OF MY POTENTIAL.
OKAY, MURDER HORNET, YOU'RE UP...TAKE OUT THAT SENTRY.
THIS SHOULD BE FUN.
BZZZZ
YEOOOWWW... WHAT THE BLOODY HELL?!
UNNN. YOU PUNCHED ABOVE YOUR WEIGHT CLASS, YOU LITTLE #$@!
BZZZZZ...

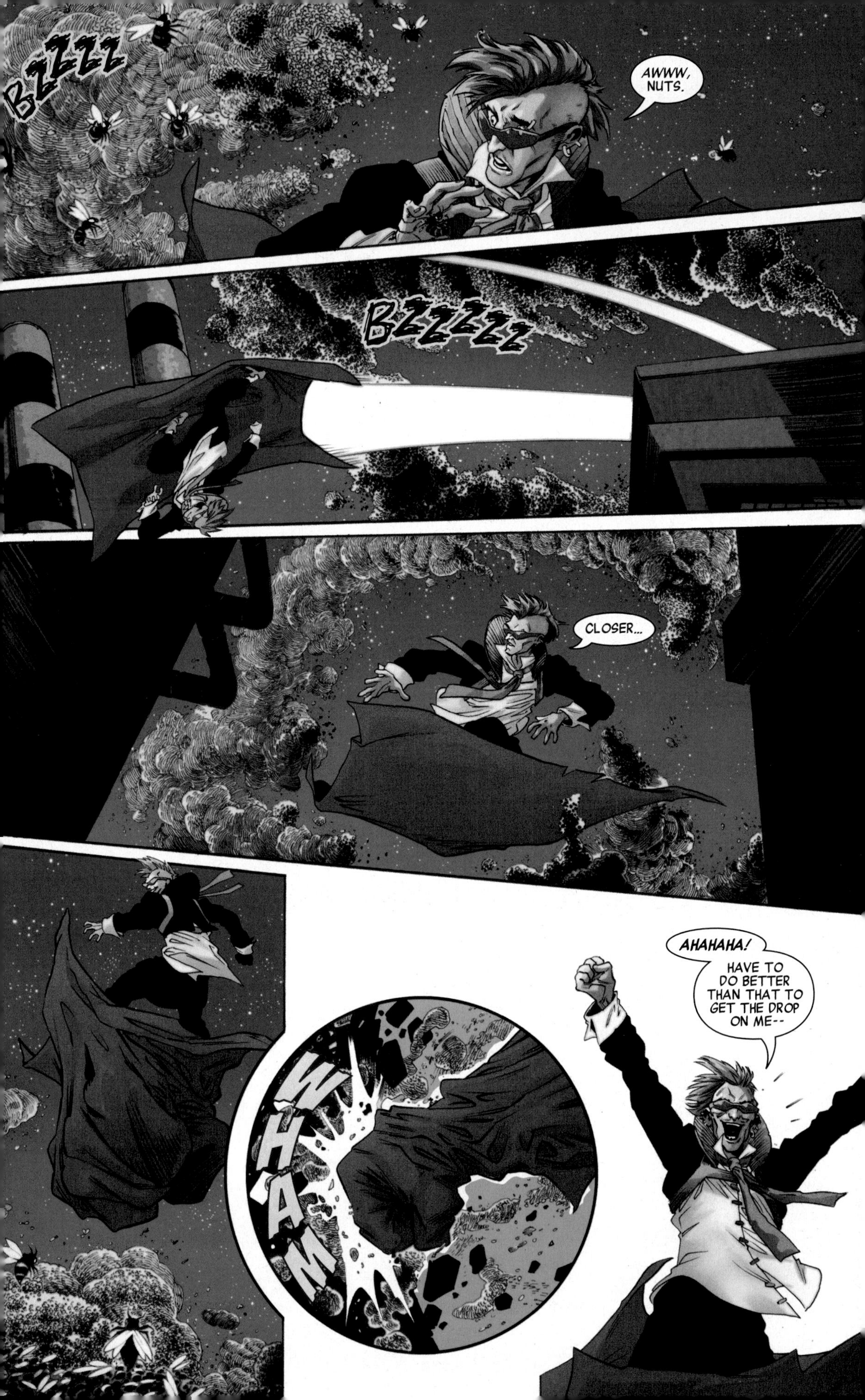
BZZZZZ
AWWW, NUTS.
BZZZZZZ
CLOSER...
WHAM
AHAHAHA!
HAVE TO DO BETTER THAN THAT TO GET THE DROP ON ME--

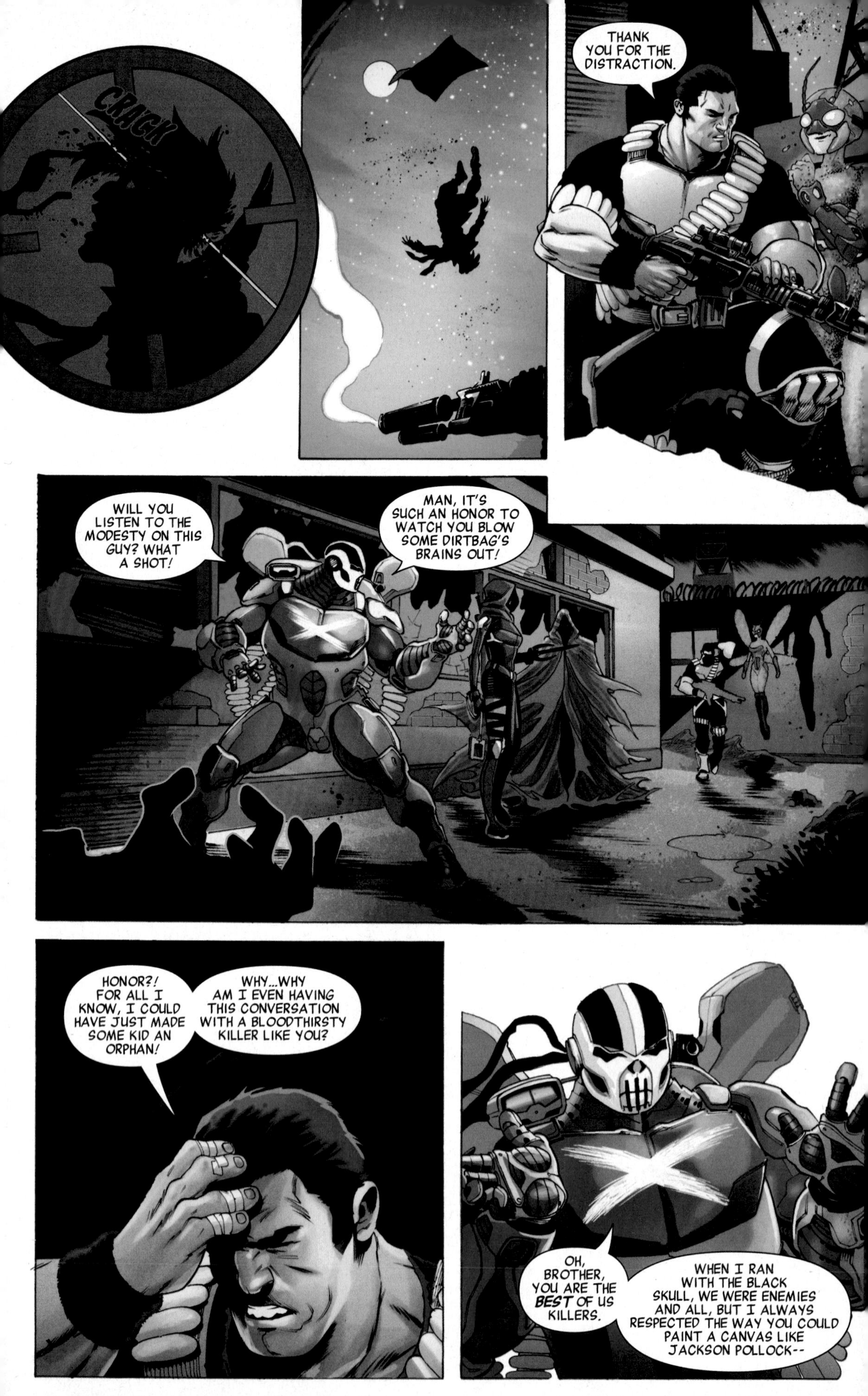
CRACK
THANK YOU FOR THE DISTRACTION.
WILL YOU LISTEN TO THE MODESTY ON THIS GUY? WHAT A SHOT!
MAN, IT'S SUCH AN HONOR TO WATCH YOU BLOW SOME DIRTBAG'S BRAINS OUT!
HONOR?! FOR ALL I KNOW, I COULD HAVE JUST MADE SOME KID AN ORPHAN!
WHY...WHY AM I EVEN HAVING THIS CONVERSATION WITH A BLOODTHIRSTY KILLER LIKE YOU?
OH, BROTHER, YOU ARE THE *BEST* OF US KILLERS.
WHEN I RAN WITH THE BLACK SKULL, WE WERE ENEMIES AND ALL, BUT I ALWAYS RESPECTED THE WAY YOU COULD PAINT A CANVAS LIKE JACKSON POLLOCK--

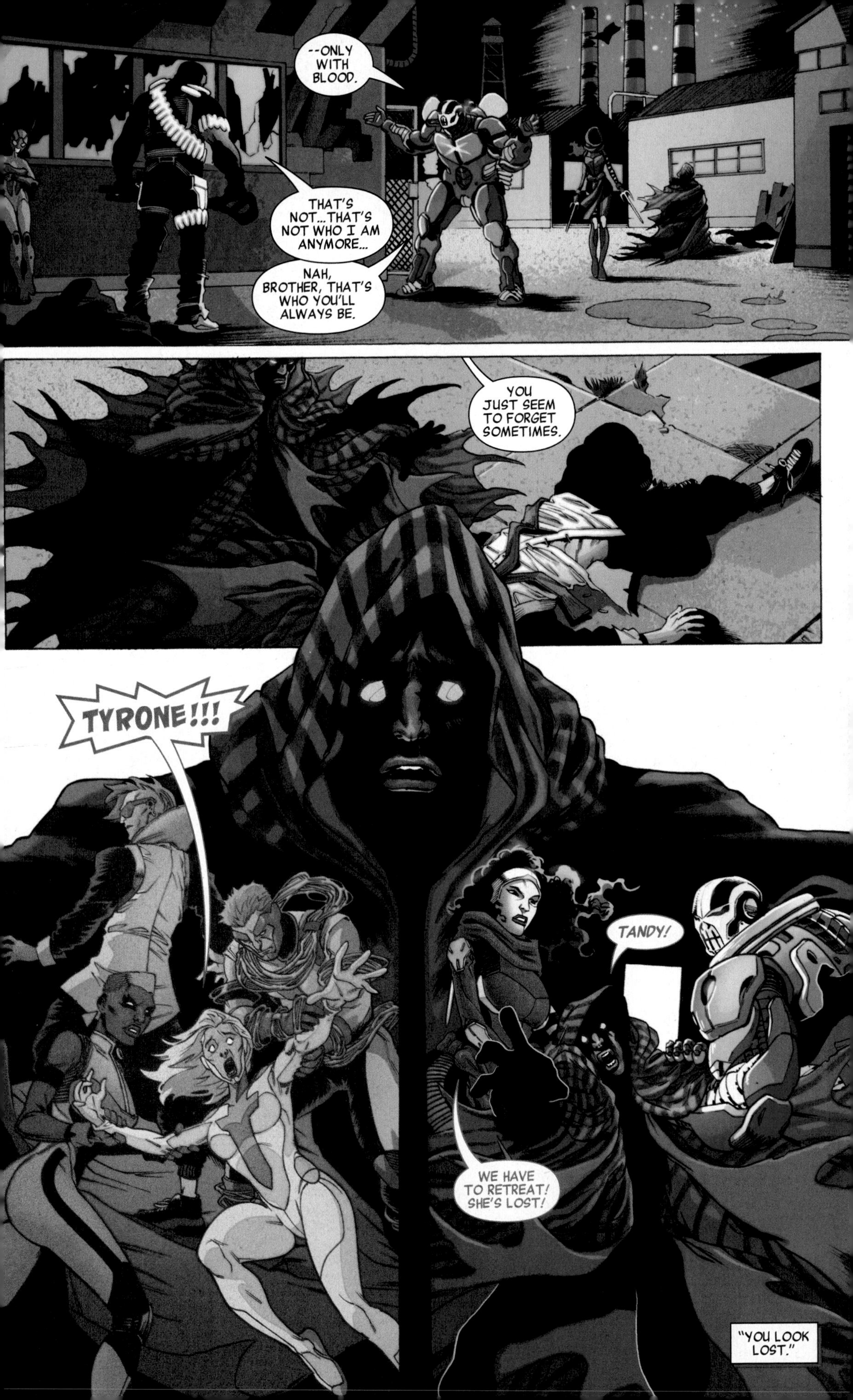
--ONLY WITH BLOOD.
THAT'S NOT...THAT'S NOT WHO I AM ANYMORE...
NAH, BROTHER, THAT'S WHO YOU'LL ALWAYS BE.
YOU JUST SEEM TO FORGET SOMETIMES.
TYRONE!!!
TANDY!
WE HAVE TO RETREAT! SHE'S LOST!
"YOU LOOK LOST."

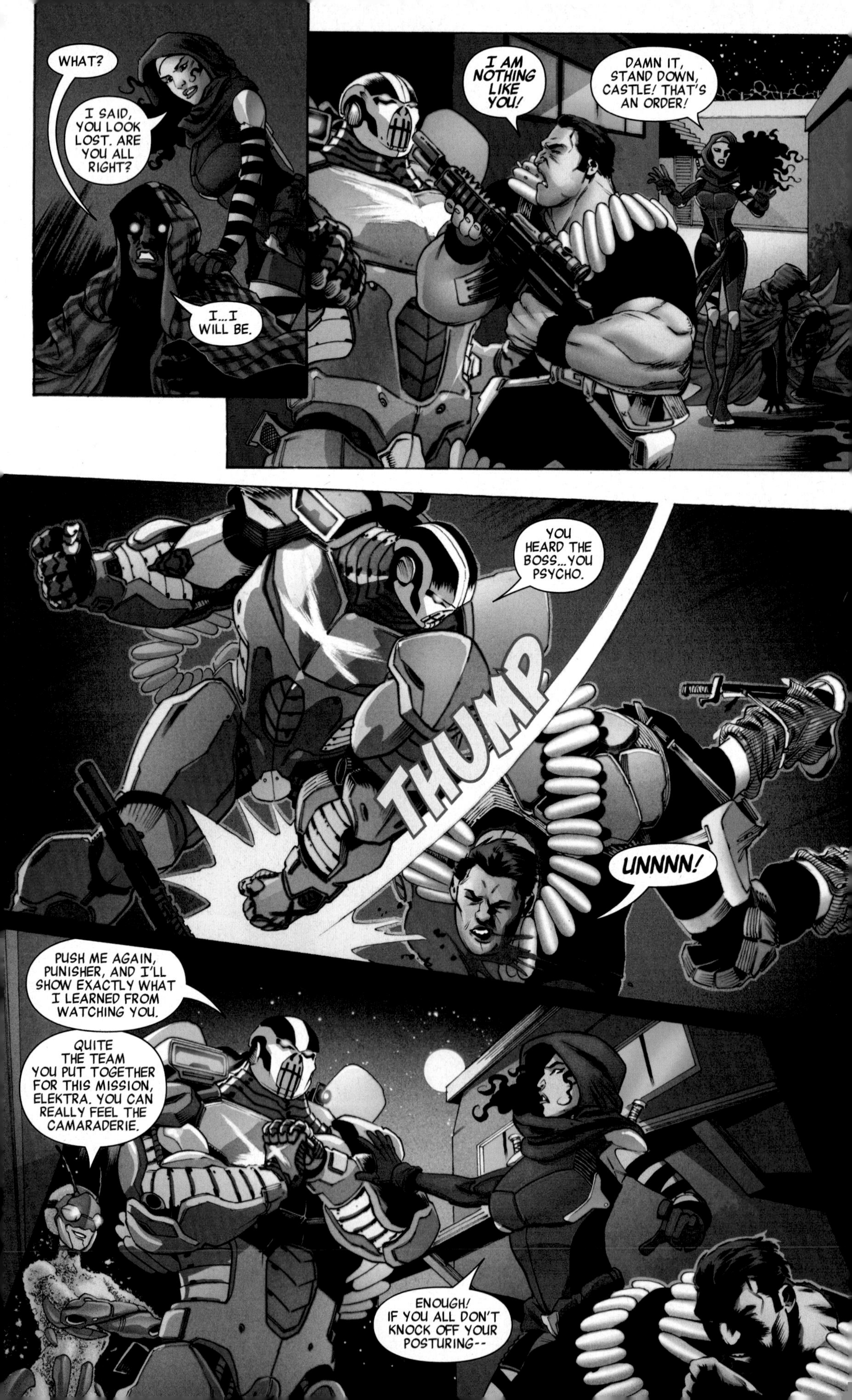
WHAT?
I SAID, YOU LOOK LOST. ARE YOU ALL RIGHT?
I...I WILL BE.
I AM NOTHING LIKE YOU!
DAMN IT, STAND DOWN, CASTLE! THAT'S AN ORDER!
YOU HEARD THE BOSS...YOU PSYCHO.
THUMP
UNNNN!
PUSH ME AGAIN, PUNISHER, AND I'LL SHOW EXACTLY WHAT I LEARNED FROM WATCHING YOU.
QUITE THE TEAM YOU PUT TOGETHER FOR THIS MISSION, ELEKTRA. YOU CAN REALLY FEEL THE CAMARADERIE.
ENOUGH! IF YOU ALL DON'T KNOCK OFF YOUR POSTURING--

"--YOU WILL BLOW THE ELEMENT OF SURPRISE... AND GET US *ALL* KILLED."

THERE...THE CAMERA AT THE NORTHEAST CORRIDOR CUT OUT FOR 22 SECONDS.

YOU'RE WORRIED OVER SOME GLITCH, FOXFIRE?

THIS SECURITY SYSTEM IS CENTURIES AHEAD OF ITS TIME.

MINK:
...ifted fighter ...rmed with ...laws.

HAYWIRE:
Projector of metallic tanglewire.

FOXFIRE:
Bringer of decay and death.

THERMITE:
Wielder of fire and ice.

MOONGLOW:
Mistress of light.

IT'S TOO ADVANCED TO "GLITCH."

BETTER TO CHECK IT OUT ANYWAY BEFORE *HE* RETURNS.

I'M MORE AFRAID OF HIM THAN *POWER PRINCESS* OR *DR. SPECTRUM.*

SEE? REMNANT IS STILL PATROLLING. NOTHING TO WORRY ABOUT.

ENHANCING...

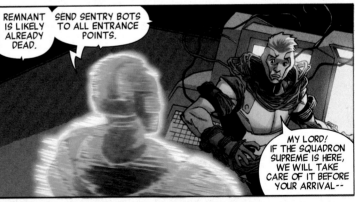

REMNANT IS LIKELY ALREADY DEAD.

SEND SENTRY BOTS TO ALL ENTRANCE POINTS.

MY LORD! IF THE SQUADRON SUPREME IS HERE, WE WILL TAKE CARE OF IT BEFORE YOUR ARRIVAL--

IF HYPERION WERE HERE, YOU WOULD ALREADY BE DEFEATED.

NO... THIS...

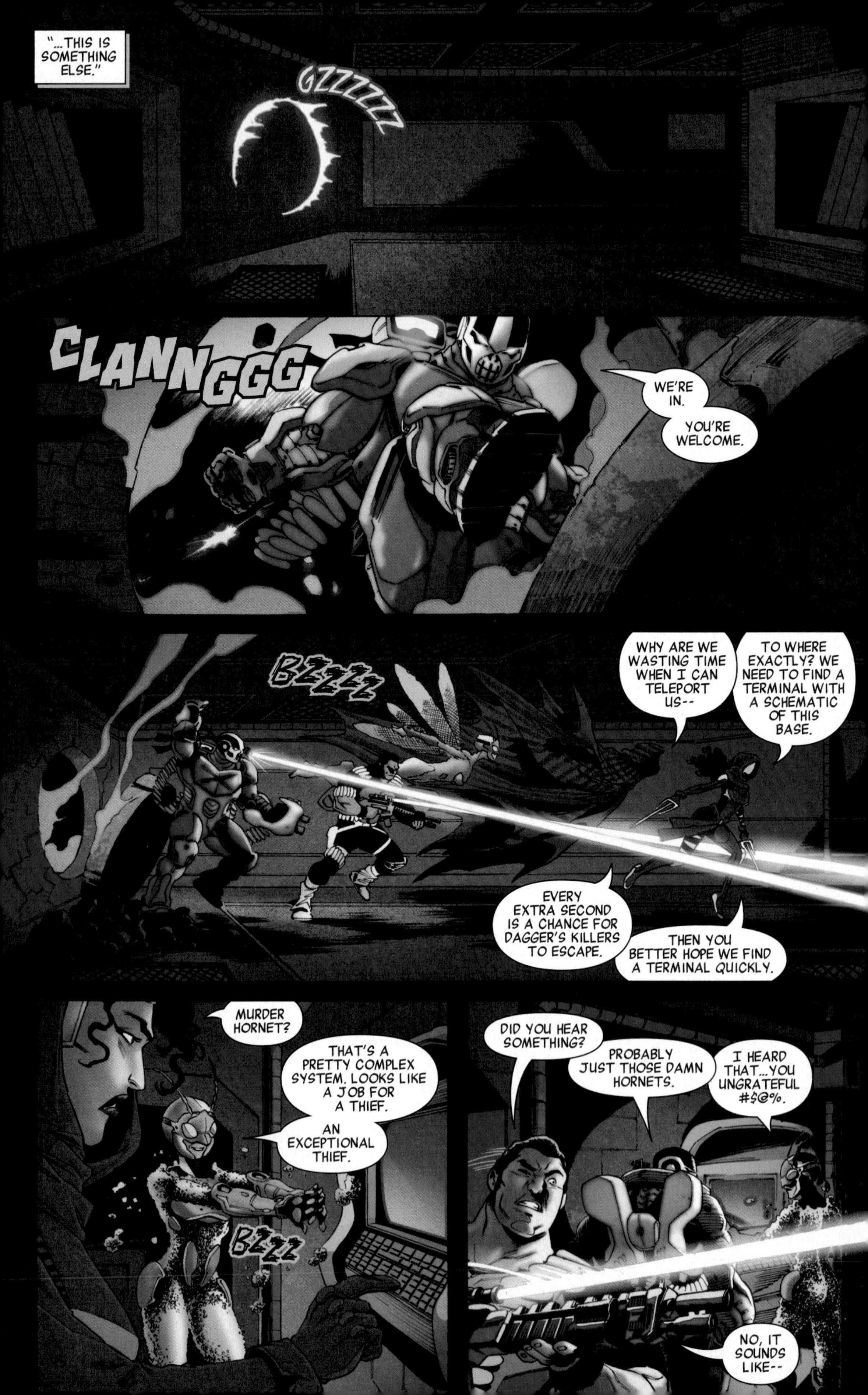
"...THIS IS SOMETHING ELSE."
GZZZZZZZ
CLANNGGG
WE'RE IN.
YOU'RE WELCOME.
BZZZZ
WHY ARE WE WASTING TIME WHEN I CAN TELEPORT US--
TO WHERE EXACTLY? WE NEED TO FIND A TERMINAL WITH A SCHEMATIC OF THIS BASE.
EVERY EXTRA SECOND IS A CHANCE FOR DAGGER'S KILLERS TO ESCAPE.
THEN YOU BETTER HOPE WE FIND A TERMINAL QUICKLY.
MURDER HORNET?
THAT'S A PRETTY COMPLEX SYSTEM. LOOKS LIKE A JOB FOR A THIEF.
AN EXCEPTIONAL THIEF.
BZZZ
DID YOU HEAR SOMETHING?
PROBABLY JUST THOSE DAMN HORNETS.
I HEARD THAT...YOU UNGRATEFUL #$@%.
NO, IT SOUNDS LIKE--

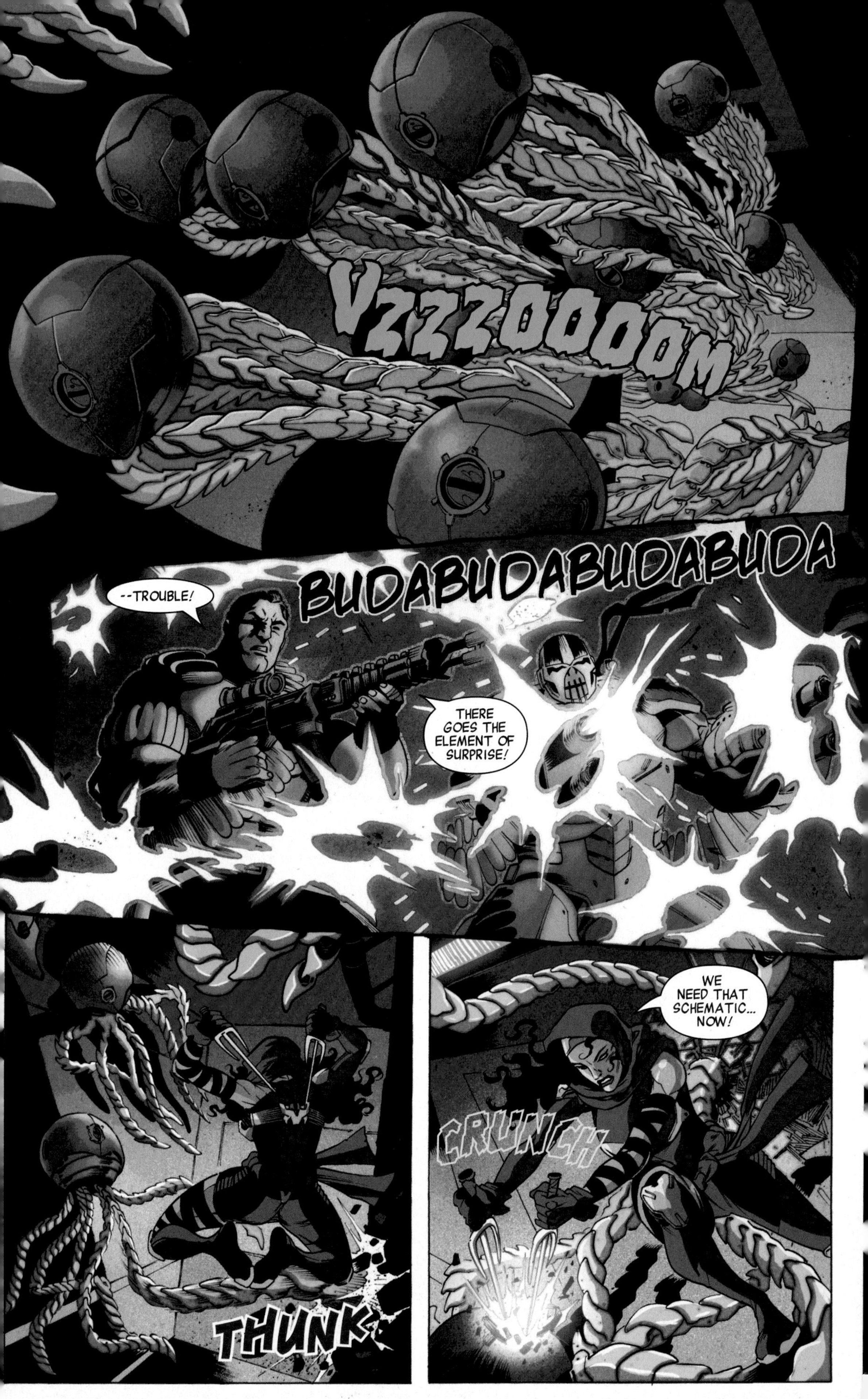
VZZZOOOOM
BUDABUDABUDABUDA
--TROUBLE!
THERE GOES THE ELEMENT OF SURPRISE!
THUNK
WE NEED THAT SCHEMATIC... NOW!
CRUNCH

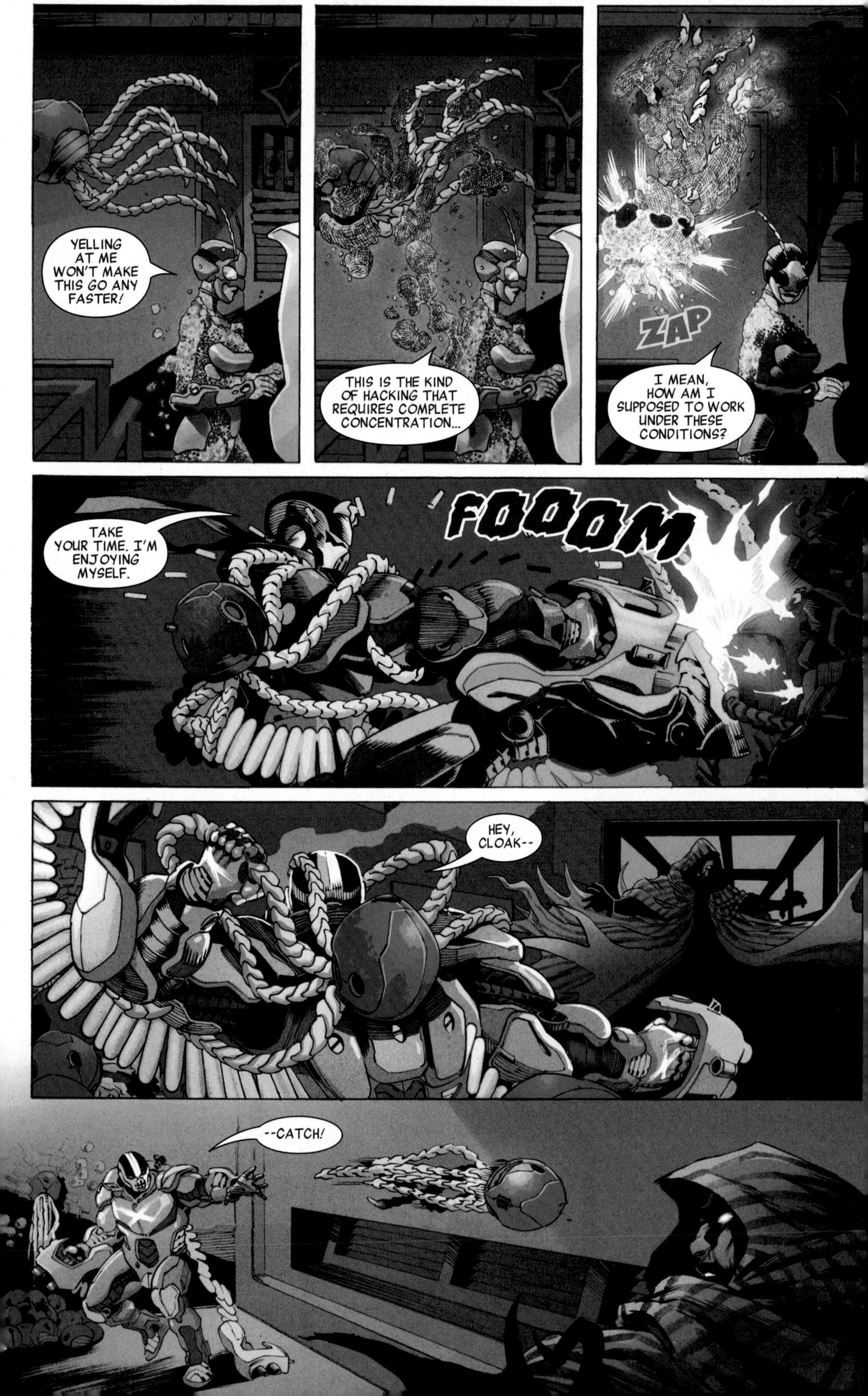
YELLING AT ME WON'T MAKE THIS GO ANY FASTER!
THIS IS THE KIND OF HACKING THAT REQUIRES COMPLETE CONCENTRATION...
ZAP
I MEAN, HOW AM I SUPPOSED TO WORK UNDER THESE CONDITIONS?
FOOOM
TAKE YOUR TIME. I'M ENJOYING MYSELF.
HEY, CLOAK--
--CATCH!

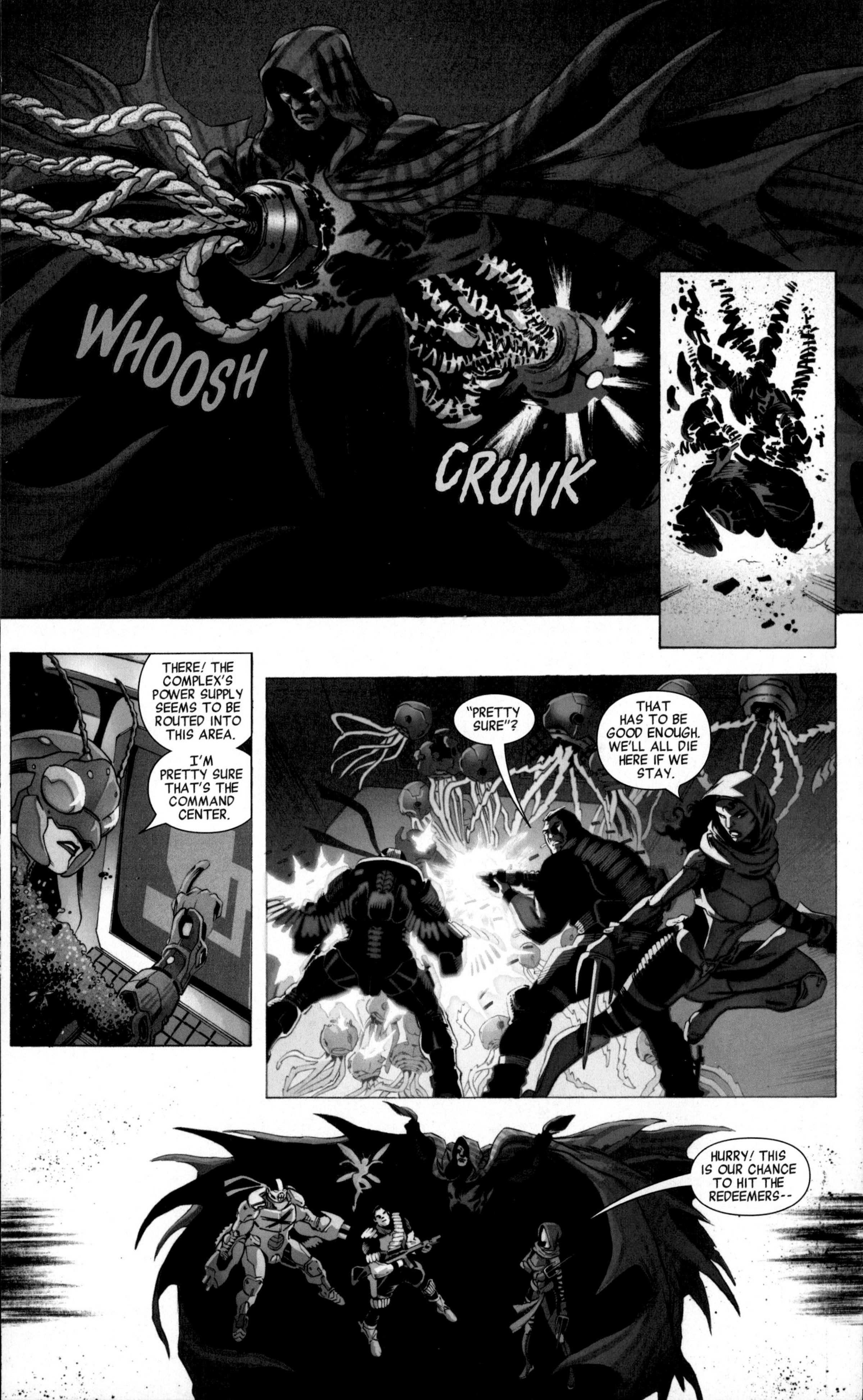
WHOOSH
CRUNK
THERE! THE COMPLEX'S POWER SUPPLY SEEMS TO BE ROUTED INTO THIS AREA.
I'M PRETTY SURE THAT'S THE COMMAND CENTER.
"PRETTY SURE"?
THAT HAS TO BE GOOD ENOUGH. WE'LL ALL DIE HERE IF WE STAY.
HURRY! THIS IS OUR CHANCE TO HIT THE REDEEMERS--

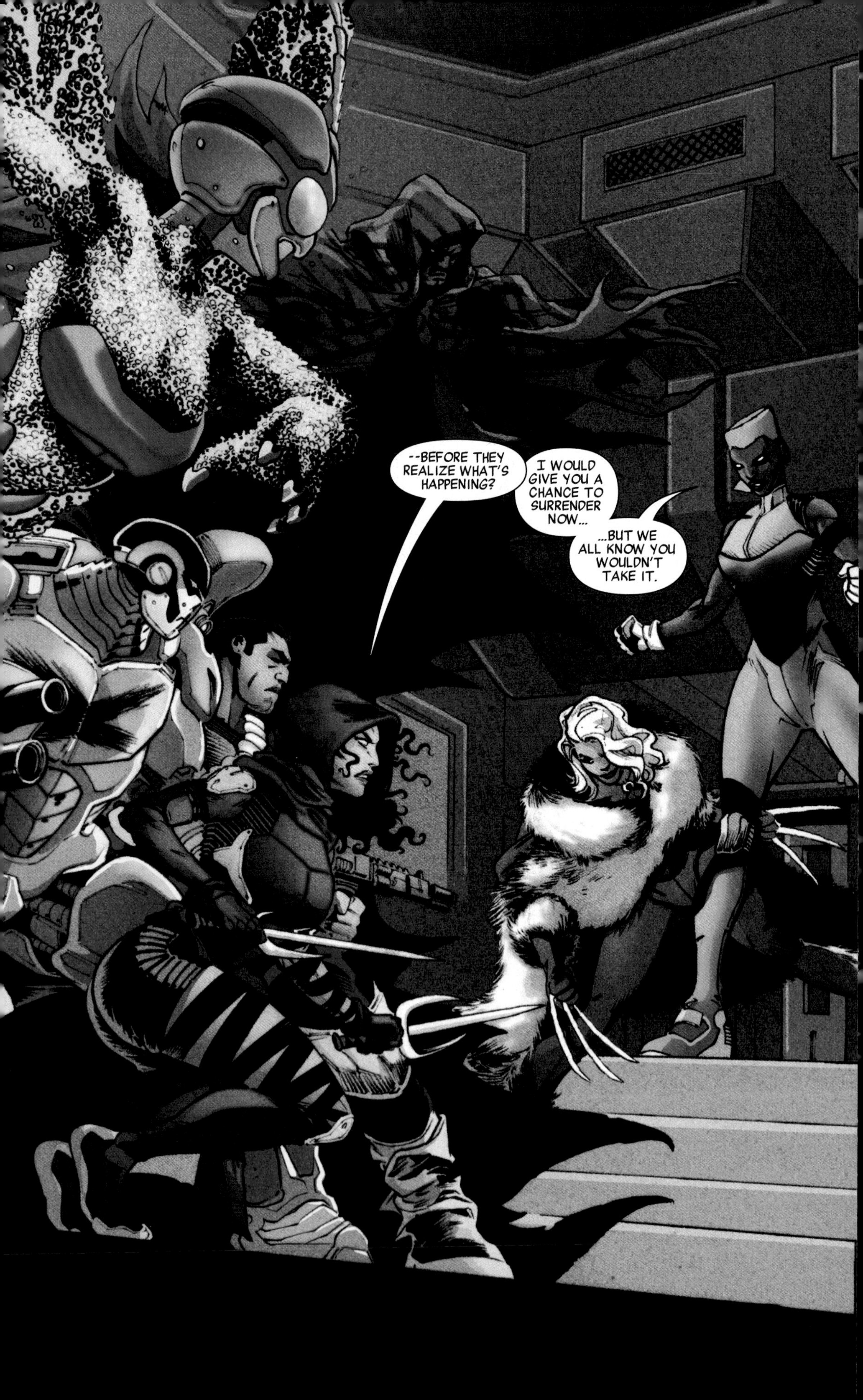
--BEFORE THEY REALIZE WHAT'S HAPPENING?
I WOULD GIVE YOU A CHANCE TO SURRENDER NOW...
...BUT WE ALL KNOW YOU WOULDN'T TAKE IT.

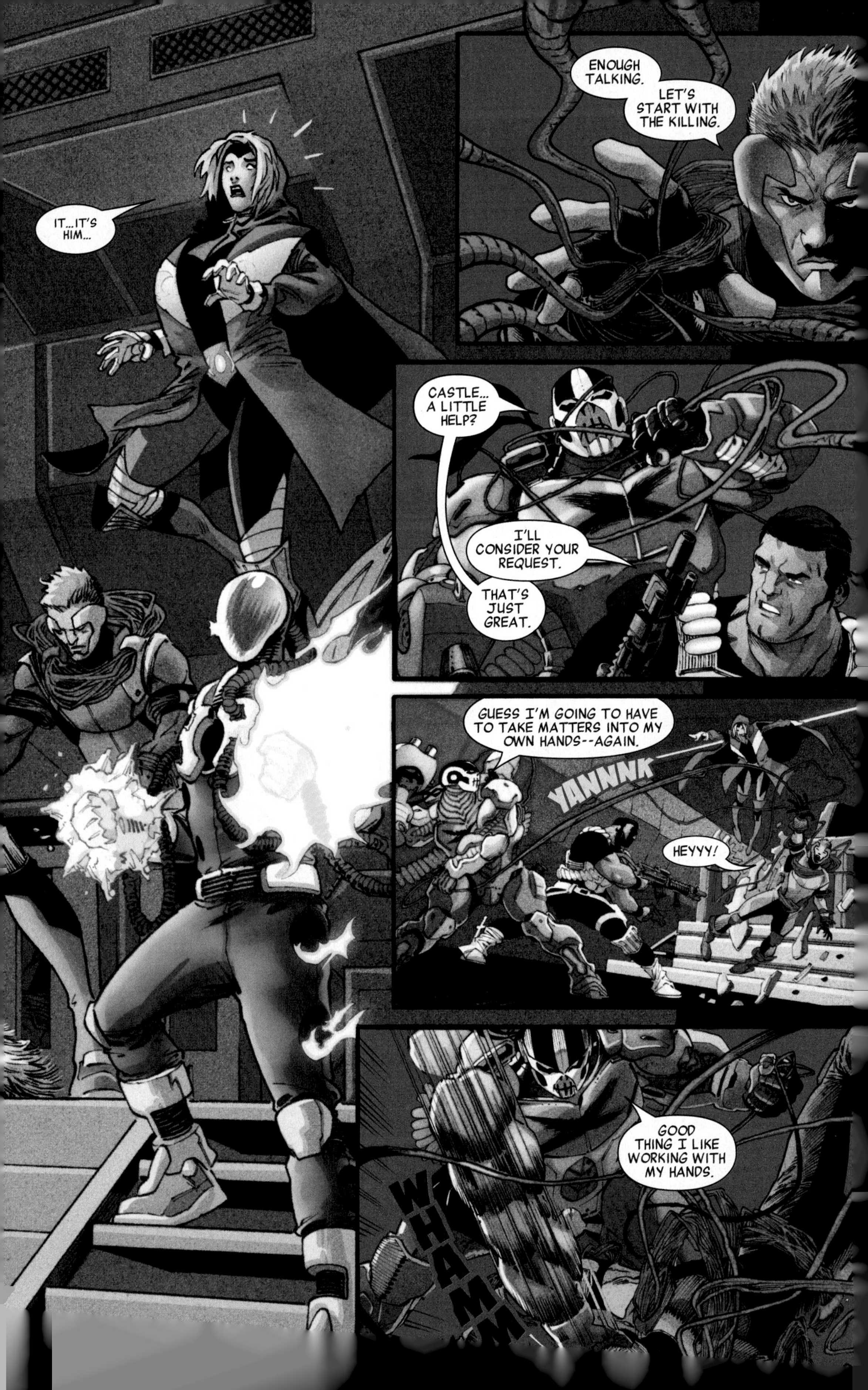
IT...IT'S HIM...
ENOUGH TALKING.
LET'S START WITH THE KILLING.
CASTLE... A LITTLE HELP?
I'LL CONSIDER YOUR REQUEST.
THAT'S JUST GREAT.
GUESS I'M GOING TO HAVE TO TAKE MATTERS INTO MY OWN HANDS--AGAIN.
YANNNK
HEYYY!
GOOD THING I LIKE WORKING WITH MY HANDS.
WHAMM

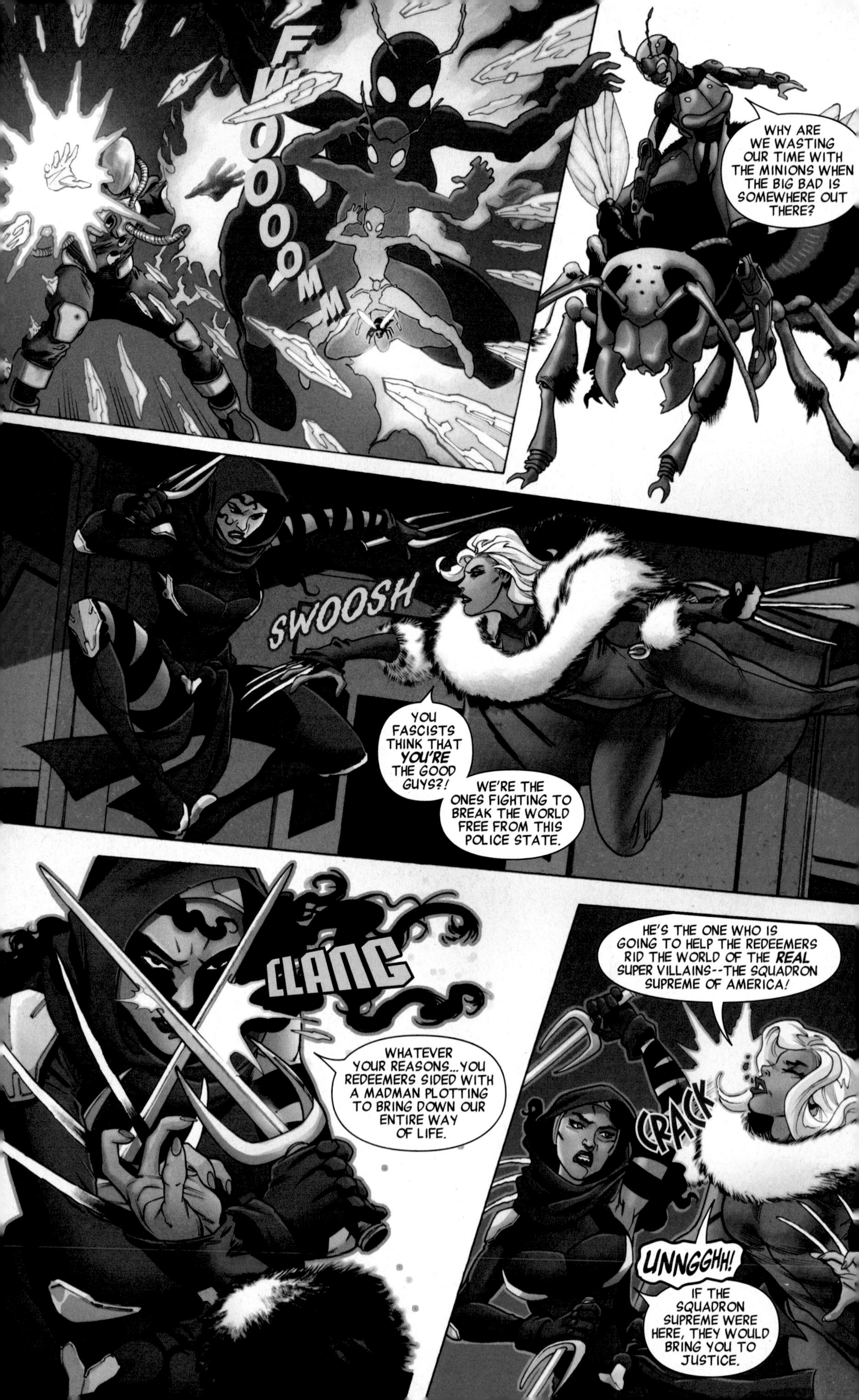
FWOOOOOMMM
WHY ARE WE WASTING OUR TIME WITH THE MINIONS WHEN THE BIG BAD IS SOMEWHERE OUT THERE?
SWOOSH
YOU FASCISTS THINK THAT YOU'RE THE GOOD GUYS?!
WE'RE THE ONES FIGHTING TO BREAK THE WORLD FREE FROM THIS POLICE STATE.
CLANG
WHATEVER YOUR REASONS...YOU REDEEMERS SIDED WITH A MADMAN PLOTTING TO BRING DOWN OUR ENTIRE WAY OF LIFE.
HE'S THE ONE WHO IS GOING TO HELP THE REDEEMERS RID THE WORLD OF THE REAL SUPER VILLAINS--THE SQUADRON SUPREME OF AMERICA!
CRACK
UNNGGHH!
IF THE SQUADRON SUPREME WERE HERE, THEY WOULD BRING YOU TO JUSTICE.

BUT THE SQUADRON I LEAD...IS MORE SAVAGE.

HURK!

YOU...YOU BASTARDS! SHE WAS MY FRIEND!

YOU ARE FIGHTING AGAINST THE INEVITABLE...

MY DARKFORCE ABSORBS ALL LIGHT.

DON'T YOU THINK I KNOW THAT...TY?

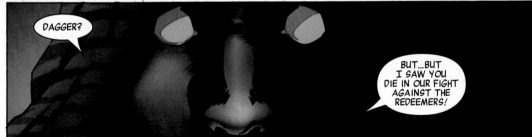

DAGGER?

BUT...BUT I SAW YOU DIE IN OUR FIGHT AGAINST THE REDEEMERS!

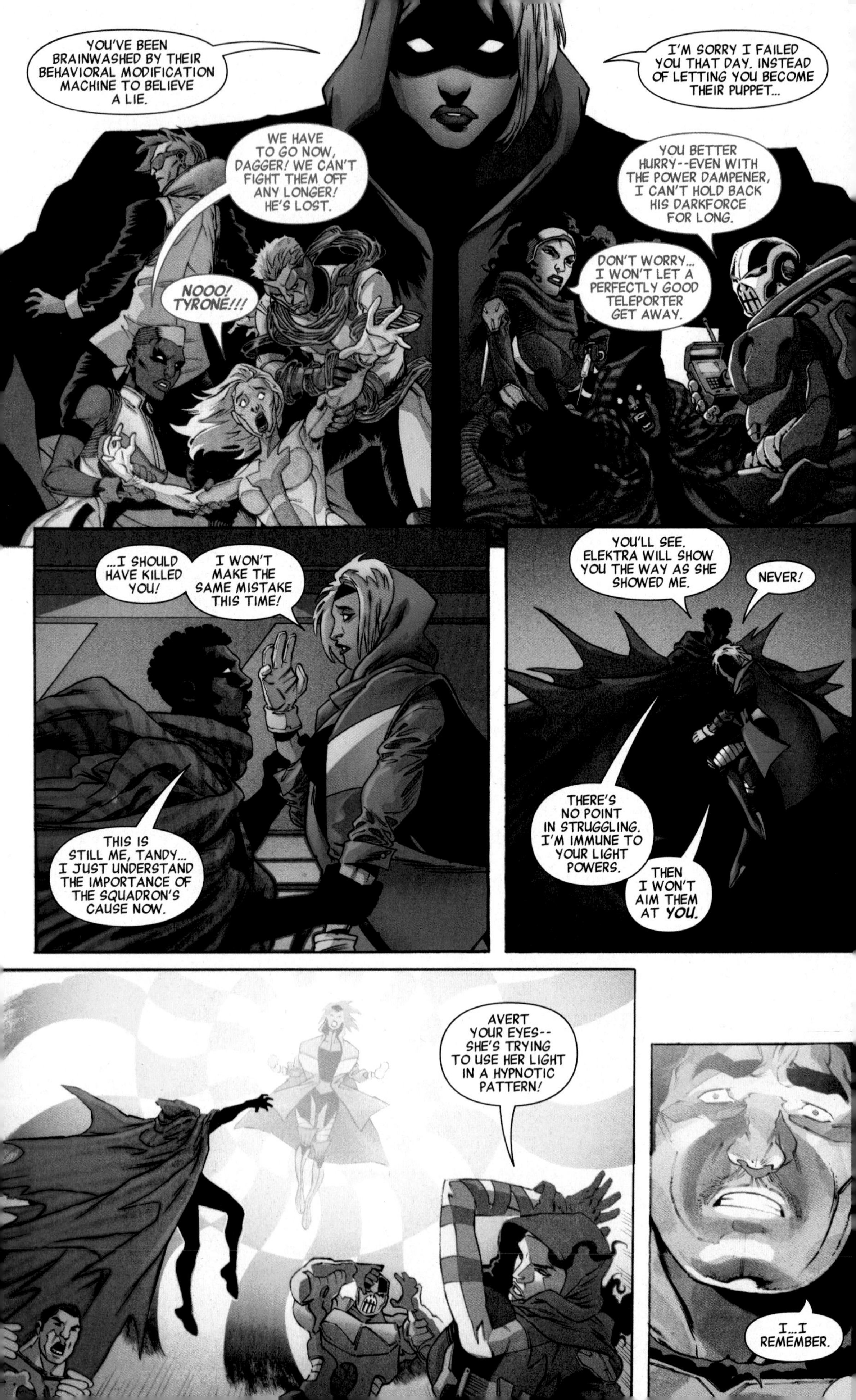
YOU'VE BEEN BRAINWASHED BY THEIR BEHAVIORAL MODIFICATION MACHINE TO BELIEVE A LIE.
I'M SORRY I FAILED YOU THAT DAY. INSTEAD OF LETTING YOU BECOME THEIR PUPPET...
WE HAVE TO GO NOW, DAGGER! WE CAN'T FIGHT THEM OFF ANY LONGER! HE'S LOST.
NOOO! TYRONE!!!
YOU BETTER HURRY--EVEN WITH THE POWER DAMPENER, I CAN'T HOLD BACK HIS DARKFORCE FOR LONG.
DON'T WORRY... I WON'T LET A PERFECTLY GOOD TELEPORTER GET AWAY.
...I SHOULD HAVE KILLED YOU!
I WON'T MAKE THE SAME MISTAKE THIS TIME!
THIS IS STILL ME, TANDY... I JUST UNDERSTAND THE IMPORTANCE OF THE SQUADRON'S CAUSE NOW.
YOU'LL SEE. ELEKTRA WILL SHOW YOU THE WAY AS SHE SHOWED ME.
NEVER!
THERE'S NO POINT IN STRUGGLING. I'M IMMUNE TO YOUR LIGHT POWERS.
THEN I WON'T AIM THEM AT YOU.
AVERT YOUR EYES-- SHE'S TRYING TO USE HER LIGHT IN A HYPNOTIC PATTERN!
I...I REMEMBER.

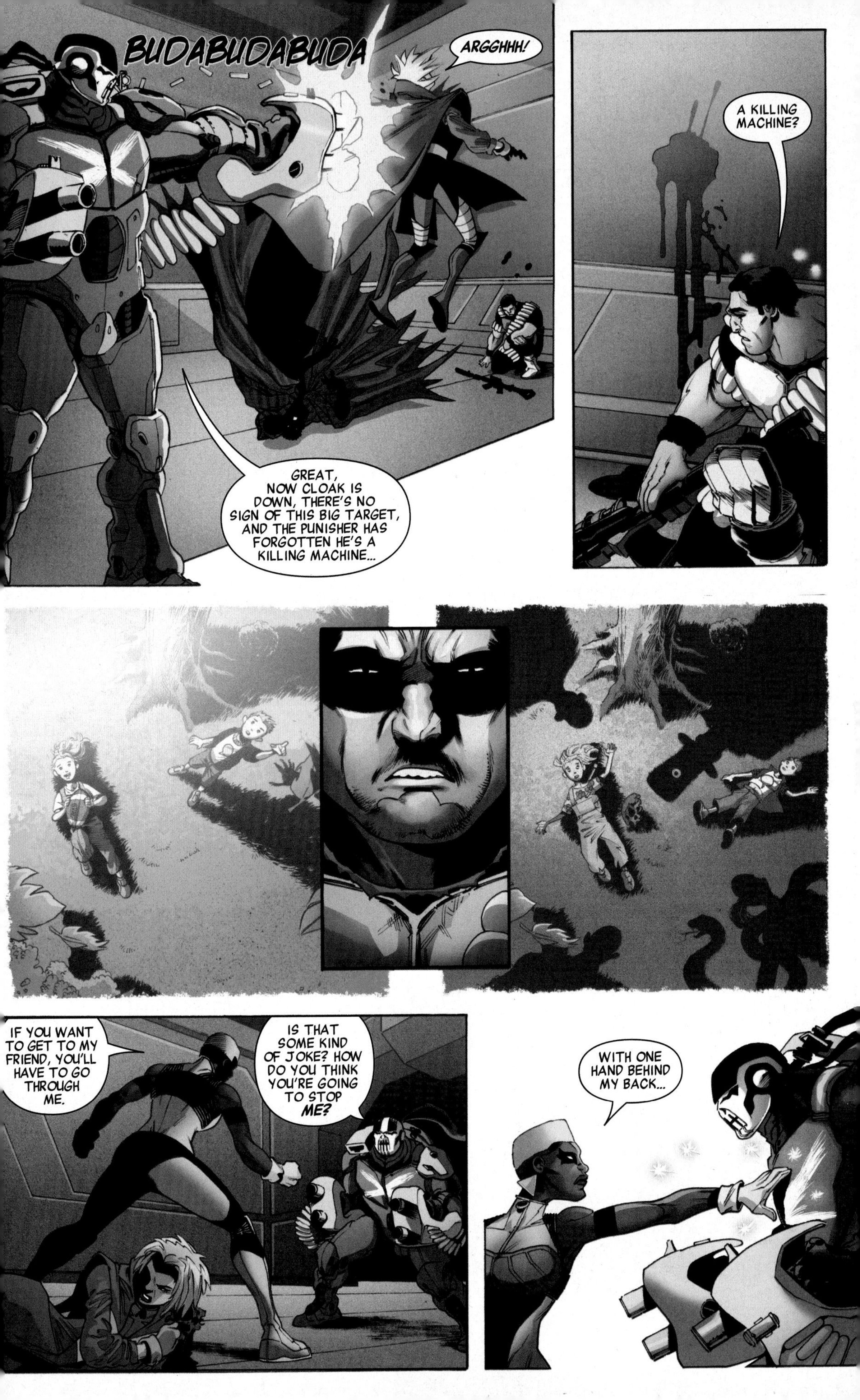
BUDABUDABUDA
ARGGHHH!
GREAT, NOW CLOAK IS DOWN, THERE'S NO SIGN OF THIS BIG TARGET, AND THE PUNISHER HAS FORGOTTEN HE'S A KILLING MACHINE...
A KILLING MACHINE?
IF YOU WANT TO GET TO MY FRIEND, YOU'LL HAVE TO GO THROUGH ME.
IS THAT SOME KIND OF JOKE? HOW DO YOU THINK YOU'RE GOING TO STOP ME?
WITH ONE HAND BEHIND MY BACK...

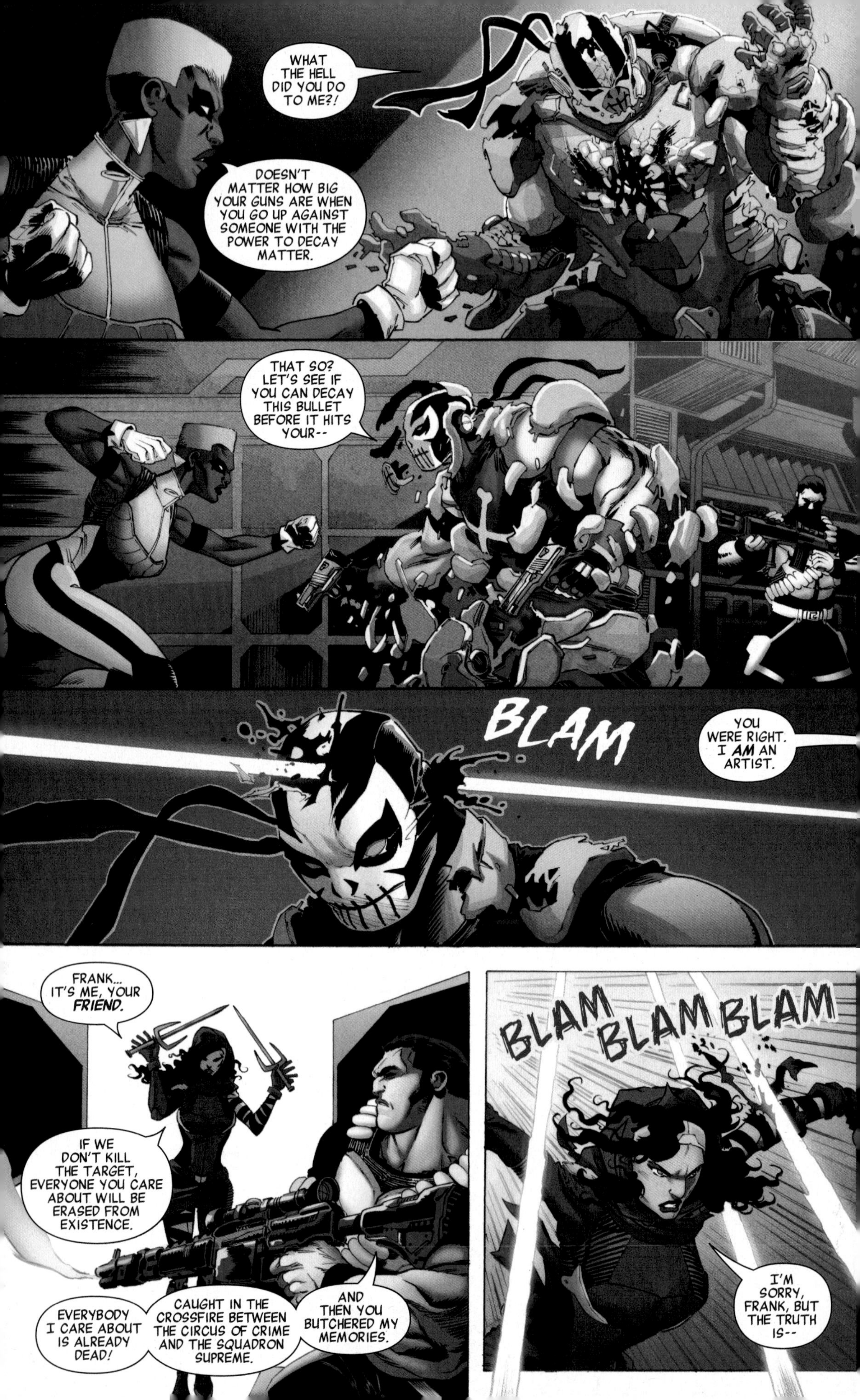
WHAT THE HELL DID YOU DO TO ME?!
DOESN'T MATTER HOW BIG YOUR GUNS ARE WHEN YOU GO UP AGAINST SOMEONE WITH THE POWER TO DECAY MATTER.
THAT SO? LET'S SEE IF YOU CAN DECAY THIS BULLET BEFORE IT HITS YOUR--
BLAM
YOU WERE RIGHT. I *AM* AN ARTIST.
FRANK... IT'S ME, YOUR *FRIEND.*
IF WE DON'T KILL THE TARGET, EVERYONE YOU CARE ABOUT WILL BE ERASED FROM EXISTENCE.
EVERYBODY I CARE ABOUT IS ALREADY DEAD!
CAUGHT IN THE CROSSFIRE BETWEEN THE CIRCUS OF CRIME AND THE SQUADRON SUPREME.
AND THEN YOU BUTCHERED MY MEMORIES.
BLAM BLAM BLAM
I'M SORRY, FRANK, BUT THE TRUTH IS--

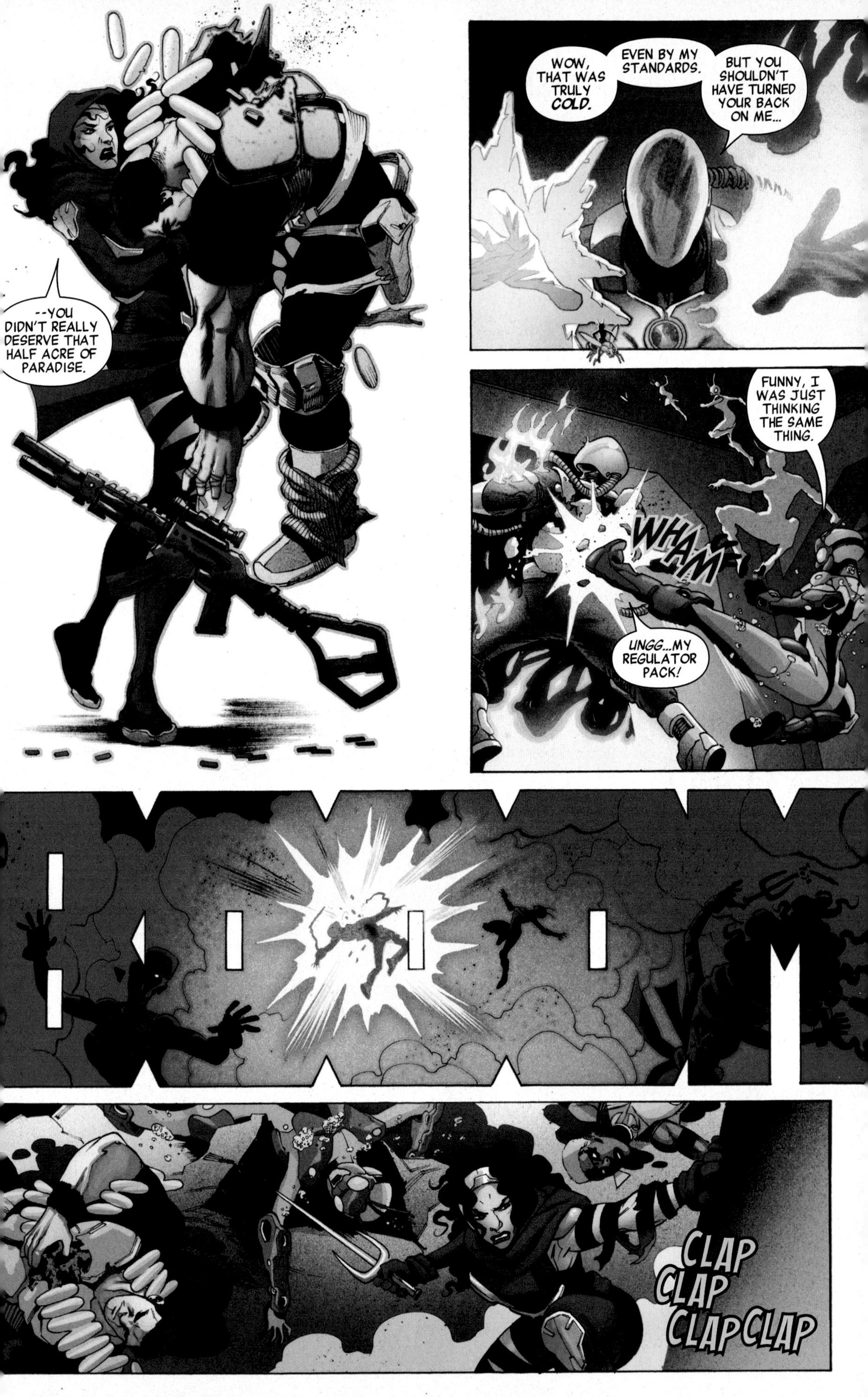
--YOU DIDN'T REALLY DESERVE THAT HALF ACRE OF PARADISE.
WOW, THAT WAS TRULY COLD.
EVEN BY MY STANDARDS.
BUT YOU SHOULDN'T HAVE TURNED YOUR BACK ON ME...
FUNNY, I WAS JUST THINKING THE SAME THING.
WHAM
UNGG...MY REGULATOR PACK!
CLAP
CLAP
CLAP CLAP

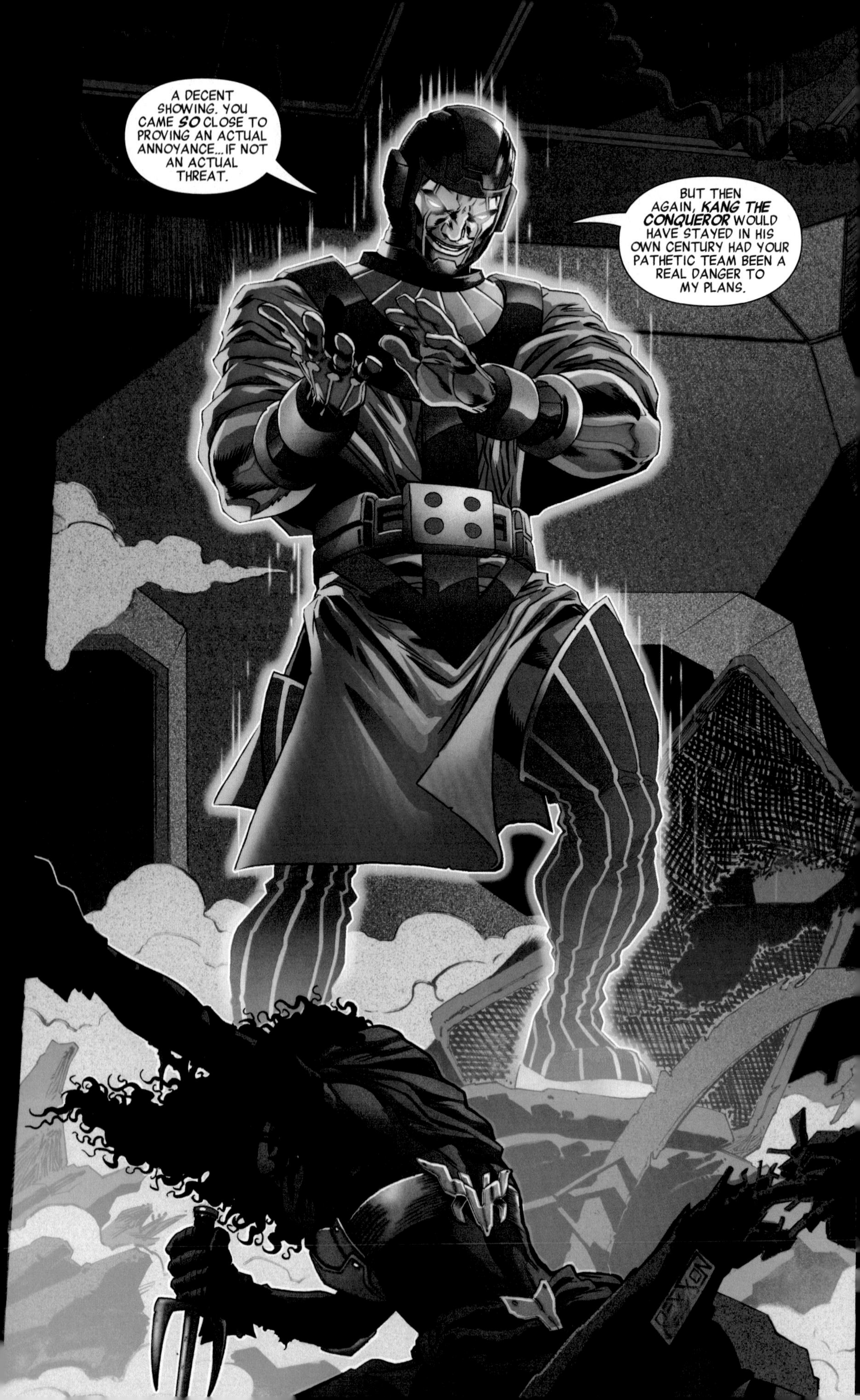
A DECENT SHOWING. YOU CAME SO CLOSE TO PROVING AN ACTUAL ANNOYANCE...IF NOT AN ACTUAL THREAT.
BUT THEN AGAIN, KANG THE CONQUEROR WOULD HAVE STAYED IN HIS OWN CENTURY HAD YOUR PATHETIC TEAM BEEN A REAL DANGER TO MY PLANS.

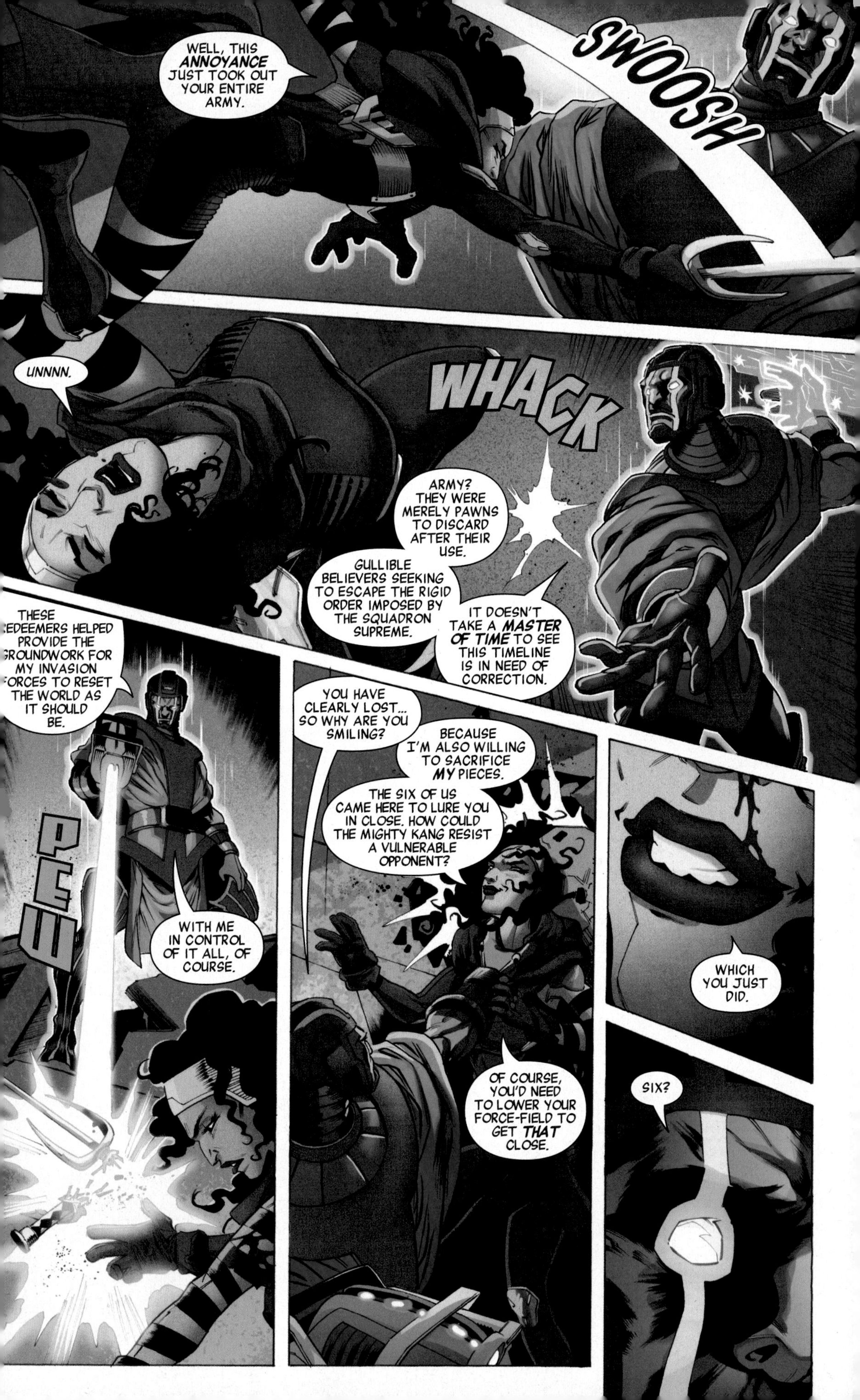
WELL, THIS ANNOYANCE JUST TOOK OUT YOUR ENTIRE ARMY.
SWOOSH
UNNNN.
WHACK
ARMY? THEY WERE MERELY PAWNS TO DISCARD AFTER THEIR USE.
GULLIBLE BELIEVERS SEEKING TO ESCAPE THE RIGID ORDER IMPOSED BY THE SQUADRON SUPREME.
IT DOESN'T TAKE A MASTER OF TIME TO SEE THIS TIMELINE IS IN NEED OF CORRECTION.
THESE EDEEMERS HELPED PROVIDE THE ROUNDWORK FOR MY INVASION ORCES TO RESET THE WORLD AS IT SHOULD BE.
PEW
WITH ME IN CONTROL OF IT ALL, OF COURSE.
YOU HAVE CLEARLY LOST... SO WHY ARE YOU SMILING?
BECAUSE I'M ALSO WILLING TO SACRIFICE MY PIECES.
THE SIX OF US CAME HERE TO LURE YOU IN CLOSE. HOW COULD THE MIGHTY KANG RESIST A VULNERABLE OPPONENT?
OF COURSE, YOU'D NEED TO LOWER YOUR FORCE-FIELD TO GET THAT CLOSE.
WHICH YOU JUST DID.
SIX?

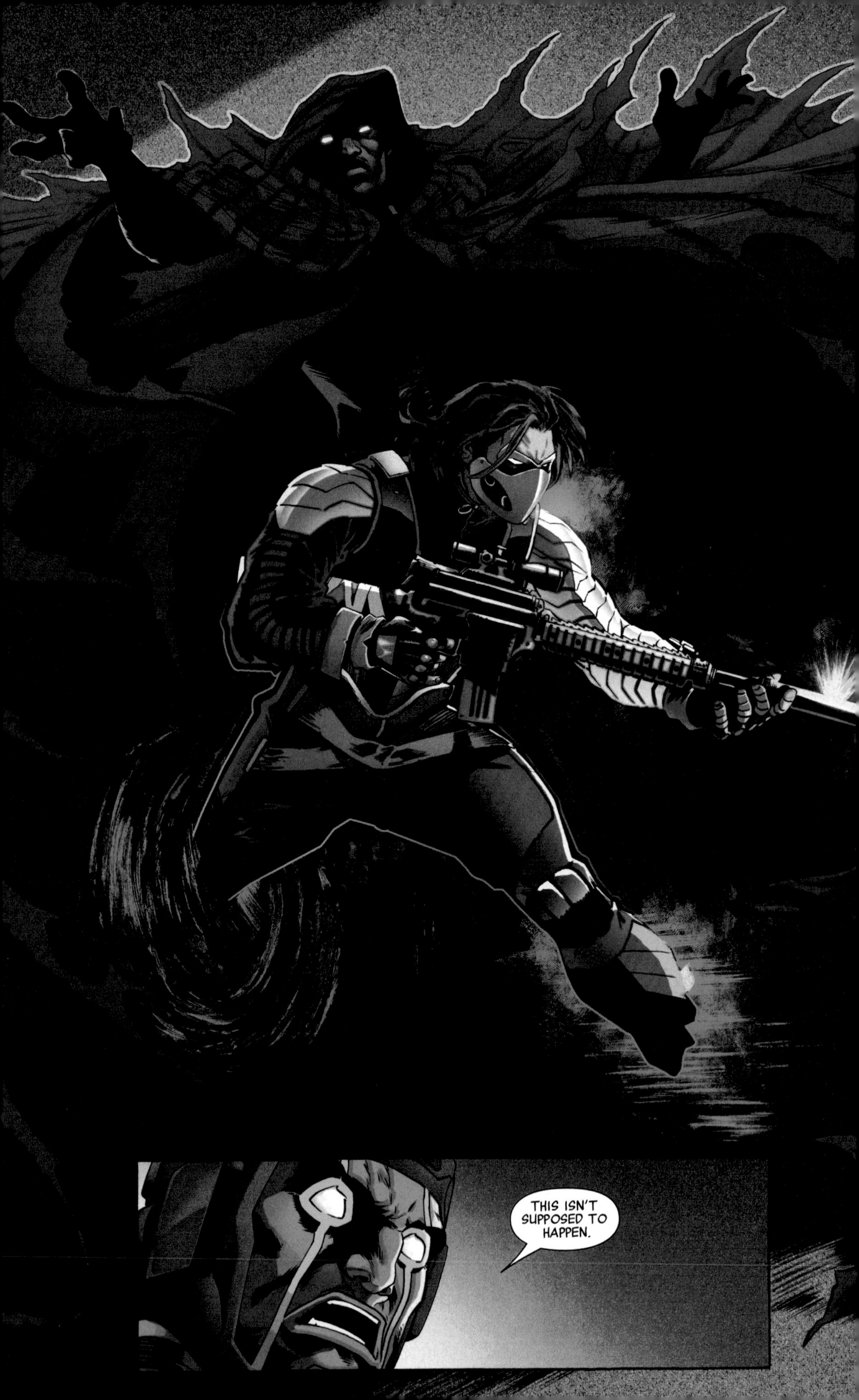
THIS ISN'T SUPPOSED TO HAPPEN.

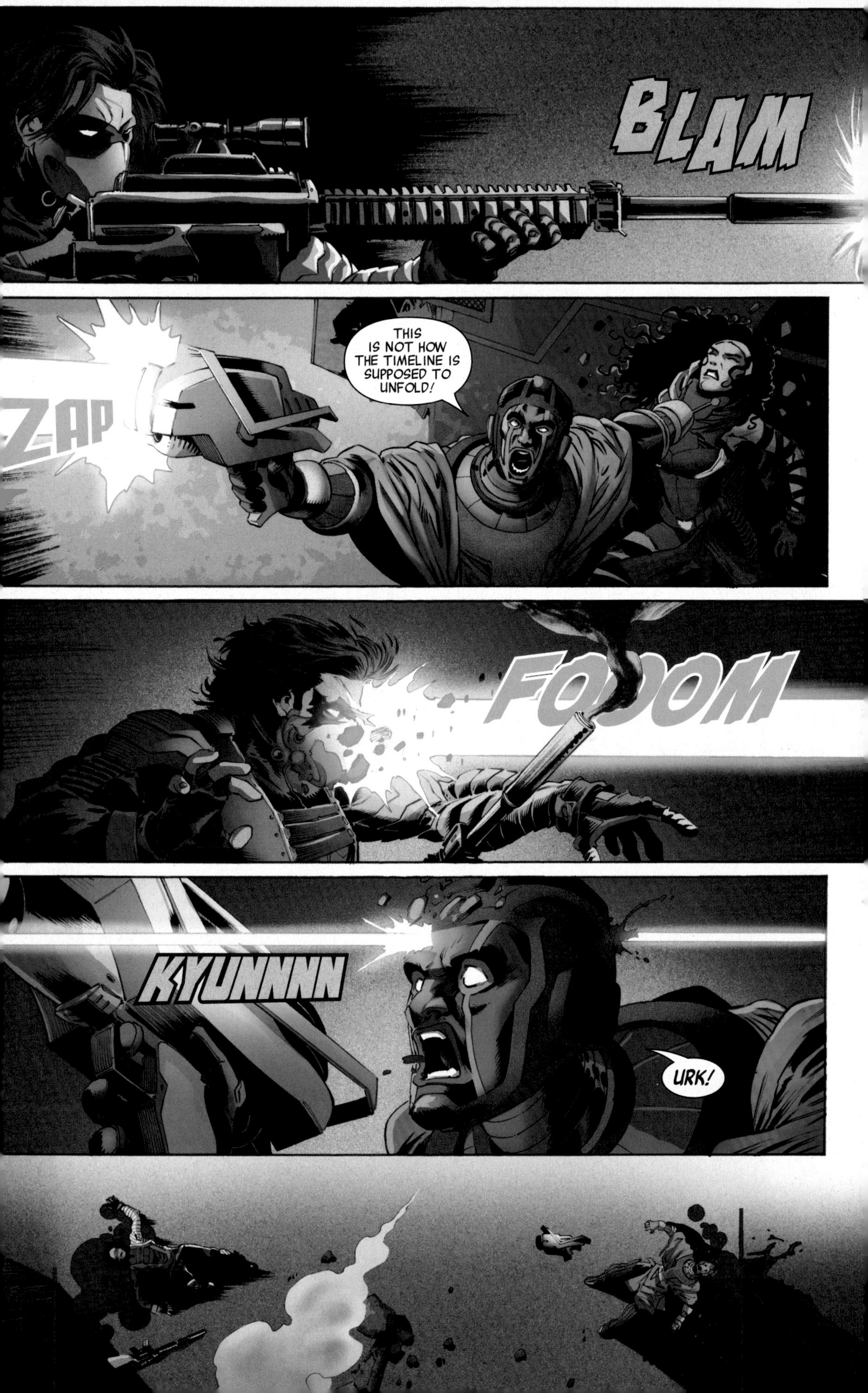
BLAM
ZAP
THIS IS NOT HOW THE TIMELINE IS SUPPOSED TO UNFOLD!
FOOOM
KYUNNNN
URK!

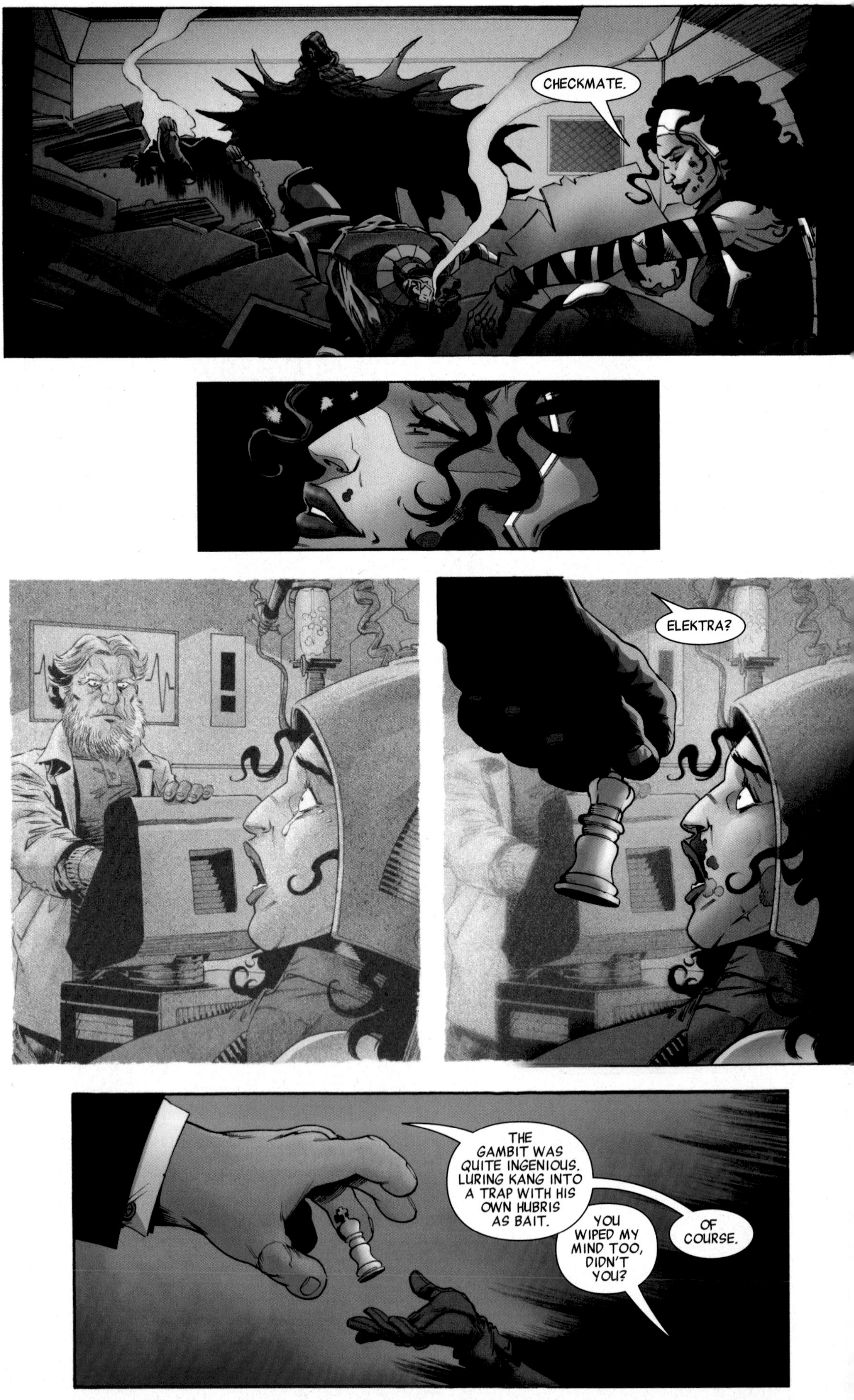
CHECKMATE.
ELEKTRA?
THE GAMBIT WAS QUITE INGENIOUS. LURING KANG INTO A TRAP WITH HIS OWN HUBRIS AS BAIT.
YOU WIPED MY MIND TOO, DIDN'T YOU?
OF COURSE.

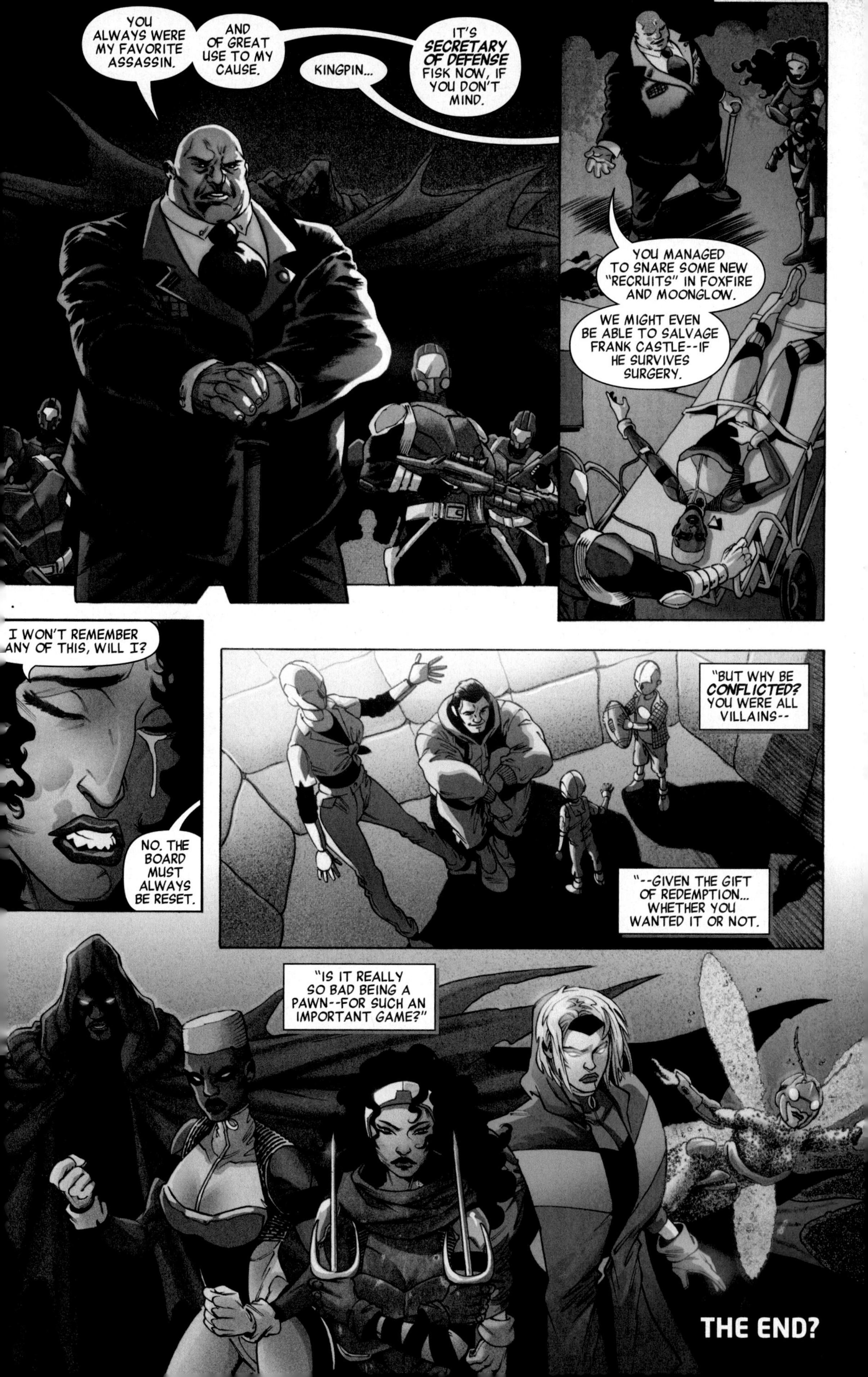
YOU ALWAYS WERE MY FAVORITE ASSASSIN.
AND OF GREAT USE TO MY CAUSE.
KINGPIN...
IT'S SECRETARY OF DEFENSE FISK NOW, IF YOU DON'T MIND.
YOU MANAGED TO SNARE SOME NEW "RECRUITS" IN FOXFIRE AND MOONGLOW.
WE MIGHT EVEN BE ABLE TO SALVAGE FRANK CASTLE--IF HE SURVIVES SURGERY.
I WON'T REMEMBER ANY OF THIS, WILL I?
NO. THE BOARD MUST ALWAYS BE RESET.
"BUT WHY BE CONFLICTED? YOU WERE ALL VILLAINS--
"--GIVEN THE GIFT OF REDEMPTION... WHETHER YOU WANTED IT OR NOT.
"IS IT REALLY SO BAD BEING A PAWN--FOR SUCH AN IMPORTANT GAME?"
THE END?

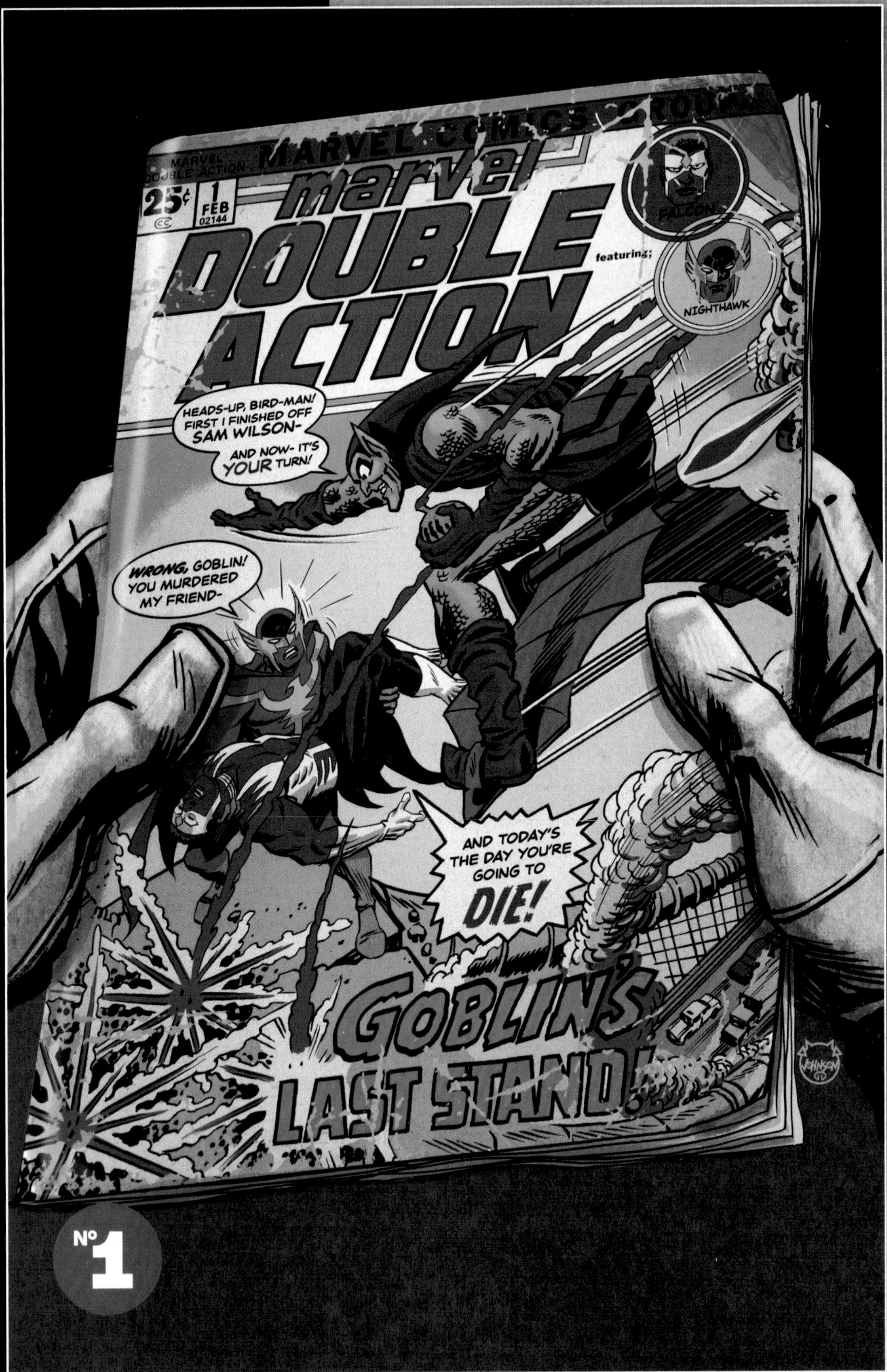
MARVEL COMICS GROUP
MARVEL DOUBLE ACTION
25¢
1 FEB 02144
marvel DOUBLE ACTION
featuring;
FALCON
NIGHTHAWK
HEADS-UP, BIRD-MAN! FIRST I FINISHED OFF SAM WILSON-
AND NOW- IT'S YOUR TURN!
WRONG, GOBLIN! YOU MURDERED MY FRIEND-
AND TODAY'S THE DAY YOU'RE GOING TO DIE!
GOBLIN'S LAST STAND!
JOHNSON
Nº 1

MARVEL
DOUBLE ACTION

“THE DEATH OF
THE DYNAMIC DOUBLE”

Marvel Comics PRESENTS: NIGHTHAWK & FALCON, THE DYNAMIC DOUBLE!

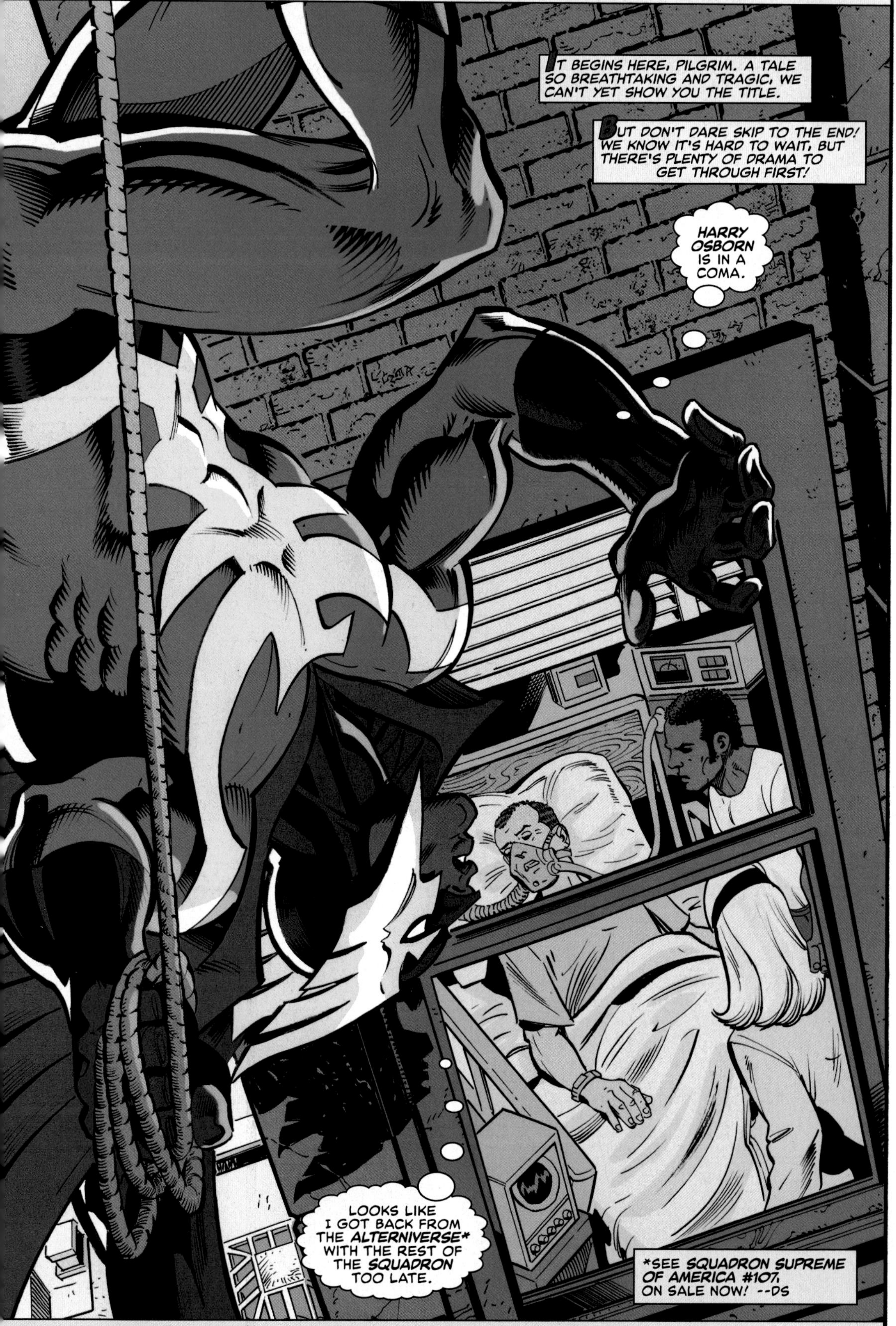
IT BEGINS HERE, PILGRIM. A TALE SO BREATHTAKING AND TRAGIC, WE CAN'T YET SHOW YOU THE TITLE.
BUT DON'T DARE SKIP TO THE END! WE KNOW IT'S HARD TO WAIT, BUT THERE'S PLENTY OF DRAMA TO GET THROUGH FIRST!
HARRY OSBORN IS IN A COMA.
LOOKS LIKE I GOT BACK FROM THE ALTERNIVERSE* WITH THE REST OF THE SQUADRON TOO LATE.
*SEE SQUADRON SUPREME OF AMERICA #107, ON SALE NOW! --DS

TIM SEELEY, SCRIPTER • DAN JURGENS, PENCILER • SCOTT HANNA, INKER

CHRIS SOTOMAYOR, COLORIST • VC'S CORY PETIT, LETTERER • DARREN SHAN, EDITOR

ORIGINALLY PRESENTED IN NIGHTHAWK #126

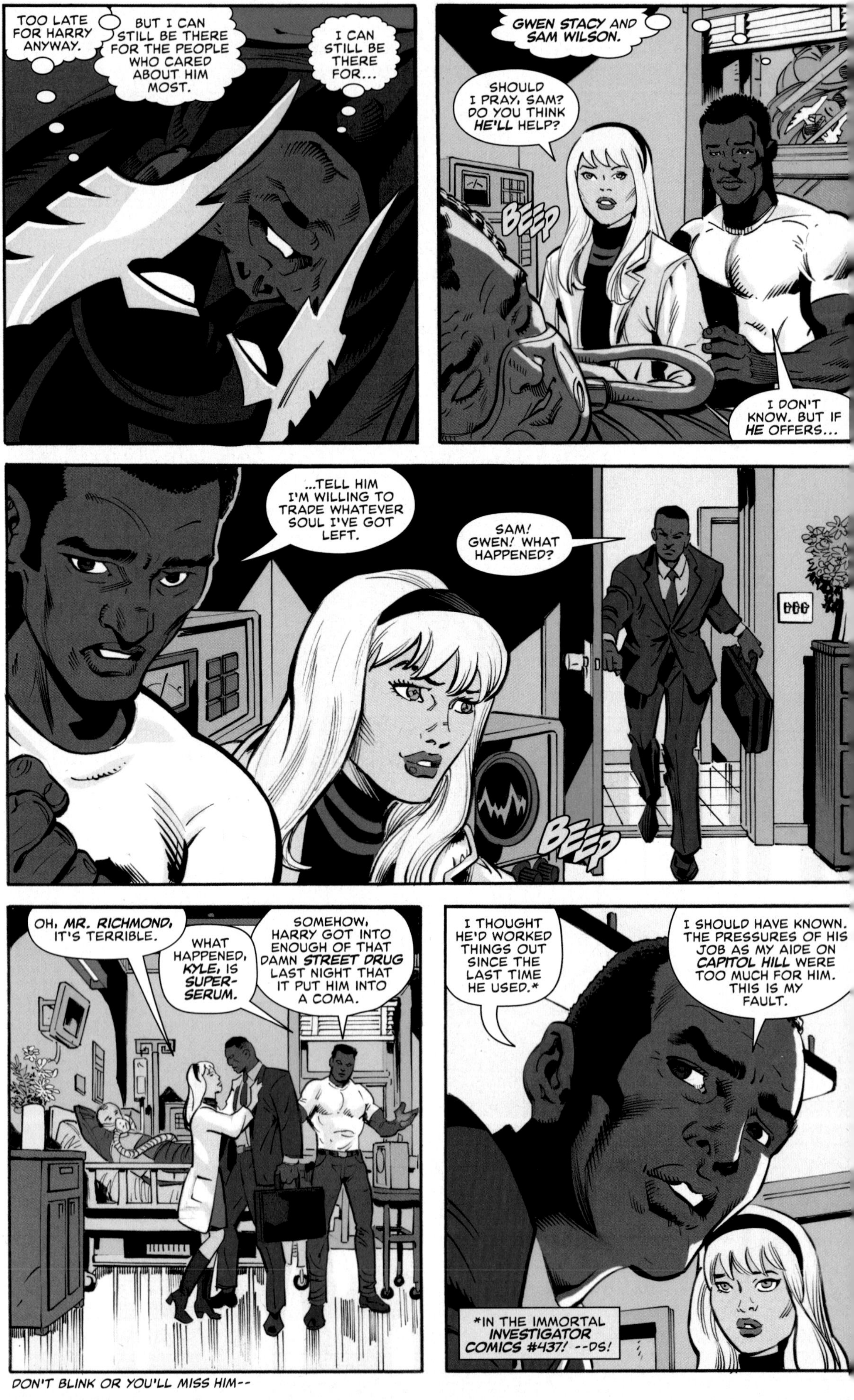
TOO LATE FOR HARRY ANYWAY.
BUT I CAN STILL BE THERE FOR THE PEOPLE WHO CARED ABOUT HIM MOST.
I CAN STILL BE THERE FOR...
GWEN STACY AND SAM WILSON.
SHOULD I PRAY, SAM? DO YOU THINK HE'LL HELP?
BEEP
I DON'T KNOW. BUT IF HE OFFERS...
...TELL HIM I'M WILLING TO TRADE WHATEVER SOUL I'VE GOT LEFT.
SAM! GWEN! WHAT HAPPENED?
BEEP
OH, MR. RICHMOND, IT'S TERRIBLE.
WHAT HAPPENED, KYLE, IS SUPER-SERUM.
SOMEHOW, HARRY GOT INTO ENOUGH OF THAT DAMN STREET DRUG LAST NIGHT THAT IT PUT HIM INTO A COMA.
I THOUGHT HE'D WORKED THINGS OUT SINCE THE LAST TIME HE USED.*
I SHOULD HAVE KNOWN. THE PRESSURES OF HIS JOB AS MY AIDE ON CAPITOL HILL WERE TOO MUCH FOR HIM. THIS IS MY FAULT.
*IN THE IMMORTAL INVESTIGATOR COMICS #437! --DS!

DON'T BLINK OR YOU'LL MISS HIM--

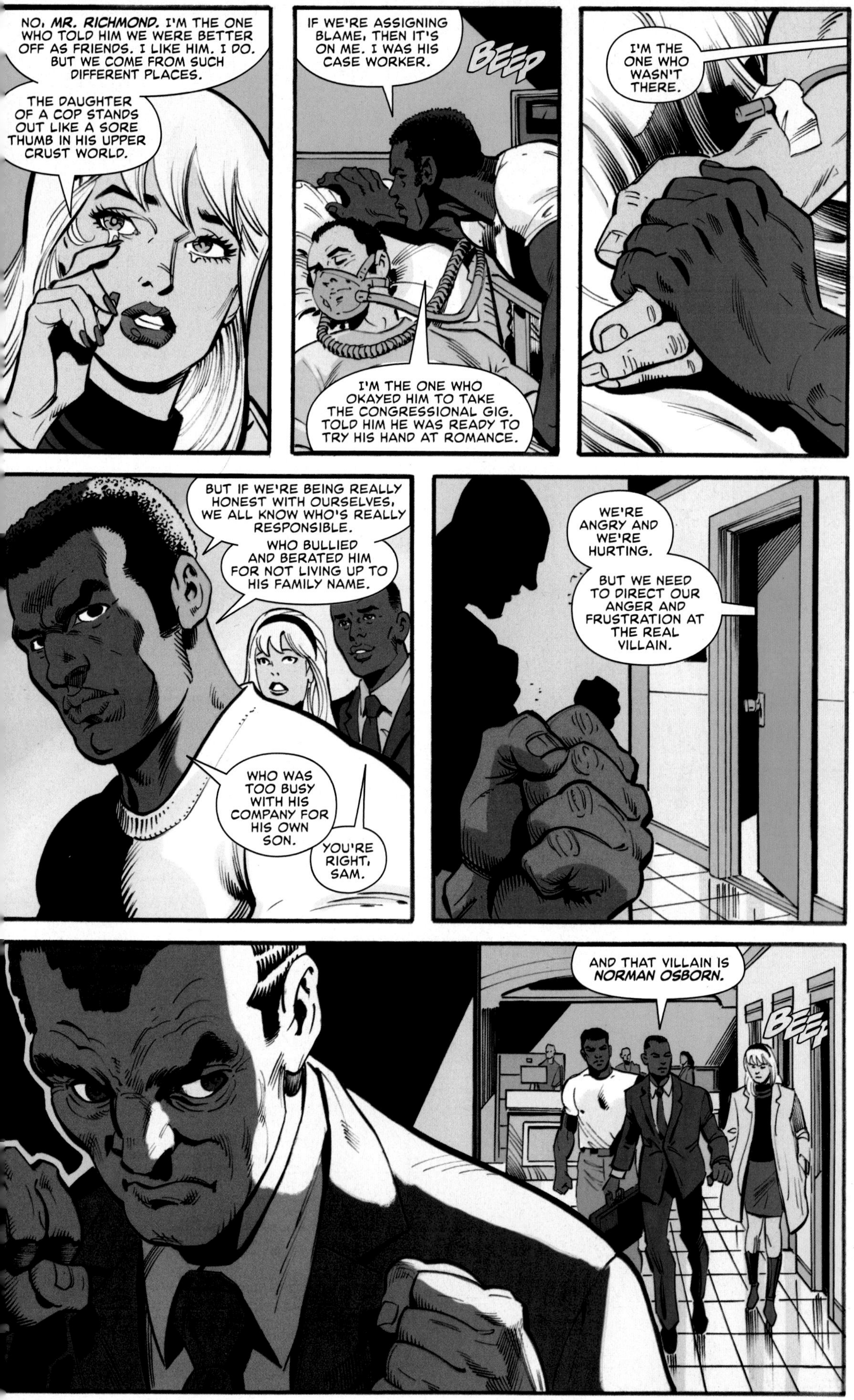
NO, MR. RICHMOND. I'M THE ONE WHO TOLD HIM WE WERE BETTER OFF AS FRIENDS. I LIKE HIM. I DO. BUT WE COME FROM SUCH DIFFERENT PLACES.
THE DAUGHTER OF A COP STANDS OUT LIKE A SORE THUMB IN HIS UPPER CRUST WORLD.
IF WE'RE ASSIGNING BLAME, THEN IT'S ON ME. I WAS HIS CASE WORKER.
BEEP
I'M THE ONE WHO OKAYED HIM TO TAKE THE CONGRESSIONAL GIG. TOLD HIM HE WAS READY TO TRY HIS HAND AT ROMANCE.
I'M THE ONE WHO WASN'T THERE.
BUT IF WE'RE BEING REALLY HONEST WITH OURSELVES, WE ALL KNOW WHO'S REALLY RESPONSIBLE.
WHO BULLIED AND BERATED HIM FOR NOT LIVING UP TO HIS FAMILY NAME.
WHO WAS TOO BUSY WITH HIS COMPANY FOR HIS OWN SON.
YOU'RE RIGHT, SAM.
WE'RE ANGRY AND WE'RE HURTING.
BUT WE NEED TO DIRECT OUR ANGER AND FRUSTRATION AT THE REAL VILLAIN.
AND THAT VILLAIN IS NORMAN OSBORN.
BEEP

*--EVERY MONTH IN **THE BLUR!***

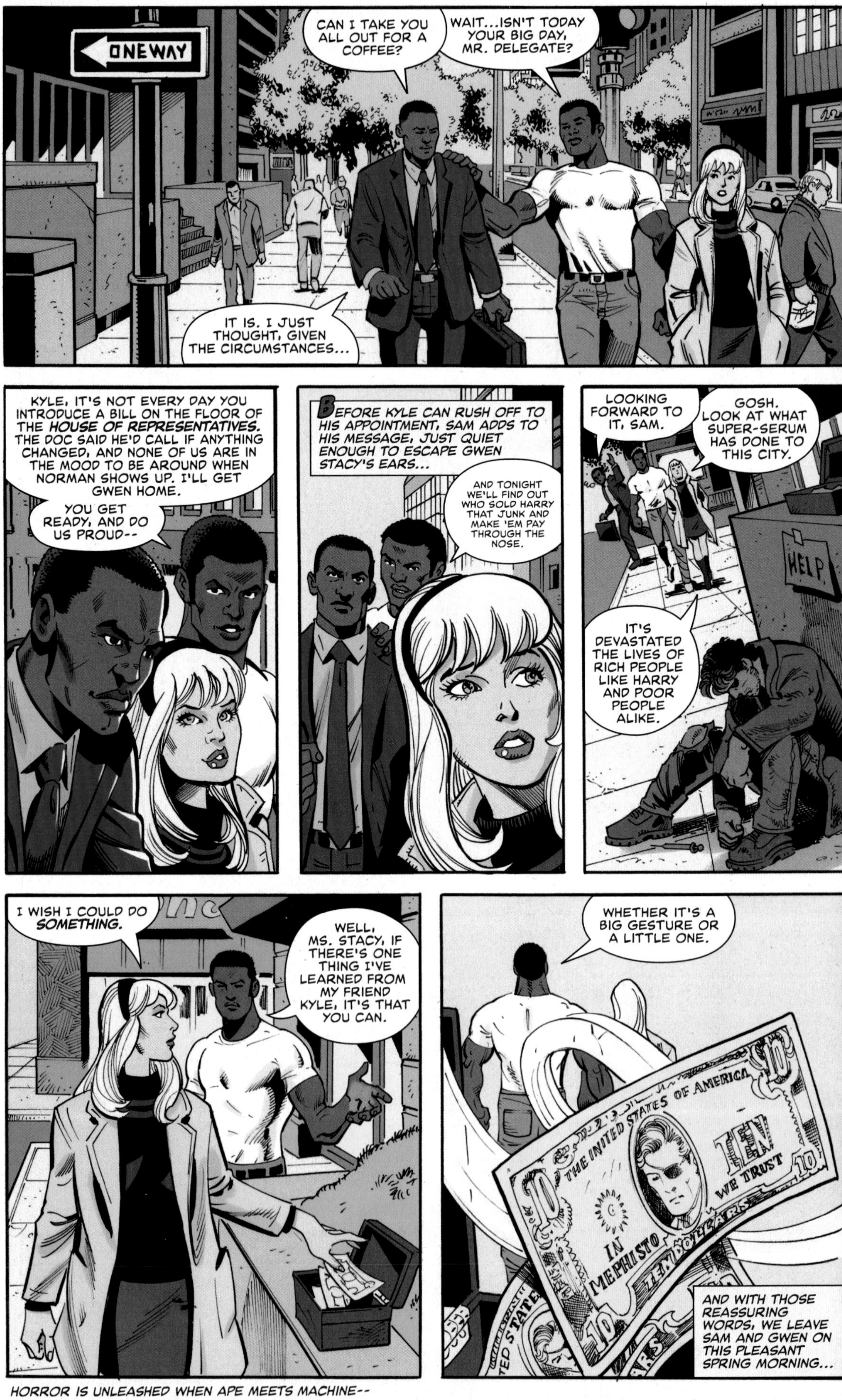
ONE WAY
CAN I TAKE YOU ALL OUT FOR A COFFEE?
WAIT...ISN'T TODAY YOUR BIG DAY, MR. DELEGATE?
IT IS. I JUST THOUGHT, GIVEN THE CIRCUMSTANCES...
KYLE, IT'S NOT EVERY DAY YOU INTRODUCE A BILL ON THE FLOOR OF THE HOUSE OF REPRESENTATIVES. THE DOC SAID HE'D CALL IF ANYTHING CHANGED, AND NONE OF US ARE IN THE MOOD TO BE AROUND WHEN NORMAN SHOWS UP. I'LL GET GWEN HOME.
YOU GET READY, AND DO US PROUD--
BEFORE KYLE CAN RUSH OFF TO HIS APPOINTMENT, SAM ADDS TO HIS MESSAGE, JUST QUIET ENOUGH TO ESCAPE GWEN STACY'S EARS...
AND TONIGHT WE'LL FIND OUT WHO SOLD HARRY THAT JUNK AND MAKE 'EM PAY THROUGH THE NOSE.
LOOKING FORWARD TO IT, SAM.
GOSH. LOOK AT WHAT SUPER-SERUM HAS DONE TO THIS CITY.
HELP.
IT'S DEVASTATED THE LIVES OF RICH PEOPLE LIKE HARRY AND POOR PEOPLE ALIKE.
I WISH I COULD DO SOMETHING.
WELL, MS. STACY, IF THERE'S ONE THING I'VE LEARNED FROM MY FRIEND KYLE, IT'S THAT YOU CAN.
WHETHER IT'S A BIG GESTURE OR A LITTLE ONE.
THE UNITED STATES OF AMERICA
TEN
IN MEPHISTO WE TRUST
AND WITH THOSE REASSURING WORDS, WE LEAVE SAM AND GWEN ON THIS PLEASANT SPRING MORNING...

HORROR IS UNLEASHED WHEN APE MEETS MACHINE--

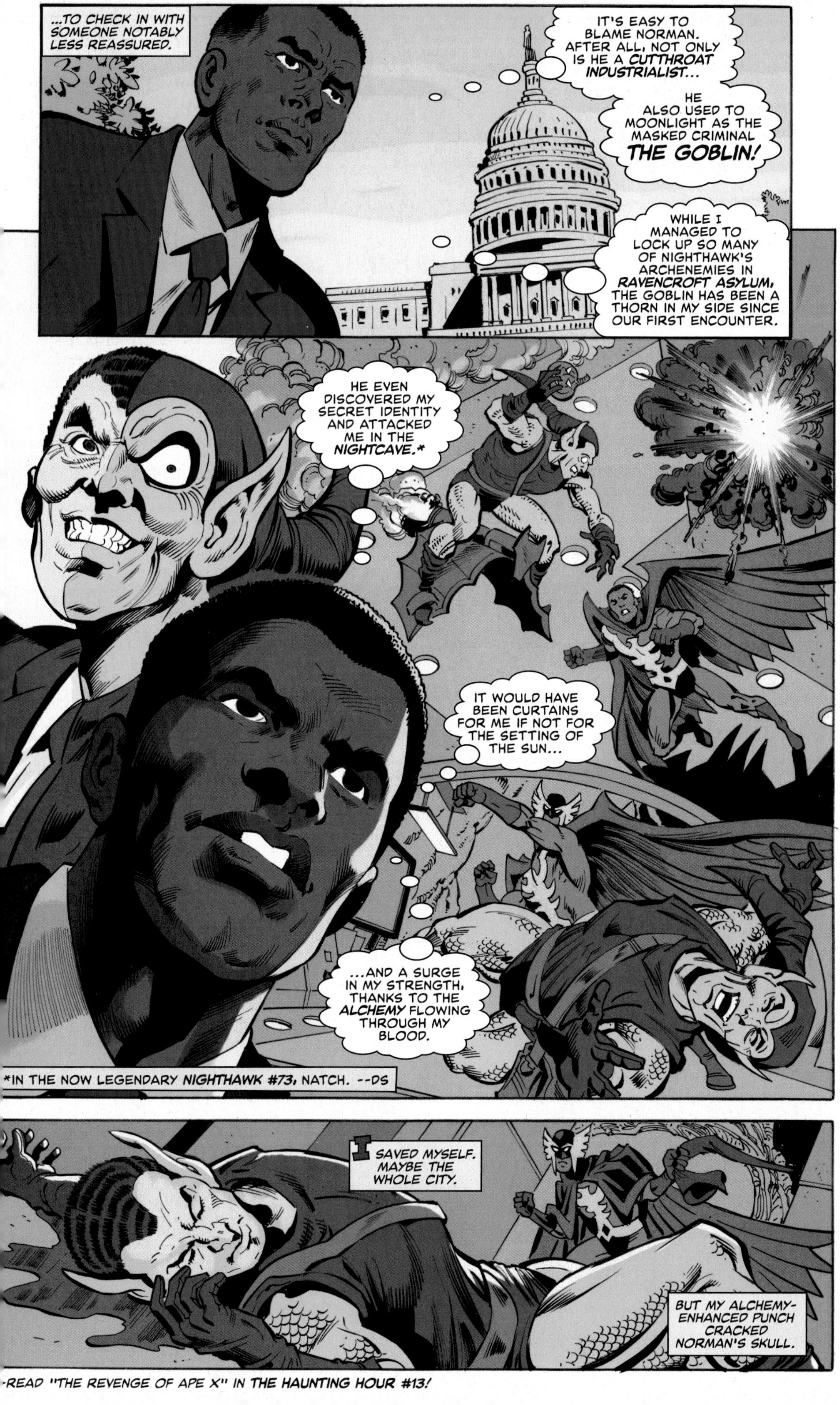
...TO CHECK IN WITH SOMEONE NOTABLY LESS REASSURED.
IT'S EASY TO BLAME NORMAN. AFTER ALL, NOT ONLY IS HE A CUTTHROAT INDUSTRIALIST...
HE ALSO USED TO MOONLIGHT AS THE MASKED CRIMINAL THE GOBLIN!
WHILE I MANAGED TO LOCK UP SO MANY OF NIGHTHAWK'S ARCHENEMIES IN RAVENCROFT ASYLUM, THE GOBLIN HAS BEEN A THORN IN MY SIDE SINCE OUR FIRST ENCOUNTER.
HE EVEN DISCOVERED MY SECRET IDENTITY AND ATTACKED ME IN THE NIGHTCAVE.*
IT WOULD HAVE BEEN CURTAINS FOR ME IF NOT FOR THE SETTING OF THE SUN...
...AND A SURGE IN MY STRENGTH, THANKS TO THE ALCHEMY FLOWING THROUGH MY BLOOD.
*IN THE NOW LEGENDARY NIGHTHAWK #73, NATCH. --DS
I SAVED MYSELF. MAYBE THE WHOLE CITY.
BUT MY ALCHEMY-ENHANCED PUNCH CRACKED NORMAN'S SKULL.
-READ "THE REVENGE OF APE X" IN THE HAUNTING HOUR #13!

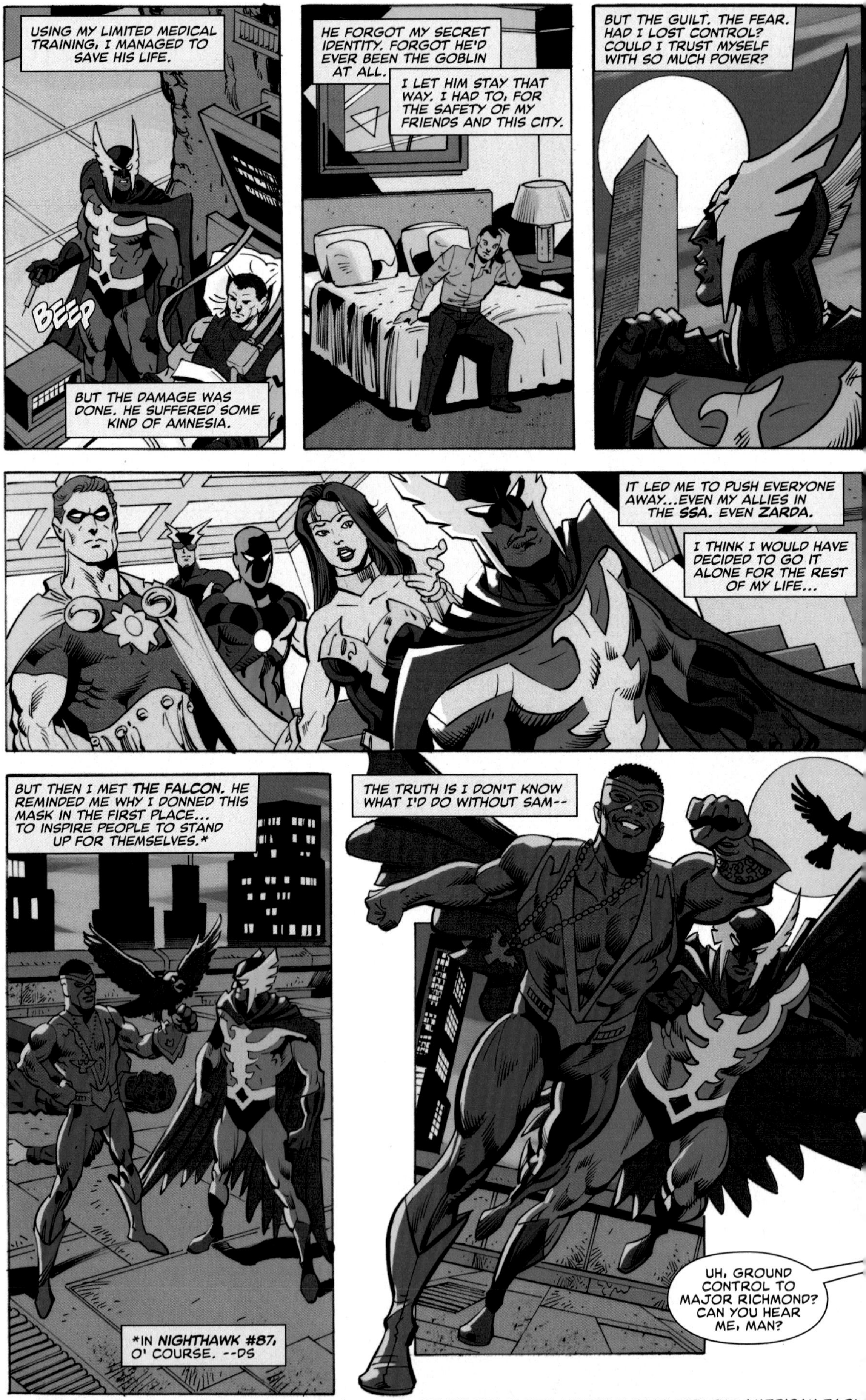
USING MY LIMITED MEDICAL TRAINING, I MANAGED TO SAVE HIS LIFE.
BEEP
BUT THE DAMAGE WAS DONE. HE SUFFERED SOME KIND OF AMNESIA.
HE FORGOT MY SECRET IDENTITY. FORGOT HE'D EVER BEEN THE GOBLIN AT ALL.
I LET HIM STAY THAT WAY. I HAD TO, FOR THE SAFETY OF MY FRIENDS AND THIS CITY.
BUT THE GUILT. THE FEAR. HAD I LOST CONTROL? COULD I TRUST MYSELF WITH SO MUCH POWER?
IT LED ME TO PUSH EVERYONE AWAY...EVEN MY ALLIES IN THE SSA. EVEN ZARDA.
I THINK I WOULD HAVE DECIDED TO GO IT ALONE FOR THE REST OF MY LIFE...
BUT THEN I MET THE FALCON. HE REMINDED ME WHY I DONNED THIS MASK IN THE FIRST PLACE... TO INSPIRE PEOPLE TO STAND UP FOR THEMSELVES.*
*IN NIGHTHAWK #87, O' COURSE. --DS
THE TRUTH IS I DON'T KNOW WHAT I'D DO WITHOUT SAM--
UH, GROUND CONTROL TO MAJOR RICHMOND? CAN YOU HEAR ME, MAN?

RELIVE THE GLORY AND TAKE WING WITH THE **AMERICAN EAGL**

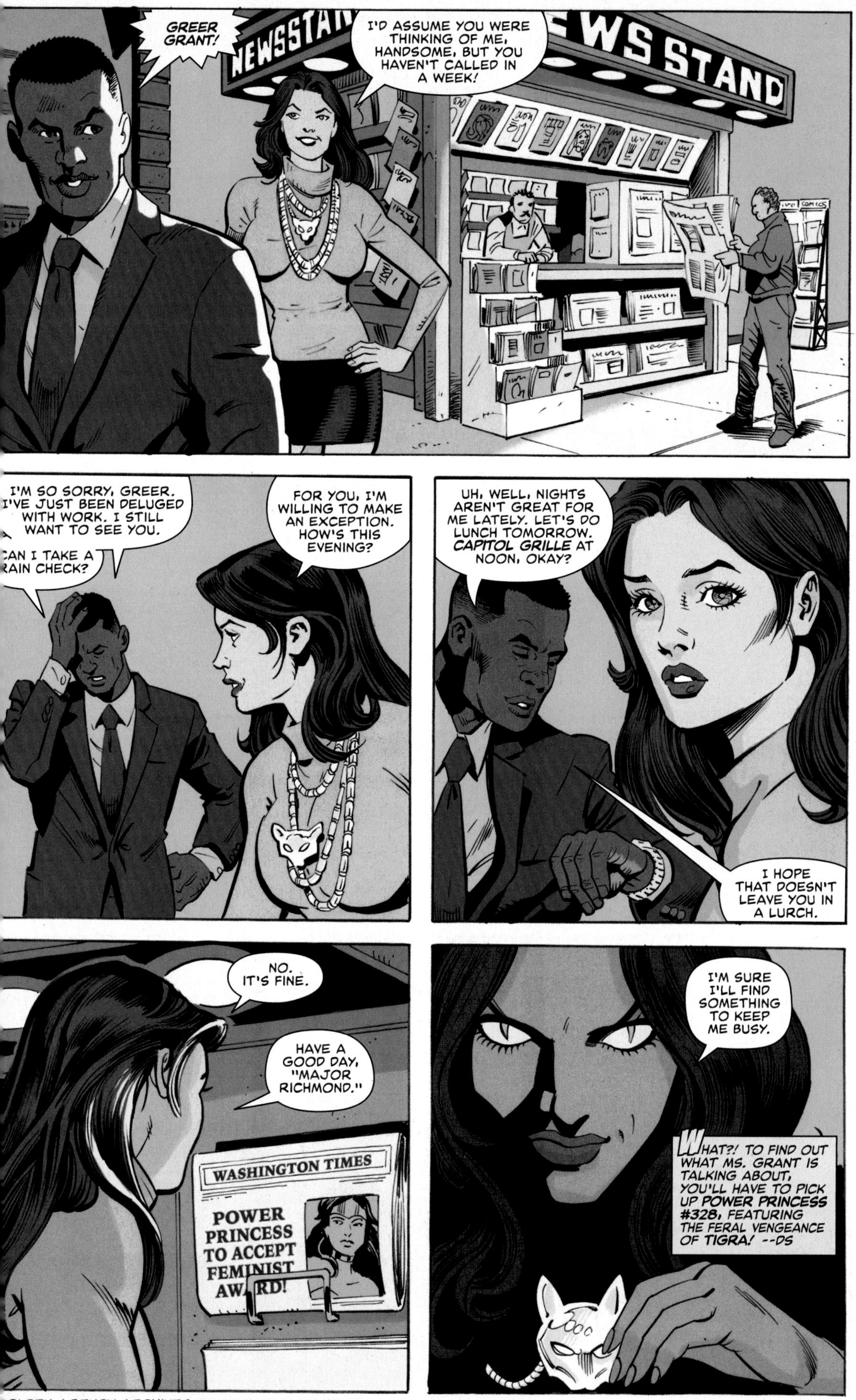
GREER GRANT!
I'D ASSUME YOU WERE THINKING OF ME, HANDSOME, BUT YOU HAVEN'T CALLED IN A WEEK!
NEWSSTAND
NEWS STAND
COMICS
I'M SO SORRY, GREER. I'VE JUST BEEN DELUGED WITH WORK. I STILL WANT TO SEE YOU.
CAN I TAKE A RAIN CHECK?
FOR YOU, I'M WILLING TO MAKE AN EXCEPTION. HOW'S THIS EVENING?
UH, WELL, NIGHTS AREN'T GREAT FOR ME LATELY. LET'S DO LUNCH TOMORROW. CAPITOL GRILLE AT NOON, OKAY?
I HOPE THAT DOESN'T LEAVE YOU IN A LURCH.
NO. IT'S FINE.
HAVE A GOOD DAY, "MAJOR RICHMOND."
WASHINGTON TIMES
POWER PRINCESS TO ACCEPT FEMINIST AWARD!
I'M SURE I'LL FIND SOMETHING TO KEEP ME BUSY.
WHAT?! TO FIND OUT WHAT MS. GRANT IS TALKING ABOUT, YOU'LL HAVE TO PICK UP POWER PRINCESS #328, FEATURING THE FERAL VENGEANCE OF TIGRA! --DS

OLDEN AGENCY ARCHIVES ON BOOKSHELVES NOW!

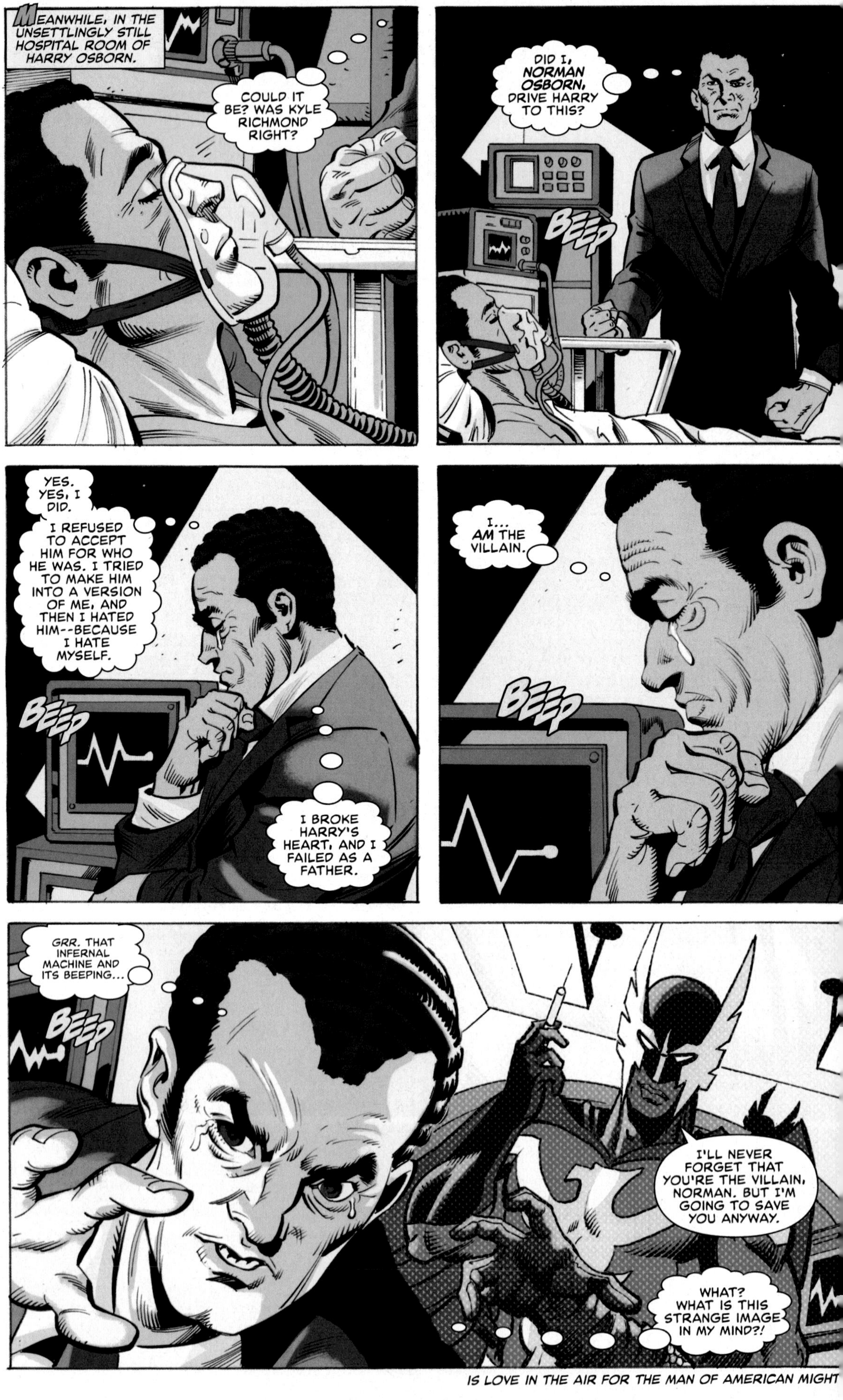
MEANWHILE, IN THE UNSETTLINGLY STILL HOSPITAL ROOM OF HARRY OSBORN.
COULD IT BE? WAS KYLE RICHMOND RIGHT?
DID I, NORMAN OSBORN, DRIVE HARRY TO THIS?
BEEP
YES. YES, I DID.
I REFUSED TO ACCEPT HIM FOR WHO HE WAS. I TRIED TO MAKE HIM INTO A VERSION OF ME, AND THEN I HATED HIM--BECAUSE I HATE MYSELF.
BEEP
I BROKE HARRY'S HEART, AND I FAILED AS A FATHER.
I... AM THE VILLAIN.
BEEP
GRR. THAT INFERNAL MACHINE AND ITS BEEPING...
BEEP
I'LL NEVER FORGET THAT YOU'RE THE VILLAIN, NORMAN. BUT I'M GOING TO SAVE YOU ANYWAY.
WHAT? WHAT IS THIS STRANGE IMAGE IN MY MIND?!

IS LOVE IN THE AIR FOR THE MAN OF AMERICAN MIGHT

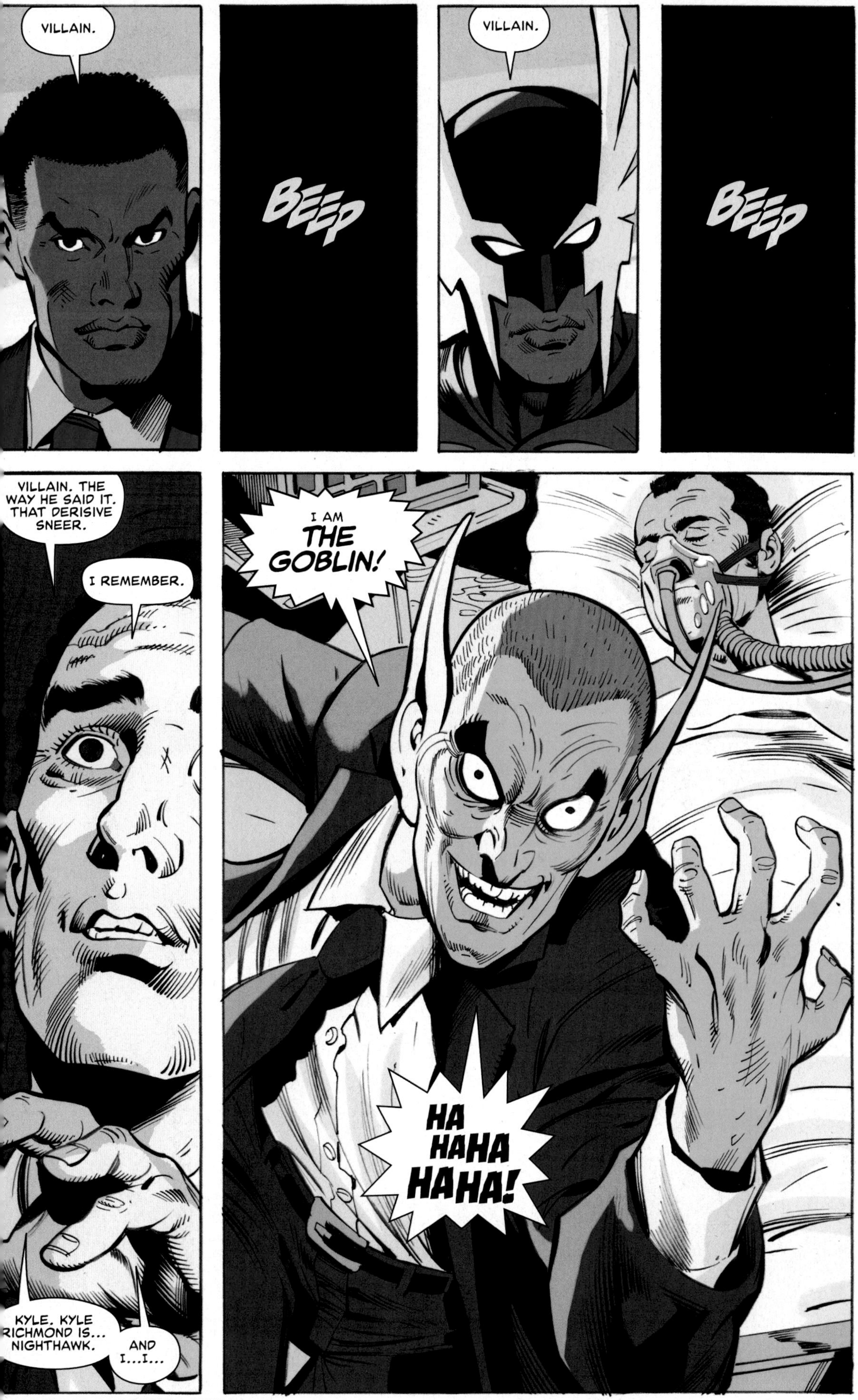
VILLAIN.
BEEP
VILLAIN.
BEEP
VILLAIN. THE WAY HE SAID IT. THAT DERISIVE SNEER.
I REMEMBER.
KYLE. KYLE RICHMOND IS... NIGHTHAWK.
AND I...I...
I AM THE GOBLIN!
HA HAHA HAHA!
MEET TITANIA IN *HYPERION #428!*

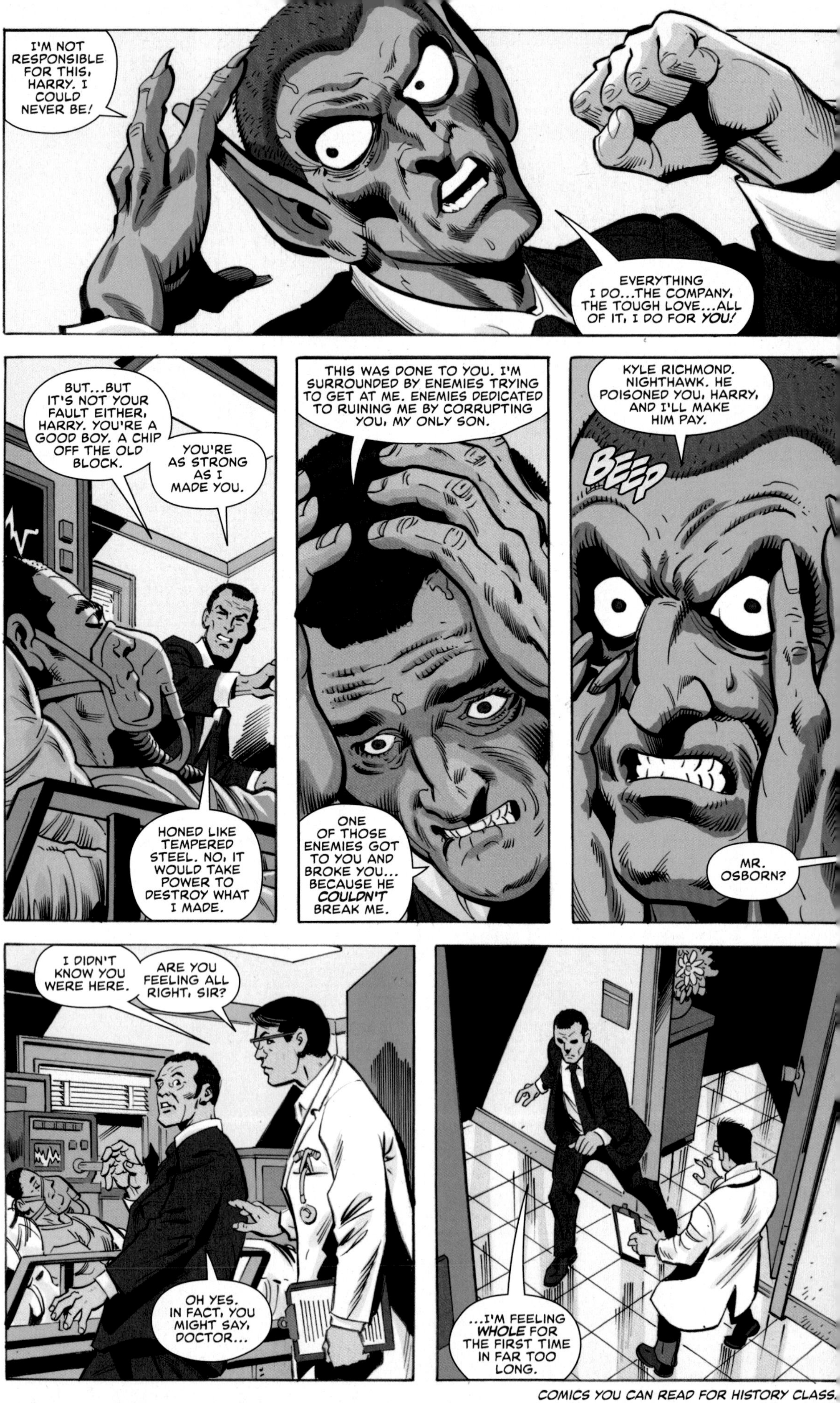
I'M NOT RESPONSIBLE FOR THIS, HARRY. I COULD NEVER BE!
EVERYTHING I DO...THE COMPANY, THE TOUGH LOVE...ALL OF IT, I DO FOR *YOU!*
BUT...BUT IT'S NOT YOUR FAULT EITHER, HARRY. YOU'RE A GOOD BOY. A CHIP OFF THE OLD BLOCK.
YOU'RE AS STRONG AS I MADE YOU.
HONED LIKE TEMPERED STEEL. NO, IT WOULD TAKE POWER TO DESTROY WHAT I MADE.
THIS WAS DONE TO YOU. I'M SURROUNDED BY ENEMIES TRYING TO GET AT ME. ENEMIES DEDICATED TO RUINING ME BY CORRUPTING YOU, MY ONLY SON.
ONE OF THOSE ENEMIES GOT TO YOU AND BROKE YOU... BECAUSE HE ***COULDN'T*** BREAK ME.
KYLE RICHMOND. NIGHTHAWK. HE POISONED YOU, HARRY, AND I'LL MAKE HIM PAY.
BEEP
MR. OSBORN?
I DIDN'T KNOW YOU WERE HERE.
ARE YOU FEELING ALL RIGHT, SIR?
OH YES. IN FACT, YOU MIGHT SAY, DOCTOR...
...I'M FEELING ***WHOLE*** FOR THE FIRST TIME IN FAR TOO LONG.

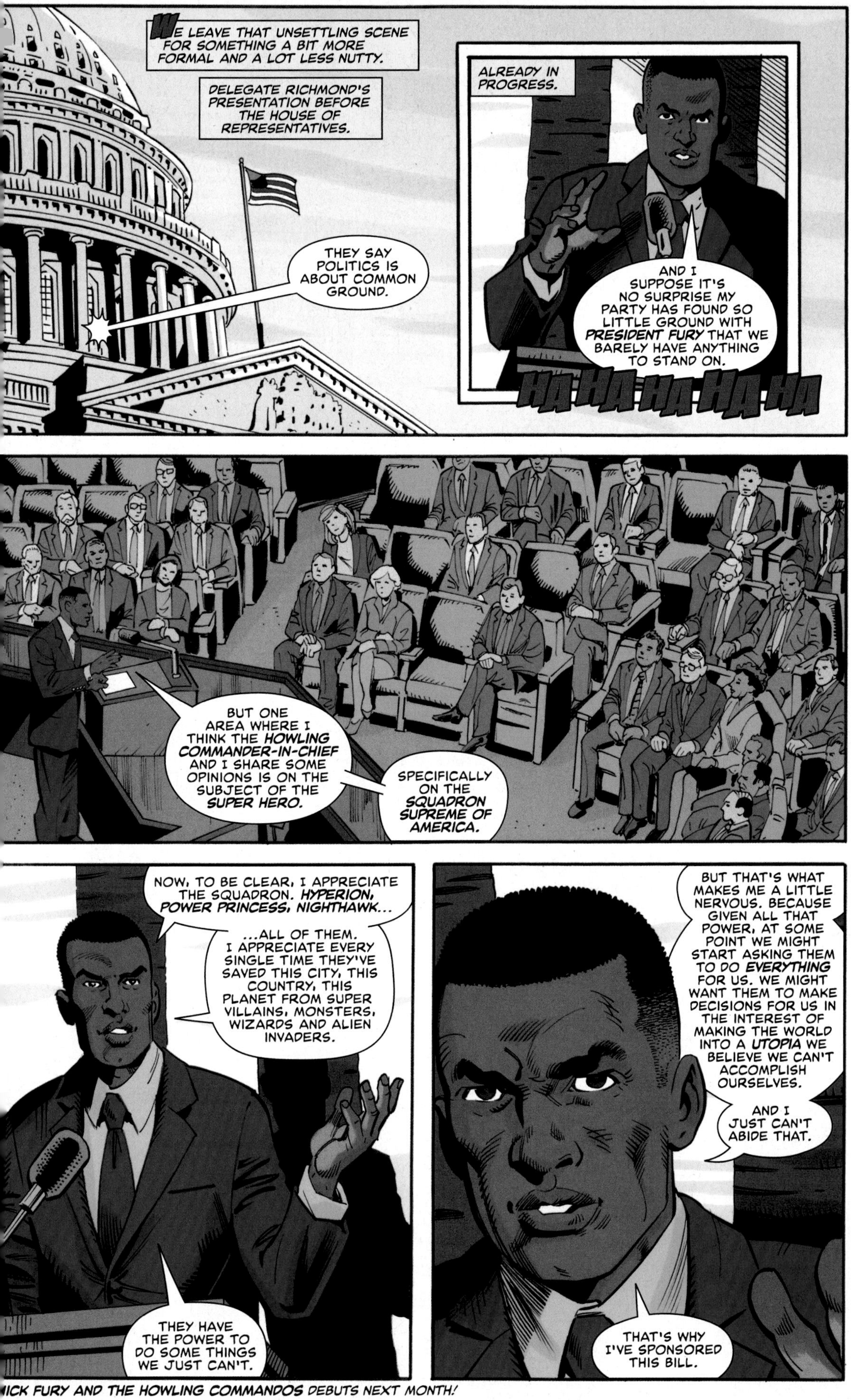
WE LEAVE THAT UNSETTLING SCENE FOR SOMETHING A BIT MORE FORMAL AND A LOT LESS NUTTY.
DELEGATE RICHMOND'S PRESENTATION BEFORE THE HOUSE OF REPRESENTATIVES.
THEY SAY POLITICS IS ABOUT COMMON GROUND.
ALREADY IN PROGRESS.
AND I SUPPOSE IT'S NO SURPRISE MY PARTY HAS FOUND SO LITTLE GROUND WITH PRESIDENT FURY THAT WE BARELY HAVE ANYTHING TO STAND ON.
HA HA HA HA HA
BUT ONE AREA WHERE I THINK THE HOWLING COMMANDER-IN-CHIEF AND I SHARE SOME OPINIONS IS ON THE SUBJECT OF THE SUPER HERO.
SPECIFICALLY ON THE SQUADRON SUPREME OF AMERICA.
NOW, TO BE CLEAR, I APPRECIATE THE SQUADRON. HYPERION, POWER PRINCESS, NIGHTHAWK...
...ALL OF THEM. I APPRECIATE EVERY SINGLE TIME THEY'VE SAVED THIS CITY, THIS COUNTRY, THIS PLANET FROM SUPER VILLAINS, MONSTERS, WIZARDS AND ALIEN INVADERS.
THEY HAVE THE POWER TO DO SOME THINGS WE JUST CAN'T.
BUT THAT'S WHAT MAKES ME A LITTLE NERVOUS. BECAUSE GIVEN ALL THAT POWER, AT SOME POINT WE MIGHT START ASKING THEM TO DO EVERYTHING FOR US. WE MIGHT WANT THEM TO MAKE DECISIONS FOR US IN THE INTEREST OF MAKING THE WORLD INTO A UTOPIA WE BELIEVE WE CAN'T ACCOMPLISH OURSELVES.
AND I JUST CAN'T ABIDE THAT.
THAT'S WHY I'VE SPONSORED THIS BILL.

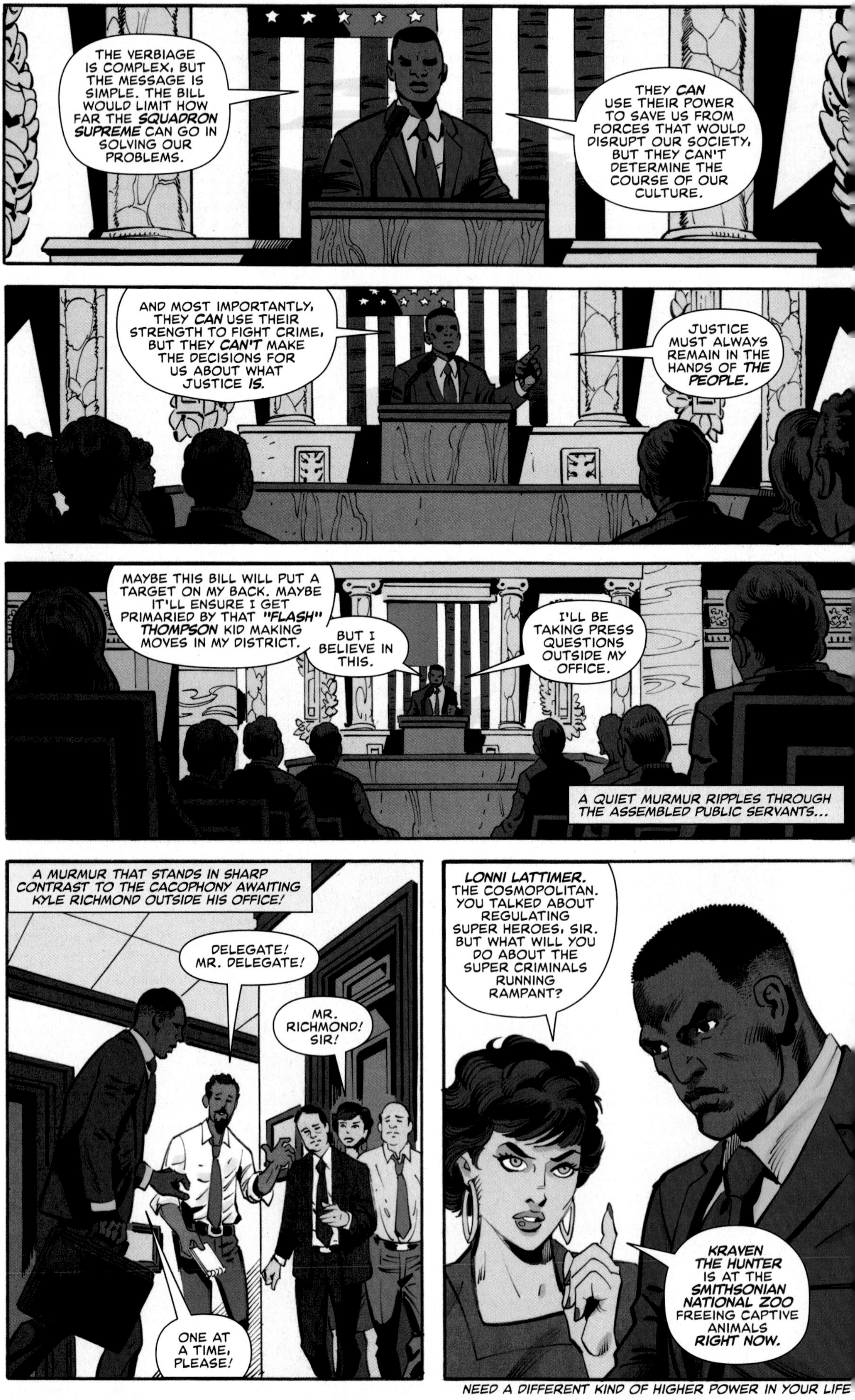
THE VERBIAGE IS COMPLEX, BUT THE MESSAGE IS SIMPLE. THE BILL WOULD LIMIT HOW FAR THE SQUADRON SUPREME CAN GO IN SOLVING OUR PROBLEMS.
THEY CAN USE THEIR POWER TO SAVE US FROM FORCES THAT WOULD DISRUPT OUR SOCIETY, BUT THEY CAN'T DETERMINE THE COURSE OF OUR CULTURE.
AND MOST IMPORTANTLY, THEY CAN USE THEIR STRENGTH TO FIGHT CRIME, BUT THEY CAN'T MAKE THE DECISIONS FOR US ABOUT WHAT JUSTICE IS.
JUSTICE MUST ALWAYS REMAIN IN THE HANDS OF THE PEOPLE.
MAYBE THIS BILL WILL PUT A TARGET ON MY BACK. MAYBE IT'LL ENSURE I GET PRIMARIED BY THAT "FLASH" THOMPSON KID MAKING MOVES IN MY DISTRICT.
BUT I BELIEVE IN THIS.
I'LL BE TAKING PRESS QUESTIONS OUTSIDE MY OFFICE.
A QUIET MURMUR RIPPLES THROUGH THE ASSEMBLED PUBLIC SERVANTS...
A MURMUR THAT STANDS IN SHARP CONTRAST TO THE CACOPHONY AWAITING KYLE RICHMOND OUTSIDE HIS OFFICE!
DELEGATE! MR. DELEGATE!
MR. RICHMOND! SIR!
ONE AT A TIME, PLEASE!
LONNI LATTIMER. THE COSMOPOLITAN. YOU TALKED ABOUT REGULATING SUPER HEROES, SIR. BUT WHAT WILL YOU DO ABOUT THE SUPER CRIMINALS RUNNING RAMPANT?
KRAVEN THE HUNTER IS AT THE SMITHSONIAN NATIONAL ZOO FREEING CAPTIVE ANIMALS RIGHT NOW.

NEED A DIFFERENT KIND OF HIGHER POWER IN YOUR LIFE

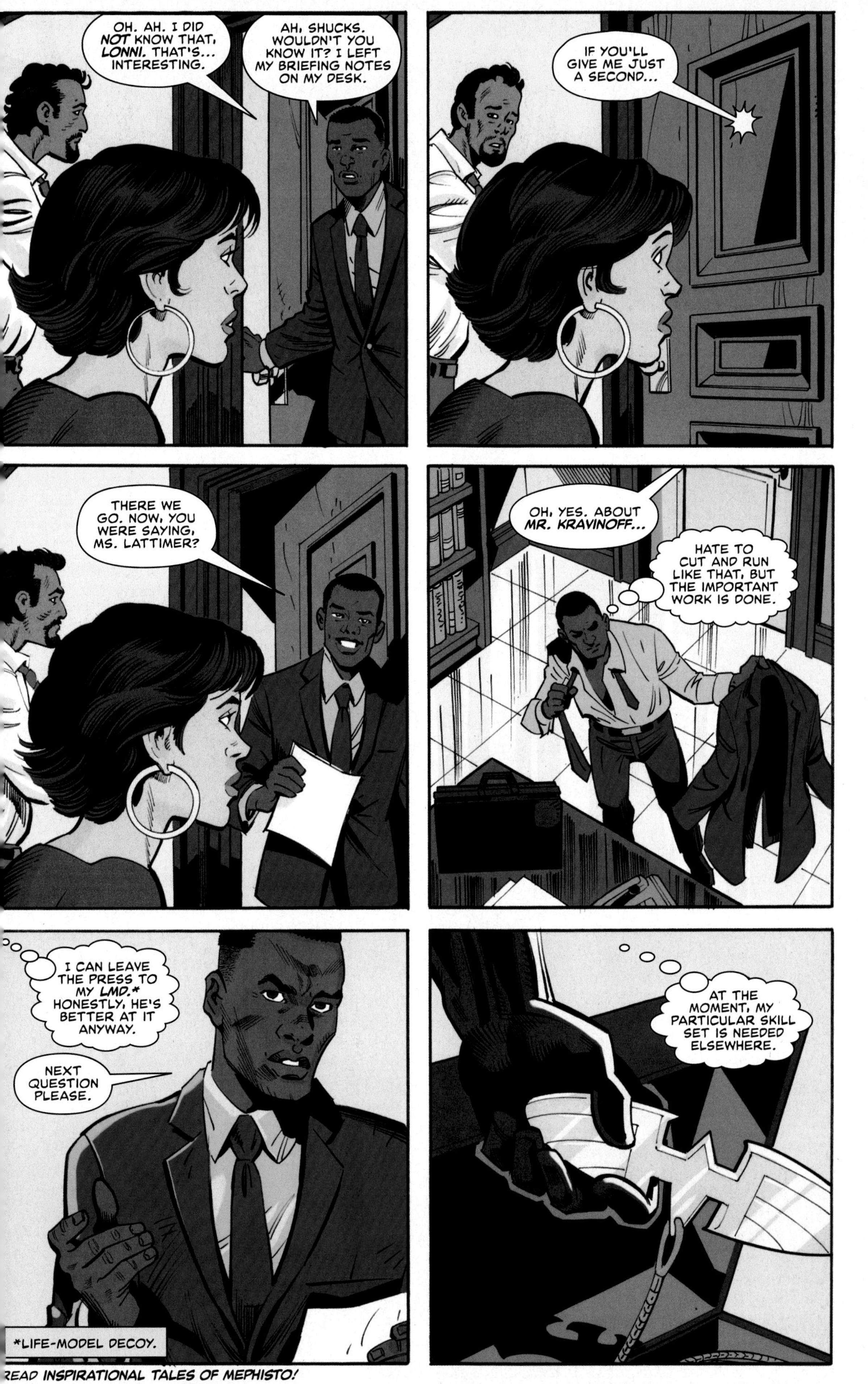
OH. AH. I DID NOT KNOW THAT, LONNI. THAT'S... INTERESTING.
AH, SHUCKS. WOULDN'T YOU KNOW IT? I LEFT MY BRIEFING NOTES ON MY DESK.
IF YOU'LL GIVE ME JUST A SECOND...
THERE WE GO. NOW, YOU WERE SAYING, MS. LATTIMER?
OH, YES. ABOUT MR. KRAVINOFF...
HATE TO CUT AND RUN LIKE THAT, BUT THE IMPORTANT WORK IS DONE.
I CAN LEAVE THE PRESS TO MY LMD.* HONESTLY, HE'S BETTER AT IT ANYWAY.
NEXT QUESTION PLEASE.
*LIFE-MODEL DECOY.
AT THE MOMENT, MY PARTICULAR SKILL SET IS NEEDED ELSEWHERE.

READ INSPIRATIONAL TALES OF MEPHISTO!

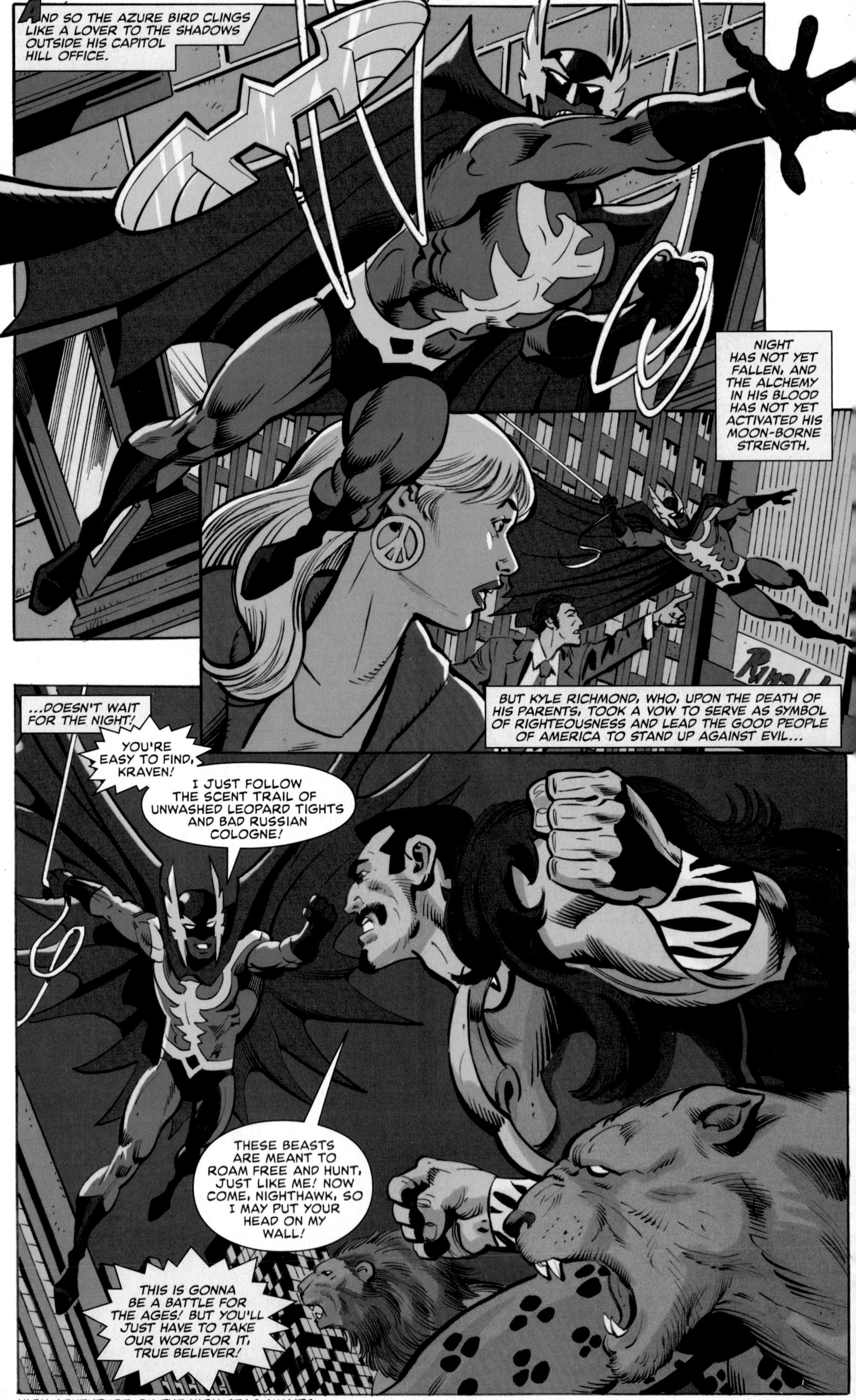
AND SO THE AZURE BIRD CLINGS LIKE A LOVER TO THE SHADOWS OUTSIDE HIS CAPITOL HILL OFFICE.
NIGHT HAS NOT YET FALLEN, AND THE ALCHEMY IN HIS BLOOD HAS NOT YET ACTIVATED HIS MOON-BORNE STRENGTH.
BUT KYLE RICHMOND, WHO, UPON THE DEATH OF HIS PARENTS, TOOK A VOW TO SERVE AS SYMBOL OF RIGHTEOUSNESS AND LEAD THE GOOD PEOPLE OF AMERICA TO STAND UP AGAINST EVIL...
...DOESN'T WAIT FOR THE NIGHT!
YOU'RE EASY TO FIND, KRAVEN!
I JUST FOLLOW THE SCENT TRAIL OF UNWASHED LEOPARD TIGHTS AND BAD RUSSIAN COLOGNE!
THESE BEASTS ARE MEANT TO ROAM FREE AND HUNT, JUST LIKE ME! NOW COME, NIGHTHAWK, SO I MAY PUT YOUR HEAD ON MY WALL!
THIS IS GONNA BE A BATTLE FOR THE AGES! BUT YOU'LL JUST HAVE TO TAKE OUR WORD FOR IT, TRUE BELIEVER!

HIGH ADVENTURE ON THE HIGH SEAS AWAITS--

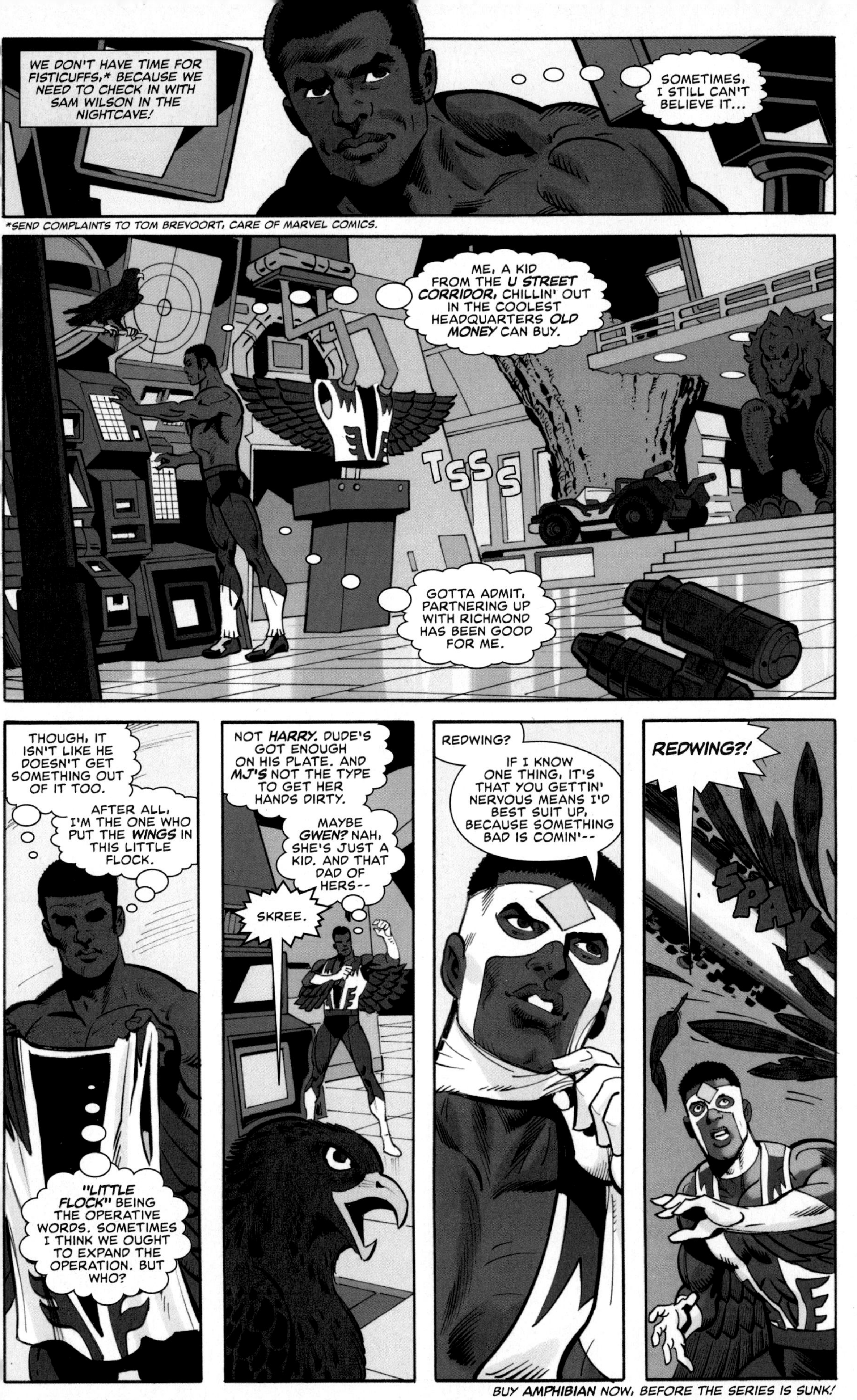
WE DON'T HAVE TIME FOR FISTICUFFS,* BECAUSE WE NEED TO CHECK IN WITH SAM WILSON IN THE NIGHTCAVE!
SOMETIMES, I STILL CAN'T BELIEVE IT...
*SEND COMPLAINTS TO TOM BREVOORT, CARE OF MARVEL COMICS.
ME, A KID FROM THE U STREET CORRIDOR, CHILLIN' OUT IN THE COOLEST HEADQUARTERS OLD MONEY CAN BUY.
TSSS
GOTTA ADMIT, PARTNERING UP WITH RICHMOND HAS BEEN GOOD FOR ME.
THOUGH, IT ISN'T LIKE HE DOESN'T GET SOMETHING OUT OF IT TOO.
AFTER ALL, I'M THE ONE WHO PUT THE WINGS IN THIS LITTLE FLOCK.
"LITTLE FLOCK" BEING THE OPERATIVE WORDS. SOMETIMES I THINK WE OUGHT TO EXPAND THE OPERATION. BUT WHO?
NOT HARRY. DUDE'S GOT ENOUGH ON HIS PLATE. AND MJ'S NOT THE TYPE TO GET HER HANDS DIRTY.
MAYBE GWEN? NAH, SHE'S JUST A KID. AND THAT DAD OF HERS--
SKREE.
REDWING?
IF I KNOW ONE THING, IT'S THAT YOU GETTIN' NERVOUS MEANS I'D BEST SUIT UP, BECAUSE SOMETHING BAD IS COMIN'--
REDWING?!
SPAK

BUY AMPHIBIAN NOW, BEFORE THE SERIES IS SUNK!

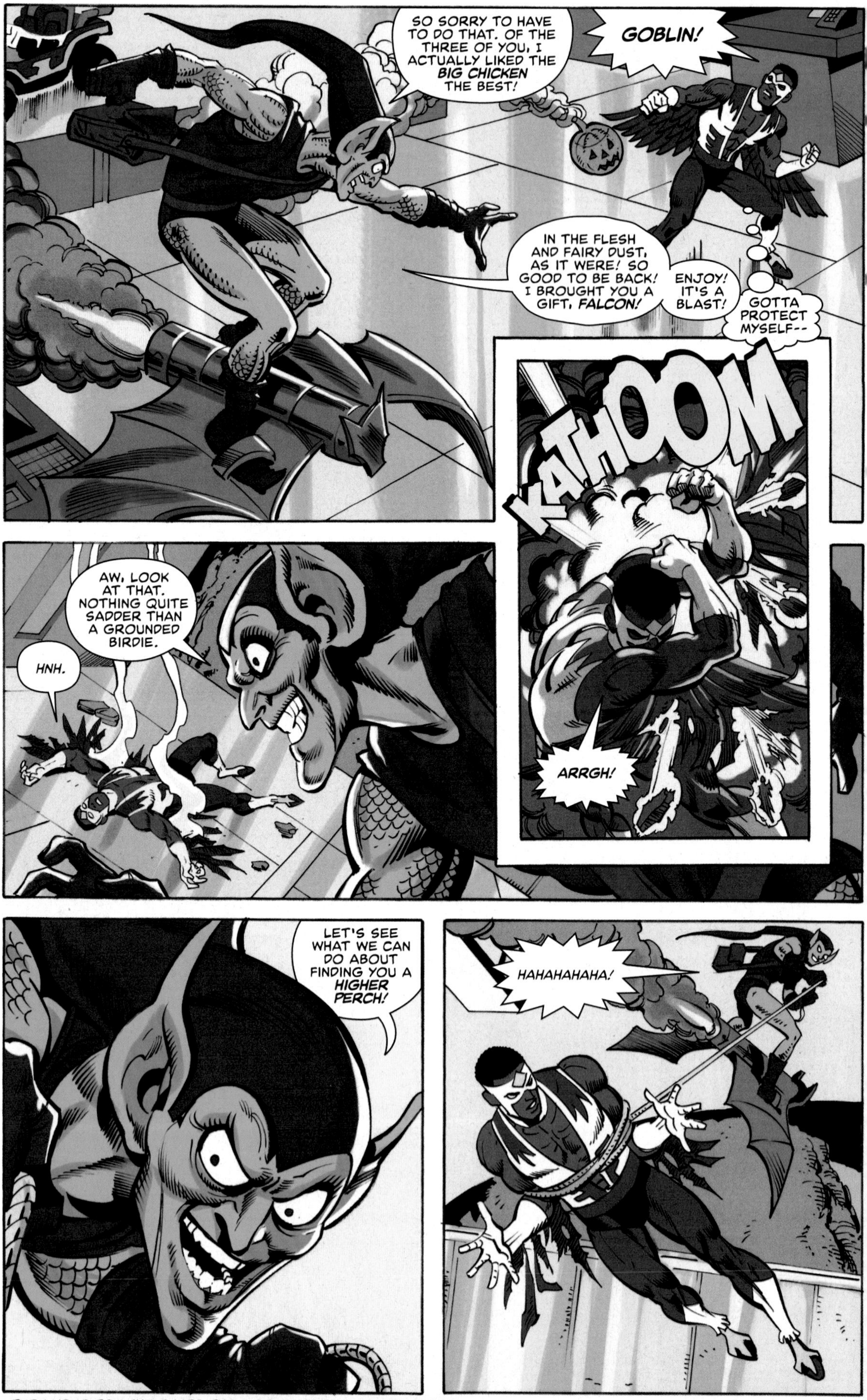
SO SORRY TO HAVE TO DO THAT. OF THE THREE OF YOU, I ACTUALLY LIKED THE BIG CHICKEN THE BEST!
GOBLIN!
IN THE FLESH AND FAIRY DUST, AS IT WERE! SO GOOD TO BE BACK! I BROUGHT YOU A GIFT, FALCON!
ENJOY! IT'S A BLAST!
GOTTA PROTECT MYSELF--
KATHOOM
ARRGH!
AW, LOOK AT THAT. NOTHING QUITE SADDER THAN A GROUNDED BIRDIE.
HNH.
LET'S SEE WHAT WE CAN DO ABOUT FINDING YOU A HIGHER PERCH!
HAHAHAHAHA!

TURN YOUR TOY SHELF INTO THE WORLD'S SLICKEST SHOWROOM--

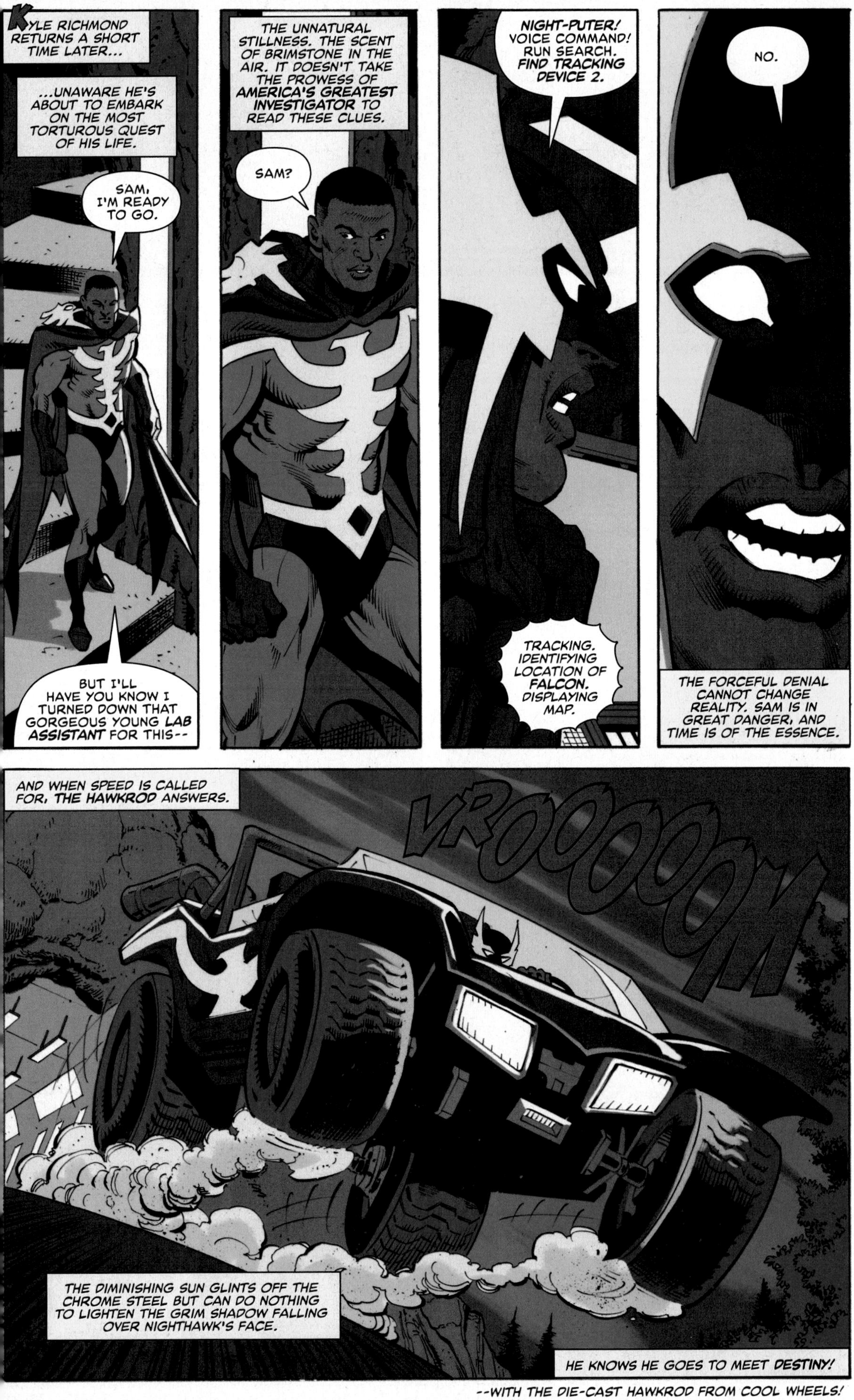
KYLE RICHMOND RETURNS A SHORT TIME LATER...
...UNAWARE HE'S ABOUT TO EMBARK ON THE MOST TORTUROUS QUEST OF HIS LIFE.
SAM, I'M READY TO GO.
BUT I'LL HAVE YOU KNOW I TURNED DOWN THAT GORGEOUS YOUNG LAB ASSISTANT FOR THIS--
THE UNNATURAL STILLNESS. THE SCENT OF BRIMSTONE IN THE AIR. IT DOESN'T TAKE THE PROWESS OF AMERICA'S GREATEST INVESTIGATOR TO READ THESE CLUES.
SAM?
NIGHT-PUTER! VOICE COMMAND! RUN SEARCH. FIND TRACKING DEVICE 2.
TRACKING. IDENTIFYING LOCATION OF FALCON. DISPLAYING MAP.
NO.
THE FORCEFUL DENIAL CANNOT CHANGE REALITY. SAM IS IN GREAT DANGER, AND TIME IS OF THE ESSENCE.
AND WHEN SPEED IS CALLED FOR, THE HAWKROD ANSWERS.
VROOOOOOM
THE DIMINISHING SUN GLINTS OFF THE CHROME STEEL BUT CAN DO NOTHING TO LIGHTEN THE GRIM SHADOW FALLING OVER NIGHTHAWK'S FACE.
HE KNOWS HE GOES TO MEET DESTINY!

--WITH THE DIE-CAST HAWKROD FROM COOL WHEELS!

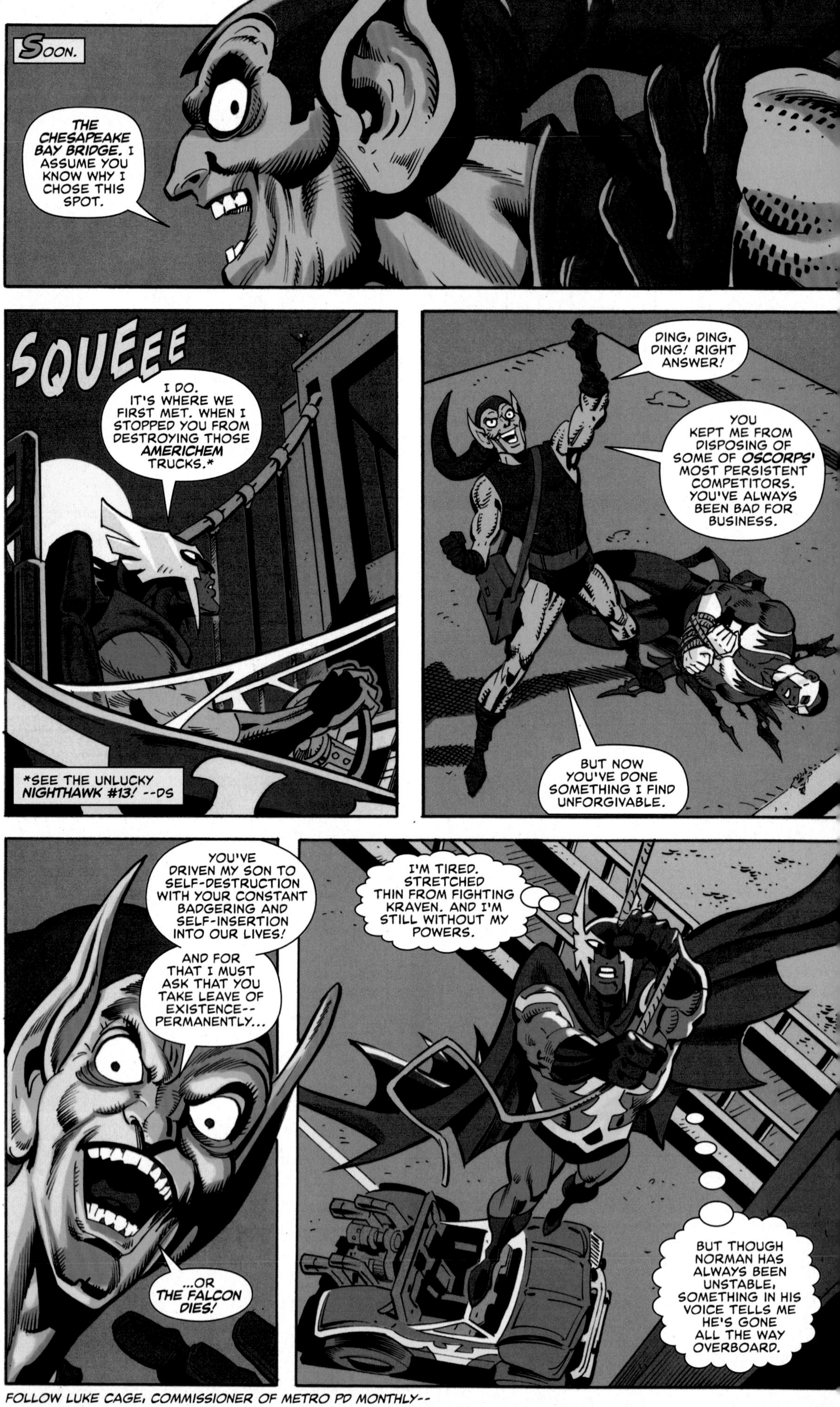
SOON.
THE CHESAPEAKE BAY BRIDGE. I ASSUME YOU KNOW WHY I CHOSE THIS SPOT.
SQUEEE
I DO. IT'S WHERE WE FIRST MET. WHEN I STOPPED YOU FROM DESTROYING THOSE AMERICHEM TRUCKS.*
*SEE THE UNLUCKY NIGHTHAWK #13! --DS
DING, DING, DING! RIGHT ANSWER!
YOU KEPT ME FROM DISPOSING OF SOME OF OSCORPS' MOST PERSISTENT COMPETITORS. YOU'VE ALWAYS BEEN BAD FOR BUSINESS.
BUT NOW YOU'VE DONE SOMETHING I FIND UNFORGIVABLE.
YOU'VE DRIVEN MY SON TO SELF-DESTRUCTION WITH YOUR CONSTANT BADGERING AND SELF-INSERTION INTO OUR LIVES!
AND FOR THAT I MUST ASK THAT YOU TAKE LEAVE OF EXISTENCE--PERMANENTLY...
...OR THE FALCON DIES!
I'M TIRED. STRETCHED THIN FROM FIGHTING KRAVEN. AND I'M STILL WITHOUT MY POWERS.
BUT THOUGH NORMAN HAS ALWAYS BEEN UNSTABLE, SOMETHING IN HIS VOICE TELLS ME HE'S GONE ALL THE WAY OVERBOARD.

FOLLOW LUKE CAGE, COMMISSIONER OF METRO PD MONTHLY--

THIS TIME HE MEANS IT!

A WORTHY ATTEMPT, MR. DELEGATE--

--BUT I CAN DODGE YOU FASTER THAN YOU DODGE THE PRESS!

THROK

HNH!

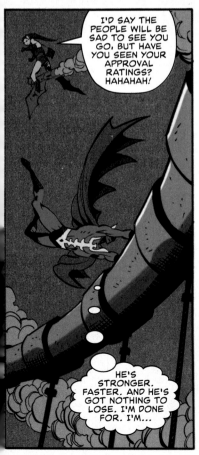

I'D SAY THE PEOPLE WILL BE SAD TO SEE YOU GO, BUT HAVE YOU SEEN YOUR APPROVAL RATINGS? HAHAHAH!

HE'S STRONGER. FASTER. AND HE'S GOT NOTHING TO LOSE. I'M DONE FOR. I'M...

NO. I'M NOT.

I TRAINED WITH THE GREATEST FIGHTERS IN THE WORLD. THE ORDER OF THE CRANE MOTHER. THE BLACK MARVEL.

PRINCESS ZARDA.

I'M MORE THAN MY SUPER-POWERS.

I'M STILL NIGHTHAWK WHEN THE SUN IS UP.

ALL I HAVE TO DO IS GIVE IT...

--IN HEROES ON CALL!

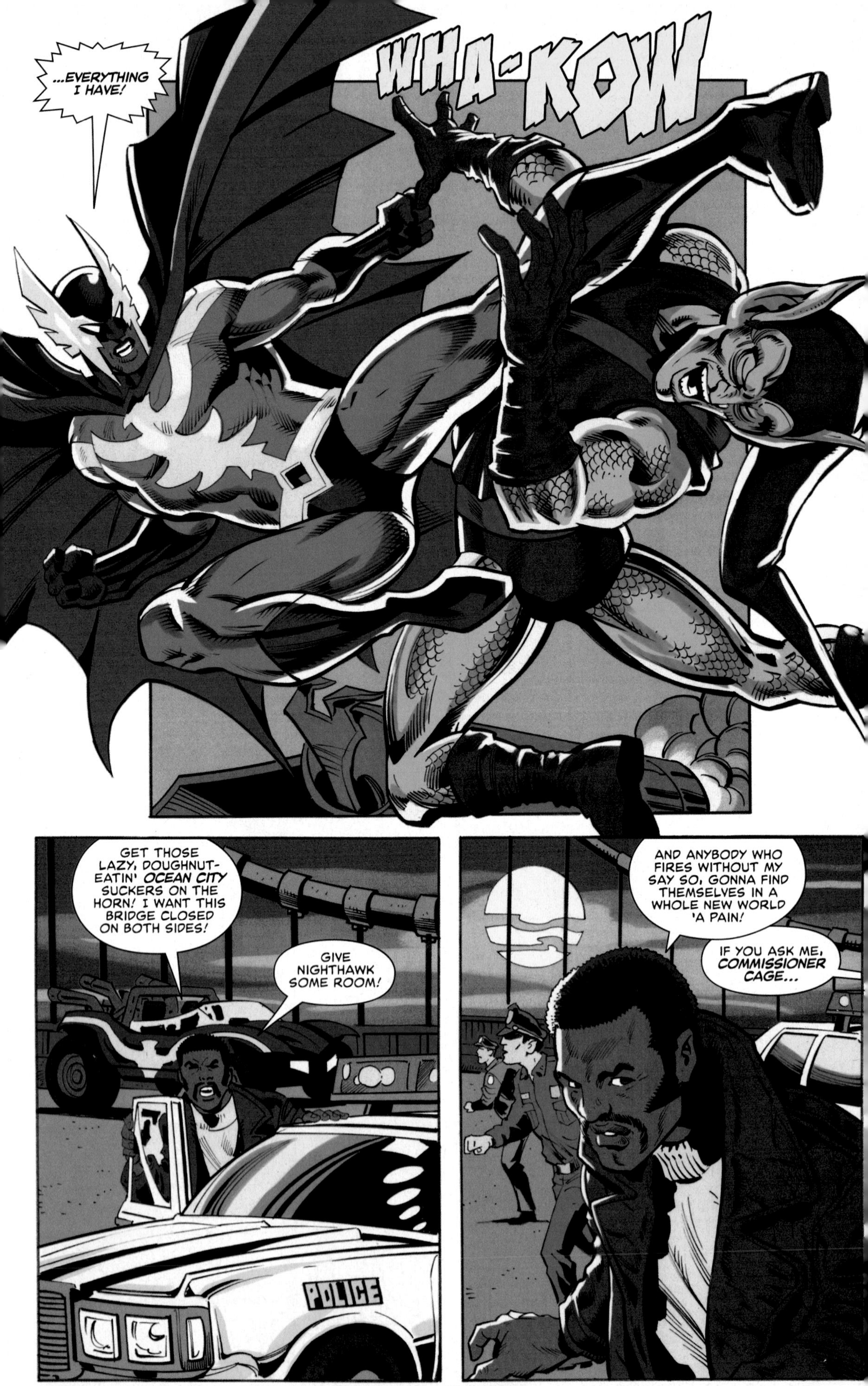
...EVERYTHING I HAVE!
WHA-KOW
GET THOSE LAZY, DOUGHNUT-EATIN' OCEAN CITY SUCKERS ON THE HORN! I WANT THIS BRIDGE CLOSED ON BOTH SIDES!
GIVE NIGHTHAWK SOME ROOM!
POLICE
AND ANYBODY WHO FIRES WITHOUT MY SAY SO, GONNA FIND THEMSELVES IN A WHOLE NEW WORLD 'A PAIN!
IF YOU ASK ME, COMMISSIONER CAGE...

MINIATURE MISCHIEF ABOUNDS WHEN HIGH FANTASY MEETS HIGH SCIENCE--

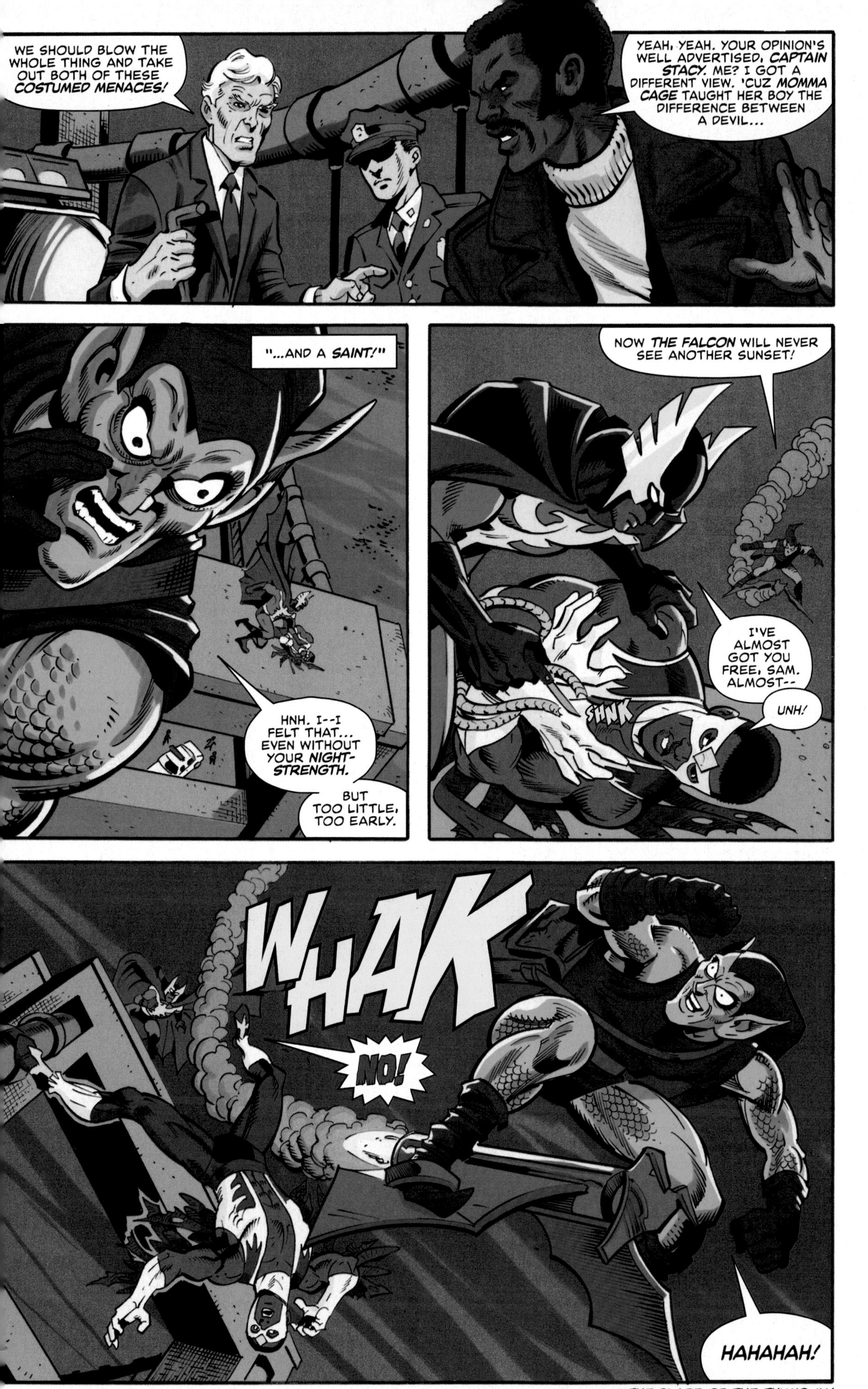
WE SHOULD BLOW THE WHOLE THING AND TAKE OUT BOTH OF THESE COSTUMED MENACES!
YEAH, YEAH. YOUR OPINION'S WELL ADVERTISED, CAPTAIN STACY. ME? I GOT A DIFFERENT VIEW. 'CUZ MOMMA CAGE TAUGHT HER BOY THE DIFFERENCE BETWEEN A DEVIL...
"...AND A SAINT!"
HNH. I--I FELT THAT... EVEN WITHOUT YOUR NIGHT-STRENGTH.
BUT TOO LITTLE, TOO EARLY.
NOW THE FALCON WILL NEVER SEE ANOTHER SUNSET!
I'VE ALMOST GOT YOU FREE, SAM. ALMOST--
SHNK
UNH!
WHAK
NO!
HAHAHAH!

--IN THE BLADE OF THE THUMB #1!

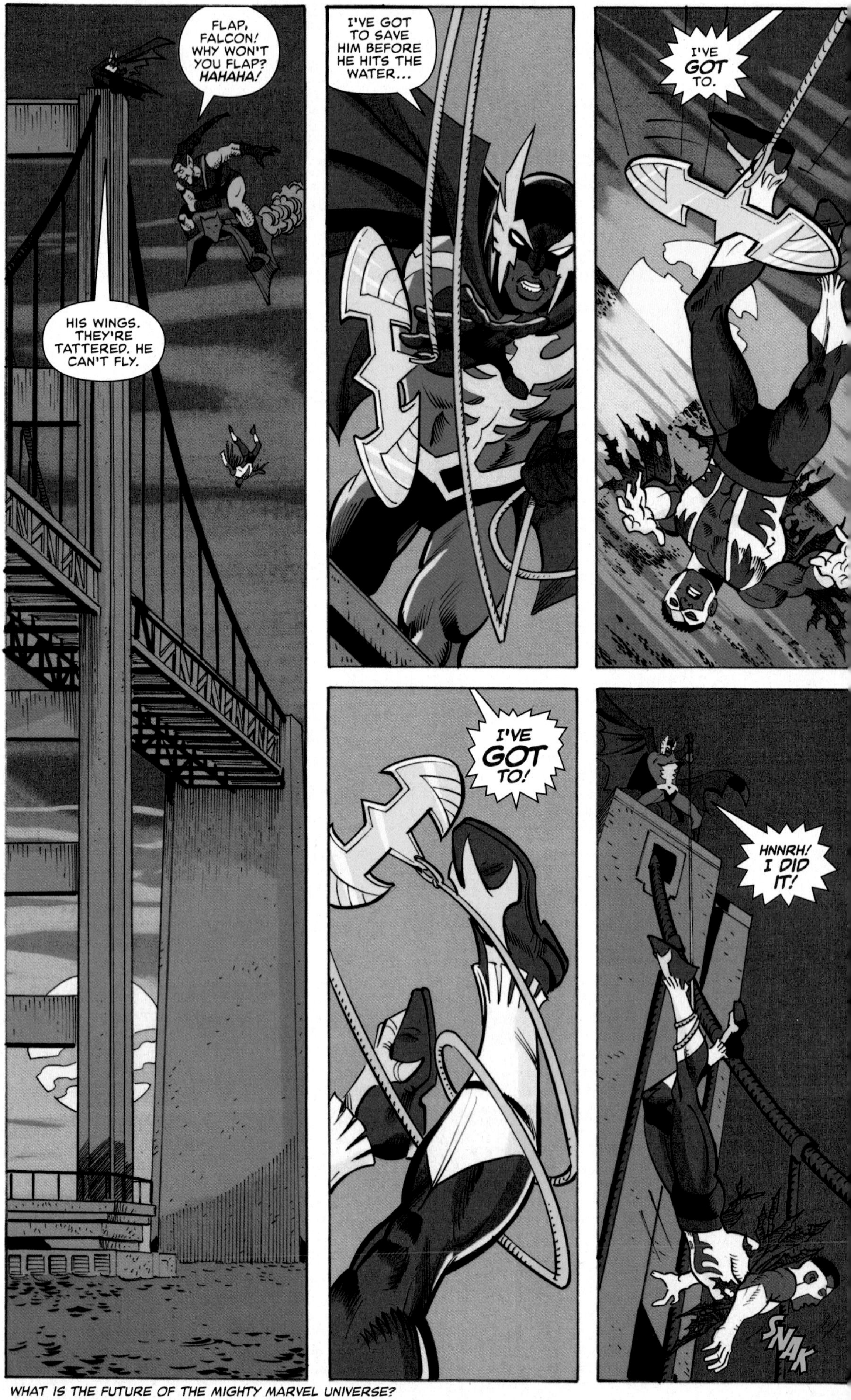
FLAP, FALCON! WHY WON'T YOU FLAP? HAHAHA!
HIS WINGS. THEY'RE TATTERED. HE CAN'T FLY.
I'VE GOT TO SAVE HIM BEFORE HE HITS THE WATER...
I'VE GOT TO.
I'VE GOT TO!
HNNRH! I DID IT!
SNAK

WHAT IS THE FUTURE OF THE MIGHTY MARVEL UNIVERSE?

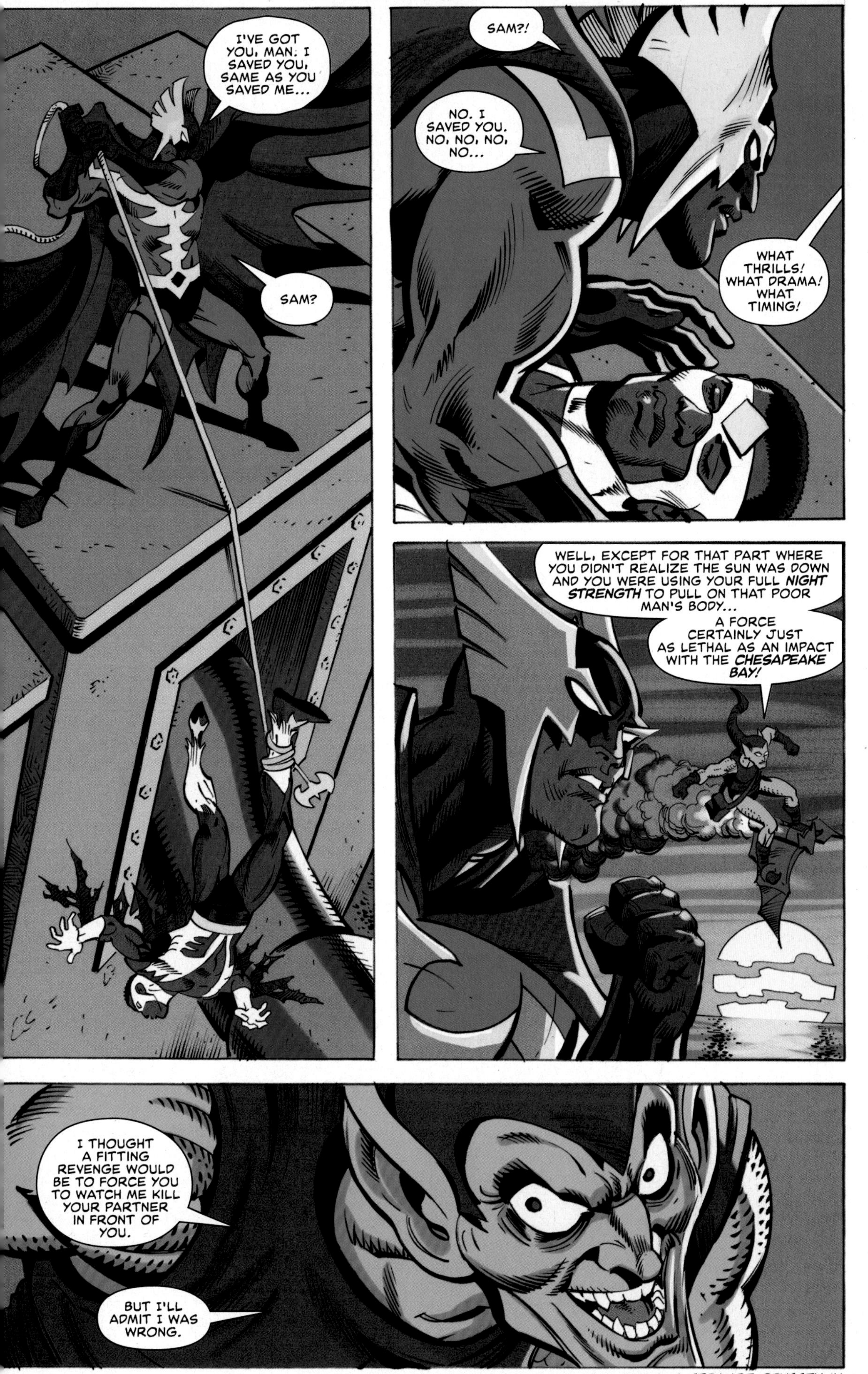
I'VE GOT YOU, MAN. I SAVED YOU, SAME AS YOU SAVED ME...
SAM?
SAM?!
NO. I SAVED YOU. NO, NO, NO, NO...
WHAT THRILLS! WHAT DRAMA! WHAT TIMING!
WELL, EXCEPT FOR THAT PART WHERE YOU DIDN'T REALIZE THE SUN WAS DOWN AND YOU WERE USING YOUR FULL NIGHT STRENGTH TO PULL ON THAT POOR MAN'S BODY...
A FORCE CERTAINLY JUST AS LETHAL AS AN IMPACT WITH THE CHESAPEAKE BAY!
I THOUGHT A FITTING REVENGE WOULD BE TO FORCE YOU TO WATCH ME KILL YOUR PARTNER IN FRONT OF YOU.
BUT I'LL ADMIT I WAS WRONG.

THE SCARLET CENTURION KNOWS IN *2000: A STRANGE ODYSSEY #1.*

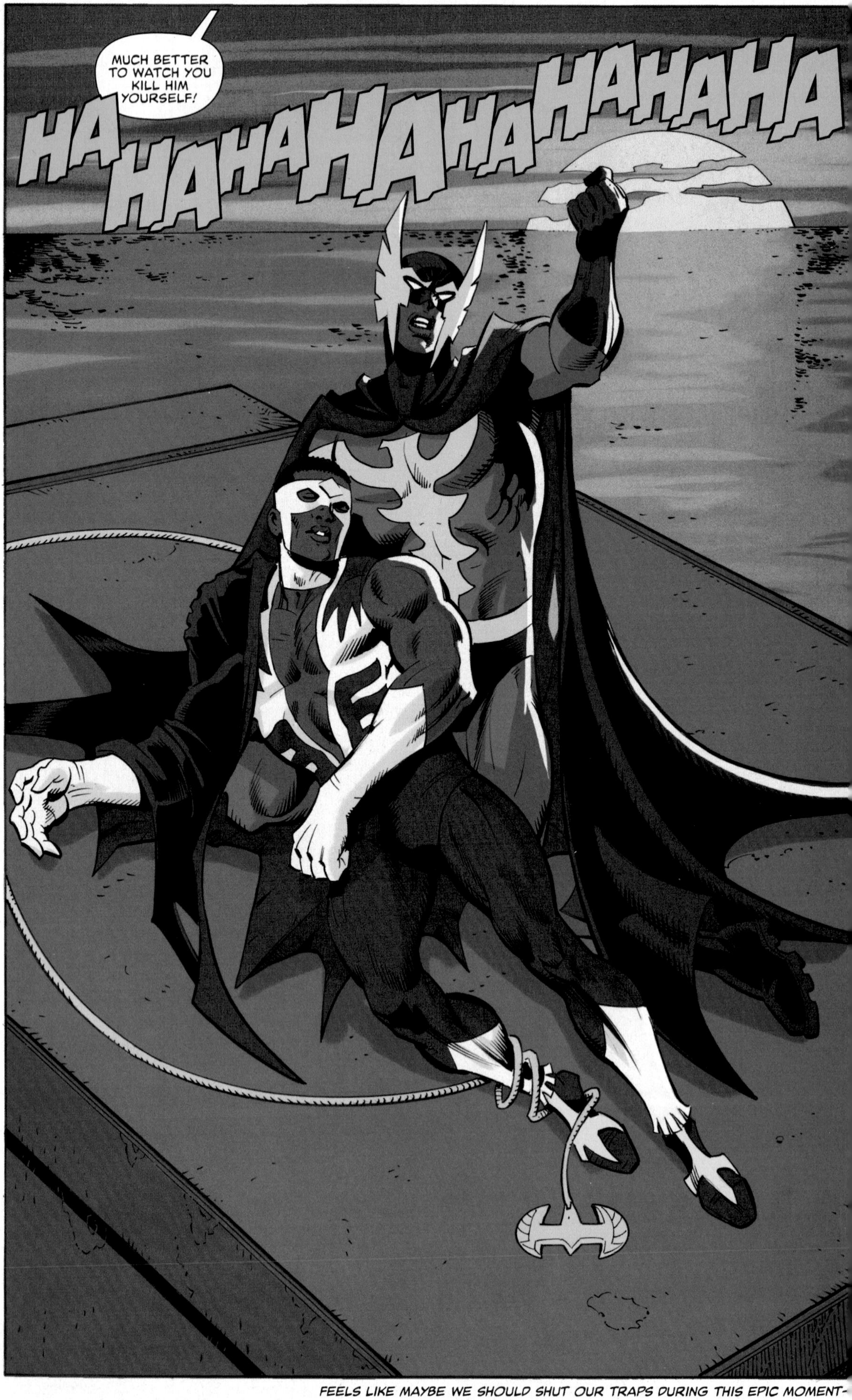
MUCH BETTER TO WATCH YOU KILL HIM YOURSELF!
HA HAHAHAHAHAHAHAHAHA

FEELS LIKE MAYBE WE SHOULD SHUT OUR TRAPS DURING THIS EPIC MOMENT-

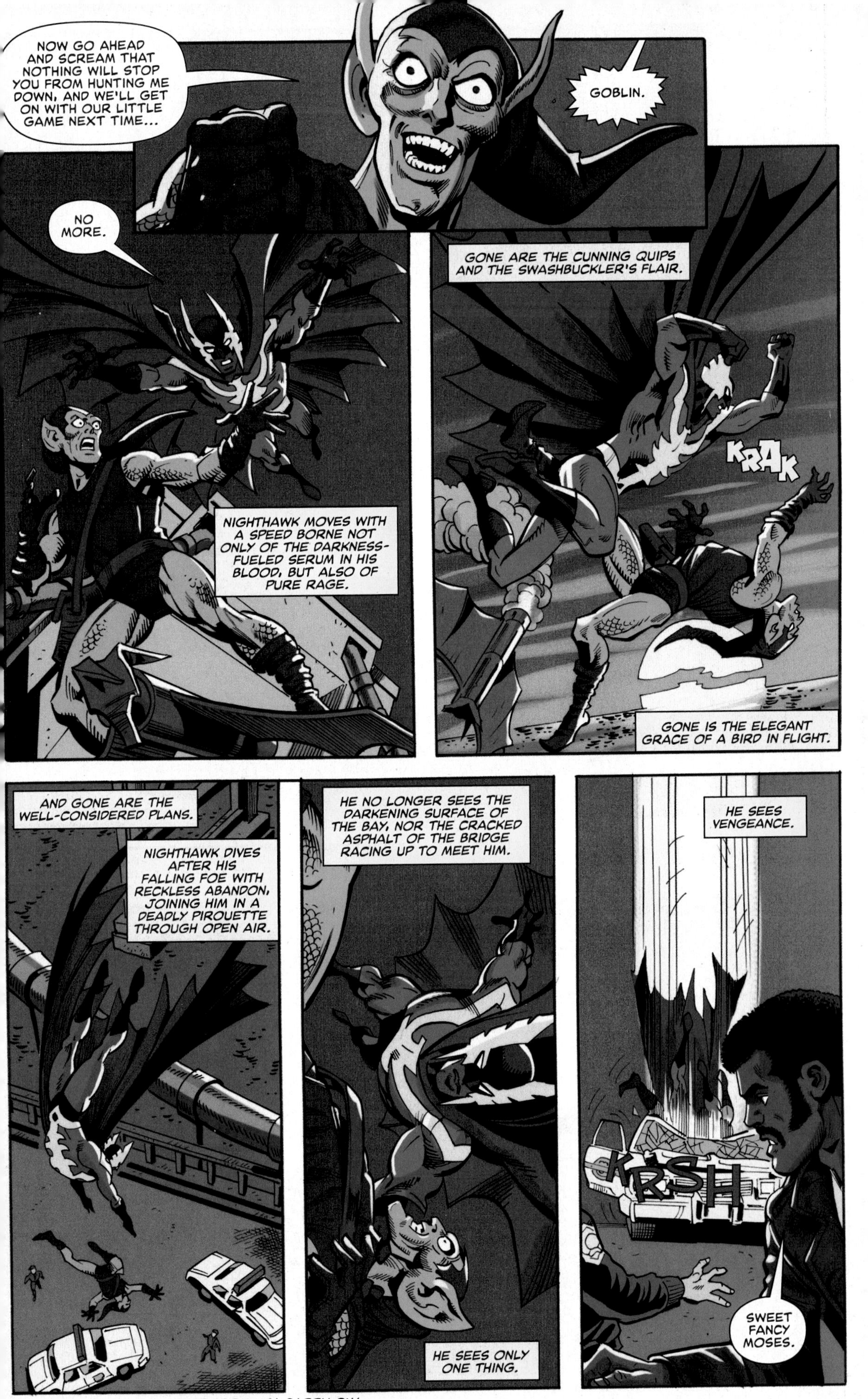
NOW GO AHEAD AND SCREAM THAT NOTHING WILL STOP YOU FROM HUNTING ME DOWN, AND WE'LL GET ON WITH OUR LITTLE GAME NEXT TIME...
GOBLIN.
NO MORE.
NIGHTHAWK MOVES WITH A SPEED BORNE NOT ONLY OF THE DARKNESS-FUELED SERUM IN HIS BLOOD, BUT ALSO OF PURE RAGE.
GONE ARE THE CUNNING QUIPS AND THE SWASHBUCKLER'S FLAIR.
KRAK
GONE IS THE ELEGANT GRACE OF A BIRD IN FLIGHT.
AND GONE ARE THE WELL-CONSIDERED PLANS.
NIGHTHAWK DIVES AFTER HIS FALLING FOE WITH RECKLESS ABANDON, JOINING HIM IN A DEADLY PIROUETTE THROUGH OPEN AIR.
HE NO LONGER SEES THE DARKENING SURFACE OF THE BAY, NOR THE CRACKED ASPHALT OF THE BRIDGE RACING UP TO MEET HIM.
HE SEES ONLY ONE THING.
HE SEES VENGEANCE.
KRSH
SWEET FANCY MOSES.

NO, SERIOUSLY! NOT A PEEP FROM US! CARRY ON!

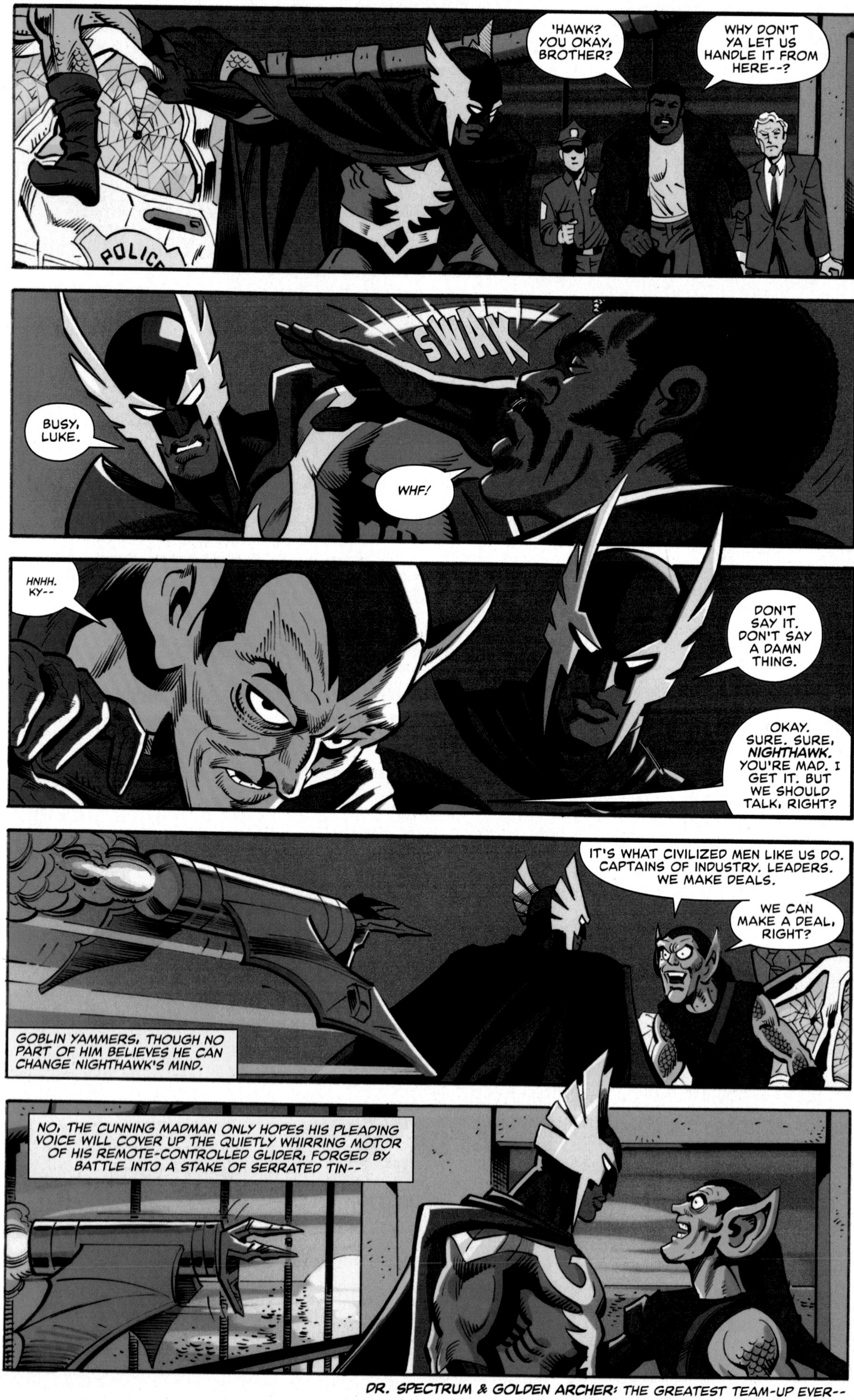
'HAWK? YOU OKAY, BROTHER?
WHY DON'T YA LET US HANDLE IT FROM HERE--?
POLICE
SWAK
BUSY, LUKE.
WHF!
HNHH. KY--
DON'T SAY IT. DON'T SAY A DAMN THING.
OKAY. SURE. SURE, NIGHTHAWK. YOU'RE MAD. I GET IT. BUT WE SHOULD TALK, RIGHT?
IT'S WHAT CIVILIZED MEN LIKE US DO. CAPTAINS OF INDUSTRY. LEADERS. WE MAKE DEALS.
WE CAN MAKE A DEAL, RIGHT?
GOBLIN YAMMERS, THOUGH NO PART OF HIM BELIEVES HE CAN CHANGE NIGHTHAWK'S MIND.
NO, THE CUNNING MADMAN ONLY HOPES HIS PLEADING VOICE WILL COVER UP THE QUIETLY WHIRRING MOTOR OF HIS REMOTE-CONTROLLED GLIDER, FORGED BY BATTLE INTO A STAKE OF SERRATED TIN--

DR. SPECTRUM & GOLDEN ARCHER: THE GREATEST TEAM-UP EVER--

PNK

SHRNCH

NIGHTHAWK GRIPS THE METAL SO HARD THAT IT CUTS THROUGH HIS LEATHER GLOVE AND INTO THE PALM OF HIS HAND.

THE PHYSICAL PAIN ISN'T ENOUGH THOUGH TO DULL HIS MENTAL ANGUISH.

AND GOBLIN... GOBLIN DOESN'T TAUNT. HE DOESN'T LAUGH. HE DOESN'T SAY ANYTHING.

HE KNOWS THERE'S NOTHING HE CAN SAY OR DO.

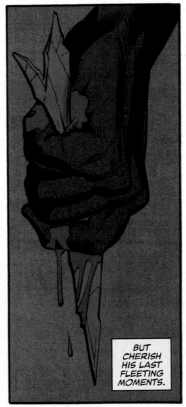

BUT CHERISH HIS LAST FLEETING MOMENTS.

THE METAL SLICES THROUGH THE MILLISECONDS ON THE WAY TO NORMAN OSBORN'S NECK.

--IF THEY CAN STOP FROM KILLING EACH OTHER! MARVEL SPOTLIGHT #221

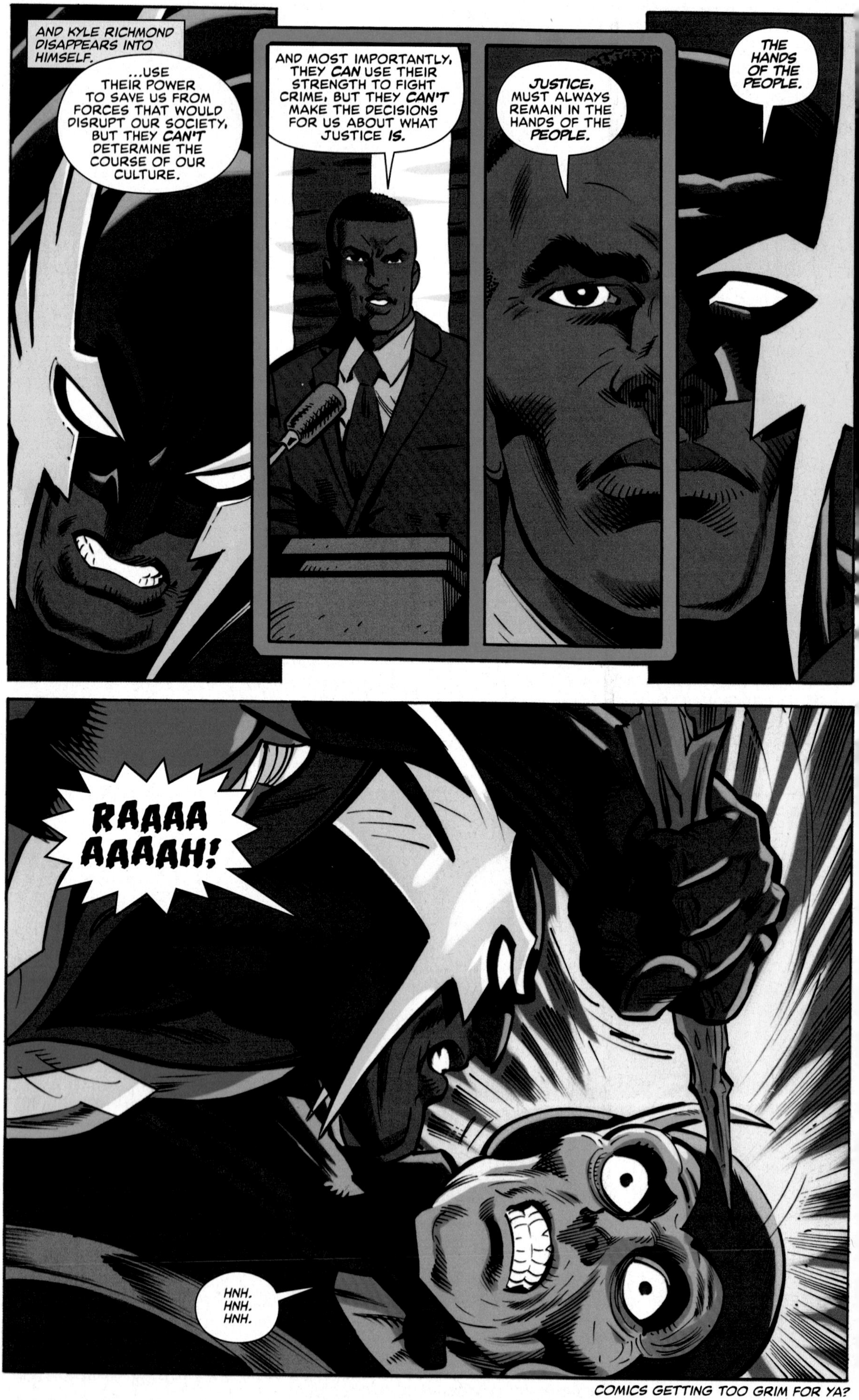
AND KYLE RICHMOND DISAPPEARS INTO HIMSELF.
...USE THEIR POWER TO SAVE US FROM FORCES THAT WOULD DISRUPT OUR SOCIETY, BUT THEY CAN'T DETERMINE THE COURSE OF OUR CULTURE.
AND MOST IMPORTANTLY, THEY CAN USE THEIR STRENGTH TO FIGHT CRIME, BUT THEY CAN'T MAKE THE DECISIONS FOR US ABOUT WHAT JUSTICE IS.
JUSTICE, MUST ALWAYS REMAIN IN THE HANDS OF THE PEOPLE.
THE HANDS OF THE PEOPLE.
RAAAA AAAAH!
HNH. HNH. HNH.

COMICS GETTING TOO GRIM FOR YA?

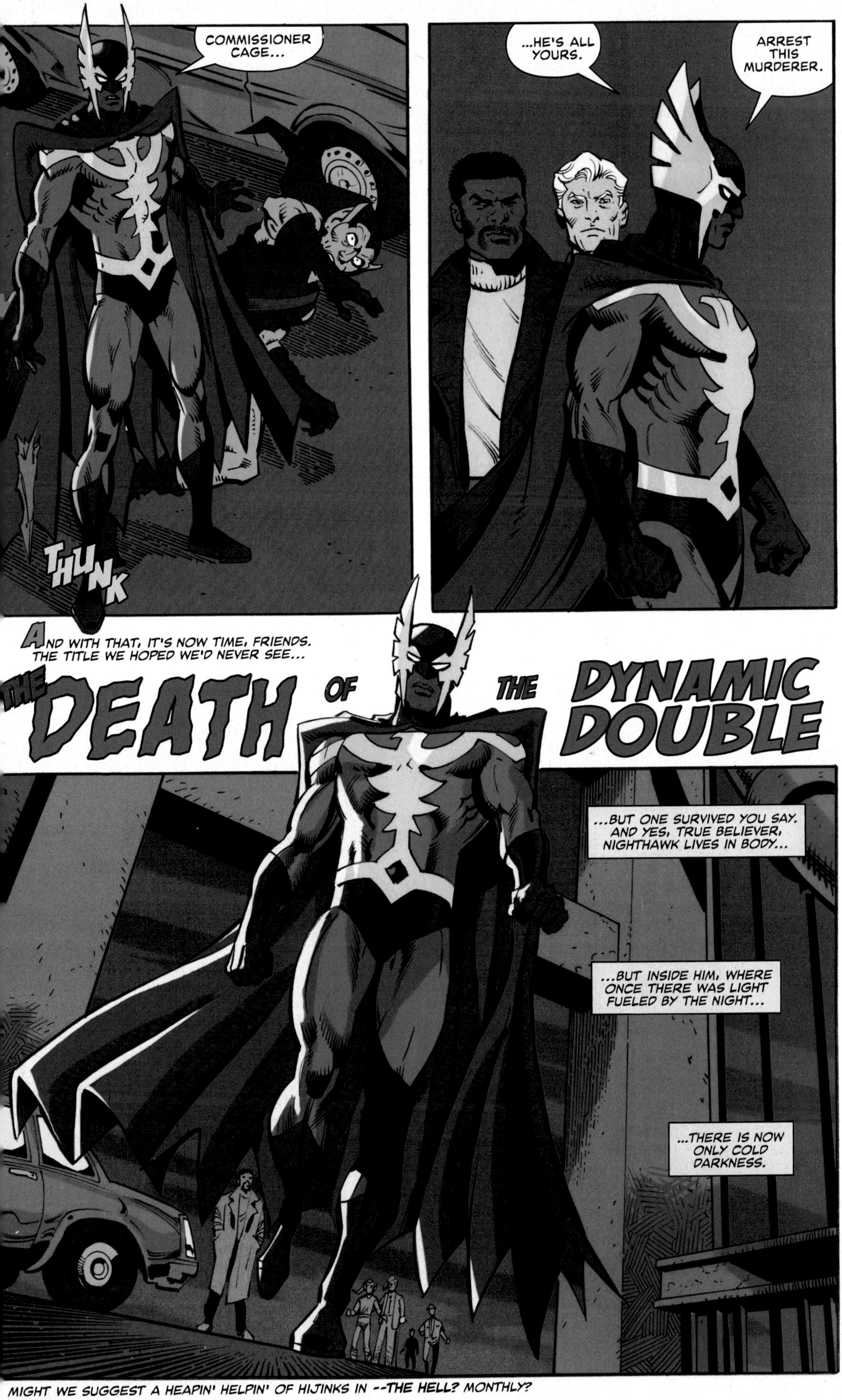
COMMISSIONER CAGE...
THUNK
...HE'S ALL YOURS.
ARREST THIS MURDERER.
AND WITH THAT, IT'S NOW TIME, FRIENDS. THE TITLE WE HOPED WE'D NEVER SEE...
THE DEATH OF THE DYNAMIC DOUBLE
...BUT ONE SURVIVED YOU SAY. AND YES, TRUE BELIEVER, NIGHTHAWK LIVES IN BODY...
...BUT INSIDE HIM, WHERE ONCE THERE WAS LIGHT FUELED BY THE NIGHT...
...THERE IS NOW ONLY COLD DARKNESS.

MIGHT WE SUGGEST A HEAPIN' HELPIN' OF HIJINKS IN --*THE HELL?* MONTHLY?

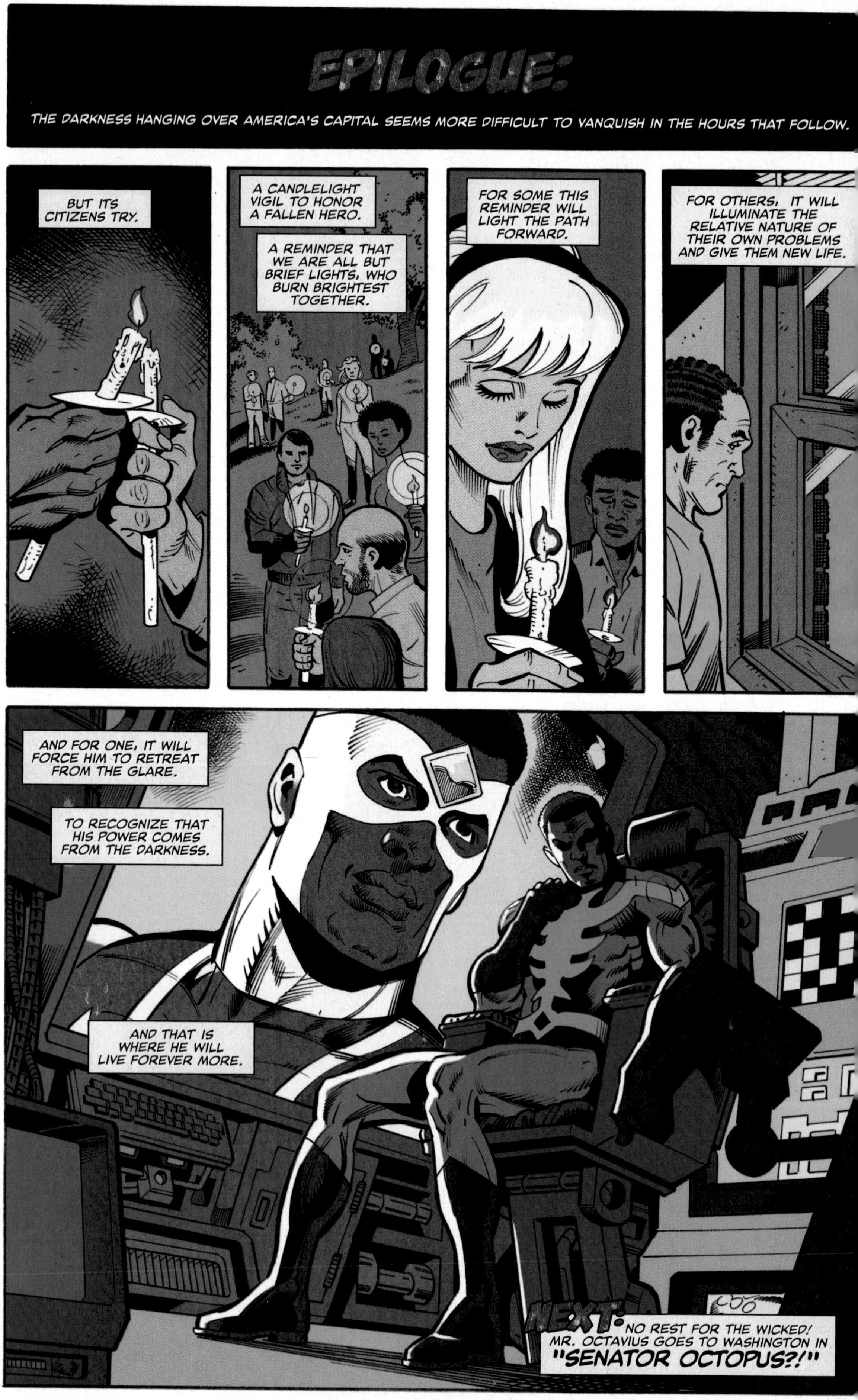
EPILOGUE:
THE DARKNESS HANGING OVER AMERICA'S CAPITAL SEEMS MORE DIFFICULT TO VANQUISH IN THE HOURS THAT FOLLOW.
BUT ITS CITIZENS TRY.
A CANDLELIGHT VIGIL TO HONOR A FALLEN HERO.
A REMINDER THAT WE ARE ALL BUT BRIEF LIGHTS, WHO BURN BRIGHTEST TOGETHER.
FOR SOME THIS REMINDER WILL LIGHT THE PATH FORWARD.
FOR OTHERS, IT WILL ILLUMINATE THE RELATIVE NATURE OF THEIR OWN PROBLEMS AND GIVE THEM NEW LIFE.
AND FOR ONE, IT WILL FORCE HIM TO RETREAT FROM THE GLARE.
TO RECOGNIZE THAT HIS POWER COMES FROM THE DARKNESS.
AND THAT IS WHERE HE WILL LIVE FOREVER MORE.
NEXT: NO REST FOR THE WICKED! MR. OCTAVIUS GOES TO WASHINGTON IN "SENATOR OCTOPUS?!"

THE HAWK'S NEST

SEND YOUR LETTERS TO:
THE MARVEL COMICS GROUP, 1290 AVENUE OF THE AMERICAS,
NEW YORK, NEW YORK 10104

We are absolutely going out of our minds waiting to hear your comments on this issue's shocking events! But until some egghead invents IMMEDIATE MAIL (I-Mail?) in the far-off future, we'll have to be patient little comic book monkeys and instead answer the letters that arrived at our office about the precursors to this precarious presentation, NIGHTHAWK issues #122 through #125! Onto your Mighty Marvel Marching Orders!

Dear Tim, Darren, Dan, Chris and whatever a "letterer" is,

This is my first letter to a comic book, and I just wanted to let you know that although I thought the conclusion to "Who's Behind the Walls of Ravencroft?" was pretty good, it was just not as good as the previous arc, "Battle of the Man-Beasts!" I'm sorry. I bet you tried pretty hard, but there's just no way a story about the Dynamic Delegate's trying to free poor incarcerated Harry Osborn from the craziest nuthouse in all of comics can match a knock 'em down, string 'em up, three-way battle between the Rhino, the Lizard and Sabretooth! I mean, sure, the psychological drama thing is cool with the college crowd, but these are super hero comics! Give us monsters! Give us slugfests! Issue 124 had some of that, but then we just spent way too much time with Gwen Stacy, and she's pretty and all, but she doesn't punch enough stuff to hold my attention. But this new Tigra lady joining the cast seems promising!

Anyway, thanks for listening, and I hope the next arc is more "Man-Beast" and less "Ravencroft!"

Until Kyle trades in the Hawkrod for a Nightbicycle, Make Mine Marvel!

Kent Mundt, Esq.
La Crosse, WI

Thanks for the letter, Kent! Hopefully this issue contained the proper balance of mind games and head punches you crave!

Dear Bullpen,

Thanks for putting out my second-favorite monthly mag, right after SQUADRON SUPREME OF AMERICA! I read NIGHTHAWK twice every month, but all the Heroes Supreme in one comic gets a third view!

All that repeat reading means I notice just about everything, so I have to point out that when Kyle Richmond said he was going to Utopia Isle to ask the Squad for their help against the Triple Beast in NIGHTHAWK #123, he was wearing a blue tie. But when he showed up in SSA #104, he was wearing a plaid tie. Now, I know you guys never make mistakes, so I bet that when Kyle went through the secret transporter, his molecules got all messed up. Now, it wasn't bad enough to hurt the Avian Investigator, but it did scramble up the threads of his tie, making it appear plaid.

That's gotta be good enough for a No-Prize right?

Cassandra Moreno
Chicago, IL

Y'know, Cassandra, the process of creating a No-Prize is so arduous, so DANGEROUS, we don't undertake it unless a reader goes above and beyond. And, well, ya did it. Expect your prize to materialize at your house soon. Let's just hope it doesn't end up plaid.

To They Who Make The Nighthawk,

I'm new to this comic (heck, to comics in general), and I've got some questions so I can get caught up on the goings-on of this series! I hope you can help, and since you're the crazy cats that made this, I figure you're better than my Uncle Clem!

1) My dad said back in World War II, he used to read about a guy named Captain America. I didn't see him here or in any issues of SQUADRON SUPREME down at the drugstore. Is he still around?

2) How does Nighthawk see out of his lenses? They're solid white! Wouldn't he just run into all kinds of walls?

3) Who would win in a fight? Hyperion or Nighthawk? Because my stupid friend Randy says Nighthawk, but as much as I like Nighthawk, he can't throw buses into space.

4) Will we ever see the Goblin again? He's the scariest Nighthawk villain!

5) Why is everybody in the letters always asking for a No-Prize?

Sincerely,
Jason Aaron
Age 9
Jasper, AL

Welcome, Jason! We're happy to have you and even happier to answer your questions!

1) Captain America hasn't been seen since back in the Atlas Comics days! Sometimes even great characters fall through the cracks. Maybe someday some talented writer will come up with a great story to bring him back! Maybe it'll be you!

2) Nighthawk's lenses are like a two-way mirror! On the side that faces his eyes, it's clear as day! Unless he sneezes in his mask. We don't recommend it.

3) Since this is his mag, we're gonna side with your smart friend Randy that Nighthawk wins the day! Nighthawk is smart, and that'll win the day over brawn anytime!

4) Norman Osborn is back in his green genes in this very issue! We hope you're happy to see the Goblin again, Jason! Because Kyle definitely isn't!

5) Well, if we're being honest, we made an offhand joke about giving out "no prizes" once, and now we are harassed day and night by legions of eager fans who make it impossible for us to move on and who occasionally make demands for what is literally nothing so vehemently that we wish we were dead.

Plus, getting one is a feather in the cap of any true fan!

Well, that's all the room we have this issue! Thanks to all our letter hacks, old and new! Let us know what you thought of this mighty issue of NIGHTHAWK! Until next time, True Believers,

MAKE YOURS MARVEL!

In a world in which the Avengers never existed, the Squadron Supreme of America are and have always been Earth's Mightiest Heroes!

MARVEL
DOUBLE ACTION

THE DEATH OF THE DYNAMIC DOUBLE"

TIM **SEELEY** WRITER

DAN **JURGENS** PENCILER

SCOTT **HANNA** INKER

CHRIS **SOTOMAYOR** COLORS

VC's CORY **PETIT** LETTERER

DAVE **JOHNSON** COVER ARTIST

ANNIE **WU** VARIANT COVER ARTIST

JAY **BOWEN** GRAPHIC DESIGN

DARREN **SHAN** EDITOR

TOM **BREVOORT** EXECUTIVE EDITOR

C.B. **CEBULSKI** EDITOR IN CHIEF

HEROES REBORN

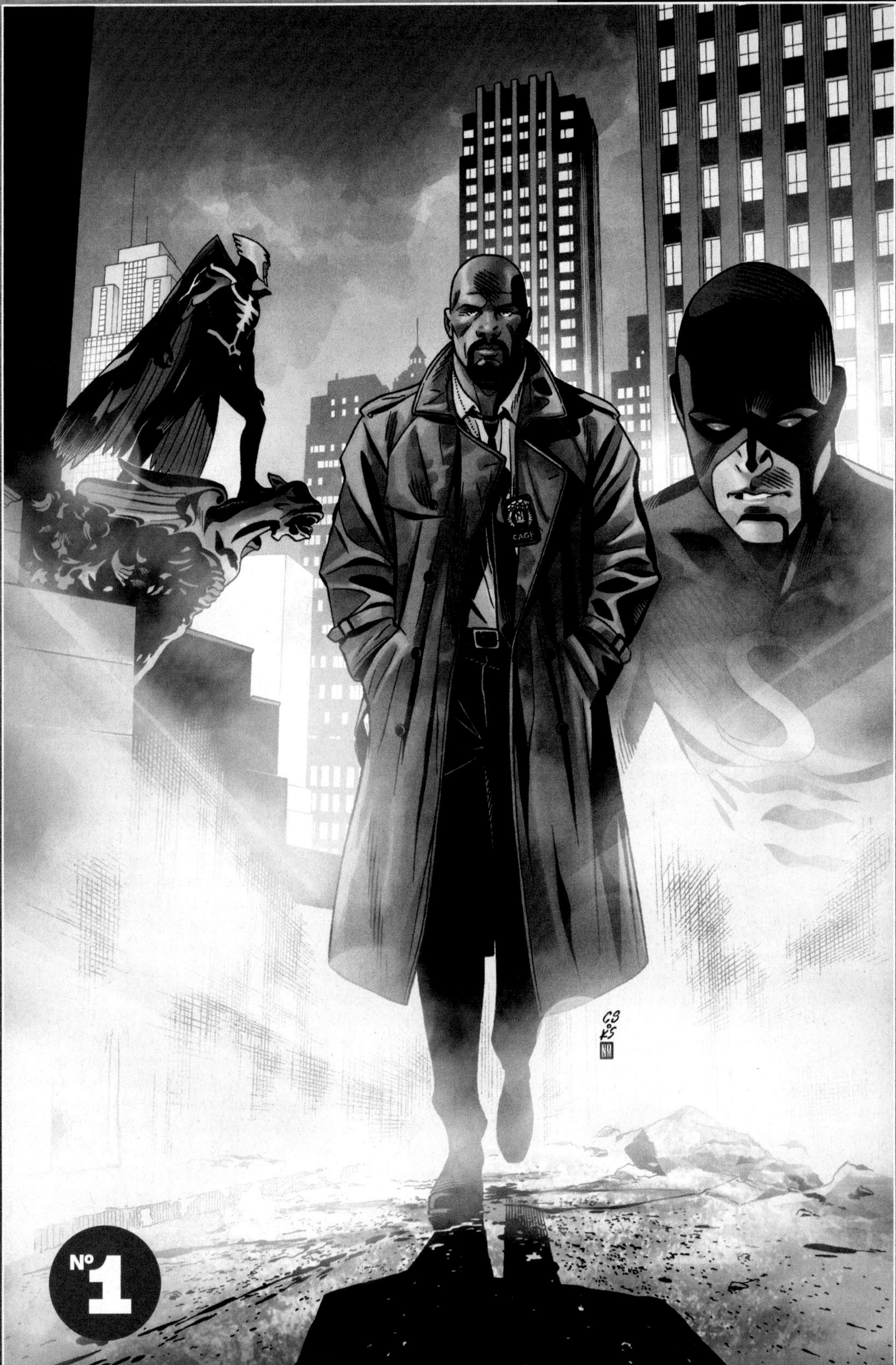
CAGE
Nº 1

AMERICAN KNIGHTS

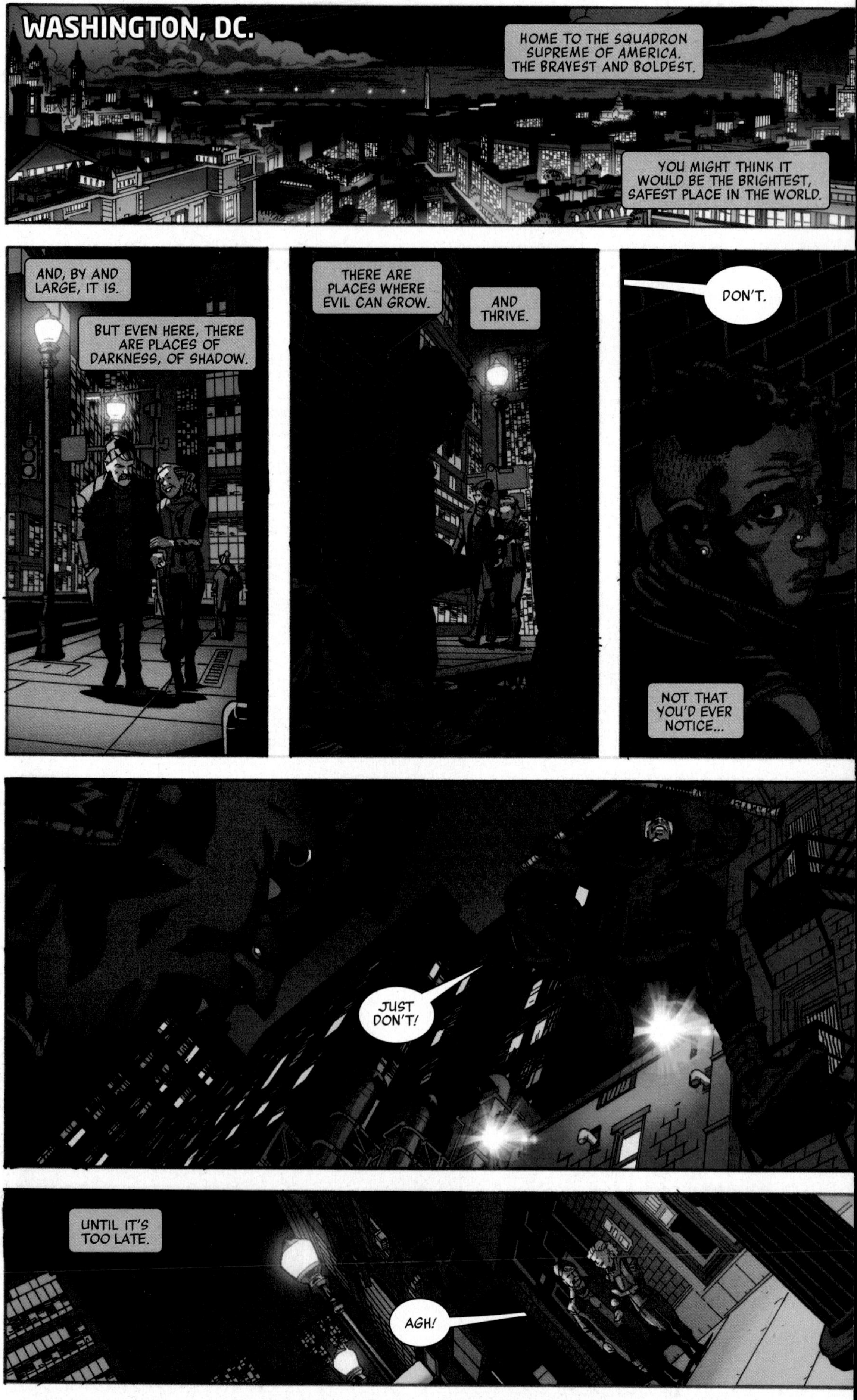
WASHINGTON, DC.
HOME TO THE SQUADRON SUPREME OF AMERICA. THE BRAVEST AND BOLDEST.
YOU MIGHT THINK IT WOULD BE THE BRIGHTEST, SAFEST PLACE IN THE WORLD.
AND, BY AND LARGE, IT IS.
BUT EVEN HERE, THERE ARE PLACES OF DARKNESS, OF SHADOW.
THERE ARE PLACES WHERE EVIL CAN GROW.
AND THRIVE.
DON'T.
NOT THAT YOU'D EVER NOTICE...
JUST DON'T!
UNTIL IT'S TOO LATE.
AGH!

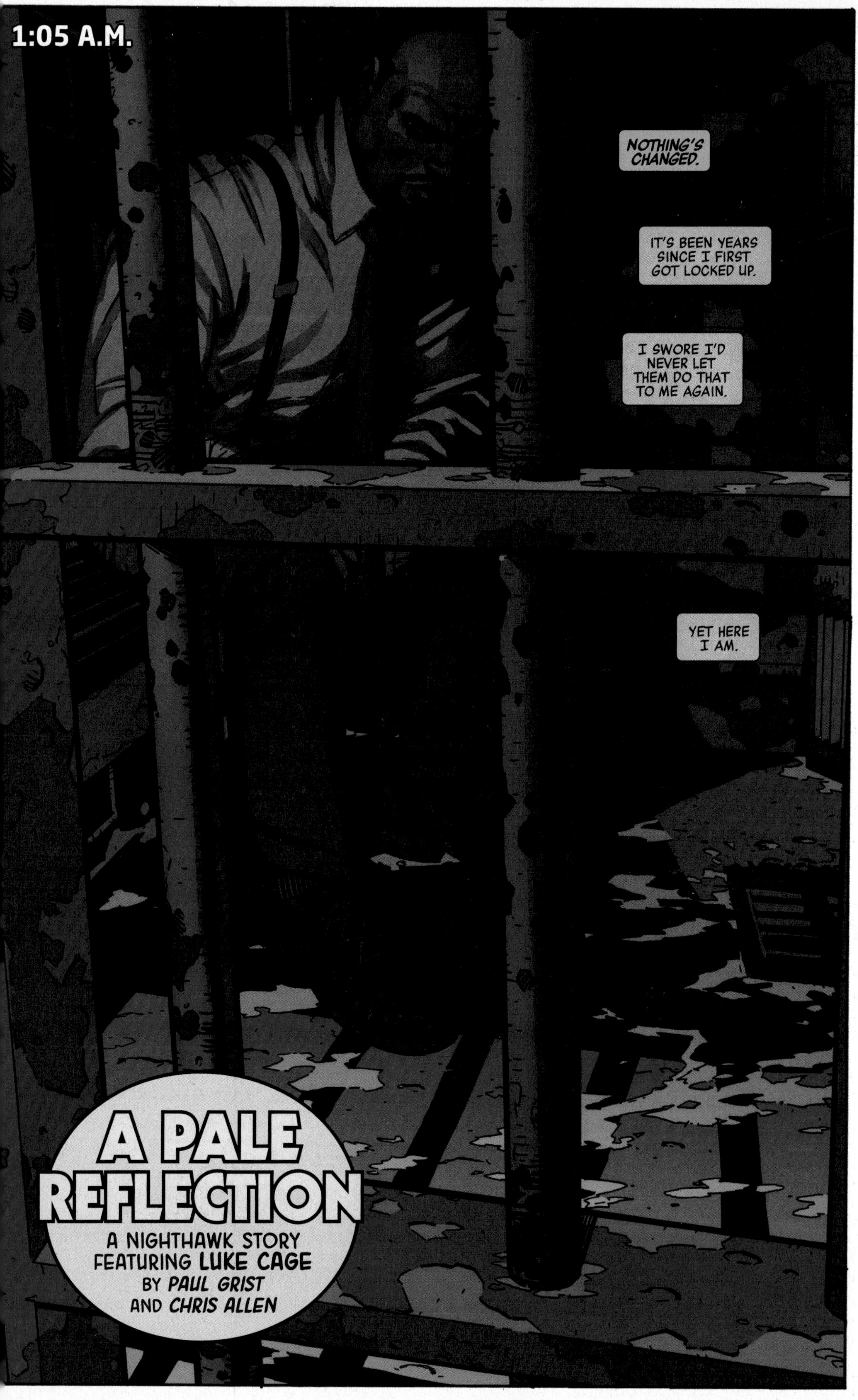
1:05 A.M.
NOTHING'S CHANGED.
IT'S BEEN YEARS SINCE I FIRST GOT LOCKED UP.
I SWORE I'D NEVER LET THEM DO THAT TO ME AGAIN.
YET HERE I AM.
A PALE REFLECTION
A NIGHTHAWK STORY FEATURING LUKE CAGE
BY PAUL GRIST AND CHRIS ALLEN

In a world in which the Avengers never existed, the Squadron Supreme of America are and have always been Earth's Mightiest Heroes!

AMERICAN KNIGHTS

LUKE CAGE is the police commissioner of Washington, D.C. When the streets get too mean for the cops, he calls in NIGHTHAWK, a member of the Squadron Supreme and the city's dark protector. But not everyone appreciates Cage's methods, or those of his super hero allies...

PAUL **GRIST** WRITER

CHRIS **ALLEN** WITH
MARC **DEERING** (INKS, PGS. 14-15, 23-25, 27-29) ARTISTS

GURU-**eFX** COLOR ARTIST

VC's CORY **PETIT** LETTERER

CHRIS **SPROUSE**, KARL **STORY** & NEERAJ **MENON** COVER ARTISTS

DECLAN **SHALVEY** VARIANT COVER ARTIST

JAY **BOWEN** GRAPHIC DESIGN

SARAH **BRUNSTAD** EDITOR

TOM **BREVOORT** EXECUTIVE EDITOR

C.B. **CEBULSKI** EDITOR IN CHIEF

HEROES REBORN

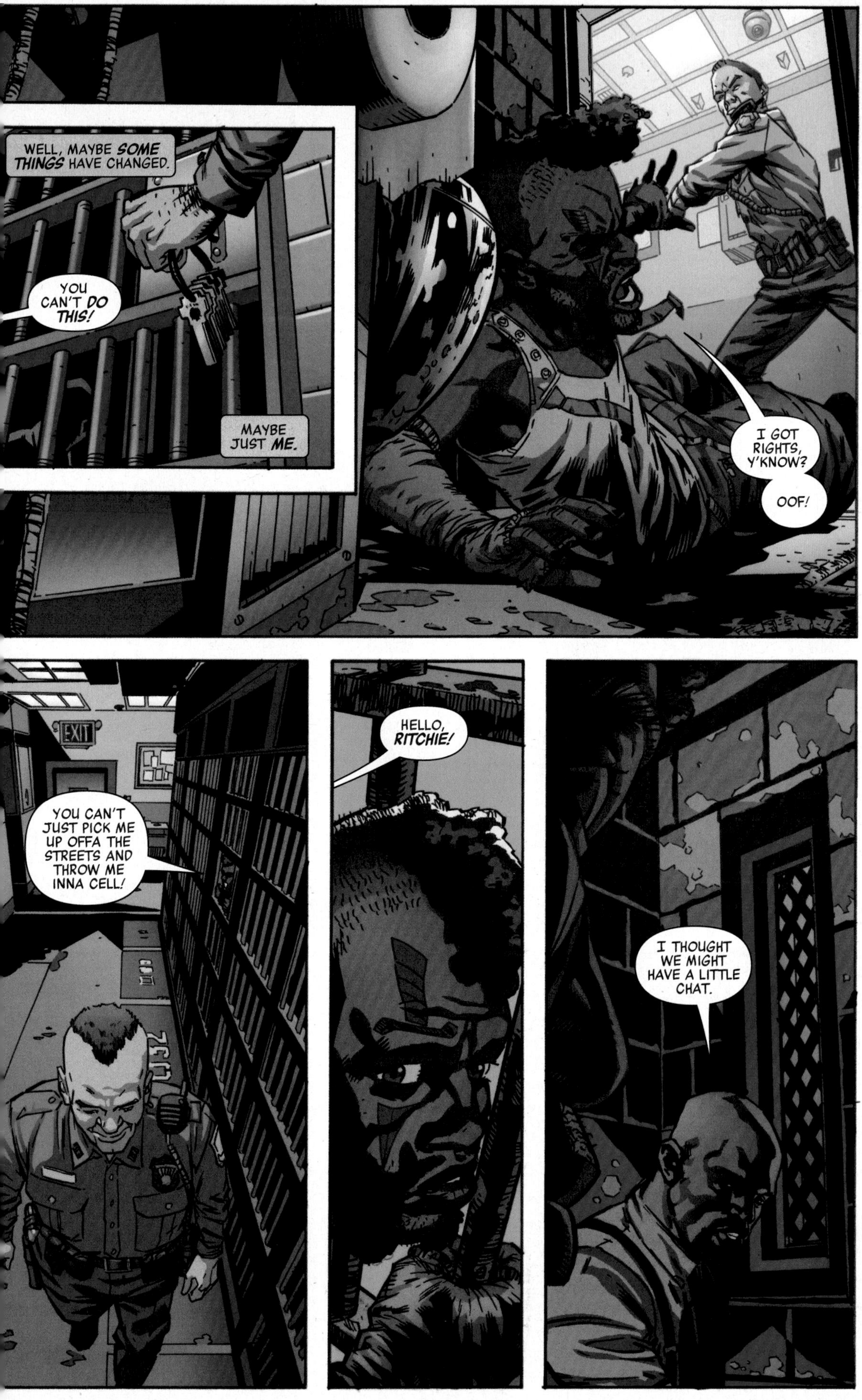
WELL, MAYBE SOME THINGS HAVE CHANGED.
YOU CAN'T DO THIS!
MAYBE JUST ME.
I GOT RIGHTS, Y'KNOW?
OOF!
YOU CAN'T JUST PICK ME UP OFFA THE STREETS AND THROW ME INNA CELL!
HELLO, RITCHIE!
I THOUGHT WE MIGHT HAVE A LITTLE CHAT.

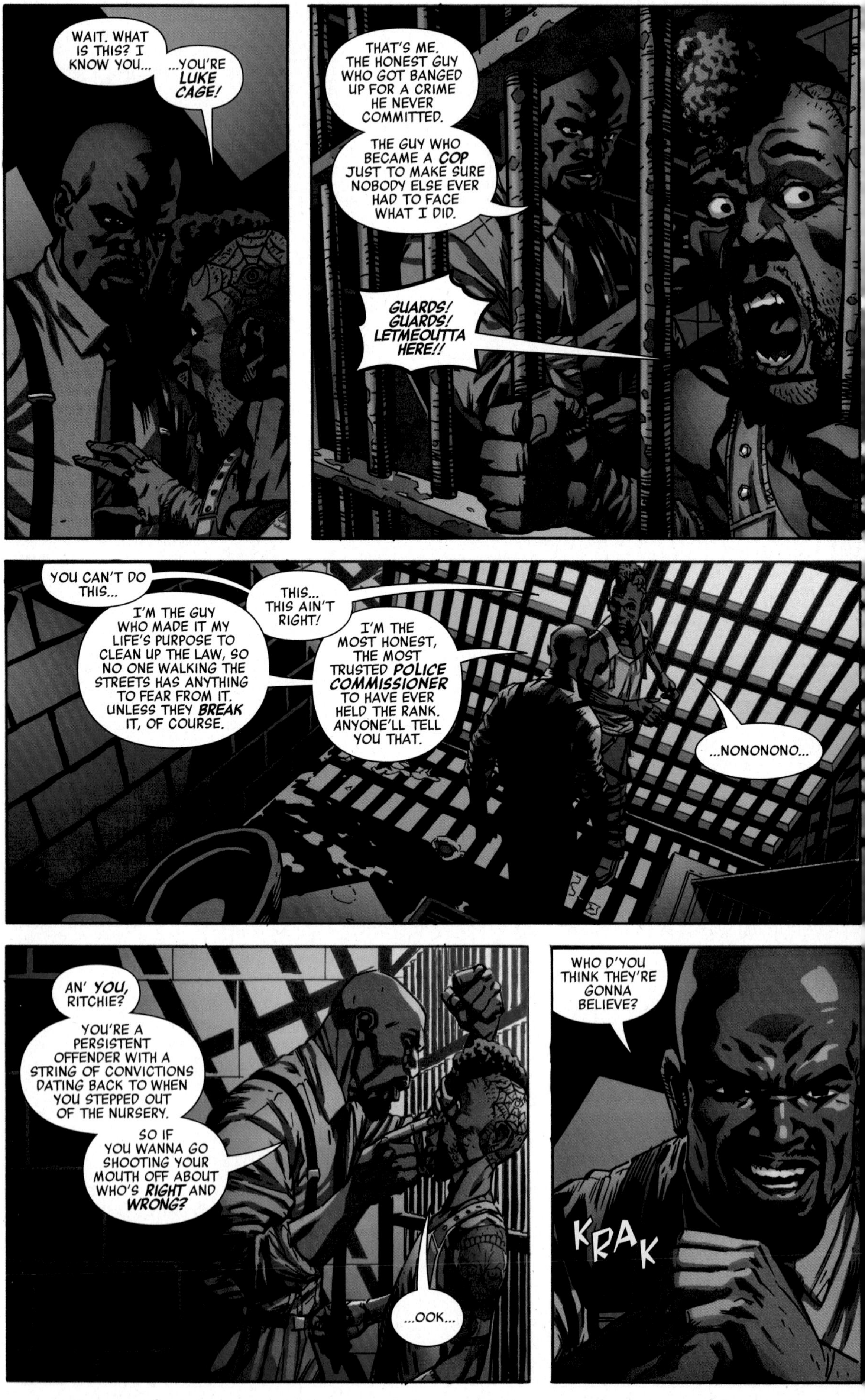

WAIT. WHAT IS THIS? I KNOW YOU...
...YOU'RE LUKE CAGE!
THAT'S ME. THE HONEST GUY WHO GOT BANGED UP FOR A CRIME HE NEVER COMMITTED.
THE GUY WHO BECAME A COP JUST TO MAKE SURE NOBODY ELSE EVER HAD TO FACE WHAT I DID.
GUARDS! GUARDS! LETMEOUTTA HERE!!
YOU CAN'T DO THIS...
I'M THE GUY WHO MADE IT MY LIFE'S PURPOSE TO CLEAN UP THE LAW, SO NO ONE WALKING THE STREETS HAS ANYTHING TO FEAR FROM IT. UNLESS THEY BREAK IT, OF COURSE.
THIS... THIS AIN'T RIGHT!
I'M THE MOST HONEST, THE MOST TRUSTED POLICE COMMISSIONER TO HAVE EVER HELD THE RANK. ANYONE'LL TELL YOU THAT.
...NONONONO...
AN' YOU, RITCHIE?
YOU'RE A PERSISTENT OFFENDER WITH A STRING OF CONVICTIONS DATING BACK TO WHEN YOU STEPPED OUT OF THE NURSERY.
SO IF YOU WANNA GO SHOOTING YOUR MOUTH OFF ABOUT WHO'S RIGHT AND WRONG?
...OOK...
WHO D'YOU THINK THEY'RE GONNA BELIEVE?
KRAK

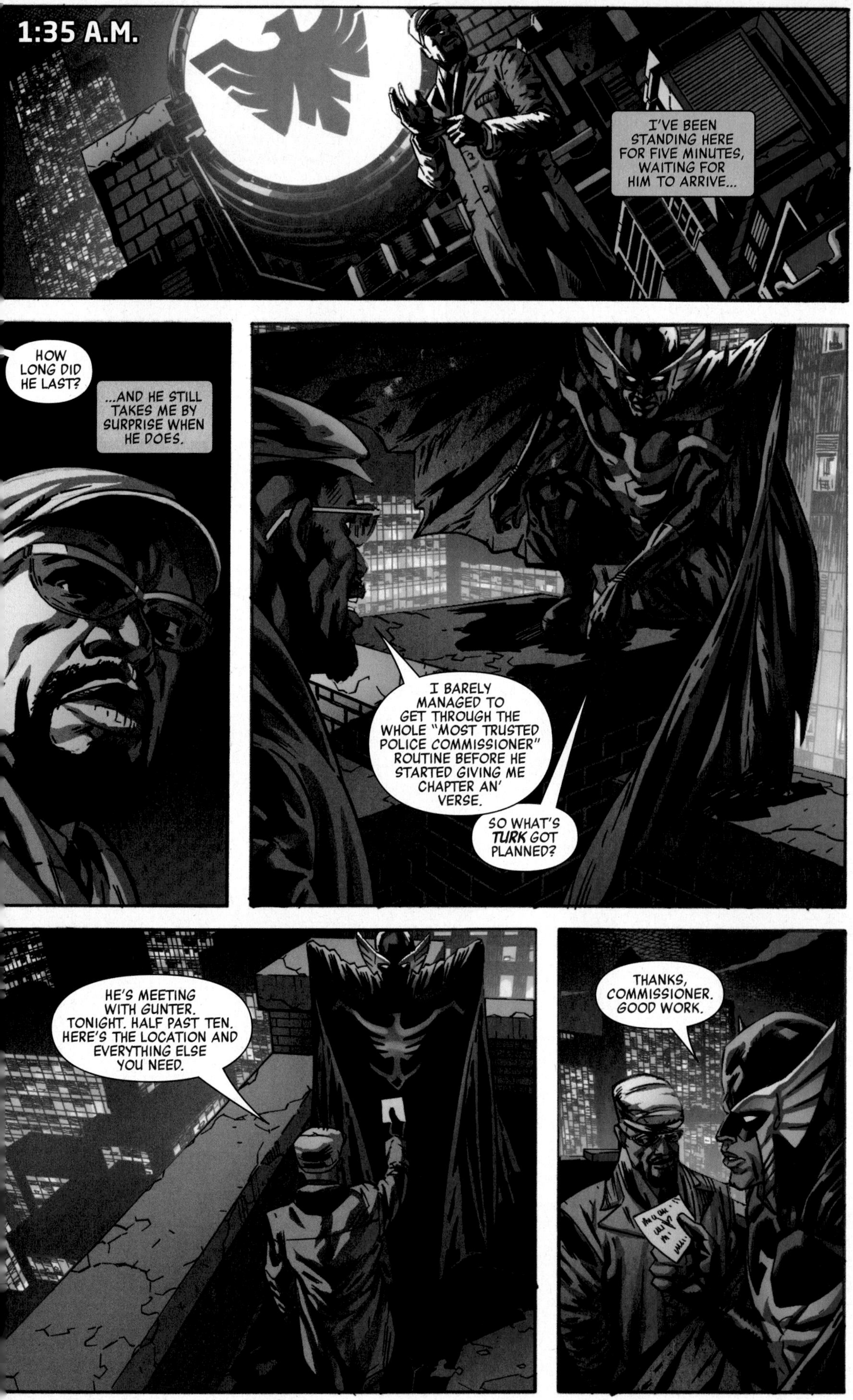
1:35 A.M.
I'VE BEEN STANDING HERE FOR FIVE MINUTES, WAITING FOR HIM TO ARRIVE...
HOW LONG DID HE LAST?
...AND HE STILL TAKES ME BY SURPRISE WHEN HE DOES.
I BARELY MANAGED TO GET THROUGH THE WHOLE "MOST TRUSTED POLICE COMMISSIONER" ROUTINE BEFORE HE STARTED GIVING ME CHAPTER AN' VERSE.
SO WHAT'S TURK GOT PLANNED?
HE'S MEETING WITH GUNTER. TONIGHT. HALF PAST TEN. HERE'S THE LOCATION AND EVERYTHING ELSE YOU NEED.
THANKS, COMMISSIONER. GOOD WORK.

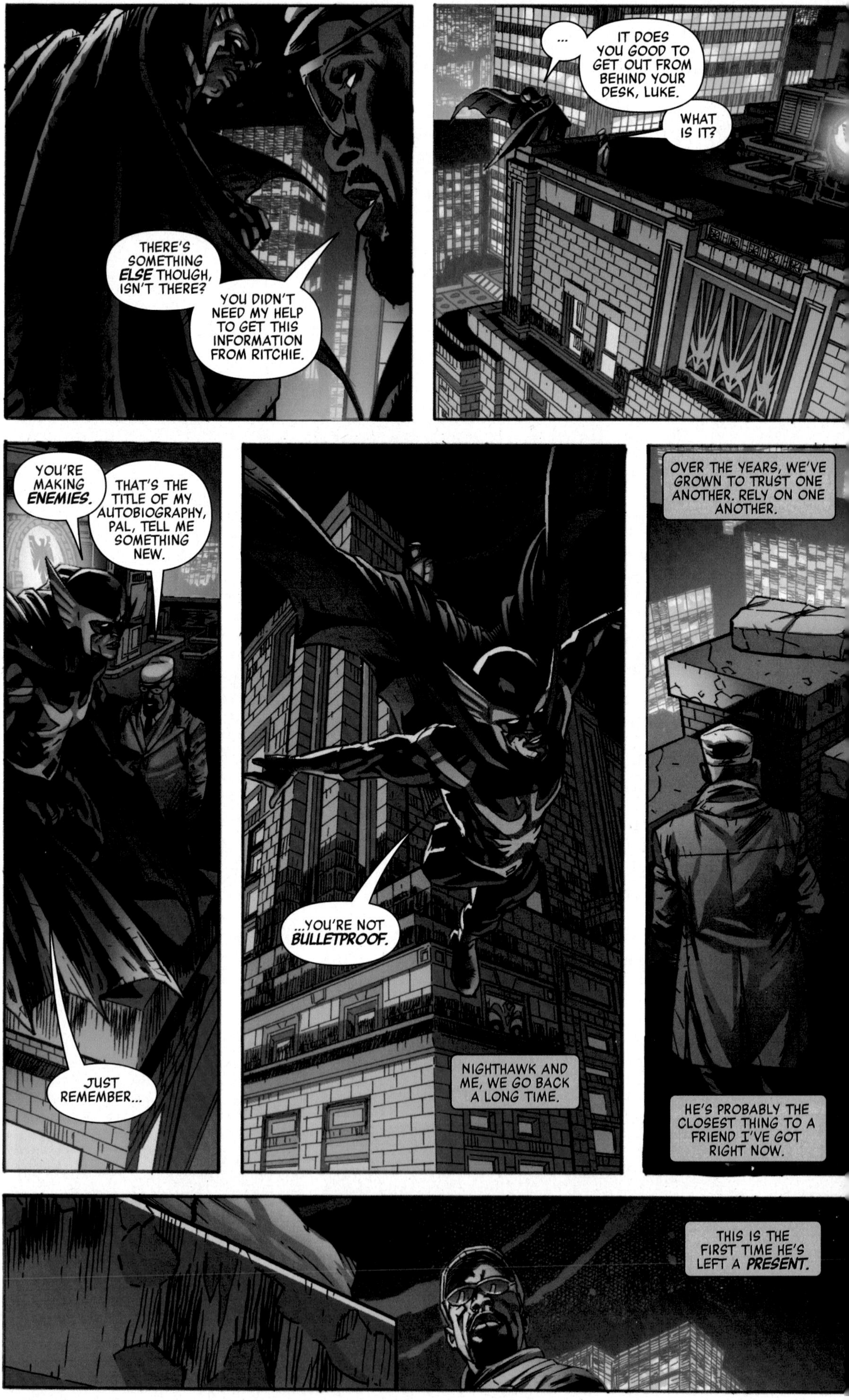
THERE'S SOMETHING ELSE THOUGH, ISN'T THERE?
YOU DIDN'T NEED MY HELP TO GET THIS INFORMATION FROM RITCHIE.
...
IT DOES YOU GOOD TO GET OUT FROM BEHIND YOUR DESK, LUKE.
WHAT IS IT?
YOU'RE MAKING ENEMIES.
THAT'S THE TITLE OF MY AUTOBIOGRAPHY, PAL, TELL ME SOMETHING NEW.
JUST REMEMBER...
...YOU'RE NOT BULLETPROOF.
NIGHTHAWK AND ME, WE GO BACK A LONG TIME.
OVER THE YEARS, WE'VE GROWN TO TRUST ONE ANOTHER. RELY ON ONE ANOTHER.
HE'S PROBABLY THE CLOSEST THING TO A FRIEND I'VE GOT RIGHT NOW.
THIS IS THE FIRST TIME HE'S LEFT A PRESENT.

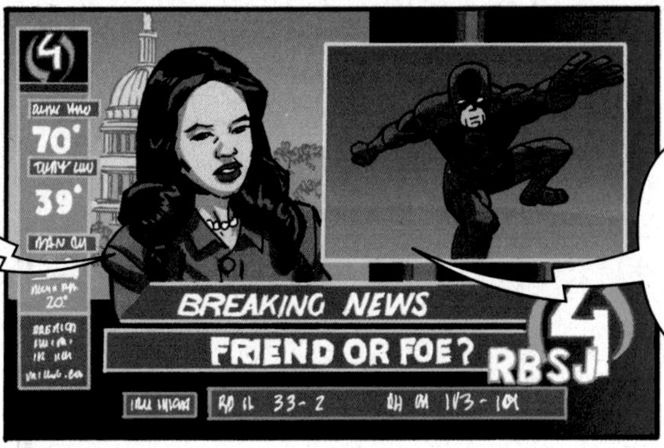
POLICE HAVE RELEASED A NEW IMAGE OF THE MASKED VIGILANTE WHO HAS BEEN ATTACKING CRIMINALS IN WASHINGTON IN RECENT WEEKS. HE HAS BEEN DUBBED THE SAINT AFTER THE DISTINCTIVE S ON HIS CHEST.
70°
39°
BREAKING NEWS
FRIEND OR FOE?
RBSJ
WHILE THE VIGILANTE'S ACTIONS HAVE RECEIVED WIDE PUBLIC SUPPORT, POLICE HAVE WARNED PEOPLE NOT TO COPY HIS ACTIONS AND TO LEAVE THE ADMINISTRATION OF JUSTICE TO OFFICIALLY APPOINTED OFFICERS.

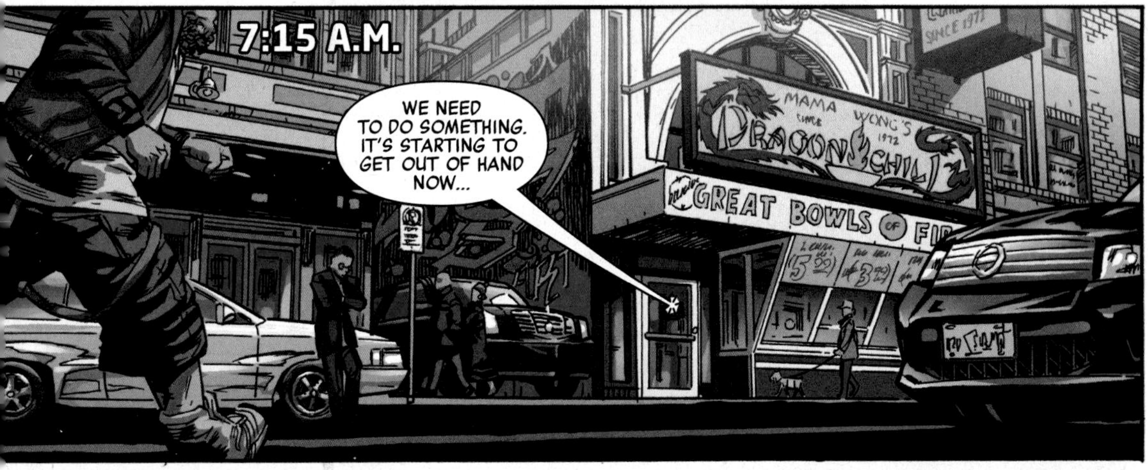
7:15 A.M.
SINCE 1972
MAMA WONG'S
DRAGON CHILI
GREAT BOWLS OF FI
WE NEED TO DO SOMETHING. IT'S STARTING TO GET OUT OF HAND NOW...

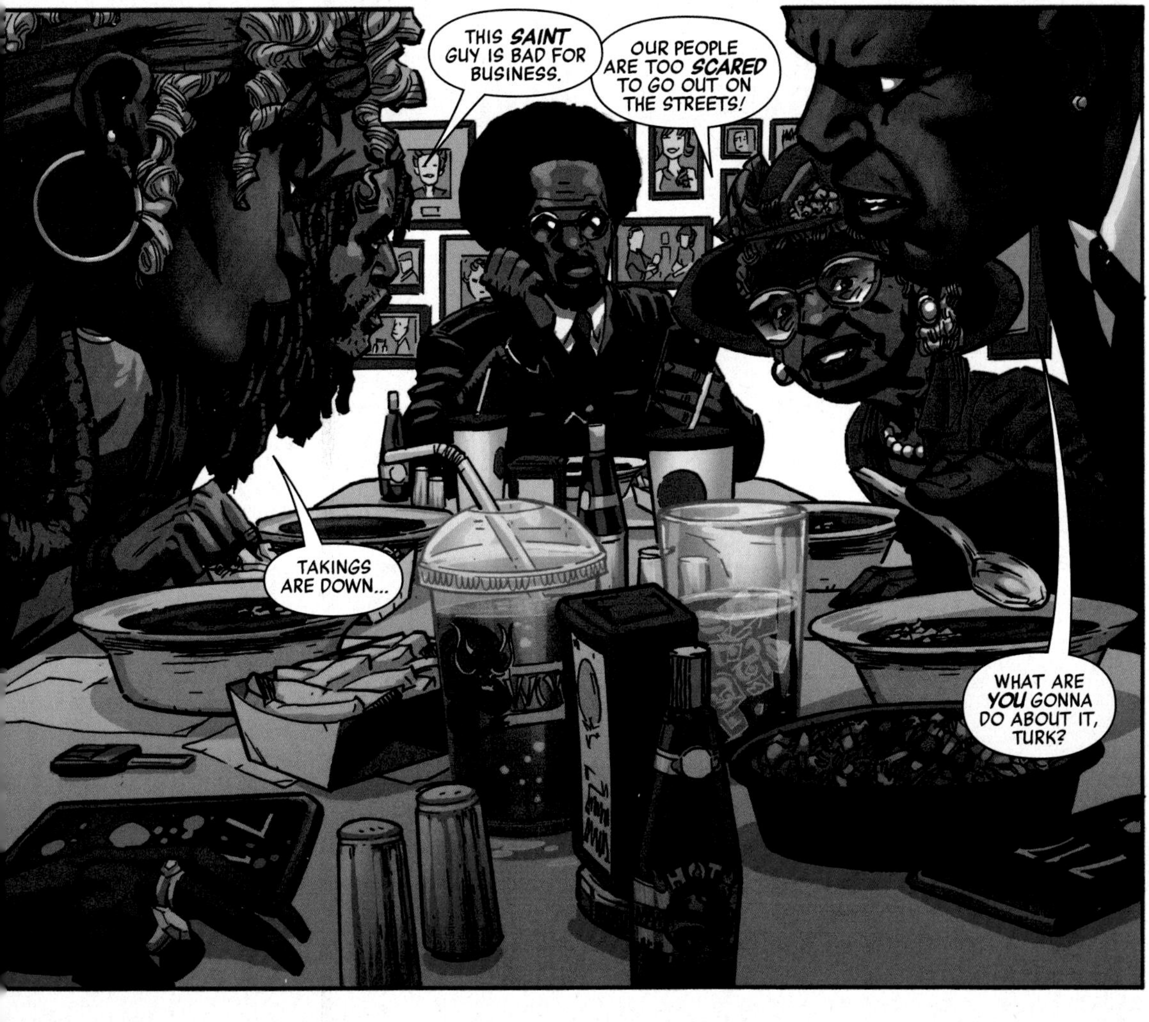
THIS SAINT GUY IS BAD FOR BUSINESS.
OUR PEOPLE ARE TOO SCARED TO GO OUT ON THE STREETS!
TAKINGS ARE DOWN...
WHAT ARE YOU GONNA DO ABOUT IT, TURK?

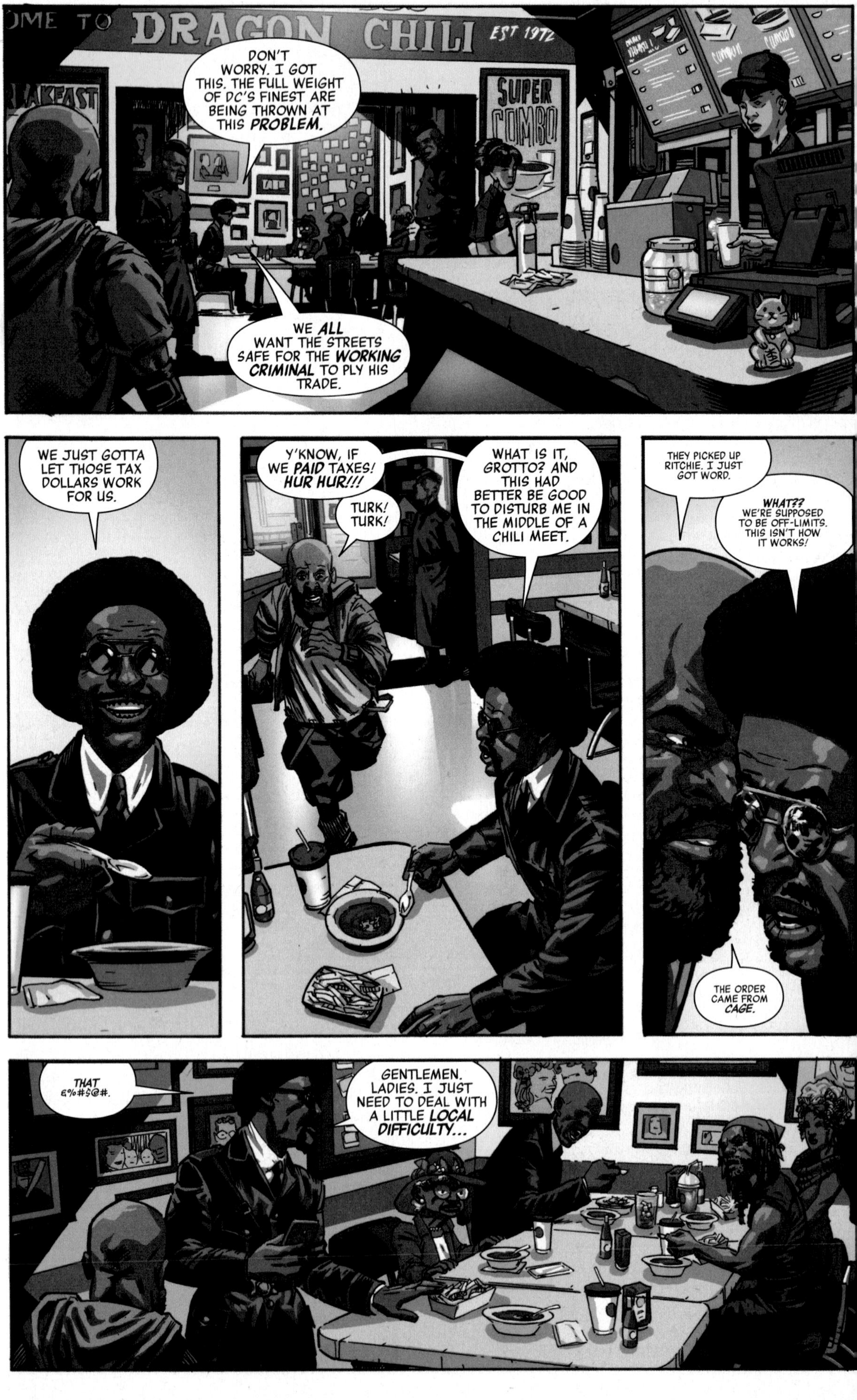

...OME TO DRAGON CHILI EST 1972
BREAKFAST
SUPER COMBO
DON'T WORRY. I GOT THIS. THE FULL WEIGHT OF DC'S FINEST ARE BEING THROWN AT THIS PROBLEM.
WE ALL WANT THE STREETS SAFE FOR THE WORKING CRIMINAL TO PLY HIS TRADE.
WE JUST GOTTA LET THOSE TAX DOLLARS WORK FOR US.
Y'KNOW, IF WE PAID TAXES! HUR HUR!!!
TURK! TURK!
WHAT IS IT, GROTTO? AND THIS HAD BETTER BE GOOD TO DISTURB ME IN THE MIDDLE OF A CHILI MEET.
THEY PICKED UP RITCHIE. I JUST GOT WORD.
WHAT?? WE'RE SUPPOSED TO BE OFF-LIMITS. THIS ISN'T HOW IT WORKS!
THE ORDER CAME FROM CAGE.
THAT £%#$@#.
GENTLEMEN. LADIES. I JUST NEED TO DEAL WITH A LITTLE LOCAL DIFFICULTY...

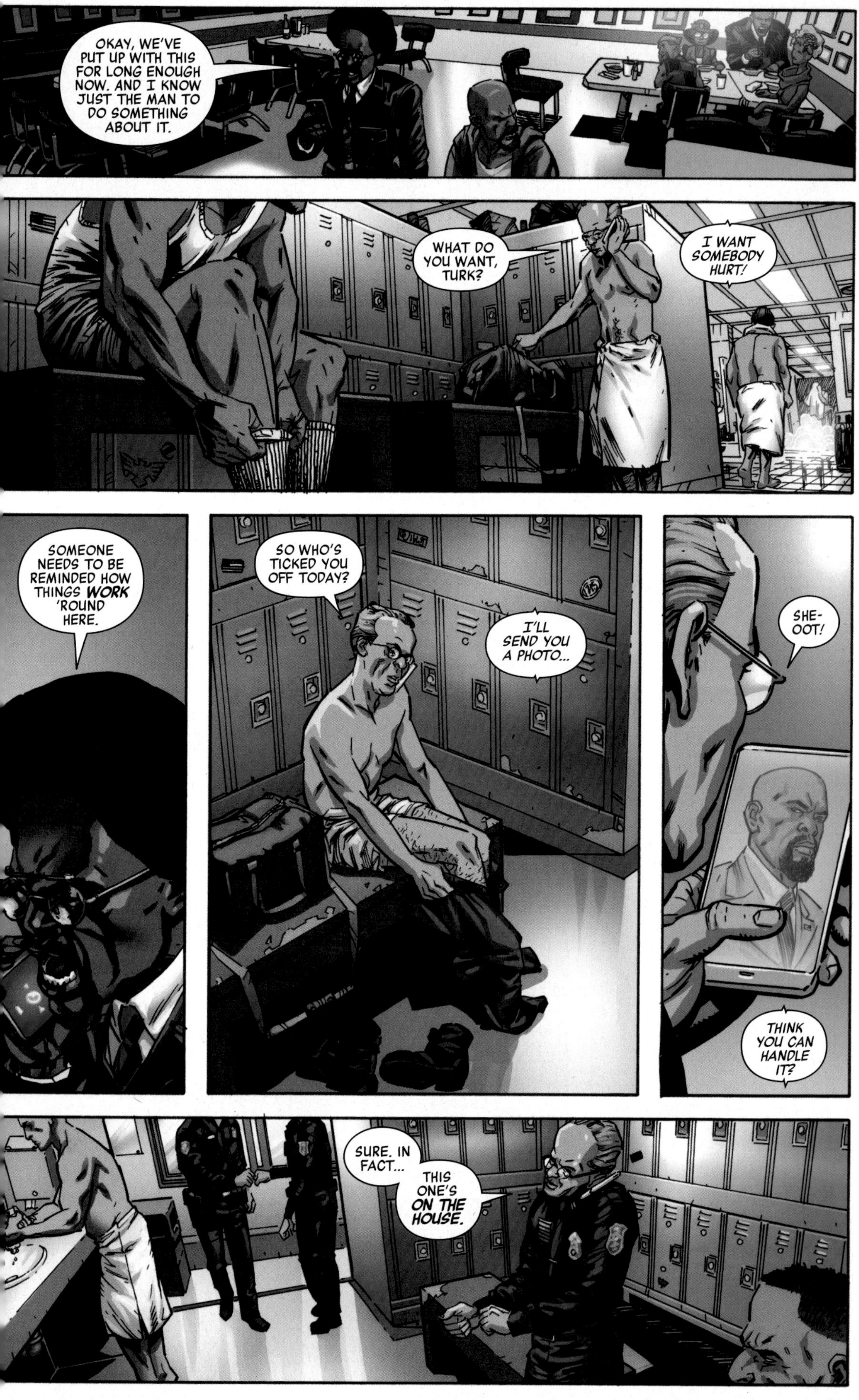
OKAY, WE'VE PUT UP WITH THIS FOR LONG ENOUGH NOW. AND I KNOW JUST THE MAN TO DO SOMETHING ABOUT IT.
WHAT DO YOU WANT, TURK?
I WANT SOMEBODY HURT!
SOMEONE NEEDS TO BE REMINDED HOW THINGS **WORK** 'ROUND HERE.
SO WHO'S TICKED YOU OFF TODAY?
I'LL SEND YOU A PHOTO...
SHE-OOT!
THINK YOU CAN HANDLE IT?
SURE. IN FACT...
THIS ONE'S **ON THE HOUSE.**

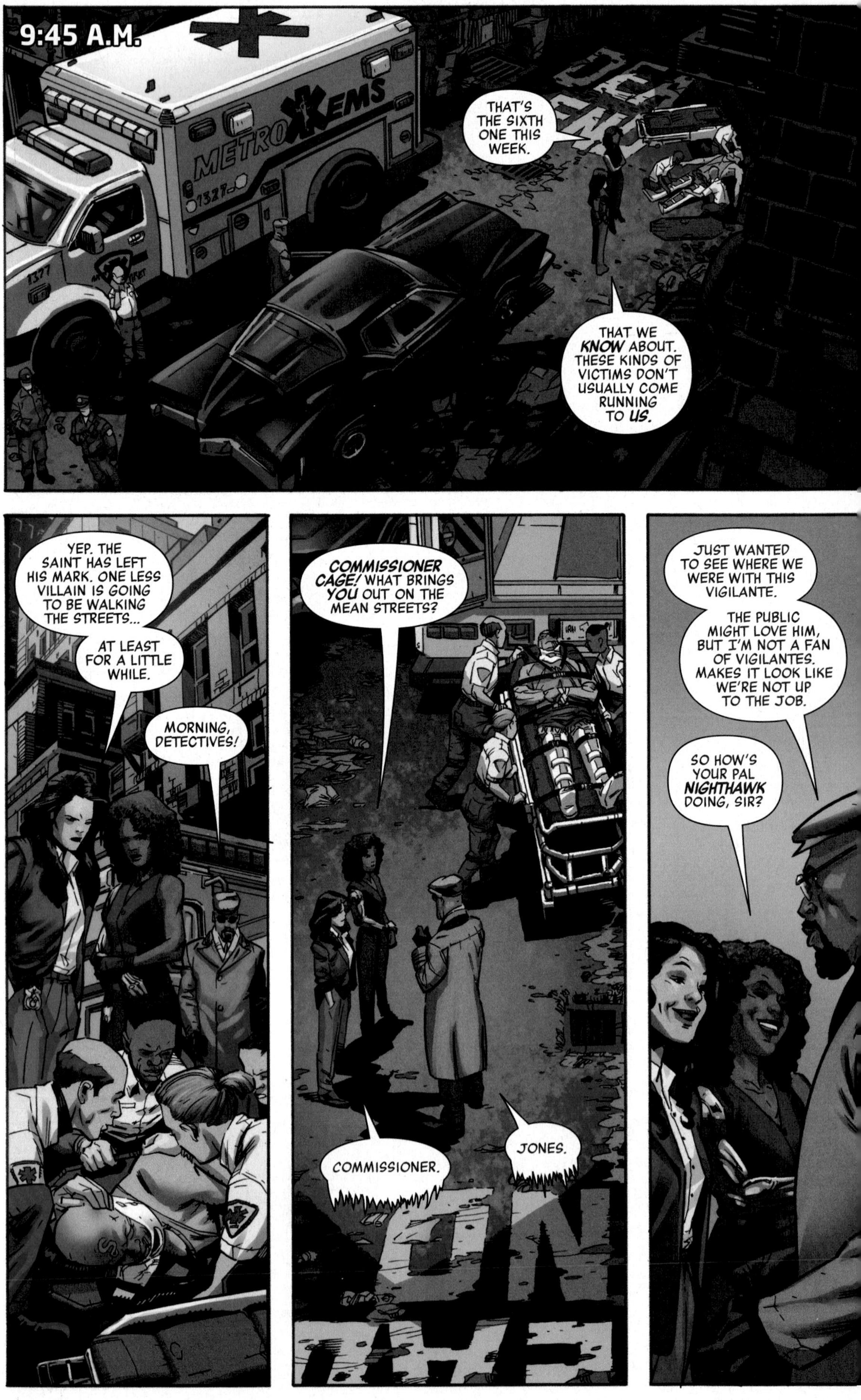
9:45 A.M.
METRO EMS
1327
THAT'S THE SIXTH ONE THIS WEEK.
THAT WE KNOW ABOUT. THESE KINDS OF VICTIMS DON'T USUALLY COME RUNNING TO US.
YEP. THE SAINT HAS LEFT HIS MARK. ONE LESS VILLAIN IS GOING TO BE WALKING THE STREETS...
AT LEAST FOR A LITTLE WHILE.
MORNING, DETECTIVES!
COMMISSIONER CAGE! WHAT BRINGS YOU OUT ON THE MEAN STREETS?
COMMISSIONER.
JONES.
JUST WANTED TO SEE WHERE WE WERE WITH THIS VIGILANTE.
THE PUBLIC MIGHT LOVE HIM, BUT I'M NOT A FAN OF VIGILANTES. MAKES IT LOOK LIKE WE'RE NOT UP TO THE JOB.
SO HOW'S YOUR PAL NIGHTHAWK DOING, SIR?

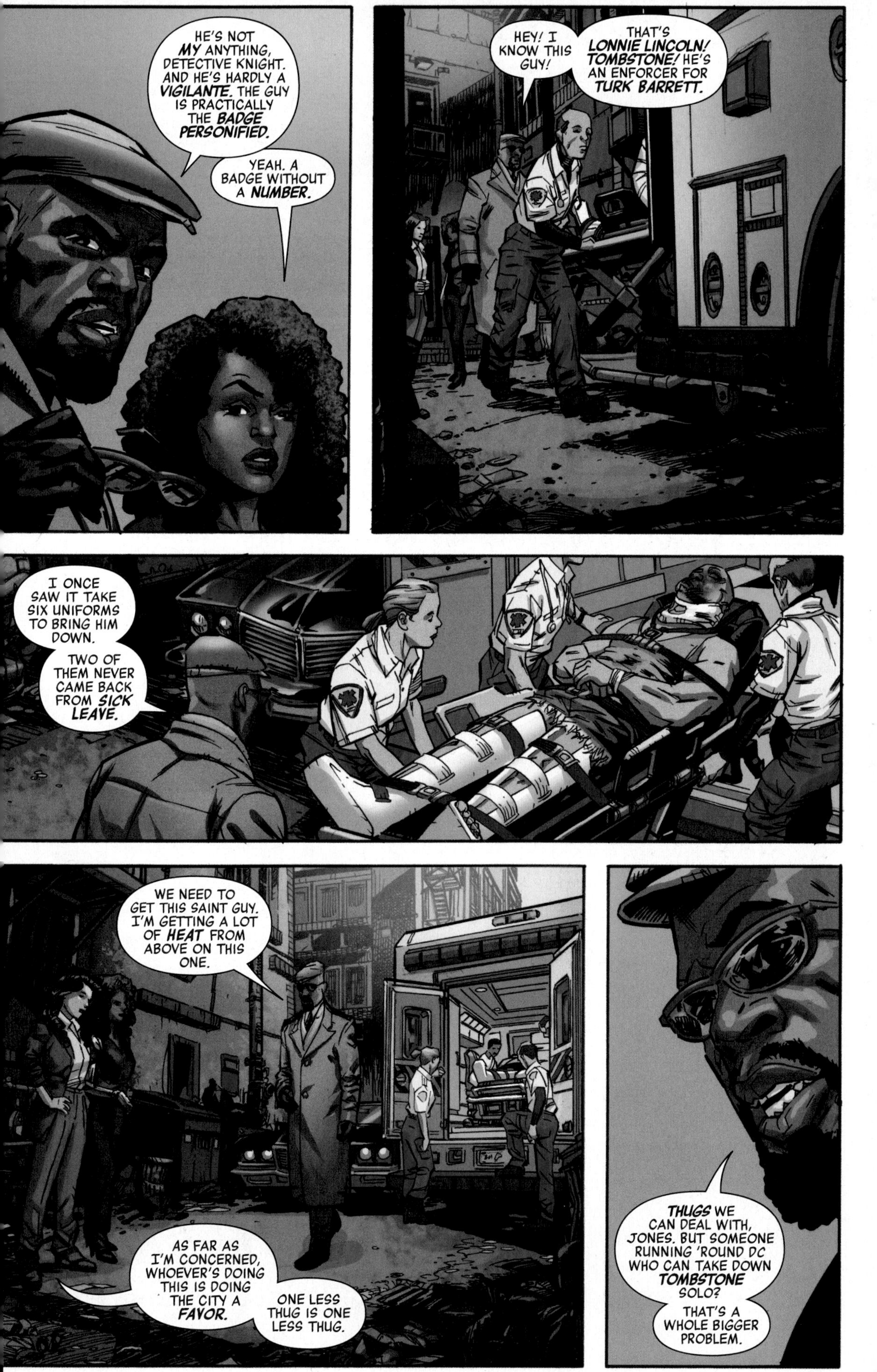
HE'S NOT MY ANYTHING, DETECTIVE KNIGHT. AND HE'S HARDLY A VIGILANTE. THE GUY IS PRACTICALLY THE BADGE PERSONIFIED.
YEAH. A BADGE WITHOUT A NUMBER.
HEY! I KNOW THIS GUY!
THAT'S LONNIE LINCOLN! TOMBSTONE! HE'S AN ENFORCER FOR TURK BARRETT.
I ONCE SAW IT TAKE SIX UNIFORMS TO BRING HIM DOWN.
TWO OF THEM NEVER CAME BACK FROM SICK LEAVE.
WE NEED TO GET THIS SAINT GUY. I'M GETTING A LOT OF HEAT FROM ABOVE ON THIS ONE.
AS FAR AS I'M CONCERNED, WHOEVER'S DOING THIS IS DOING THE CITY A FAVOR.
ONE LESS THUG IS ONE LESS THUG.
THUGS WE CAN DEAL WITH, JONES. BUT SOMEONE RUNNING 'ROUND DC WHO CAN TAKE DOWN TOMBSTONE SOLO?
THAT'S A WHOLE BIGGER PROBLEM.

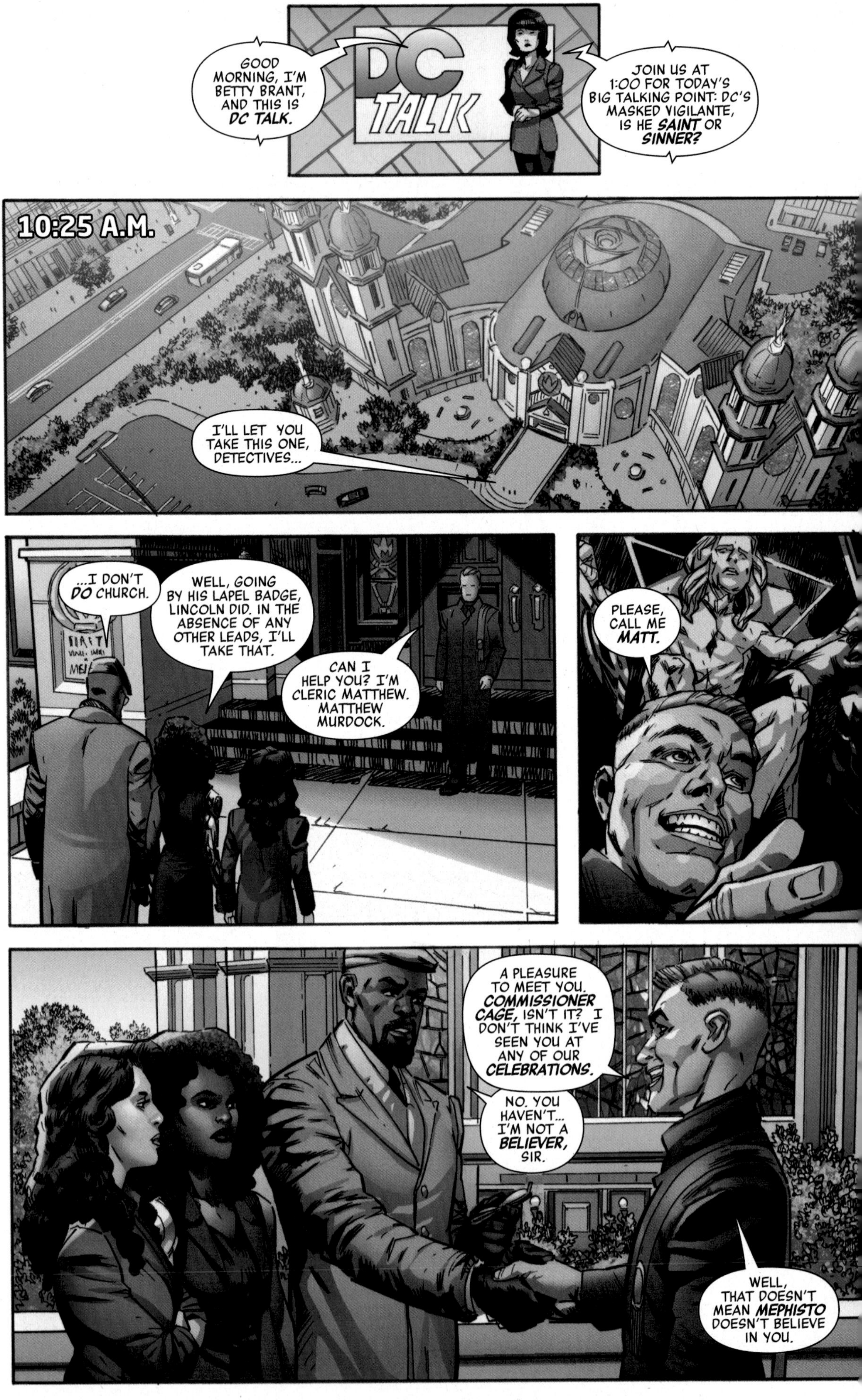
GOOD MORNING, I'M BETTY BRANT, AND THIS IS DC TALK.
DC TALK
JOIN US AT 1:00 FOR TODAY'S BIG TALKING POINT: DC'S MASKED VIGILANTE, IS HE SAINT OR SINNER?
10:25 A.M.
I'LL LET YOU TAKE THIS ONE, DETECTIVES...
...I DON'T DO CHURCH.
WELL, GOING BY HIS LAPEL BADGE, LINCOLN DID. IN THE ABSENCE OF ANY OTHER LEADS, I'LL TAKE THAT.
CAN I HELP YOU? I'M CLERIC MATTHEW. MATTHEW MURDOCK.
PLEASE, CALL ME MATT.
A PLEASURE TO MEET YOU. COMMISSIONER CAGE, ISN'T IT? I DON'T THINK I'VE SEEN YOU AT ANY OF OUR CELEBRATIONS.
NO. YOU HAVEN'T... I'M NOT A BELIEVER, SIR.
WELL, THAT DOESN'T MEAN MEPHISTO DOESN'T BELIEVE IN YOU.

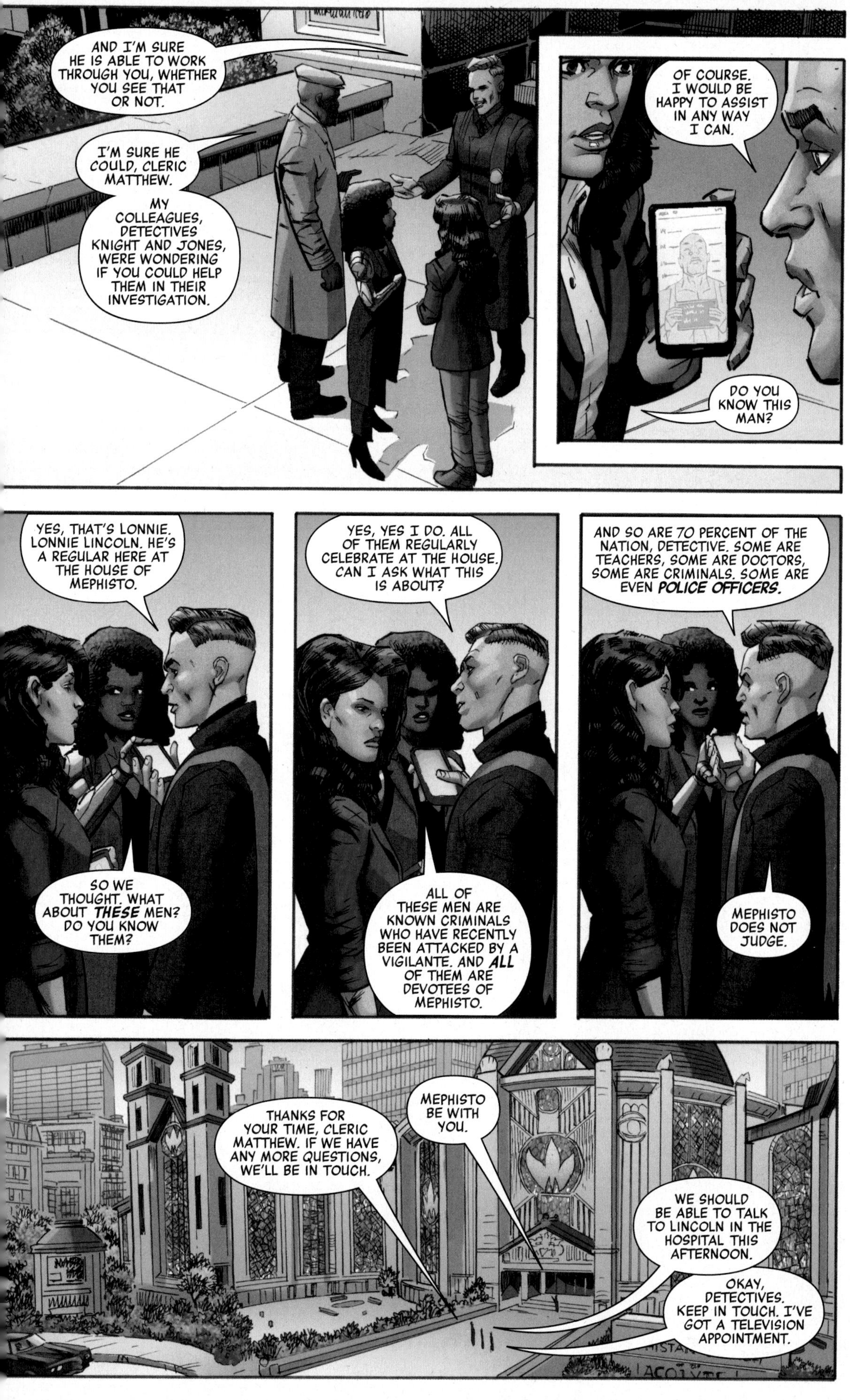
AND I'M SURE HE IS ABLE TO WORK THROUGH YOU, WHETHER YOU SEE THAT OR NOT.
I'M SURE HE COULD, CLERIC MATTHEW.
MY COLLEAGUES, DETECTIVES KNIGHT AND JONES, WERE WONDERING IF YOU COULD HELP THEM IN THEIR INVESTIGATION.
OF COURSE. I WOULD BE HAPPY TO ASSIST IN ANY WAY I CAN.
DO YOU KNOW THIS MAN?
YES, THAT'S LONNIE. LONNIE LINCOLN. HE'S A REGULAR HERE AT THE HOUSE OF MEPHISTO.
SO WE THOUGHT. WHAT ABOUT *THESE* MEN? DO YOU KNOW THEM?
YES, YES I DO. ALL OF THEM REGULARLY CELEBRATE AT THE HOUSE. CAN I ASK WHAT THIS IS ABOUT?
ALL OF THESE MEN ARE KNOWN CRIMINALS WHO HAVE RECENTLY BEEN ATTACKED BY A VIGILANTE. AND *ALL* OF THEM ARE DEVOTEES OF MEPHISTO.
AND SO ARE 70 PERCENT OF THE NATION, DETECTIVE. SOME ARE TEACHERS, SOME ARE DOCTORS, SOME ARE CRIMINALS. SOME ARE EVEN *POLICE OFFICERS.*
MEPHISTO DOES NOT JUDGE.
THANKS FOR YOUR TIME, CLERIC MATTHEW. IF WE HAVE ANY MORE QUESTIONS, WE'LL BE IN TOUCH.
MEPHISTO BE WITH YOU.
WE SHOULD BE ABLE TO TALK TO LINCOLN IN THE HOSPITAL THIS AFTERNOON.
OKAY, DETECTIVES. KEEP IN TOUCH. I'VE GOT A TELEVISION APPOINTMENT.

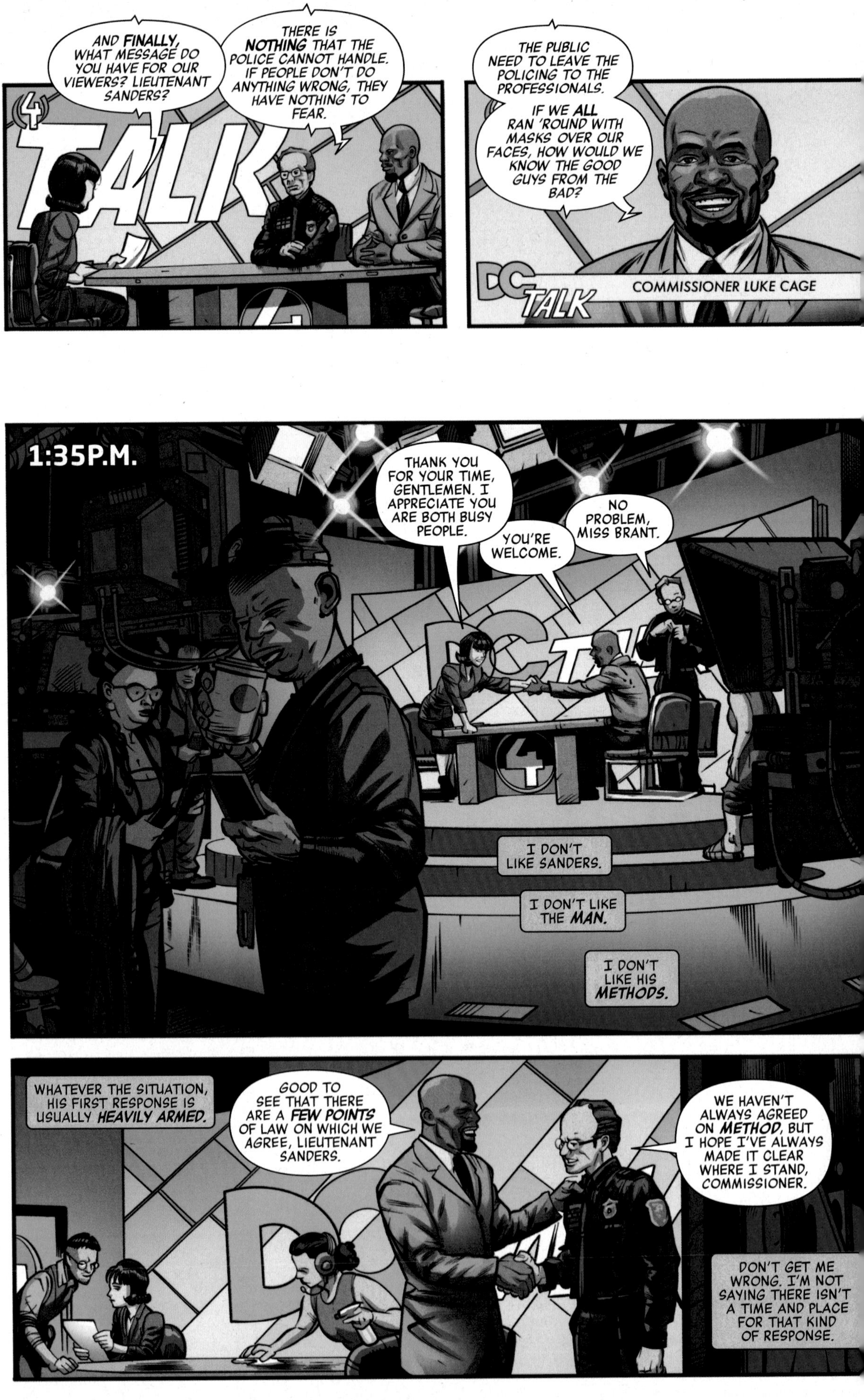
AND FINALLY, WHAT MESSAGE DO YOU HAVE FOR OUR VIEWERS? LIEUTENANT SANDERS?
THERE IS NOTHING THAT THE POLICE CANNOT HANDLE. IF PEOPLE DON'T DO ANYTHING WRONG, THEY HAVE NOTHING TO FEAR.
TALK
THE PUBLIC NEED TO LEAVE THE POLICING TO THE PROFESSIONALS.
IF WE ALL RAN 'ROUND WITH MASKS OVER OUR FACES, HOW WOULD WE KNOW THE GOOD GUYS FROM THE BAD?
DC TALK
COMMISSIONER LUKE CAGE
1:35P.M.
THANK YOU FOR YOUR TIME, GENTLEMEN. I APPRECIATE YOU ARE BOTH BUSY PEOPLE.
YOU'RE WELCOME.
NO PROBLEM, MISS BRANT.
I DON'T LIKE SANDERS.
I DON'T LIKE THE MAN.
I DON'T LIKE HIS METHODS.
WHATEVER THE SITUATION, HIS FIRST RESPONSE IS USUALLY HEAVILY ARMED.
GOOD TO SEE THAT THERE ARE A FEW POINTS OF LAW ON WHICH WE AGREE, LIEUTENANT SANDERS.
WE HAVEN'T ALWAYS AGREED ON METHOD, BUT I HOPE I'VE ALWAYS MADE IT CLEAR WHERE I STAND, COMMISSIONER.
DON'T GET ME WRONG. I'M NOT SAYING THERE ISN'T A TIME AND PLACE FOR THAT KIND OF RESPONSE.

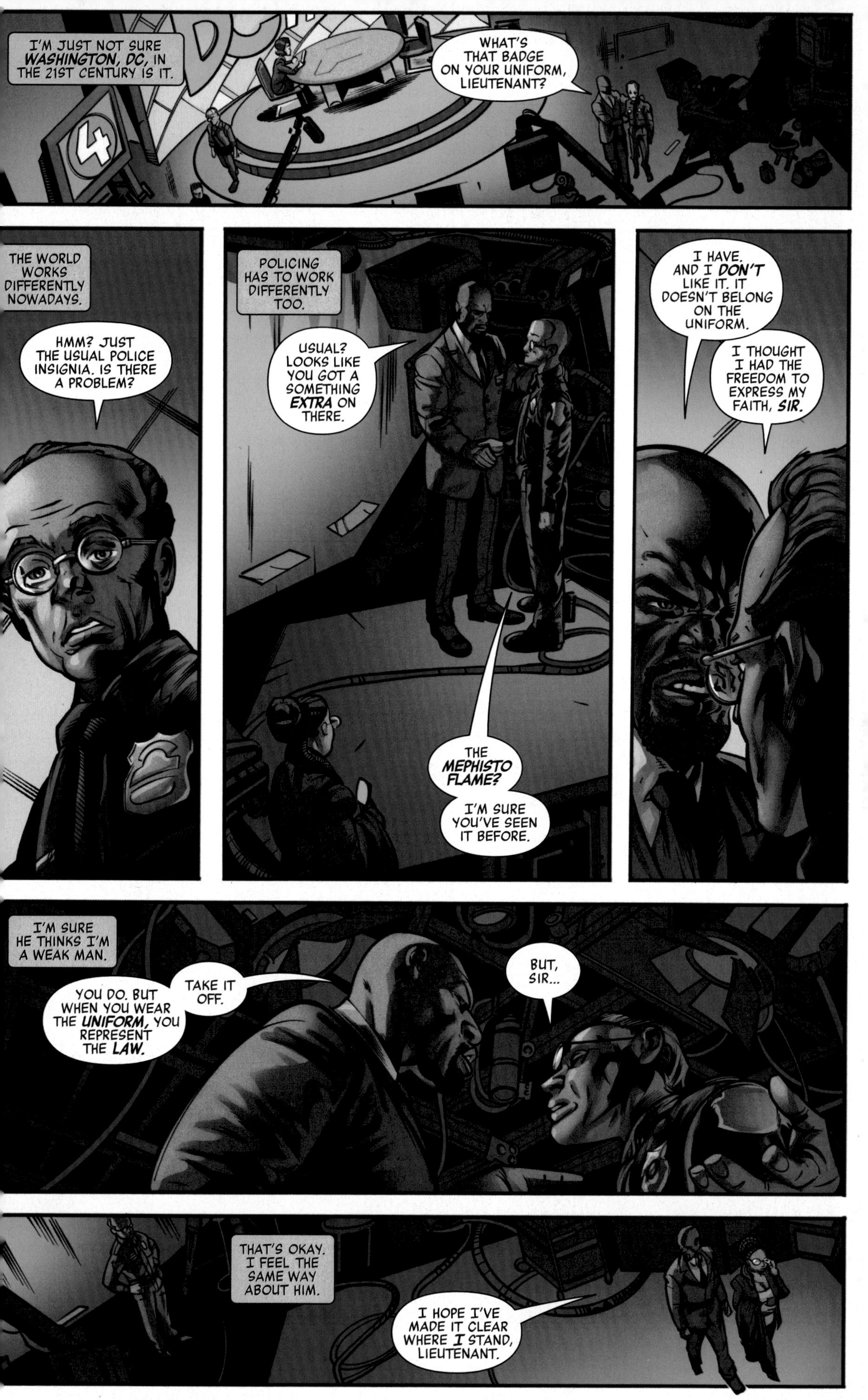
I'M JUST NOT SURE WASHINGTON, DC, IN THE 21ST CENTURY IS IT.
WHAT'S THAT BADGE ON YOUR UNIFORM, LIEUTENANT?
THE WORLD WORKS DIFFERENTLY NOWADAYS.
HMM? JUST THE USUAL POLICE INSIGNIA. IS THERE A PROBLEM?
POLICING HAS TO WORK DIFFERENTLY TOO.
USUAL? LOOKS LIKE YOU GOT A SOMETHING EXTRA ON THERE.
THE MEPHISTO FLAME?
I'M SURE YOU'VE SEEN IT BEFORE.
I HAVE. AND I DON'T LIKE IT. IT DOESN'T BELONG ON THE UNIFORM.
I THOUGHT I HAD THE FREEDOM TO EXPRESS MY FAITH, SIR.
I'M SURE HE THINKS I'M A WEAK MAN.
TAKE IT OFF.
BUT, SIR...
YOU DO. BUT WHEN YOU WEAR THE UNIFORM, YOU REPRESENT THE LAW.
THAT'S OKAY. I FEEL THE SAME WAY ABOUT HIM.
I HOPE I'VE MADE IT CLEAR WHERE I STAND, LIEUTENANT.

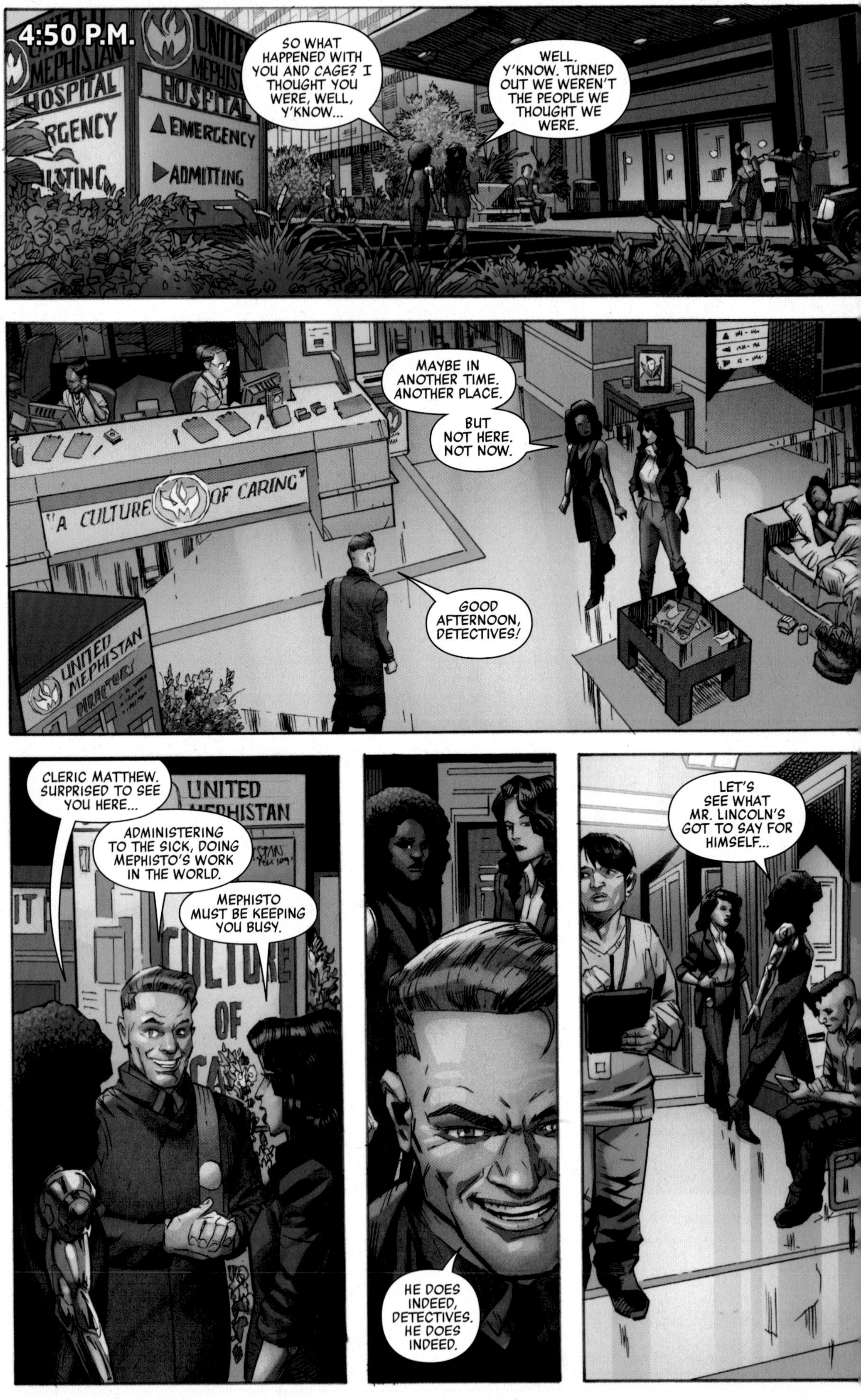
4:50 P.M.
UNITED MEPHISTAN HOSPITAL
EMERGENCY
ADMITTING
SO WHAT HAPPENED WITH YOU AND CAGE? I THOUGHT YOU WERE, WELL, Y'KNOW...
WELL. Y'KNOW. TURNED OUT WE WEREN'T THE PEOPLE WE THOUGHT WE WERE.
MAYBE IN ANOTHER TIME. ANOTHER PLACE.
BUT NOT HERE. NOT NOW.
"A CULTURE OF CARING"
GOOD AFTERNOON, DETECTIVES!
UNITED MEPHISTAN
CLERIC MATTHEW. SURPRISED TO SEE YOU HERE...
ADMINISTERING TO THE SICK, DOING MEPHISTO'S WORK IN THE WORLD.
MEPHISTO MUST BE KEEPING YOU BUSY.
HE DOES INDEED, DETECTIVES. HE DOES INDEED.
LET'S SEE WHAT MR. LINCOLN'S GOT TO SAY FOR HIMSELF...

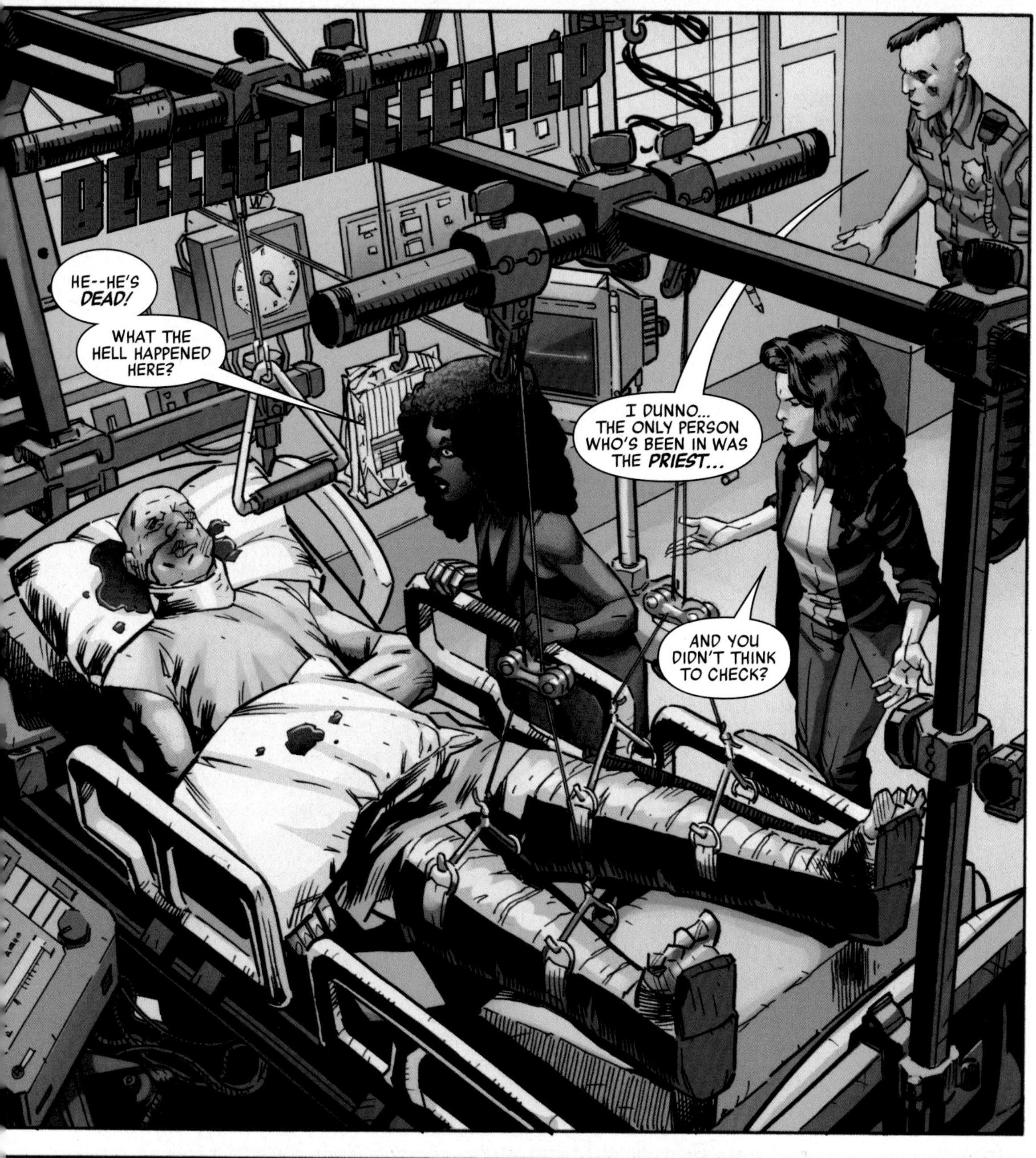
BEEEEEEEEEEEEEEEP
HE--HE'S DEAD!
WHAT THE HELL HAPPENED HERE?
I DUNNO... THE ONLY PERSON WHO'S BEEN IN WAS THE PRIEST...
AND YOU DIDN'T THINK TO CHECK?

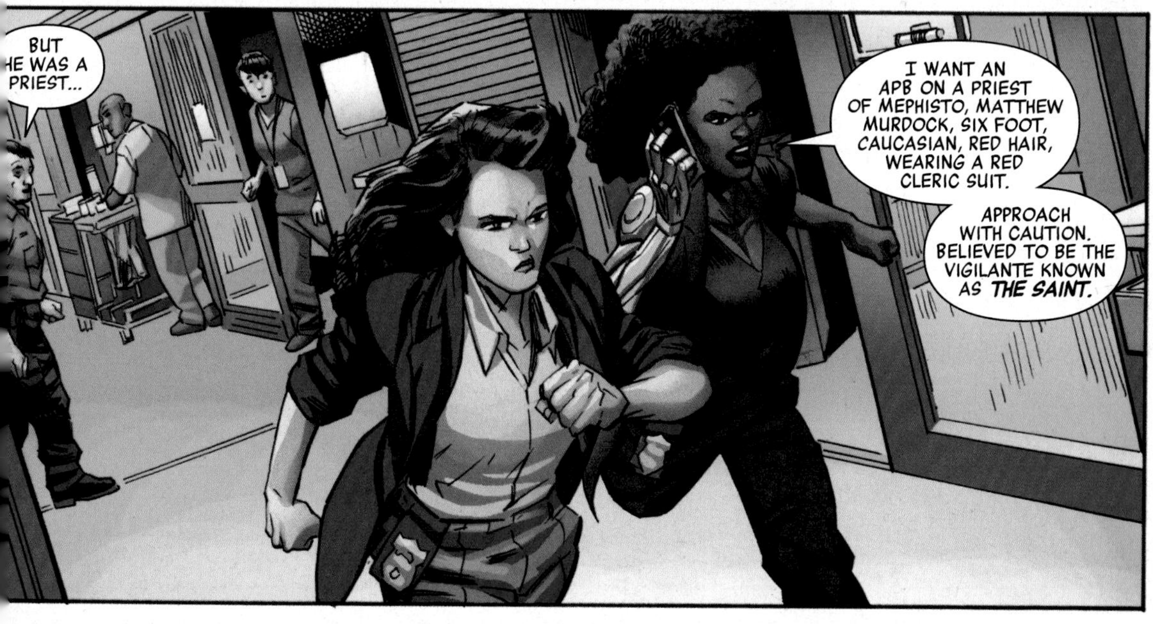
BUT HE WAS A PRIEST...
I WANT AN APB ON A PRIEST OF MEPHISTO, MATTHEW MURDOCK, SIX FOOT, CAUCASIAN, RED HAIR, WEARING A RED CLERIC SUIT.
APPROACH WITH CAUTION. BELIEVED TO BE THE VIGILANTE KNOWN AS THE SAINT.

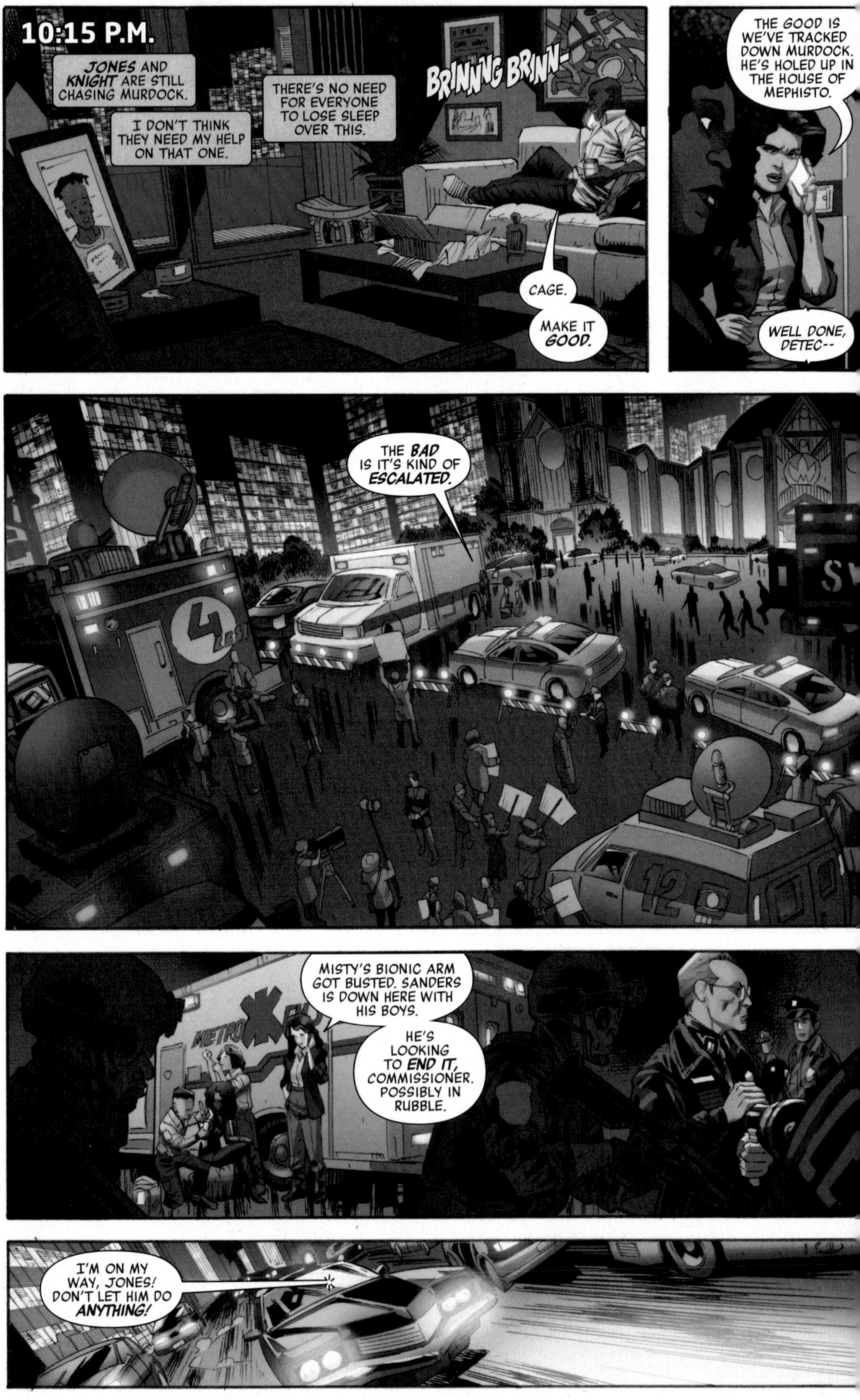
10:15 P.M.
JONES AND KNIGHT ARE STILL CHASING MURDOCK.
I DON'T THINK THEY NEED MY HELP ON THAT ONE.
THERE'S NO NEED FOR EVERYONE TO LOSE SLEEP OVER THIS.
BRINNNG BRINN-
CAGE.
MAKE IT GOOD.
THE GOOD IS WE'VE TRACKED DOWN MURDOCK. HE'S HOLED UP IN THE HOUSE OF MEPHISTO.
WELL DONE, DETEC--
THE BAD IS IT'S KIND OF ESCALATED.
MISTY'S BIONIC ARM GOT BUSTED. SANDERS IS DOWN HERE WITH HIS BOYS.
HE'S LOOKING TO END IT, COMMISSIONER. POSSIBLY IN RUBBLE.
I'M ON MY WAY, JONES! DON'T LET HIM DO ANYTHING!

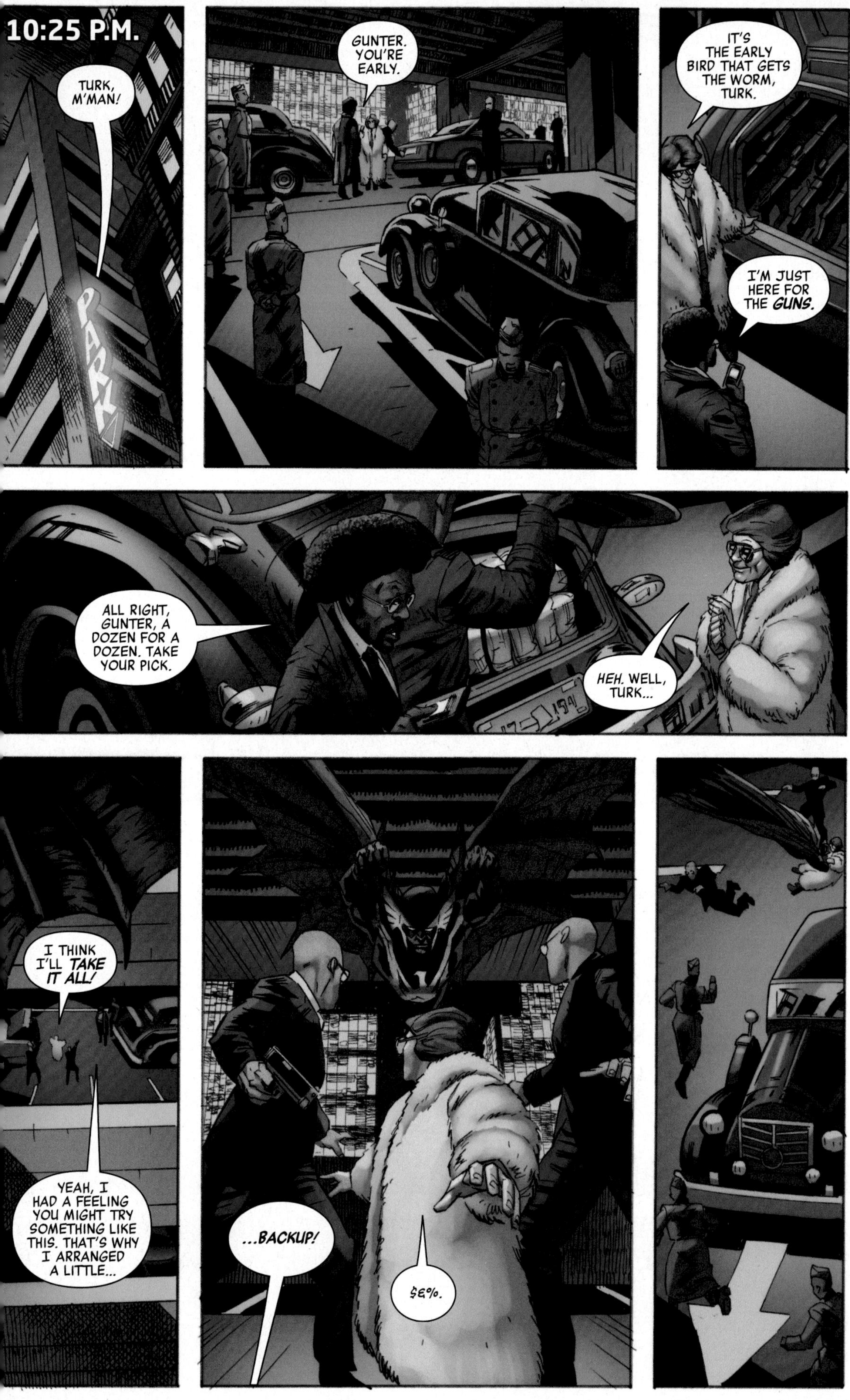
10:25 P.M.
TURK, M'MAN!
PARK
GUNTER. YOU'RE EARLY.
IT'S THE EARLY BIRD THAT GETS THE WORM, TURK.
I'M JUST HERE FOR THE GUNS.
ALL RIGHT, GUNTER, A DOZEN FOR A DOZEN. TAKE YOUR PICK.
HEH. WELL, TURK...
I THINK I'LL TAKE IT ALL!
YEAH, I HAD A FEELING YOU MIGHT TRY SOMETHING LIKE THIS. THAT'S WHY I ARRANGED A LITTLE...
...BACKUP!
$&%.

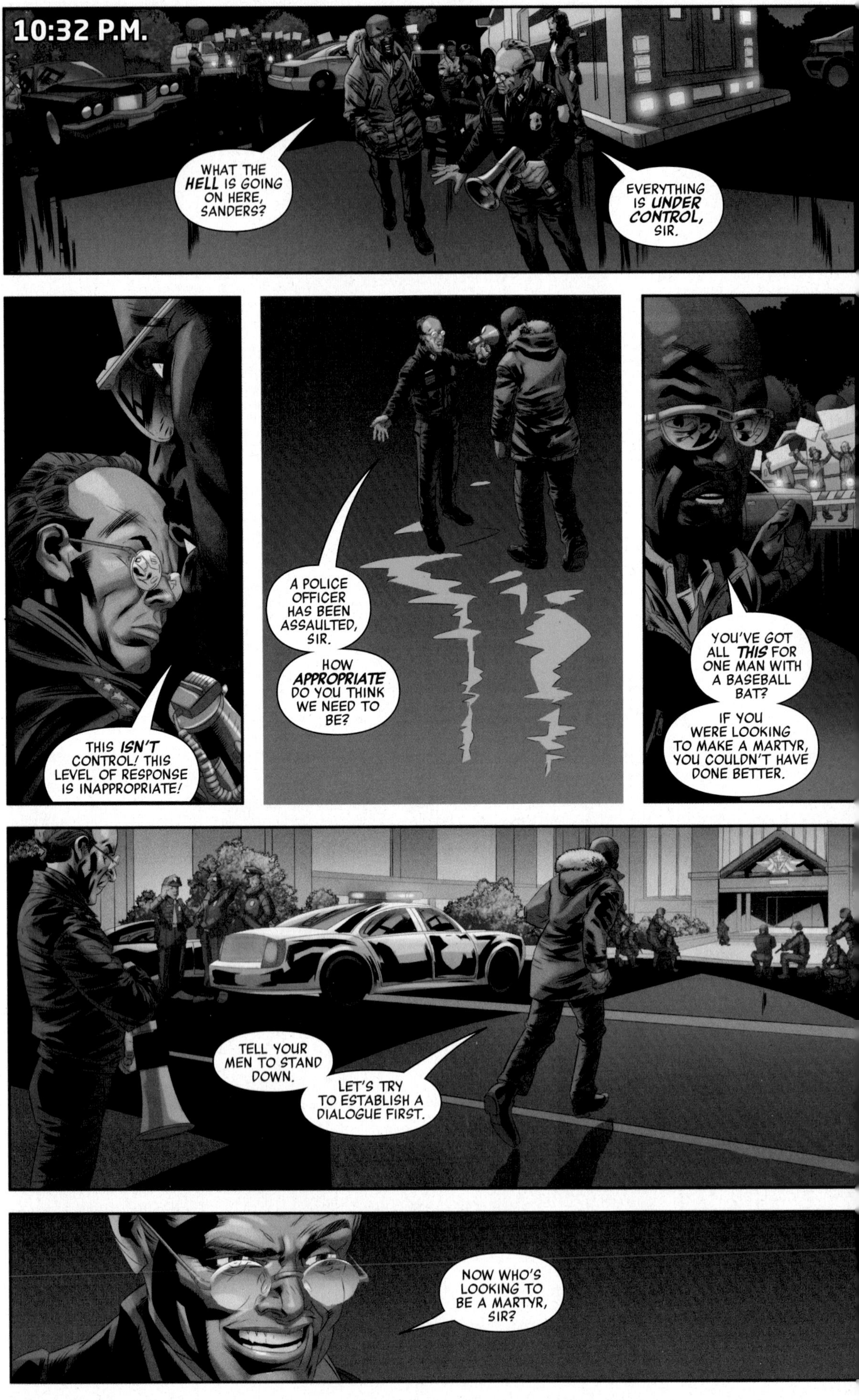
10:32 P.M.
WHAT THE HELL IS GOING ON HERE, SANDERS?
EVERYTHING IS UNDER CONTROL, SIR.
THIS ISN'T CONTROL! THIS LEVEL OF RESPONSE IS INAPPROPRIATE!
A POLICE OFFICER HAS BEEN ASSAULTED, SIR.
HOW APPROPRIATE DO YOU THINK WE NEED TO BE?
YOU'VE GOT ALL THIS FOR ONE MAN WITH A BASEBALL BAT?
IF YOU WERE LOOKING TO MAKE A MARTYR, YOU COULDN'T HAVE DONE BETTER.
TELL YOUR MEN TO STAND DOWN.
LET'S TRY TO ESTABLISH A DIALOGUE FIRST.
NOW WHO'S LOOKING TO BE A MARTYR, SIR?

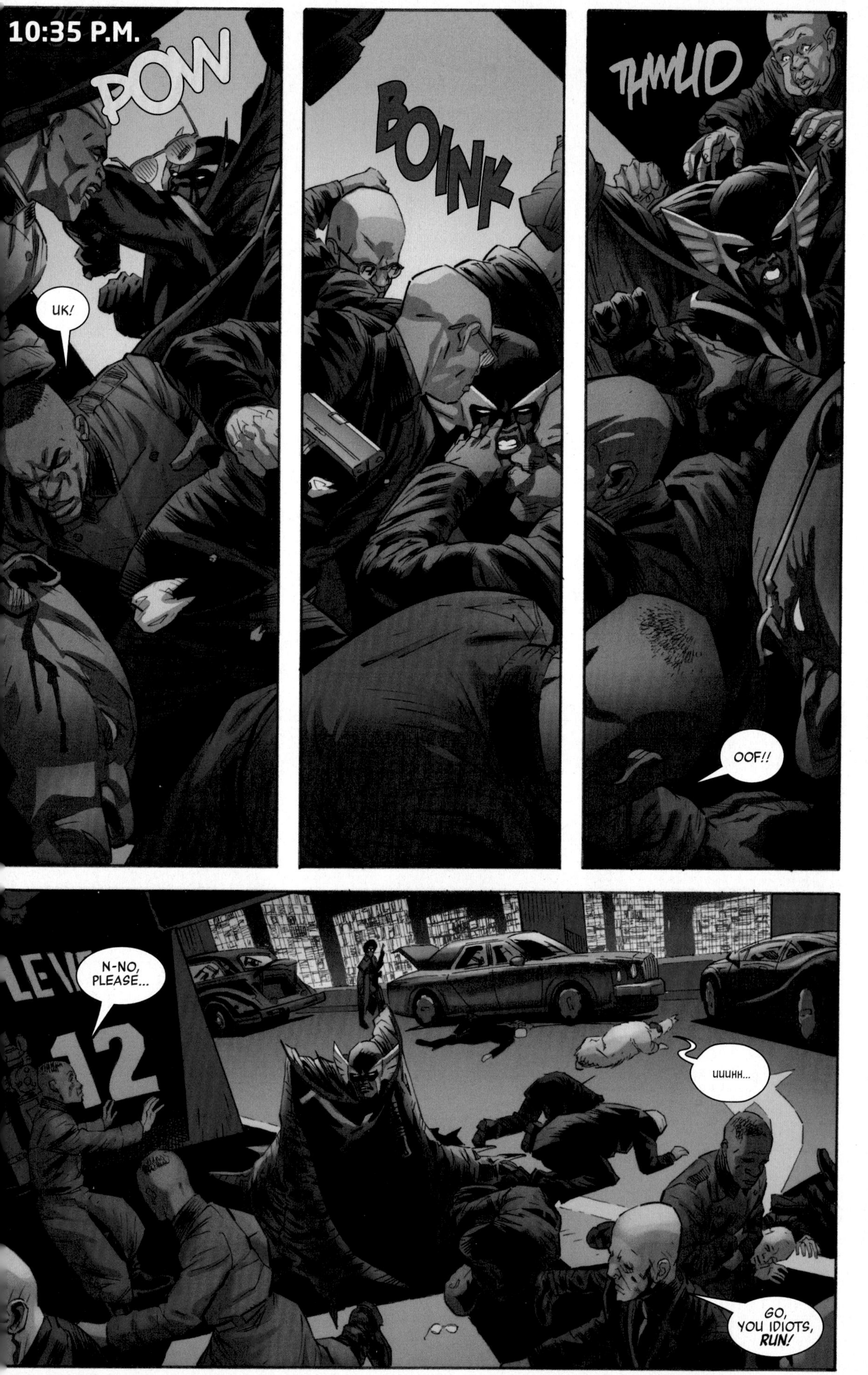
10:35 P.M.
POW
UK!
BOINK
THWUD
OOF!!
N-NO, PLEASE...
LEVEL 12
UUUHH...
GO, YOU IDIOTS, RUN!

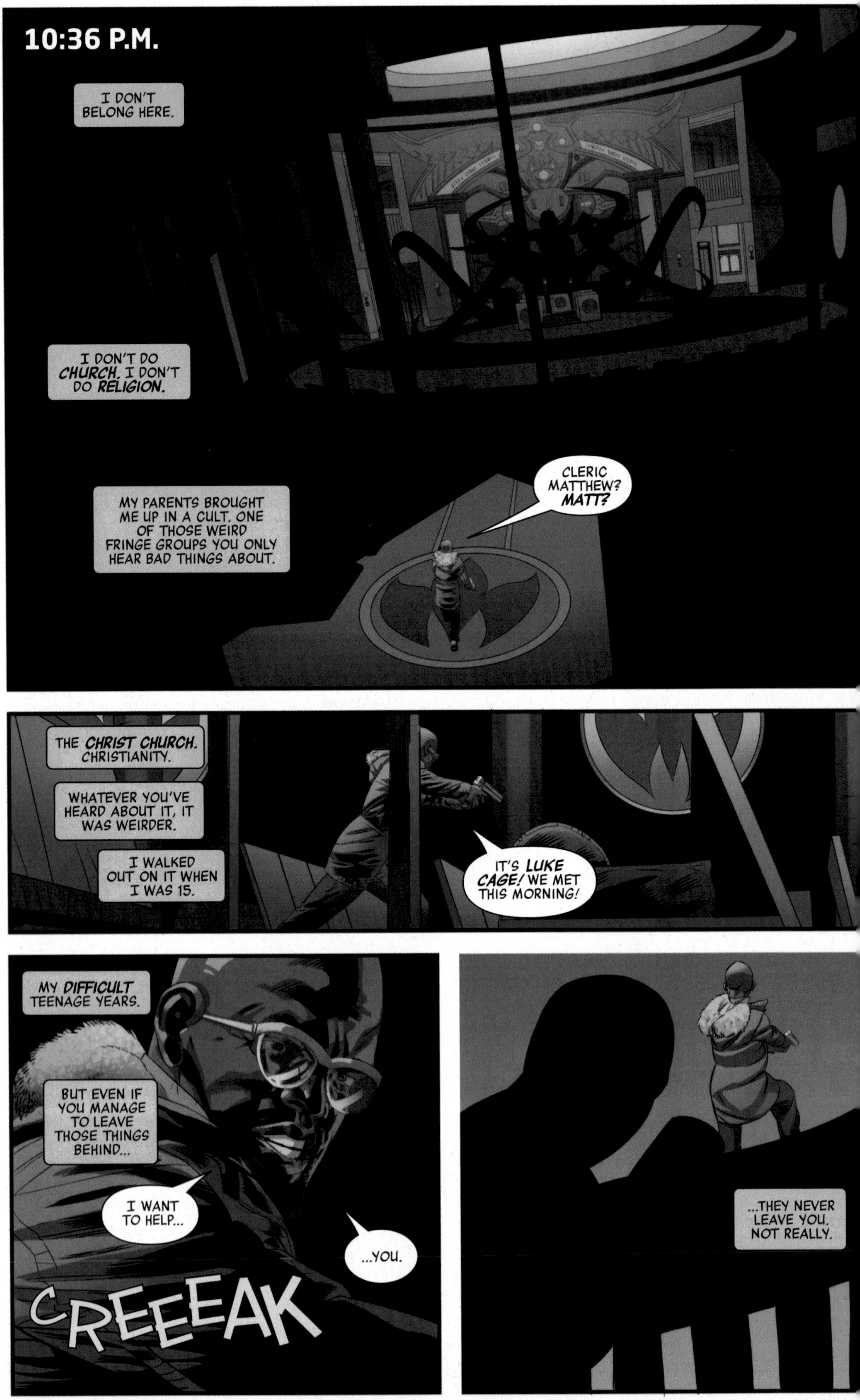
10:36 P.M.
I DON'T BELONG HERE.
I DON'T DO CHURCH. I DON'T DO RELIGION.
MY PARENTS BROUGHT ME UP IN A CULT. ONE OF THOSE WEIRD FRINGE GROUPS YOU ONLY HEAR BAD THINGS ABOUT.
CLERIC MATTHEW? MATT?
THE CHRIST CHURCH. CHRISTIANITY.
WHATEVER YOU'VE HEARD ABOUT IT, IT WAS WEIRDER.
I WALKED OUT ON IT WHEN I WAS 15.
IT'S LUKE CAGE! WE MET THIS MORNING!
MY DIFFICULT TEENAGE YEARS.
BUT EVEN IF YOU MANAGE TO LEAVE THOSE THINGS BEHIND...
I WANT TO HELP...
...YOU.
CREEEAK
...THEY NEVER LEAVE YOU. NOT REALLY.

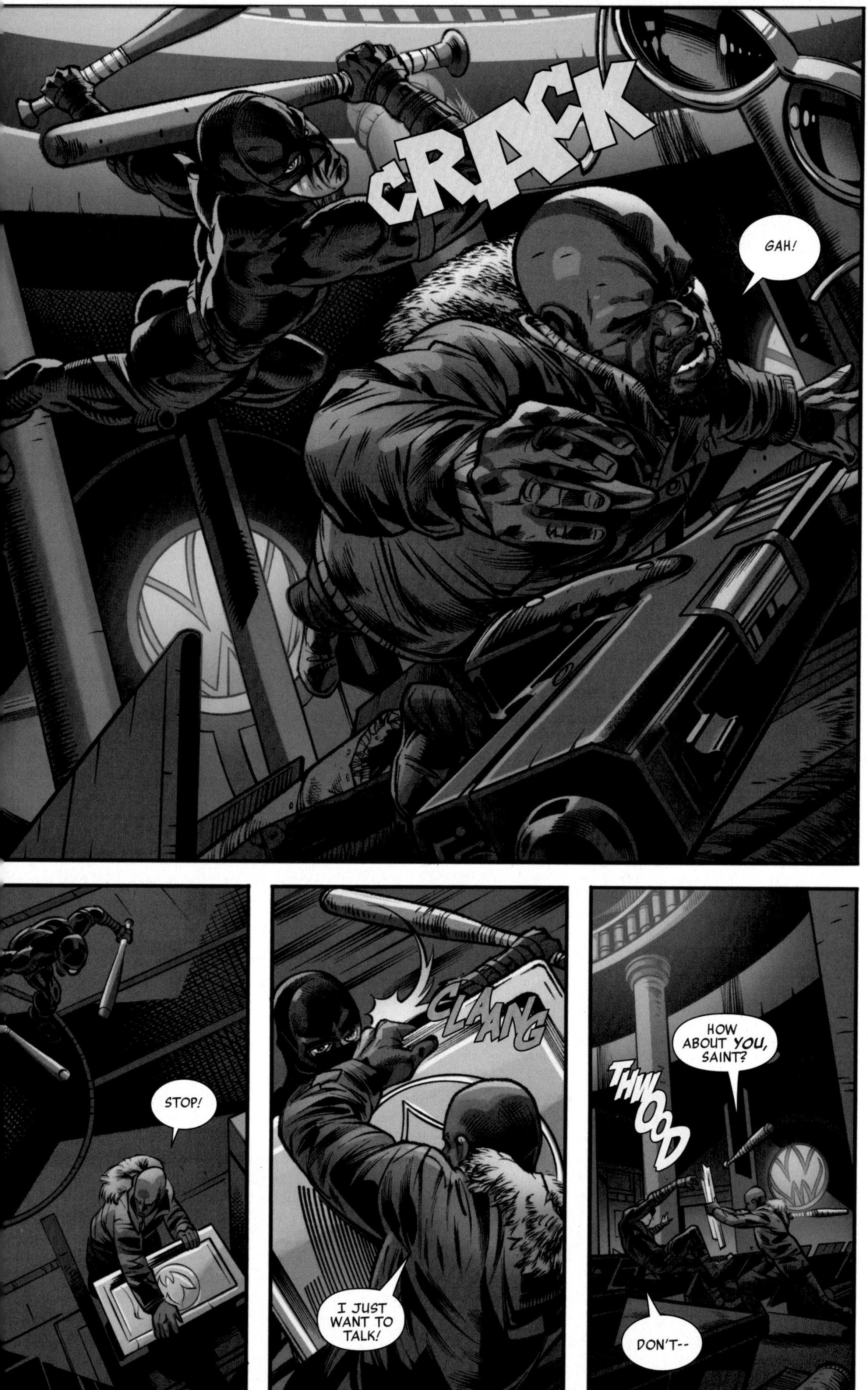
CRACK
GAH!
STOP!
CLANG
I JUST WANT TO TALK!
THWOOD
HOW ABOUT YOU, SAINT?
DON'T--

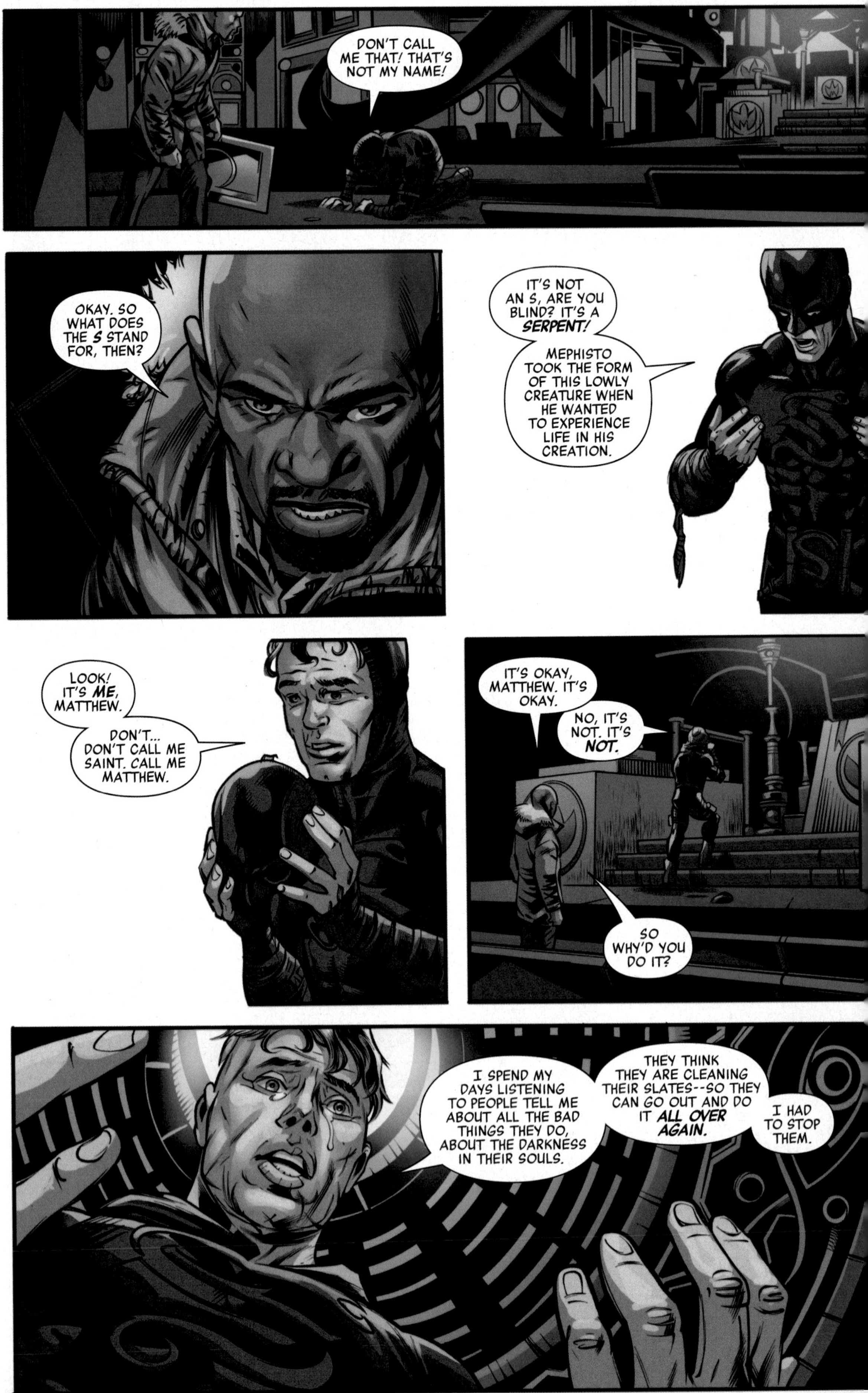
DON'T CALL ME THAT! THAT'S NOT MY NAME!
OKAY. SO WHAT DOES THE S STAND FOR, THEN?
IT'S NOT AN S, ARE YOU BLIND? IT'S A SERPENT!
MEPHISTO TOOK THE FORM OF THIS LOWLY CREATURE WHEN HE WANTED TO EXPERIENCE LIFE IN HIS CREATION.
LOOK! IT'S ME, MATTHEW.
DON'T... DON'T CALL ME SAINT. CALL ME MATTHEW.
IT'S OKAY, MATTHEW. IT'S OKAY.
NO, IT'S NOT. IT'S NOT.
SO WHY'D YOU DO IT?
I SPEND MY DAYS LISTENING TO PEOPLE TELL ME ABOUT ALL THE BAD THINGS THEY DO, ABOUT THE DARKNESS IN THEIR SOULS.
THEY THINK THEY ARE CLEANING THEIR SLATES--SO THEY CAN GO OUT AND DO IT ALL OVER AGAIN.
I HAD TO STOP THEM.

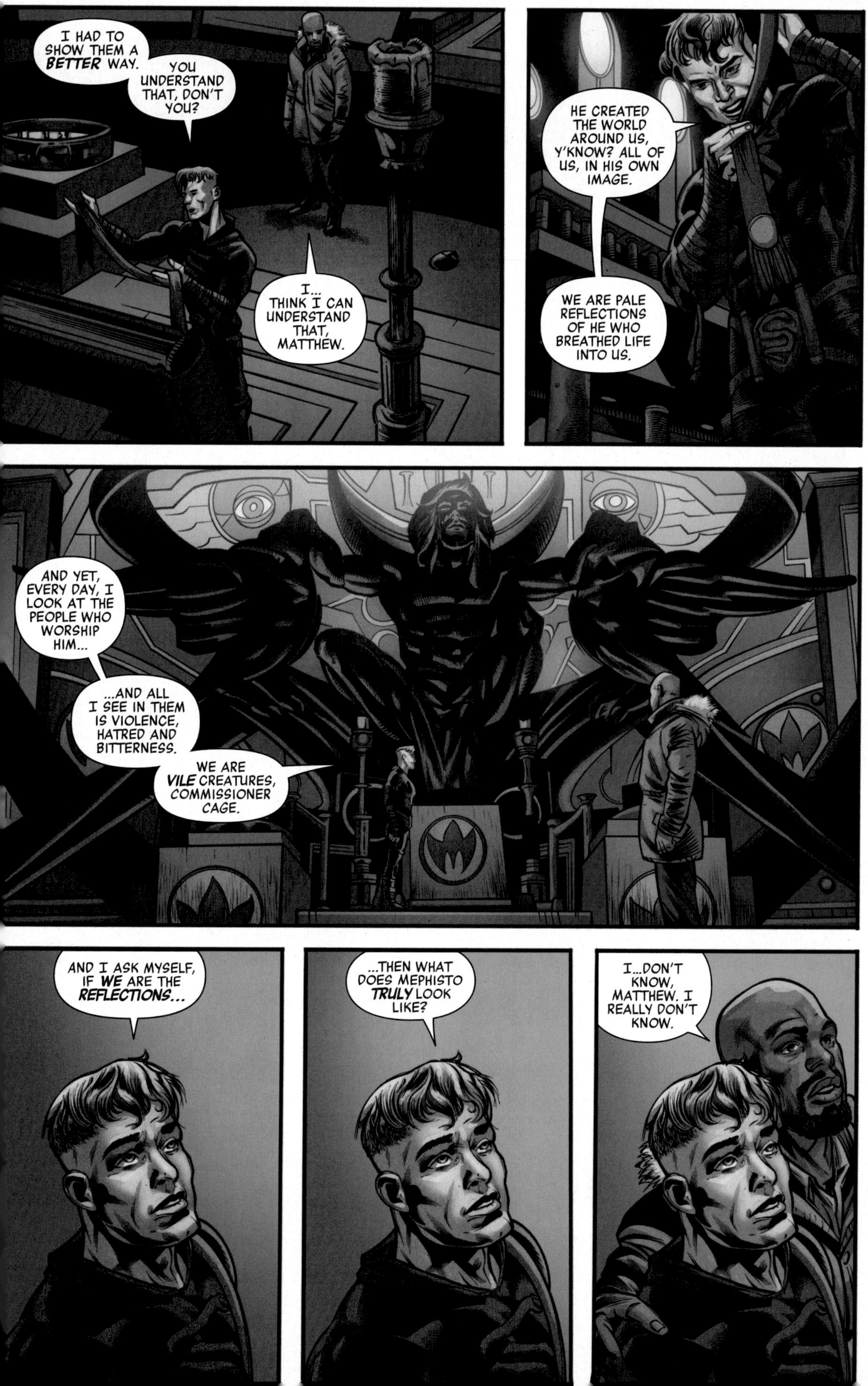
I HAD TO SHOW THEM A BETTER WAY.
YOU UNDERSTAND THAT, DON'T YOU?
I... THINK I CAN UNDERSTAND THAT, MATTHEW.
HE CREATED THE WORLD AROUND US, Y'KNOW? ALL OF US, IN HIS OWN IMAGE.
WE ARE PALE REFLECTIONS OF HE WHO BREATHED LIFE INTO US.
AND YET, EVERY DAY, I LOOK AT THE PEOPLE WHO WORSHIP HIM...
...AND ALL I SEE IN THEM IS VIOLENCE, HATRED AND BITTERNESS.
WE ARE VILE CREATURES, COMMISSIONER CAGE.
AND I ASK MYSELF, IF WE ARE THE REFLECTIONS...
...THEN WHAT DOES MEPHISTO TRULY LOOK LIKE?
I...DON'T KNOW, MATTHEW. I REALLY DON'T KNOW.

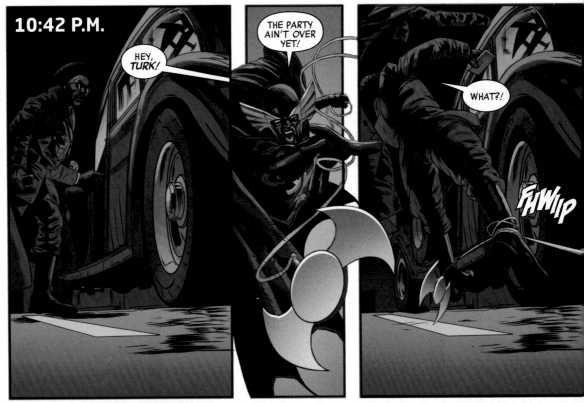

10:42 P.M.

HEY, *TURK!*

THE PARTY AIN'T OVER YET!

WHAT?!

FHWIIP

I'D HATE FOR YOU TO MISS OUT ON THE FUN!

WHOOA!!!

HEY, YOU GOT ME, HERO!

--WE BRING YOU THE LATEST UPDATE FROM THE HOUSE OF MEPHISTO, WHERE POLICE COMMISSIONER LUKE CAGE HAS ENTERED THE BUILDING IN PURSUIT OF THE MASKED VIGILANTE KNOWN AS THE SAINT--

LIVE

(4) BREAKING

TEMPLE STANDOFF

BUT WHO'S GOT YOUR MAN *CAGE?*

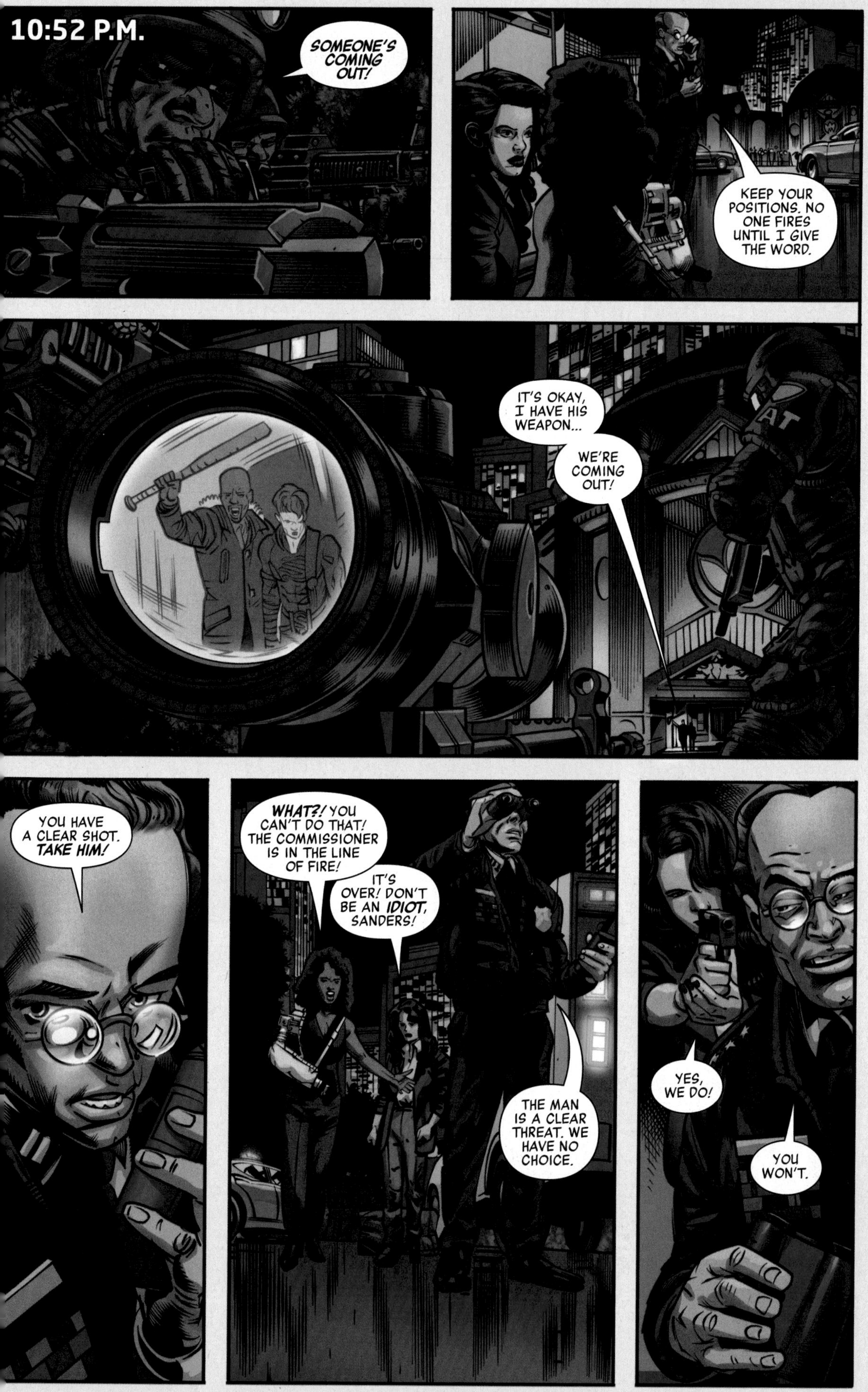
10:52 P.M.
SOMEONE'S COMING OUT!
KEEP YOUR POSITIONS. NO ONE FIRES UNTIL I GIVE THE WORD.
IT'S OKAY, I HAVE HIS WEAPON...
WE'RE COMING OUT!
YOU HAVE A CLEAR SHOT. TAKE HIM!
WHAT?! YOU CAN'T DO THAT! THE COMMISSIONER IS IN THE LINE OF FIRE!
IT'S OVER! DON'T BE AN IDIOT, SANDERS!
THE MAN IS A CLEAR THREAT. WE HAVE NO CHOICE.
YES, WE DO!
YOU WON'T.

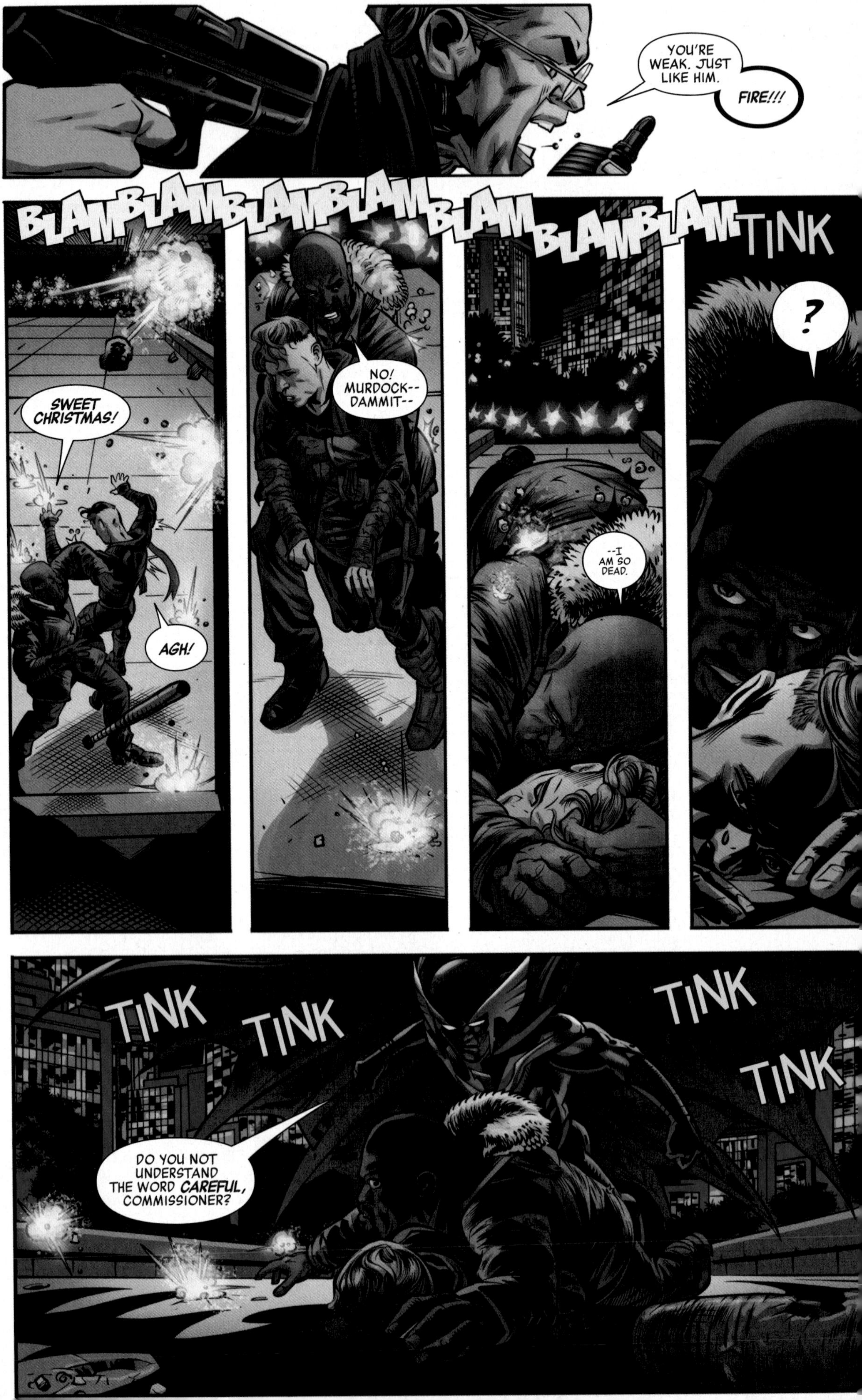
YOU'RE WEAK. JUST LIKE HIM.
FIRE!!!
BLAMBLAMBLAMBLAMBLAMBLAMBLAM
TINK
SWEET CHRISTMAS!
AGH!
NO! MURDOCK-- DAMMIT--
--I AM SO DEAD.
?
TINK
TINK
TINK
TINK
DO YOU NOT UNDERSTAND THE WORD CAREFUL, COMMISSIONER?

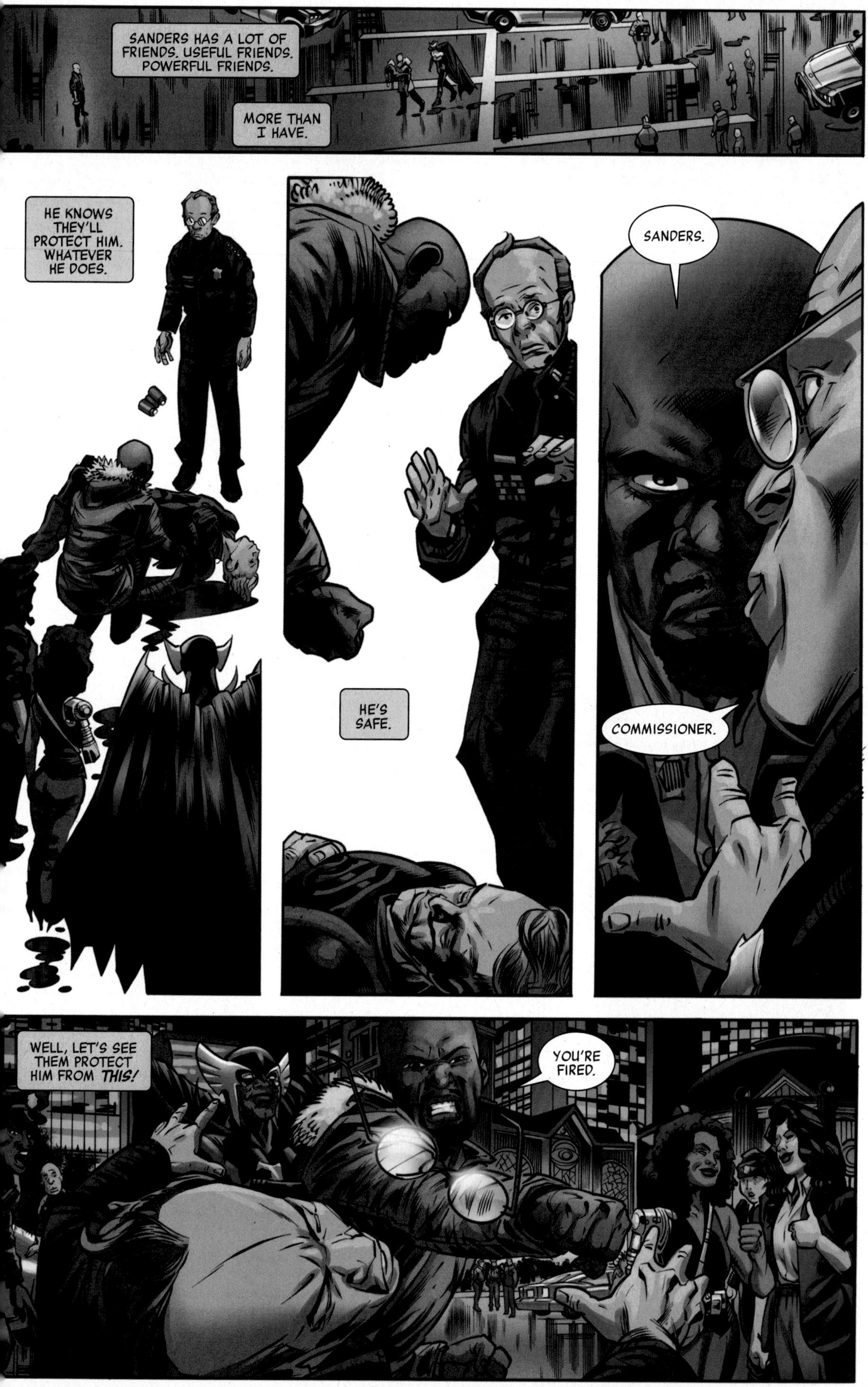
SANDERS HAS A LOT OF FRIENDS. USEFUL FRIENDS. POWERFUL FRIENDS.
MORE THAN I HAVE.
HE KNOWS THEY'LL PROTECT HIM. WHATEVER HE DOES.
HE'S SAFE.
SANDERS.
COMMISSIONER.
WELL, LET'S SEE THEM PROTECT HIM FROM *THIS!*
YOU'RE FIRED.

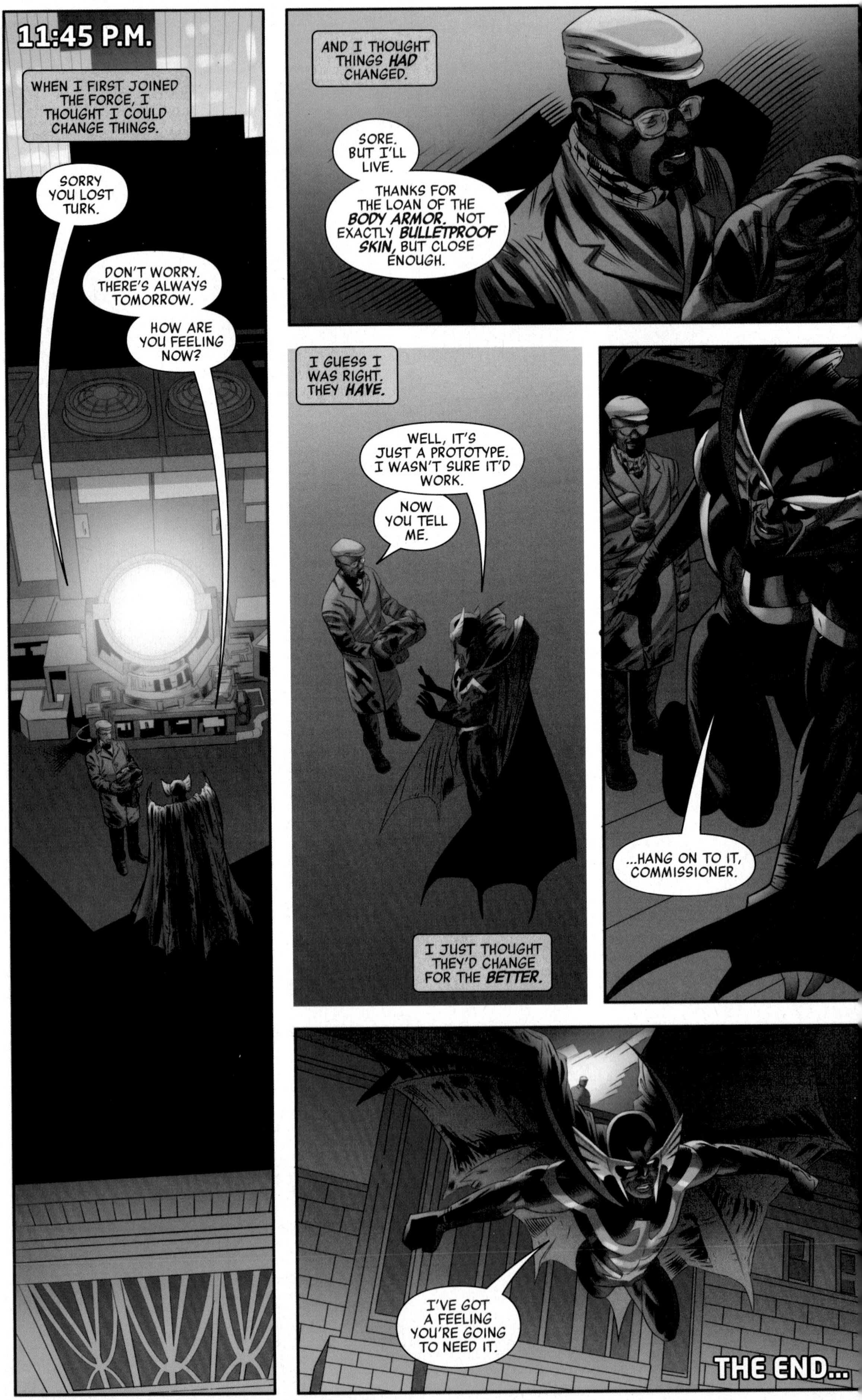
11:45 P.M.
WHEN I FIRST JOINED THE FORCE, I THOUGHT I COULD CHANGE THINGS.
SORRY YOU LOST TURK.
DON'T WORRY. THERE'S ALWAYS TOMORROW.
HOW ARE YOU FEELING NOW?
AND I THOUGHT THINGS HAD CHANGED.
SORE. BUT I'LL LIVE.
THANKS FOR THE LOAN OF THE BODY ARMOR. NOT EXACTLY BULLETPROOF SKIN, BUT CLOSE ENOUGH.
I GUESS I WAS RIGHT. THEY HAVE.
WELL, IT'S JUST A PROTOTYPE. I WASN'T SURE IT'D WORK.
NOW YOU TELL ME.
I JUST THOUGHT THEY'D CHANGE FOR THE BETTER.
...HANG ON TO IT, COMMISSIONER.
I'VE GOT A FEELING YOU'RE GOING TO NEED IT.
THE END...

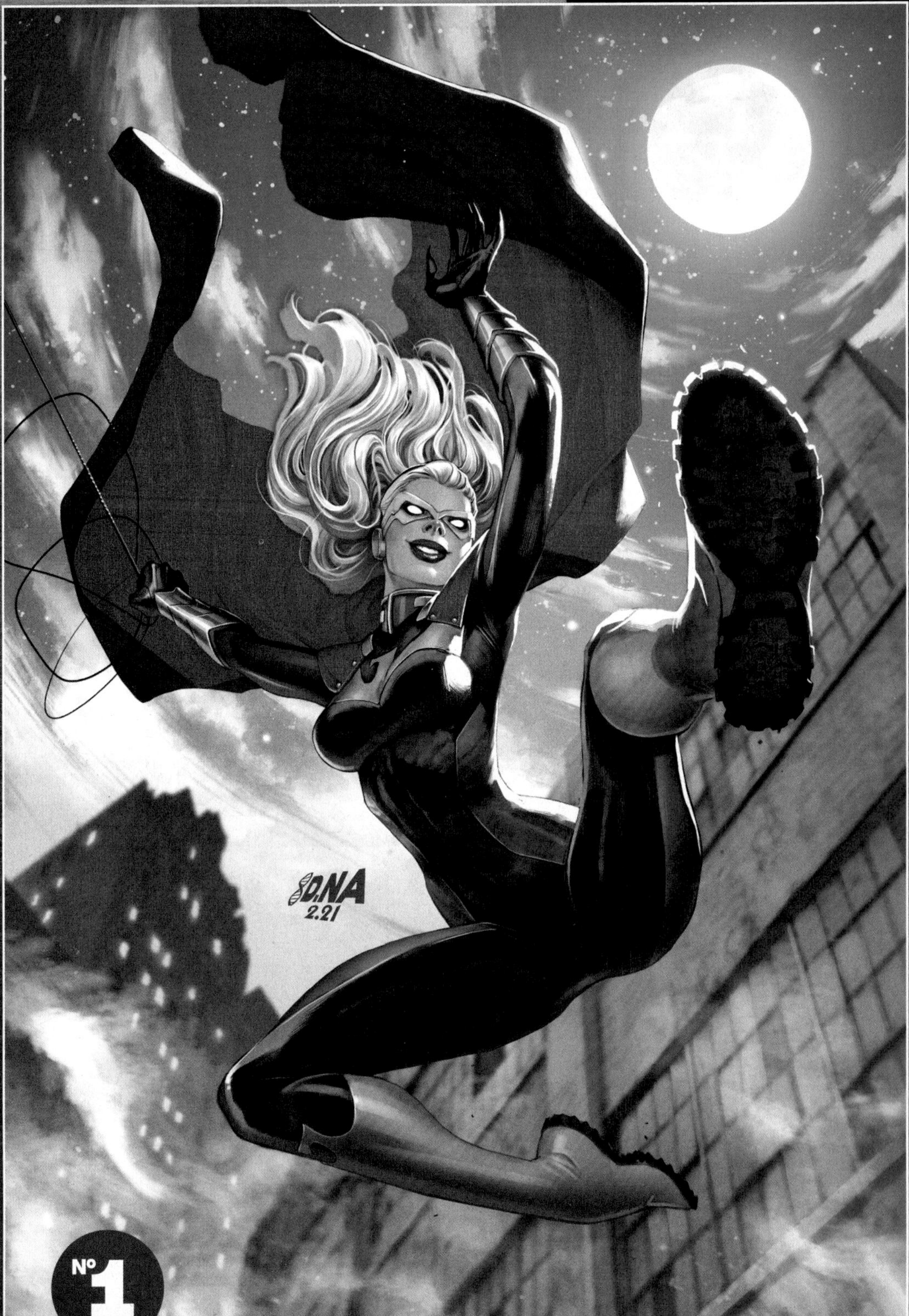
D.NA
2.21
Nº 1

"HUNTERS & PREY"

NIGHT-GWEN

In a world in which the Avengers never existed, the Squadron Supreme of America are and have always been Earth's Mightiest Heroes!

NIGHT-GWEN

"HUNTERS & PREY"

VITA **AYALA** WRITER

FARID **KARAMI** ARTIST

ERICK **ARCINIEGA** COLORS

VC's CORY **PETIT** LETTERER

DAVID **NAKAYAMA** COVER ARTIST

TAKESHI **MIYAZAWA** & IAN **HERRING**;
JAVIER **GARRÓN** VARIANT COVER ARTISTS

JAY **BOWEN** GRAPHIC DESIGN

DARREN **SHAN** EDITOR

TOM **BREVOORT** EXECUTIVE EDITOR

C.B. **CEBULSKI** EDITOR IN CHIEF

HEROES REBORN

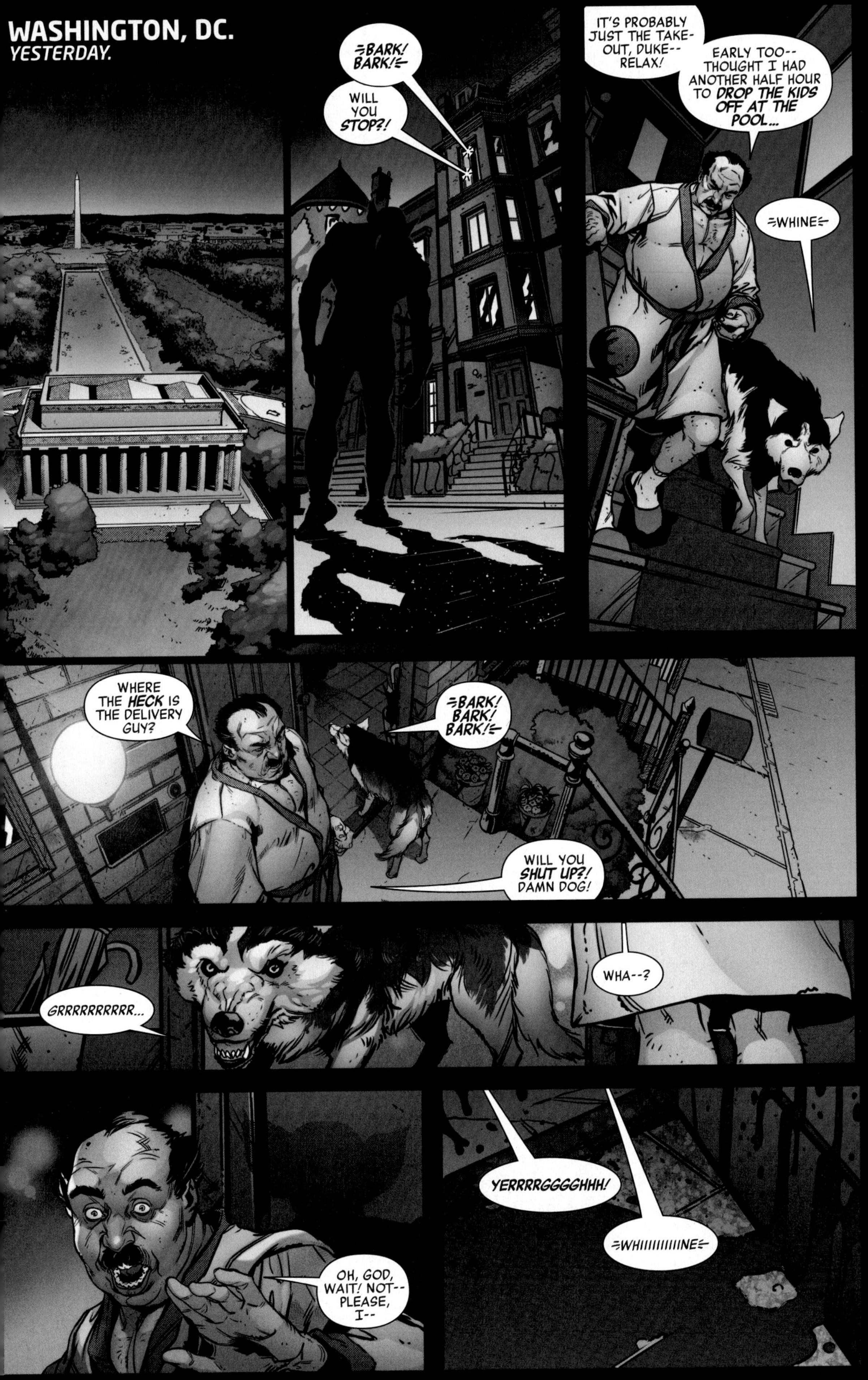
WASHINGTON, DC.
YESTERDAY.
BARK! BARK!
WILL YOU STOP?!
IT'S PROBABLY JUST THE TAKE-OUT, DUKE--RELAX!
EARLY TOO--THOUGHT I HAD ANOTHER HALF HOUR TO DROP THE KIDS OFF AT THE POOL...
WHINE
WHERE THE HECK IS THE DELIVERY GUY?
BARK! BARK! BARK!
WILL YOU SHUT UP?! DAMN DOG!
GRRRRRRRRRR...
WHA--?
OH, GOD, WAIT! NOT--PLEASE, I--
YERRRRGGGGHHH!
WHIIIIIIIIIIINE

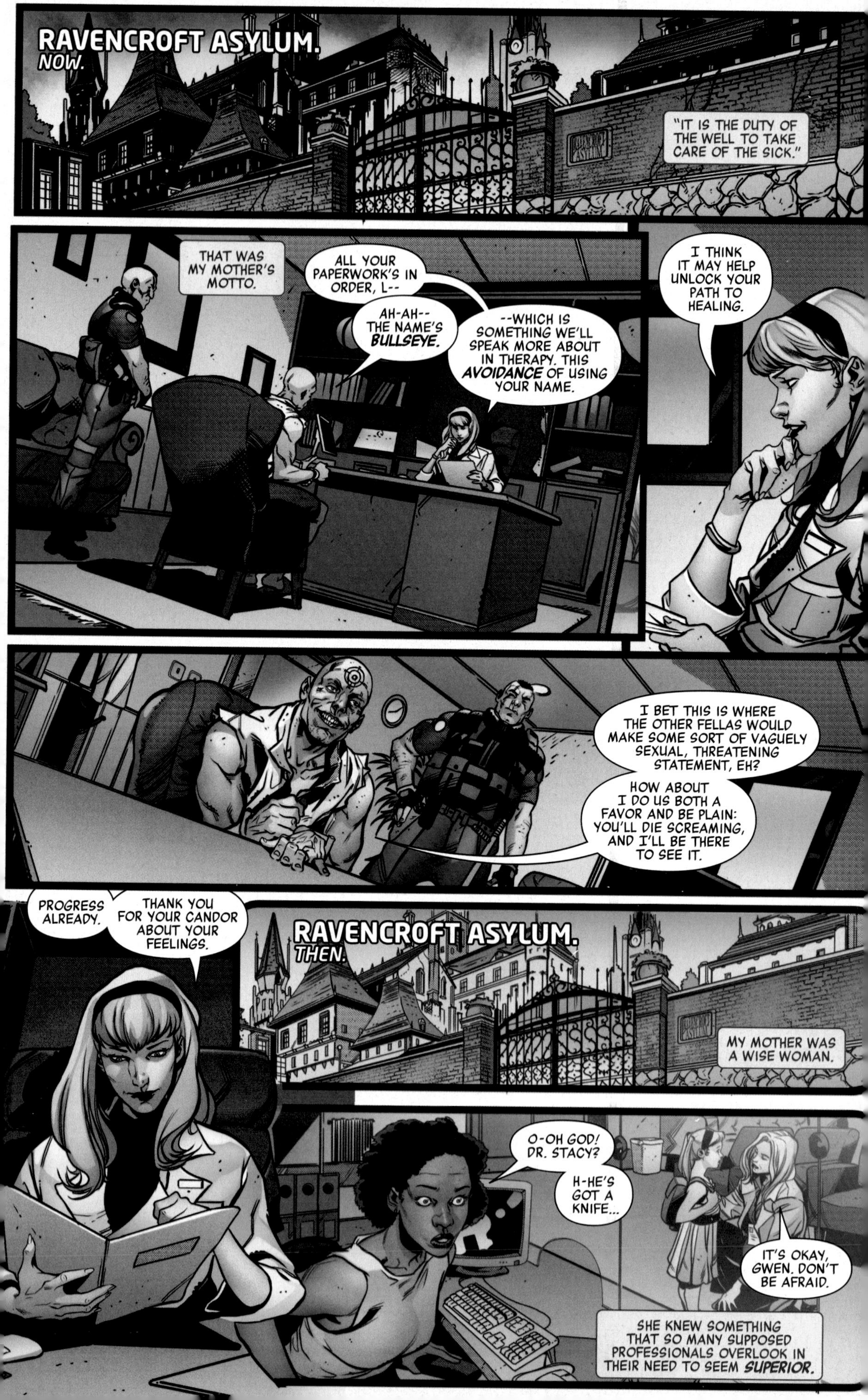
RAVENCROFT ASYLUM.
NOW.
"IT IS THE DUTY OF THE WELL TO TAKE CARE OF THE SICK."
THAT WAS MY MOTHER'S MOTTO.
ALL YOUR PAPERWORK'S IN ORDER, L--
AH-AH-- THE NAME'S BULLSEYE.
--WHICH IS SOMETHING WE'LL SPEAK MORE ABOUT IN THERAPY. THIS AVOIDANCE OF USING YOUR NAME.
I THINK IT MAY HELP UNLOCK YOUR PATH TO HEALING.
I BET THIS IS WHERE THE OTHER FELLAS WOULD MAKE SOME SORT OF VAGUELY SEXUAL, THREATENING STATEMENT, EH?
HOW ABOUT I DO US BOTH A FAVOR AND BE PLAIN: YOU'LL DIE SCREAMING, AND I'LL BE THERE TO SEE IT.
PROGRESS ALREADY.
THANK YOU FOR YOUR CANDOR ABOUT YOUR FEELINGS.
RAVENCROFT ASYLUM.
THEN.
MY MOTHER WAS A WISE WOMAN.
O-OH GOD! DR. STACY?
H-HE'S GOT A KNIFE...
IT'S OKAY, GWEN. DON'T BE AFRAID.
SHE KNEW SOMETHING THAT SO MANY SUPPOSED PROFESSIONALS OVERLOOK IN THEIR NEED TO SEEM SUPERIOR.

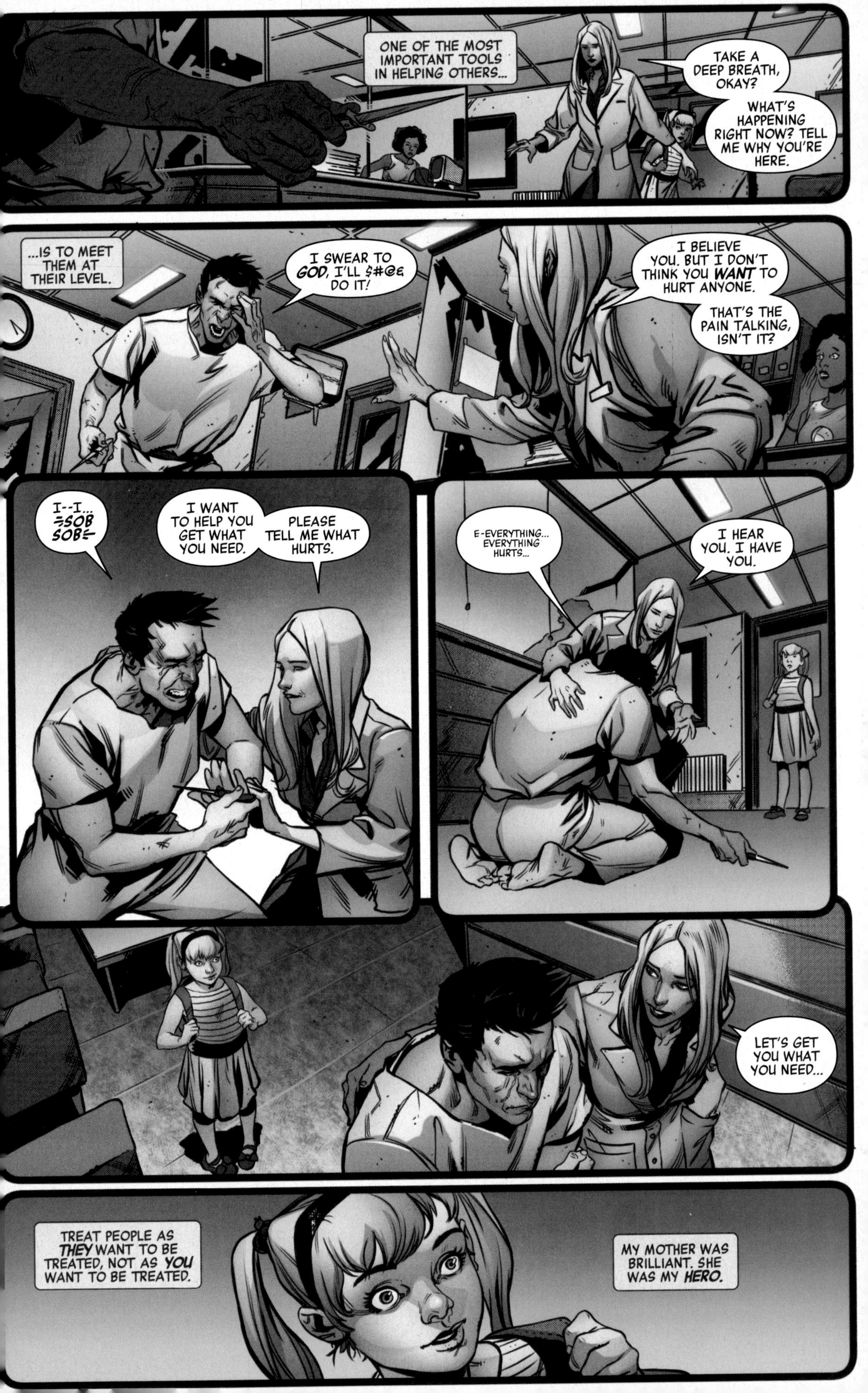
ONE OF THE MOST IMPORTANT TOOLS IN HELPING OTHERS...
TAKE A DEEP BREATH, OKAY?
WHAT'S HAPPENING RIGHT NOW? TELL ME WHY YOU'RE HERE.
...IS TO MEET THEM AT THEIR LEVEL.
I SWEAR TO GOD, I'LL $#@& DO IT!
I BELIEVE YOU. BUT I DON'T THINK YOU WANT TO HURT ANYONE.
THAT'S THE PAIN TALKING, ISN'T IT?
I--I... SOB SOB
I WANT TO HELP YOU GET WHAT YOU NEED.
PLEASE TELL ME WHAT HURTS.
E-EVERYTHING... EVERYTHING HURTS...
I HEAR YOU. I HAVE YOU.
LET'S GET YOU WHAT YOU NEED...
TREAT PEOPLE AS THEY WANT TO BE TREATED, NOT AS YOU WANT TO BE TREATED.
MY MOTHER WAS BRILLIANT. SHE WAS MY HERO.

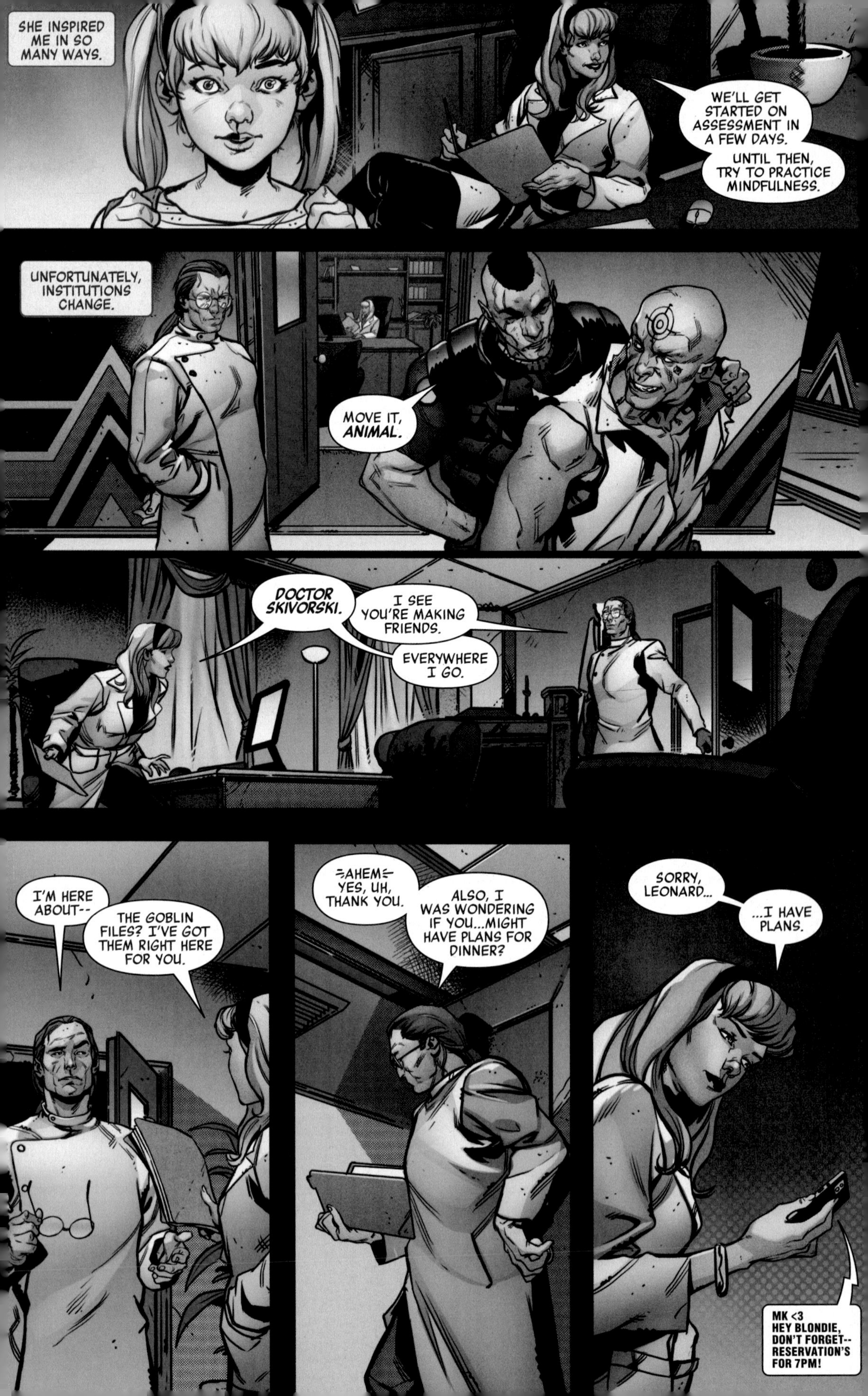
SHE INSPIRED ME IN SO MANY WAYS.
WE'LL GET STARTED ON ASSESSMENT IN A FEW DAYS.
UNTIL THEN, TRY TO PRACTICE MINDFULNESS.
UNFORTUNATELY, INSTITUTIONS CHANGE.
MOVE IT, *ANIMAL.*
DOCTOR SKIVORSKI.
I SEE YOU'RE MAKING FRIENDS.
EVERYWHERE I GO.
I'M HERE ABOUT--
THE GOBLIN FILES? I'VE GOT THEM RIGHT HERE FOR YOU.
=AHEM= YES, UH, THANK YOU.
ALSO, I WAS WONDERING IF YOU...MIGHT HAVE PLANS FOR DINNER?
SORRY, LEONARD...
...I HAVE PLANS.
MK <3
HEY BLONDIE, DON'T FORGET-- RESERVATION'S FOR 7PM!

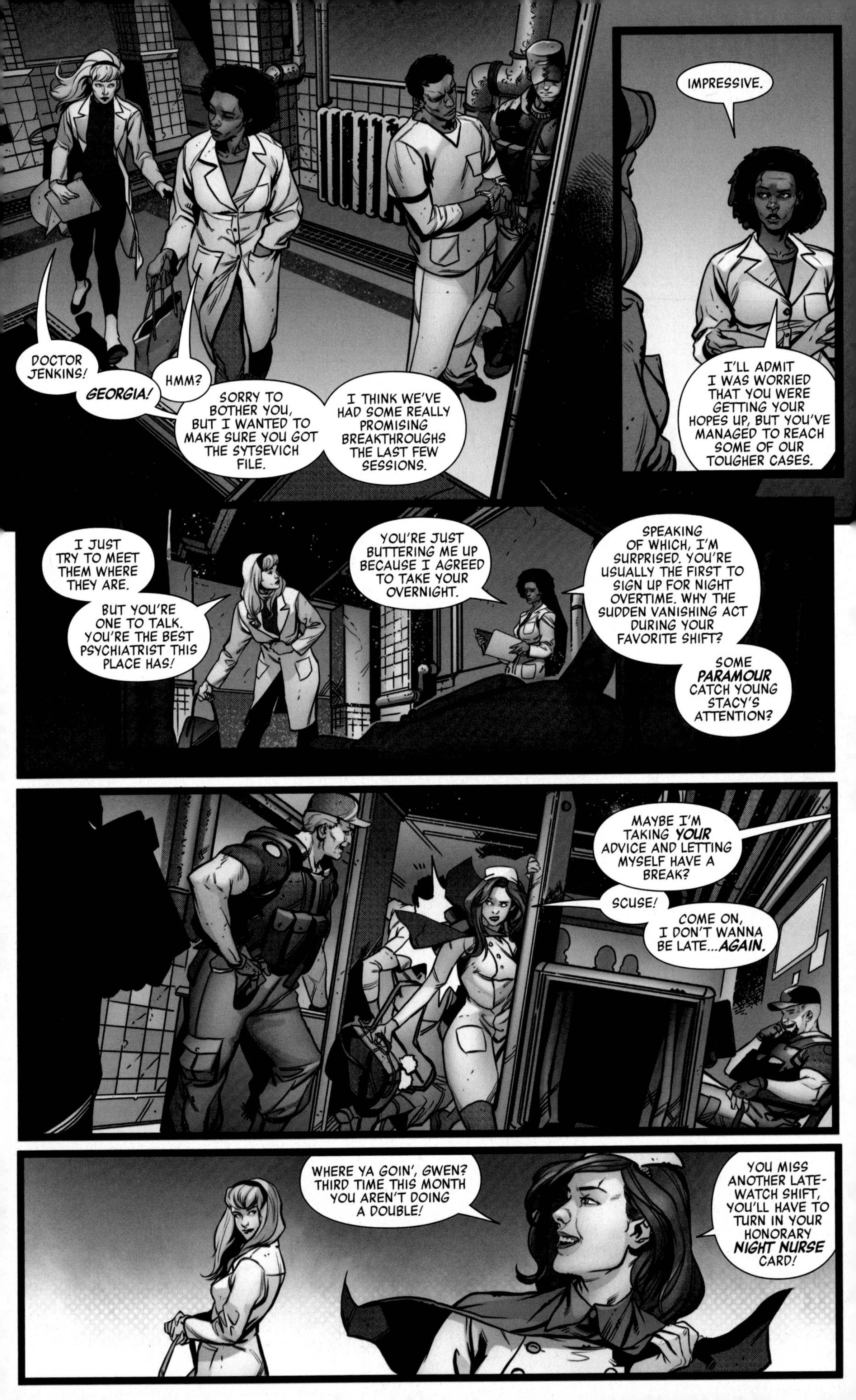
DOCTOR JENKINS!
GEORGIA!
HMM?
SORRY TO BOTHER YOU, BUT I WANTED TO MAKE SURE YOU GOT THE SYTSEVICH FILE.
I THINK WE'VE HAD SOME REALLY PROMISING BREAKTHROUGHS THE LAST FEW SESSIONS.
IMPRESSIVE.
I'LL ADMIT I WAS WORRIED THAT YOU WERE GETTING YOUR HOPES UP, BUT YOU'VE MANAGED TO REACH SOME OF OUR TOUGHER CASES.
I JUST TRY TO MEET THEM WHERE THEY ARE.
BUT YOU'RE ONE TO TALK. YOU'RE THE BEST PSYCHIATRIST THIS PLACE HAS!
YOU'RE JUST BUTTERING ME UP BECAUSE I AGREED TO TAKE YOUR OVERNIGHT.
SPEAKING OF WHICH, I'M SURPRISED. YOU'RE USUALLY THE FIRST TO SIGN UP FOR NIGHT OVERTIME. WHY THE SUDDEN VANISHING ACT DURING YOUR FAVORITE SHIFT?
SOME PARAMOUR CATCH YOUNG STACY'S ATTENTION?
MAYBE I'M TAKING YOUR ADVICE AND LETTING MYSELF HAVE A BREAK?
SCUSE!
COME ON, I DON'T WANNA BE LATE...AGAIN.
WHERE YA GOIN', GWEN? THIRD TIME THIS MONTH YOU AREN'T DOING A DOUBLE!
YOU MISS ANOTHER LATE-WATCH SHIFT, YOU'LL HAVE TO TURN IN YOUR HONORARY NIGHT NURSE CARD!

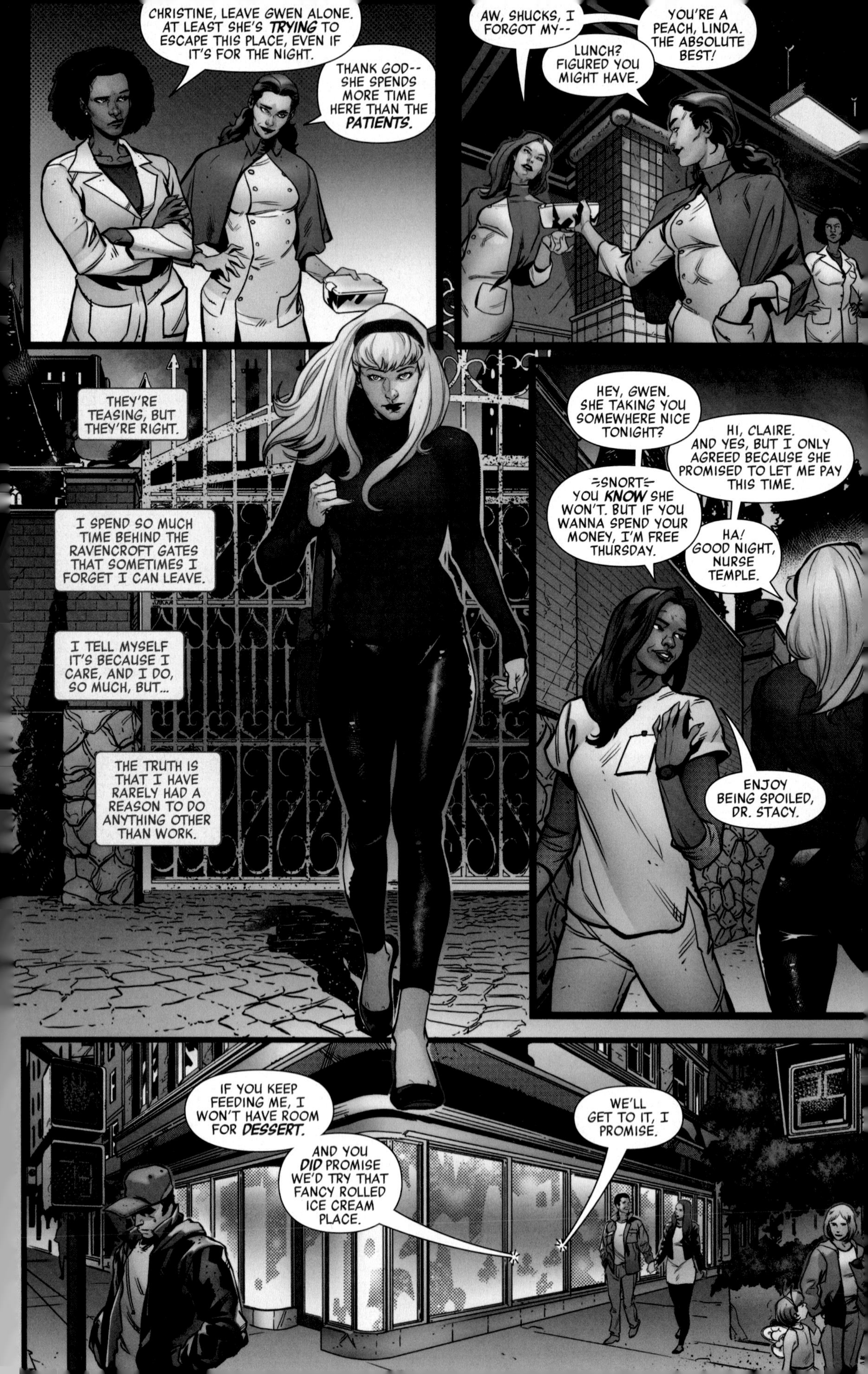
CHRISTINE, LEAVE GWEN ALONE. AT LEAST SHE'S TRYING TO ESCAPE THIS PLACE, EVEN IF IT'S FOR THE NIGHT.
THANK GOD-- SHE SPENDS MORE TIME HERE THAN THE PATIENTS.
AW, SHUCKS, I FORGOT MY--
LUNCH? FIGURED YOU MIGHT HAVE.
YOU'RE A PEACH, LINDA. THE ABSOLUTE BEST!
THEY'RE TEASING, BUT THEY'RE RIGHT.
I SPEND SO MUCH TIME BEHIND THE RAVENCROFT GATES THAT SOMETIMES I FORGET I CAN LEAVE.
I TELL MYSELF IT'S BECAUSE I CARE, AND I DO, SO MUCH, BUT...
THE TRUTH IS THAT I HAVE RARELY HAD A REASON TO DO ANYTHING OTHER THAN WORK.
HEY, GWEN. SHE TAKING YOU SOMEWHERE NICE TONIGHT?
HI, CLAIRE. AND YES, BUT I ONLY AGREED BECAUSE SHE PROMISED TO LET ME PAY THIS TIME.
=SNORT= YOU KNOW SHE WON'T. BUT IF YOU WANNA SPEND YOUR MONEY, I'M FREE THURSDAY.
HA! GOOD NIGHT, NURSE TEMPLE.
ENJOY BEING SPOILED, DR. STACY.
IF YOU KEEP FEEDING ME, I WON'T HAVE ROOM FOR DESSERT.
AND YOU DID PROMISE WE'D TRY THAT FANCY ROLLED ICE CREAM PLACE.
WE'LL GET TO IT, I PROMISE.

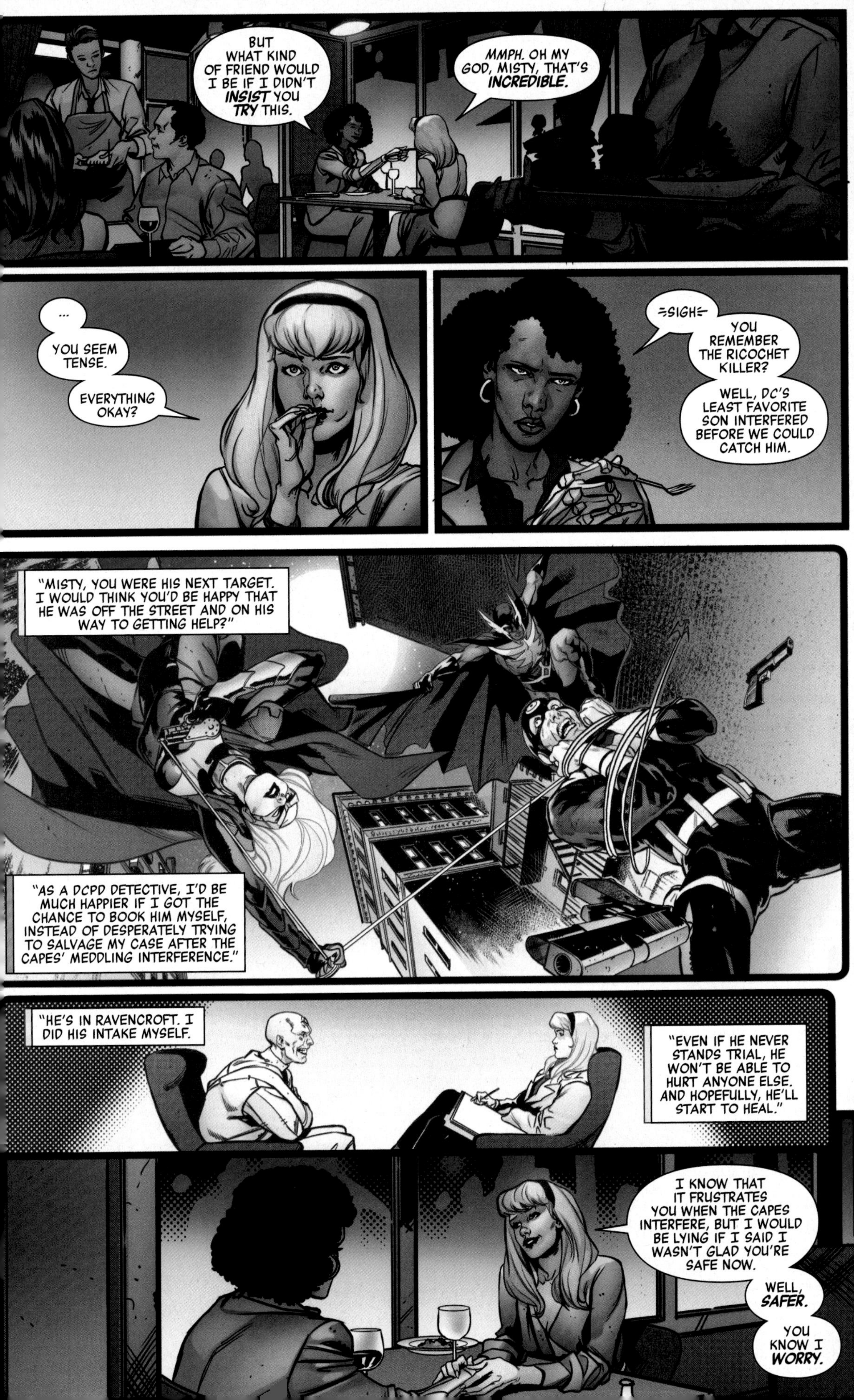

BUT WHAT KIND OF FRIEND WOULD I BE IF I DIDN'T INSIST YOU TRY THIS.
MMPH. OH MY GOD, MISTY, THAT'S INCREDIBLE.
...
YOU SEEM TENSE.
EVERYTHING OKAY?
=SIGH=
YOU REMEMBER THE RICOCHET KILLER?
WELL, DC'S LEAST FAVORITE SON INTERFERED BEFORE WE COULD CATCH HIM.
"MISTY, YOU WERE HIS NEXT TARGET. I WOULD THINK YOU'D BE HAPPY THAT HE WAS OFF THE STREET AND ON HIS WAY TO GETTING HELP?"
"AS A DCPD DETECTIVE, I'D BE MUCH HAPPIER IF I GOT THE CHANCE TO BOOK HIM MYSELF, INSTEAD OF DESPERATELY TRYING TO SALVAGE MY CASE AFTER THE CAPES' MEDDLING INTERFERENCE."
"HE'S IN RAVENCROFT. I DID HIS INTAKE MYSELF.
"EVEN IF HE NEVER STANDS TRIAL, HE WON'T BE ABLE TO HURT ANYONE ELSE. AND HOPEFULLY, HE'LL START TO HEAL."
I KNOW THAT IT FRUSTRATES YOU WHEN THE CAPES INTERFERE, BUT I WOULD BE LYING IF I SAID I WASN'T GLAD YOU'RE SAFE NOW.
WELL, SAFER.
YOU KNOW I WORRY.

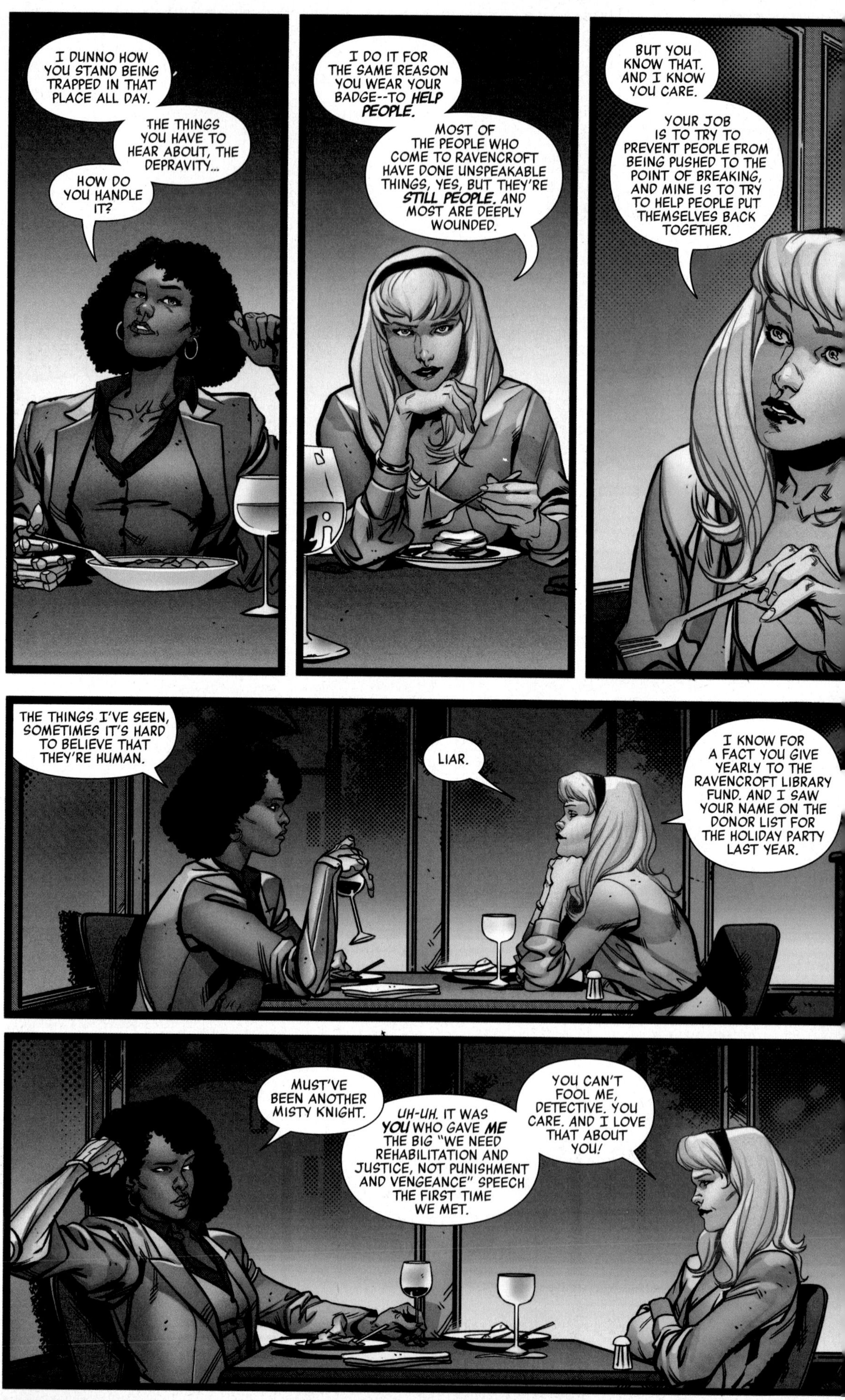
I DUNNO HOW YOU STAND BEING TRAPPED IN THAT PLACE ALL DAY.
THE THINGS YOU HAVE TO HEAR ABOUT, THE DEPRAVITY...
HOW DO YOU HANDLE IT?
I DO IT FOR THE SAME REASON YOU WEAR YOUR BADGE--TO HELP PEOPLE.
MOST OF THE PEOPLE WHO COME TO RAVENCROFT HAVE DONE UNSPEAKABLE THINGS, YES, BUT THEY'RE STILL PEOPLE. AND MOST ARE DEEPLY WOUNDED.
BUT YOU KNOW THAT. AND I KNOW YOU CARE.
YOUR JOB IS TO TRY TO PREVENT PEOPLE FROM BEING PUSHED TO THE POINT OF BREAKING, AND MINE IS TO TRY TO HELP PEOPLE PUT THEMSELVES BACK TOGETHER.
THE THINGS I'VE SEEN, SOMETIMES IT'S HARD TO BELIEVE THAT THEY'RE HUMAN.
LIAR.
I KNOW FOR A FACT YOU GIVE YEARLY TO THE RAVENCROFT LIBRARY FUND. AND I SAW YOUR NAME ON THE DONOR LIST FOR THE HOLIDAY PARTY LAST YEAR.
MUST'VE BEEN ANOTHER MISTY KNIGHT.
UH-UH. IT WAS YOU WHO GAVE ME THE BIG "WE NEED REHABILITATION AND JUSTICE, NOT PUNISHMENT AND VENGEANCE" SPEECH THE FIRST TIME WE MET.
YOU CAN'T FOOL ME, DETECTIVE. YOU CARE. AND I LOVE THAT ABOUT YOU!

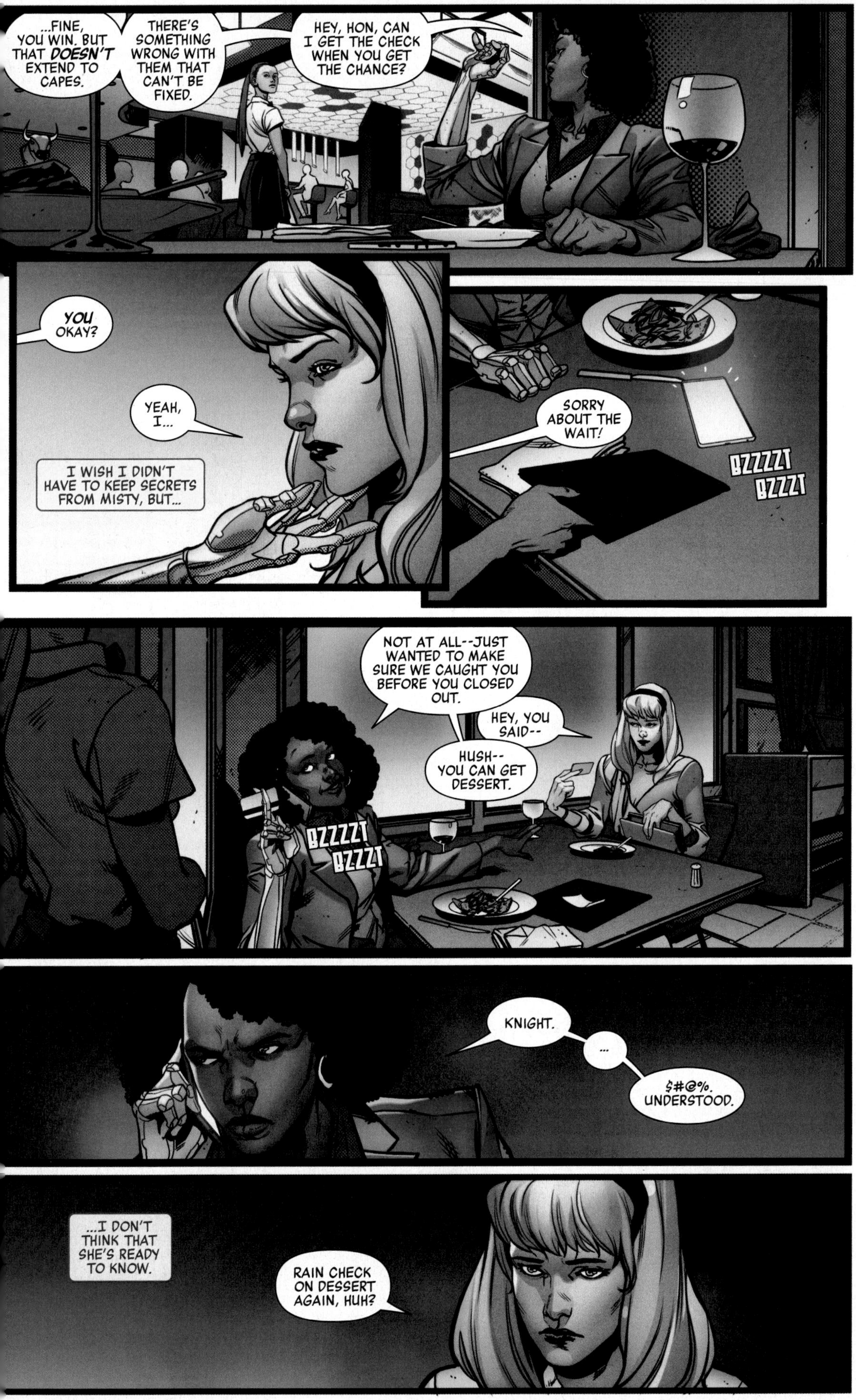

...FINE, YOU WIN. BUT THAT DOESN'T EXTEND TO CAPES.
THERE'S SOMETHING WRONG WITH THEM THAT CAN'T BE FIXED.
HEY, HON, CAN I GET THE CHECK WHEN YOU GET THE CHANCE?
YOU OKAY?
YEAH, I...
I WISH I DIDN'T HAVE TO KEEP SECRETS FROM MISTY, BUT...
SORRY ABOUT THE WAIT!
BZZZZT
BZZZT
NOT AT ALL--JUST WANTED TO MAKE SURE WE CAUGHT YOU BEFORE YOU CLOSED OUT.
HEY, YOU SAID--
HUSH-- YOU CAN GET DESSERT.
BZZZZT
BZZZT
KNIGHT.
...
$#@%. UNDERSTOOD.
...I DON'T THINK THAT SHE'S READY TO KNOW.
RAIN CHECK ON DESSERT AGAIN, HUH?

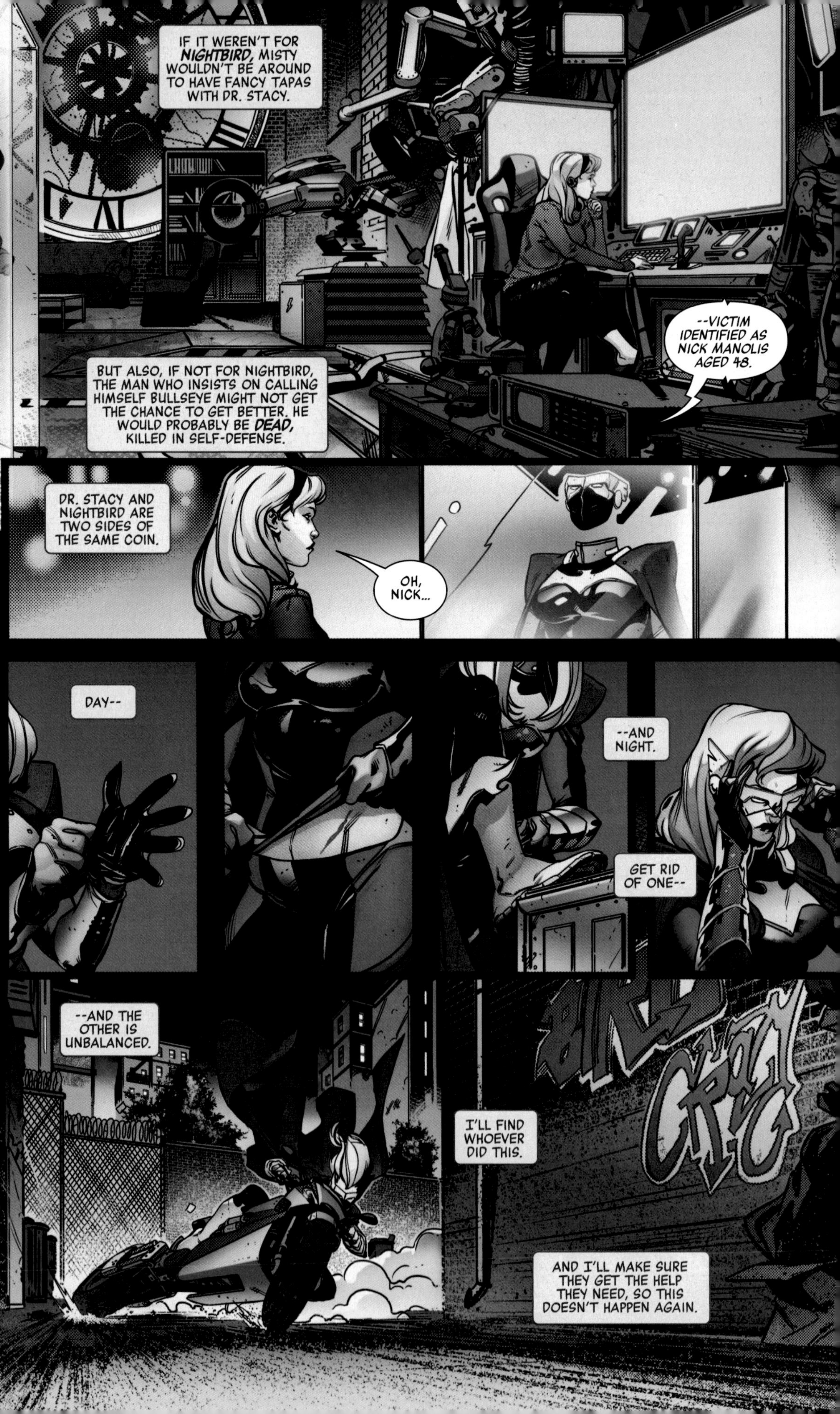
IF IT WEREN'T FOR NIGHTBIRD, MISTY WOULDN'T BE AROUND TO HAVE FANCY TAPAS WITH DR. STACY.
BUT ALSO, IF NOT FOR NIGHTBIRD, THE MAN WHO INSISTS ON CALLING HIMSELF BULLSEYE MIGHT NOT GET THE CHANCE TO GET BETTER. HE WOULD PROBABLY BE DEAD, KILLED IN SELF-DEFENSE.
--VICTIM IDENTIFIED AS NICK MANOLIS AGED 48.
DR. STACY AND NIGHTBIRD ARE TWO SIDES OF THE SAME COIN.
OH, NICK...
DAY--
--AND NIGHT.
GET RID OF ONE--
--AND THE OTHER IS UNBALANCED.
I'LL FIND WHOEVER DID THIS.
AND I'LL MAKE SURE THEY GET THE HELP THEY NEED, SO THIS DOESN'T HAPPEN AGAIN.

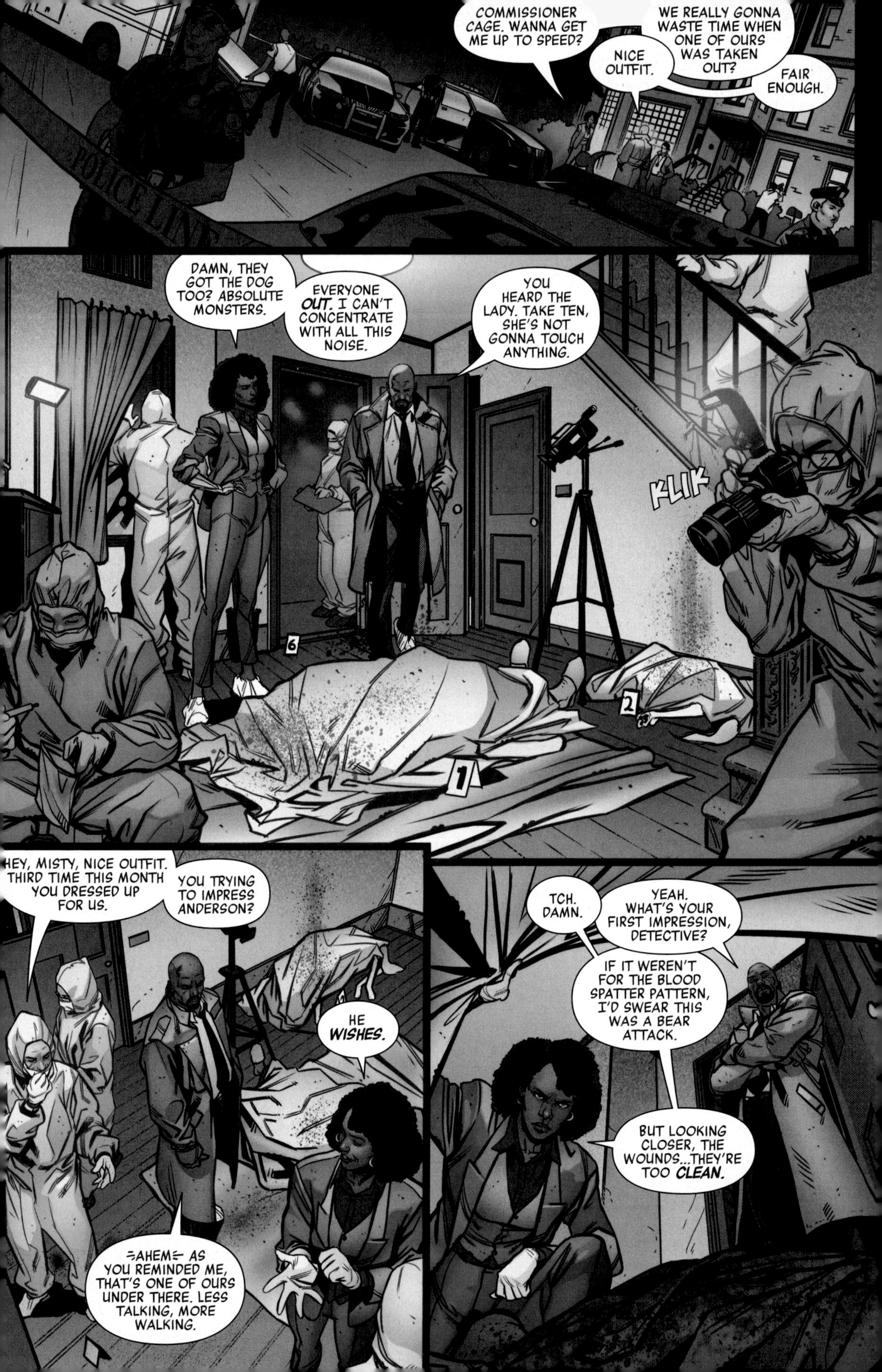
COMMISSIONER CAGE. WANNA GET ME UP TO SPEED?
NICE OUTFIT.
WE REALLY GONNA WASTE TIME WHEN ONE OF OURS WAS TAKEN OUT?
FAIR ENOUGH.
POLICE LINE
DAMN, THEY GOT THE DOG TOO? ABSOLUTE MONSTERS.
EVERYONE OUT. I CAN'T CONCENTRATE WITH ALL THIS NOISE.
YOU HEARD THE LADY. TAKE TEN, SHE'S NOT GONNA TOUCH ANYTHING.
KLIK
HEY, MISTY, NICE OUTFIT. THIRD TIME THIS MONTH YOU DRESSED UP FOR US.
YOU TRYING TO IMPRESS ANDERSON?
HE WISHES.
=AHEM= AS YOU REMINDED ME, THAT'S ONE OF OURS UNDER THERE. LESS TALKING, MORE WALKING.
TCH. DAMN.
YEAH. WHAT'S YOUR FIRST IMPRESSION, DETECTIVE?
IF IT WEREN'T FOR THE BLOOD SPATTER PATTERN, I'D SWEAR THIS WAS A BEAR ATTACK.
BUT LOOKING CLOSER, THE WOUNDS...THEY'RE TOO CLEAN.

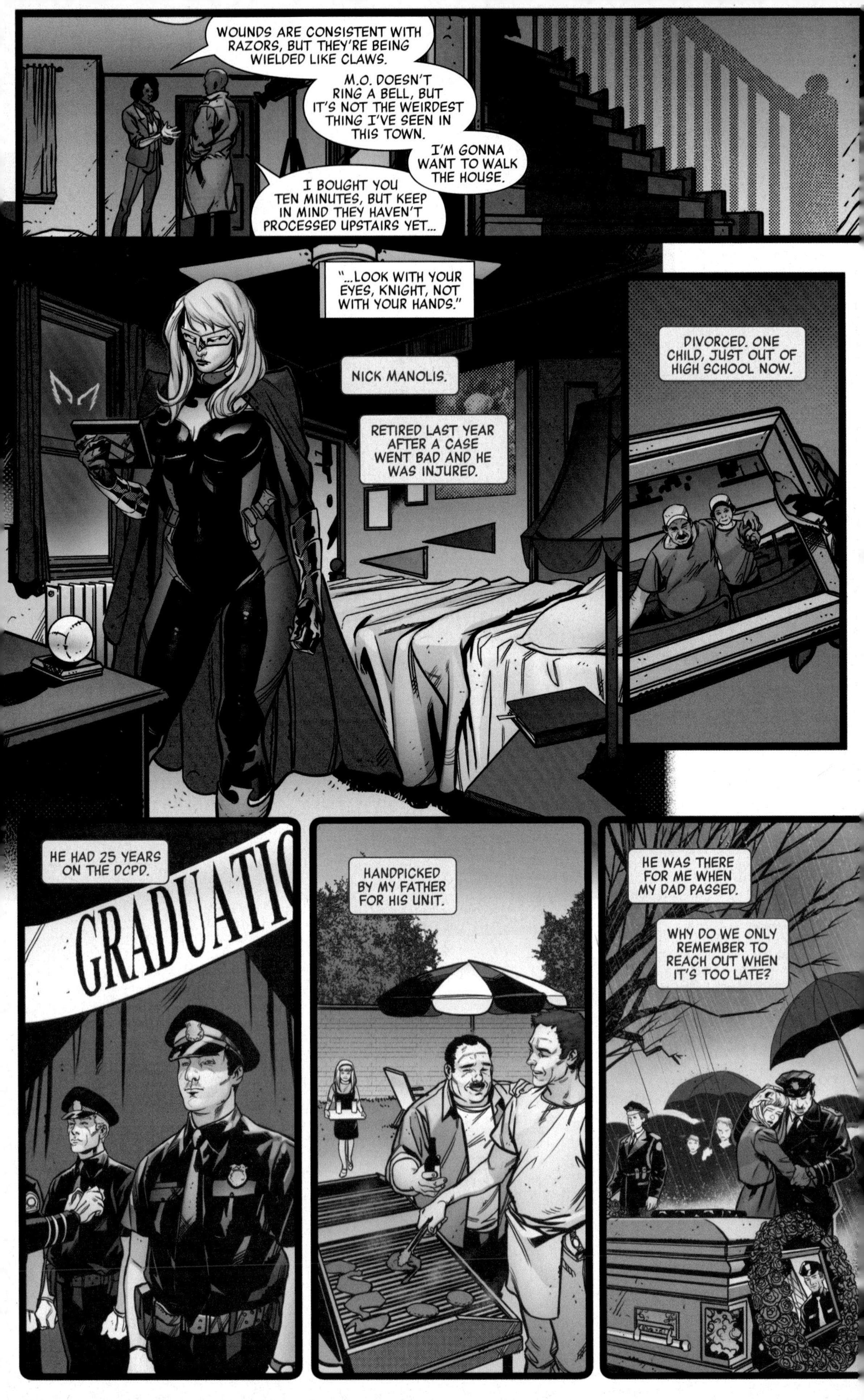
WOUNDS ARE CONSISTENT WITH RAZORS, BUT THEY'RE BEING WIELDED LIKE CLAWS.
M.O. DOESN'T RING A BELL, BUT IT'S NOT THE WEIRDEST THING I'VE SEEN IN THIS TOWN.
I'M GONNA WANT TO WALK THE HOUSE.
I BOUGHT YOU TEN MINUTES, BUT KEEP IN MIND THEY HAVEN'T PROCESSED UPSTAIRS YET...
"...LOOK WITH YOUR EYES, KNIGHT, NOT WITH YOUR HANDS."
NICK MANOLIS.
RETIRED LAST YEAR AFTER A CASE WENT BAD AND HE WAS INJURED.
DIVORCED. ONE CHILD, JUST OUT OF HIGH SCHOOL NOW.
HE HAD 25 YEARS ON THE DCPD.
GRADUATIO
HANDPICKED BY MY FATHER FOR HIS UNIT.
HE WAS THERE FOR ME WHEN MY DAD PASSED.
WHY DO WE ONLY REMEMBER TO REACH OUT WHEN IT'S TOO LATE?

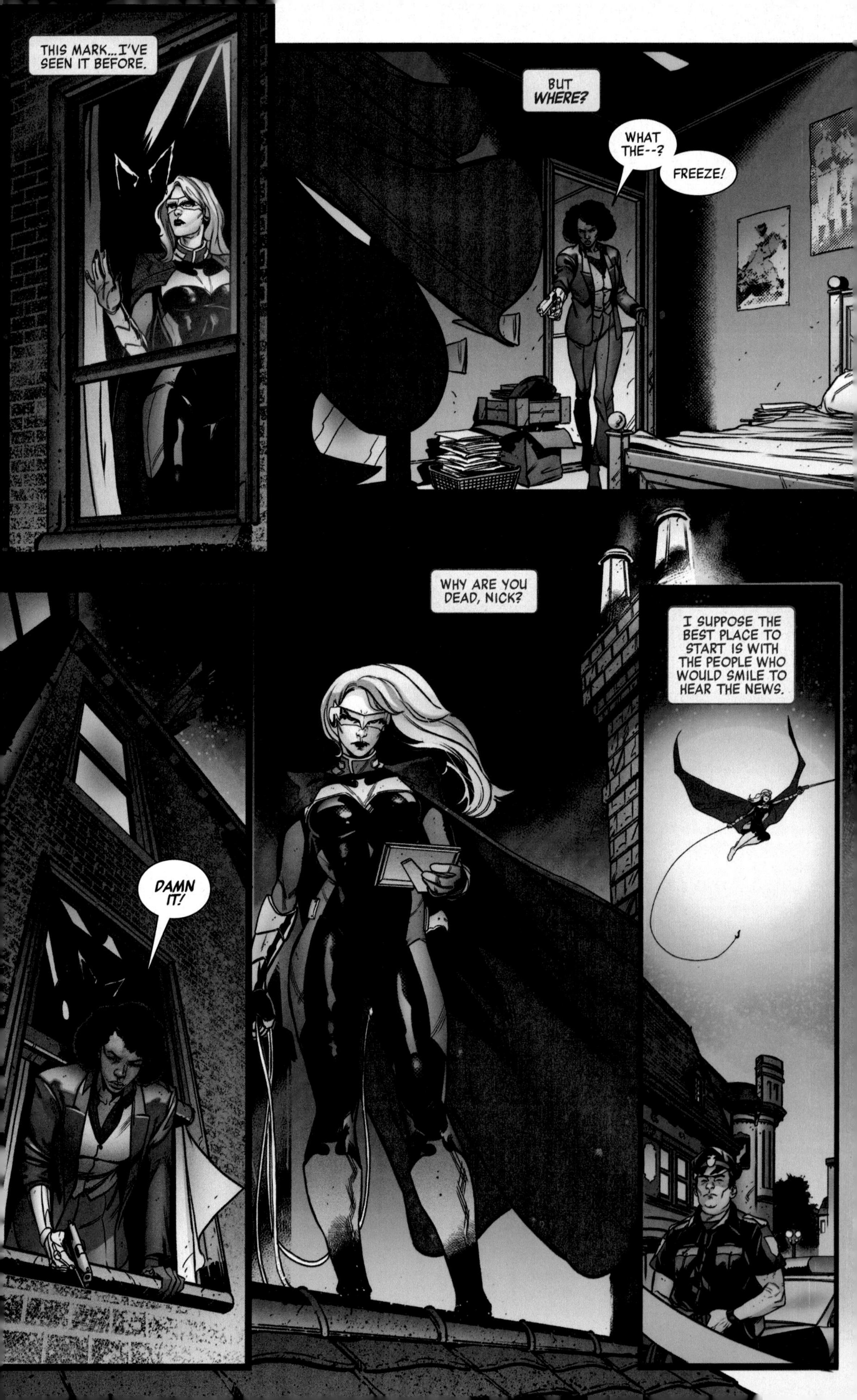
THIS MARK...I'VE SEEN IT BEFORE.
BUT *WHERE?*
WHAT THE--?
FREEZE!
WHY ARE YOU DEAD, NICK?
DAMN IT!
I SUPPOSE THE BEST PLACE TO START IS WITH THE PEOPLE WHO WOULD SMILE TO HEAR THE NEWS.

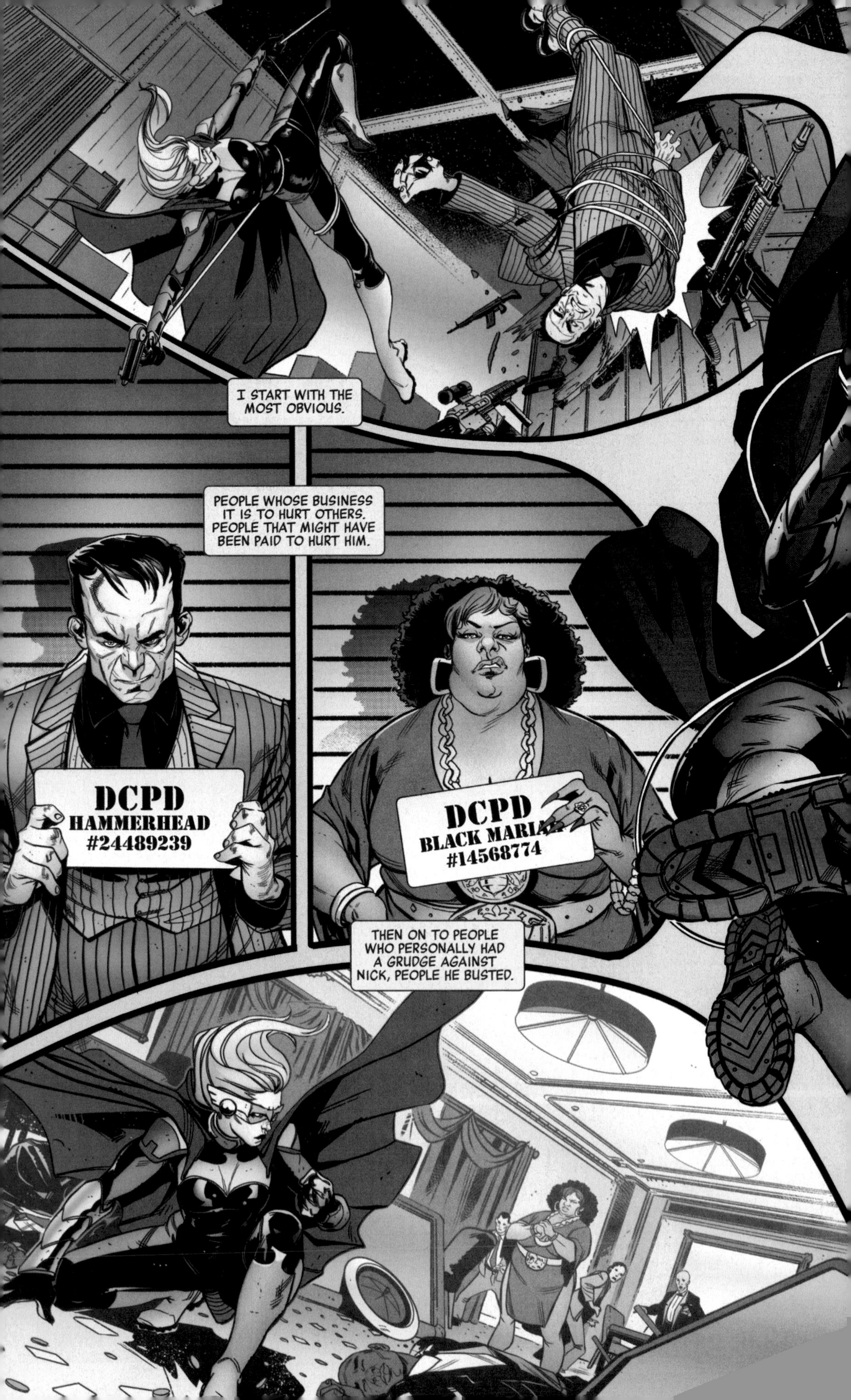
I START WITH THE MOST OBVIOUS.
PEOPLE WHOSE BUSINESS IT IS TO HURT OTHERS. PEOPLE THAT MIGHT HAVE BEEN PAID TO HURT HIM.
DCPD
HAMMERHEAD
#24489239
DCPD
BLACK MARIA
#14568774
THEN ON TO PEOPLE WHO PERSONALLY HAD A GRUDGE AGAINST NICK, PEOPLE HE BUSTED.

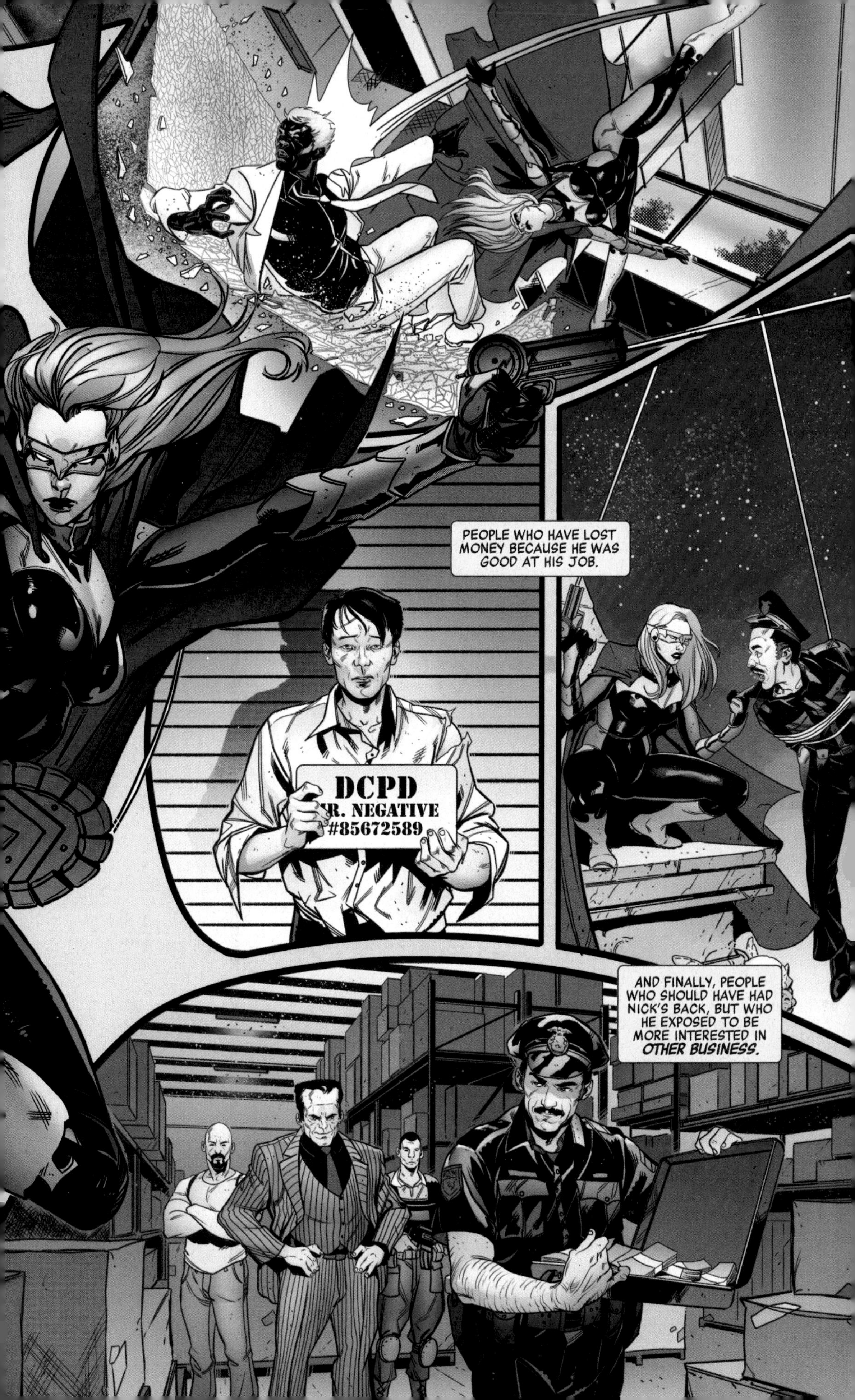
PEOPLE WHO HAVE LOST MONEY BECAUSE HE WAS GOOD AT HIS JOB.
DCPD
R. NEGATIVE
#85672589
AND FINALLY, PEOPLE WHO SHOULD HAVE HAD NICK'S BACK, BUT WHO HE EXPOSED TO BE MORE INTERESTED IN OTHER BUSINESS.

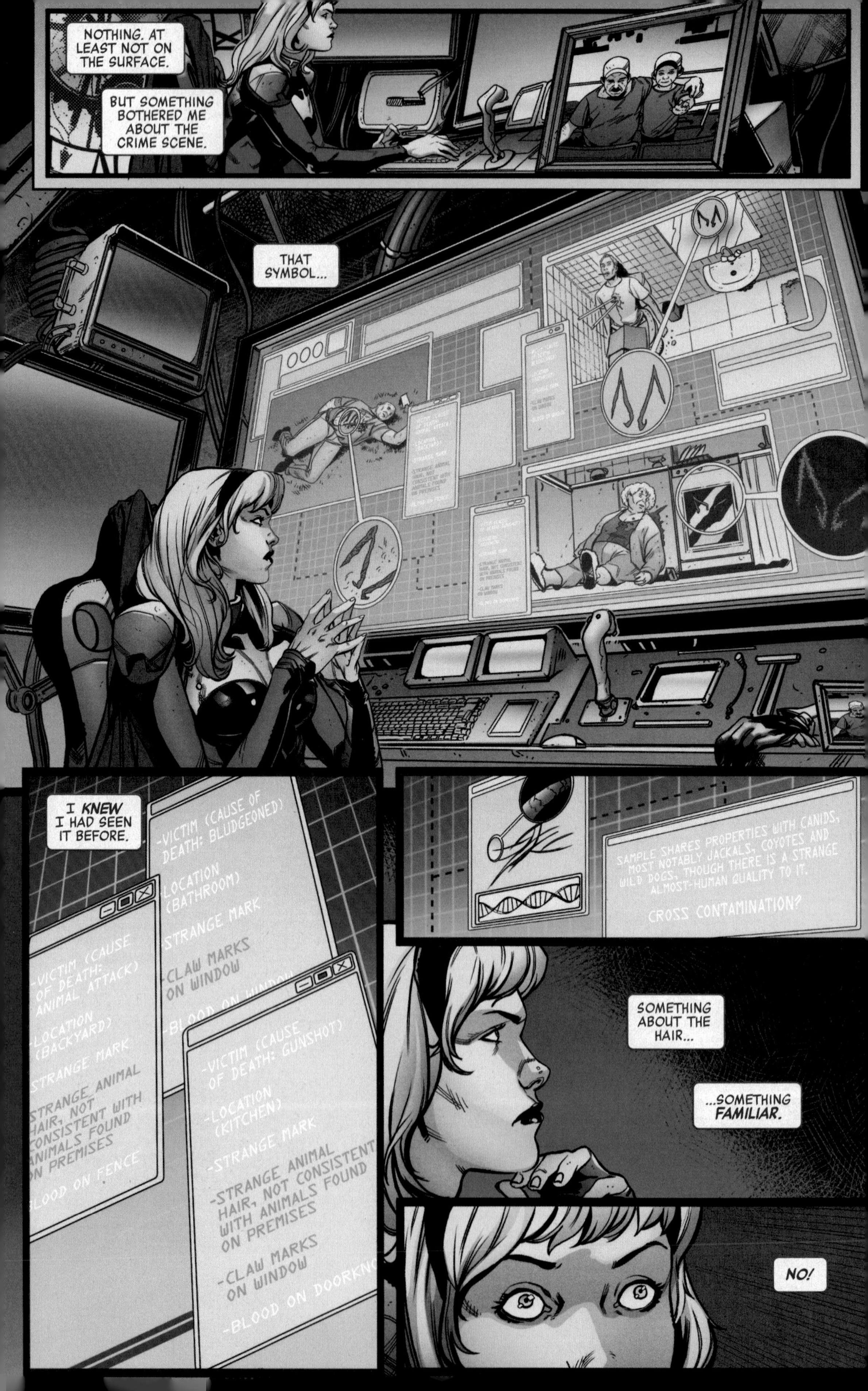
NOTHING. AT LEAST NOT ON THE SURFACE.
BUT SOMETHING BOTHERED ME ABOUT THE CRIME SCENE.
THAT SYMBOL...
I KNEW I HAD SEEN IT BEFORE.
-VICTIM (CAUSE OF DEATH: BLUDGEONED)
LOCATION (BATHROOM)
STRANGE MARK
-CLAW MARKS ON WINDOW
-VICTIM (CAUSE OF DEATH: ANIMAL ATTACK)
-LOCATION (BACKYARD)
-STRANGE MARK
-STRANGE ANIMAL HAIR, NOT CONSISTENT WITH ANIMALS FOUND ON PREMISES
-BLOOD ON FENCE
-VICTIM (CAUSE OF DEATH: GUNSHOT)
-LOCATION (KITCHEN)
-STRANGE MARK
-STRANGE ANIMAL HAIR, NOT CONSISTENT WITH ANIMALS FOUND ON PREMISES
-CLAW MARKS ON WINDOW
SAMPLE SHARES PROPERTIES WITH CANIDS, MOST NOTABLY JACKALS, COYOTES AND WILD DOGS, THOUGH THERE IS A STRANGE ALMOST-HUMAN QUALITY TO IT.
CROSS CONTAMINATION?
SOMETHING ABOUT THE HAIR...
...SOMETHING FAMILIAR.
NO!

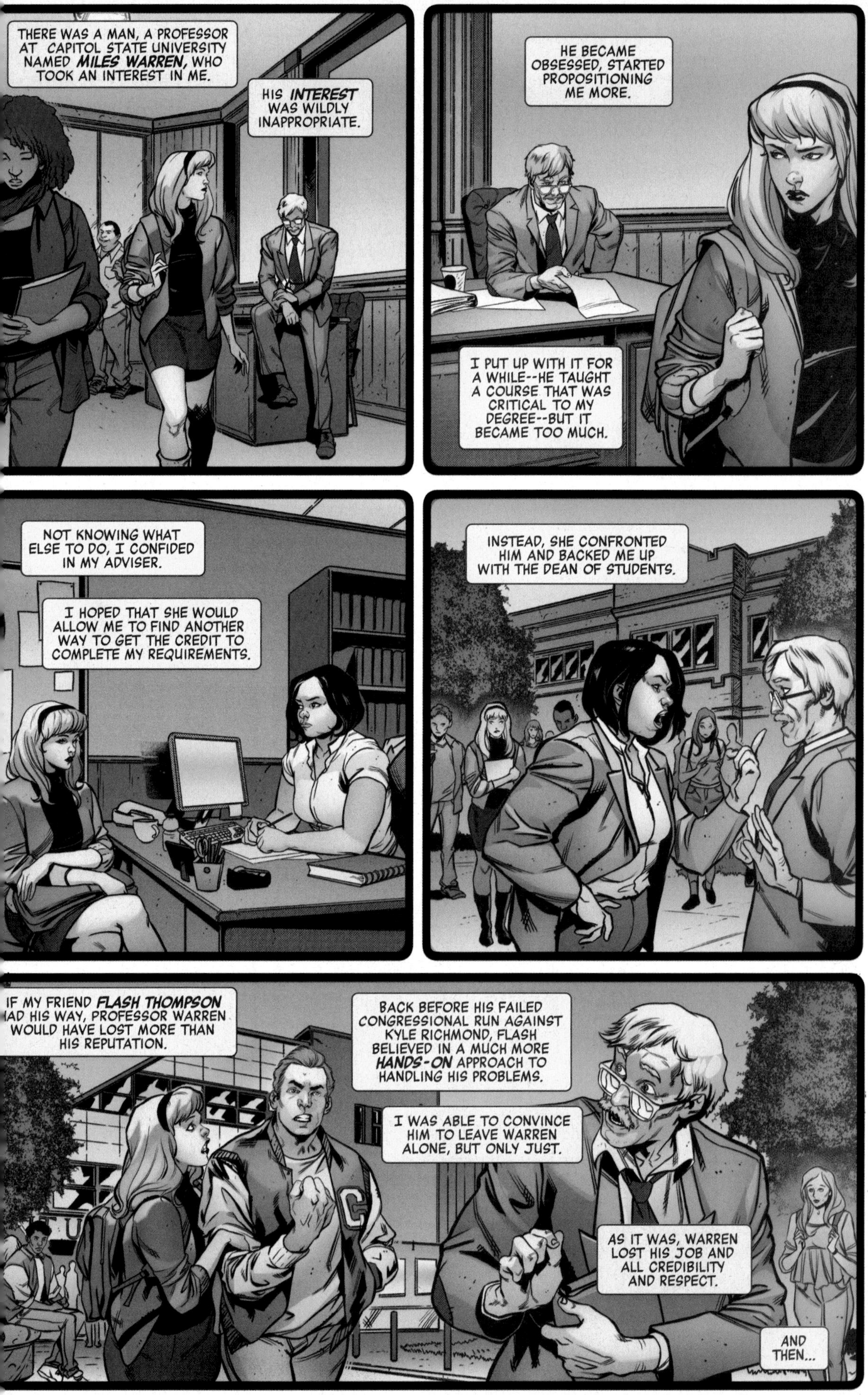
THERE WAS A MAN, A PROFESSOR AT CAPITOL STATE UNIVERSITY NAMED MILES WARREN, WHO TOOK AN INTEREST IN ME.
HIS INTEREST WAS WILDLY INAPPROPRIATE.
HE BECAME OBSESSED, STARTED PROPOSITIONING ME MORE.
I PUT UP WITH IT FOR A WHILE--HE TAUGHT A COURSE THAT WAS CRITICAL TO MY DEGREE--BUT IT BECAME TOO MUCH.
NOT KNOWING WHAT ELSE TO DO, I CONFIDED IN MY ADVISER.
I HOPED THAT SHE WOULD ALLOW ME TO FIND ANOTHER WAY TO GET THE CREDIT TO COMPLETE MY REQUIREMENTS.
INSTEAD, SHE CONFRONTED HIM AND BACKED ME UP WITH THE DEAN OF STUDENTS.
IF MY FRIEND FLASH THOMPSON HAD HIS WAY, PROFESSOR WARREN WOULD HAVE LOST MORE THAN HIS REPUTATION.
BACK BEFORE HIS FAILED CONGRESSIONAL RUN AGAINST KYLE RICHMOND, FLASH BELIEVED IN A MUCH MORE HANDS-ON APPROACH TO HANDLING HIS PROBLEMS.
I WAS ABLE TO CONVINCE HIM TO LEAVE WARREN ALONE, BUT ONLY JUST.
AS IT WAS, WARREN LOST HIS JOB AND ALL CREDIBILITY AND RESPECT.
AND THEN...

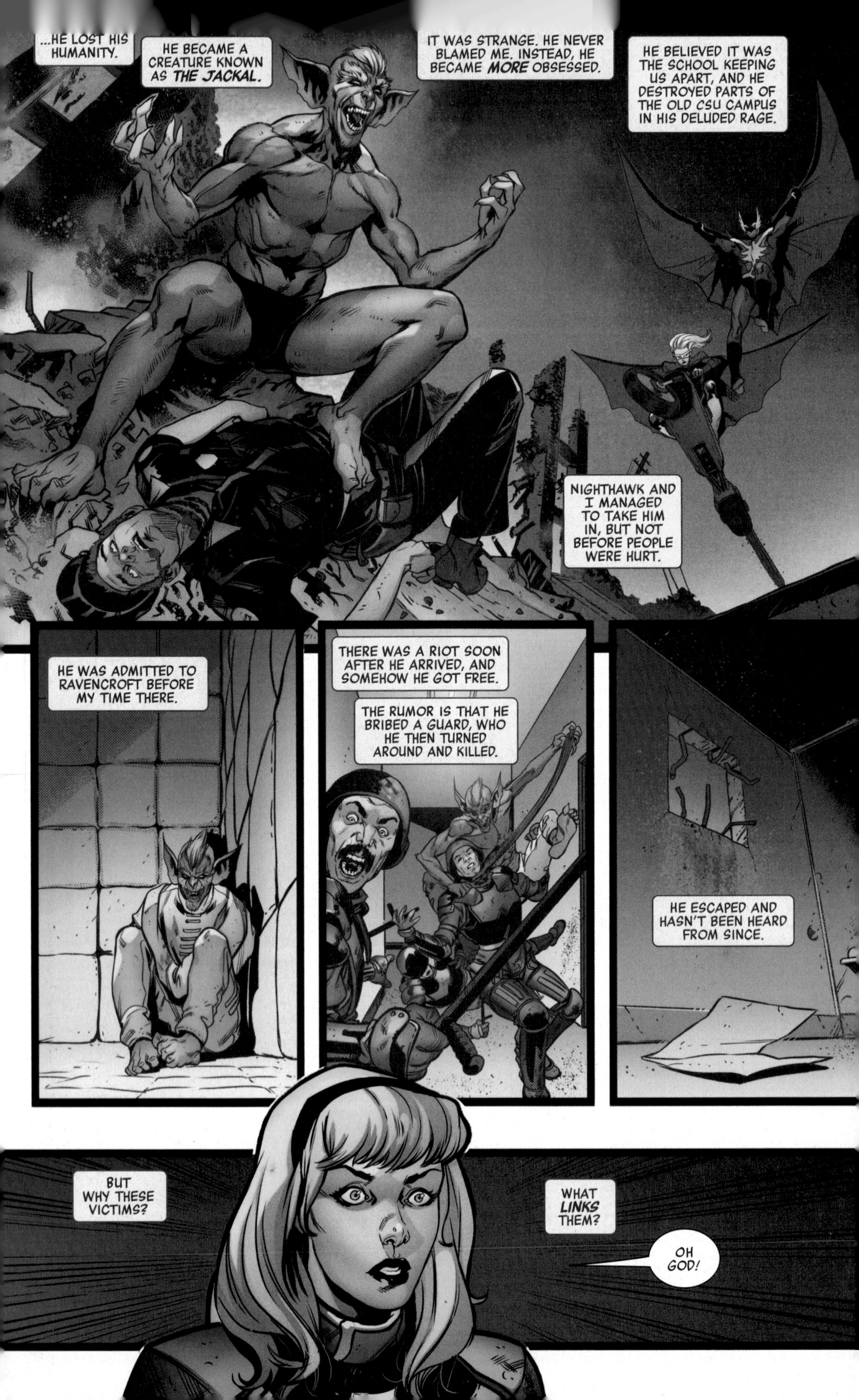
...HE LOST HIS HUMANITY.
HE BECAME A CREATURE KNOWN AS THE JACKAL.
IT WAS STRANGE. HE NEVER BLAMED ME. INSTEAD, HE BECAME MORE OBSESSED.
HE BELIEVED IT WAS THE SCHOOL KEEPING US APART, AND HE DESTROYED PARTS OF THE OLD CSU CAMPUS IN HIS DELUDED RAGE.
NIGHTHAWK AND I MANAGED TO TAKE HIM IN, BUT NOT BEFORE PEOPLE WERE HURT.
HE WAS ADMITTED TO RAVENCROFT BEFORE MY TIME THERE.
THERE WAS A RIOT SOON AFTER HE ARRIVED, AND SOMEHOW HE GOT FREE.
THE RUMOR IS THAT HE BRIBED A GUARD, WHO HE THEN TURNED AROUND AND KILLED.
HE ESCAPED AND HASN'T BEEN HEARD FROM SINCE.
BUT WHY THESE VICTIMS?
WHAT LINKS THEM?
OH GOD!

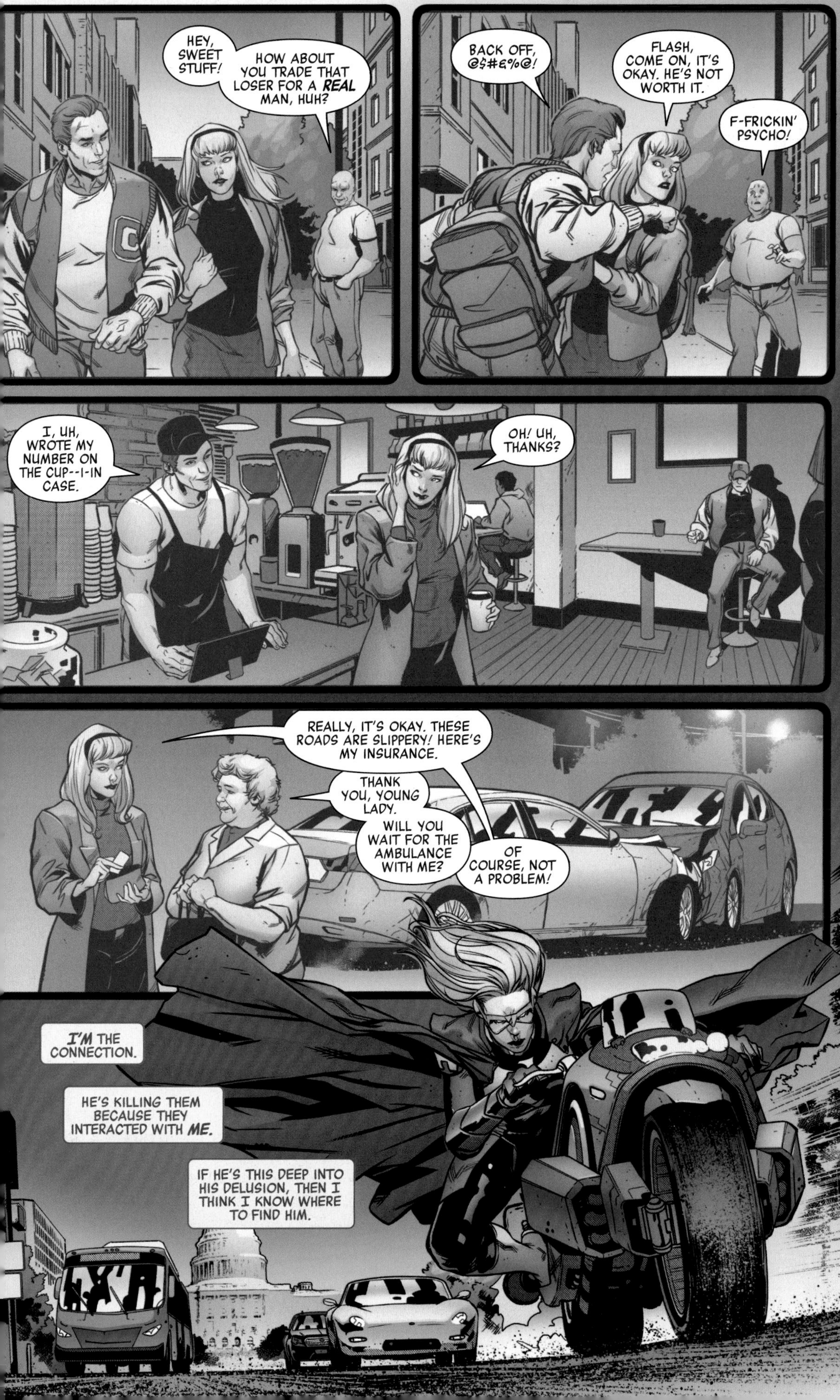
HEY, SWEET STUFF!
HOW ABOUT YOU TRADE THAT LOSER FOR A REAL MAN, HUH?
BACK OFF, @$#&%@!
FLASH, COME ON, IT'S OKAY. HE'S NOT WORTH IT.
F-FRICKIN' PSYCHO!
I, UH, WROTE MY NUMBER ON THE CUP--I-IN CASE.
OH! UH, THANKS?
REALLY, IT'S OKAY. THESE ROADS ARE SLIPPERY! HERE'S MY INSURANCE.
THANK YOU, YOUNG LADY.
WILL YOU WAIT FOR THE AMBULANCE WITH ME?
OF COURSE, NOT A PROBLEM!
I'M THE CONNECTION.
HE'S KILLING THEM BECAUSE THEY INTERACTED WITH ME.
IF HE'S THIS DEEP INTO HIS DELUSION, THEN I THINK I KNOW WHERE TO FIND HIM.

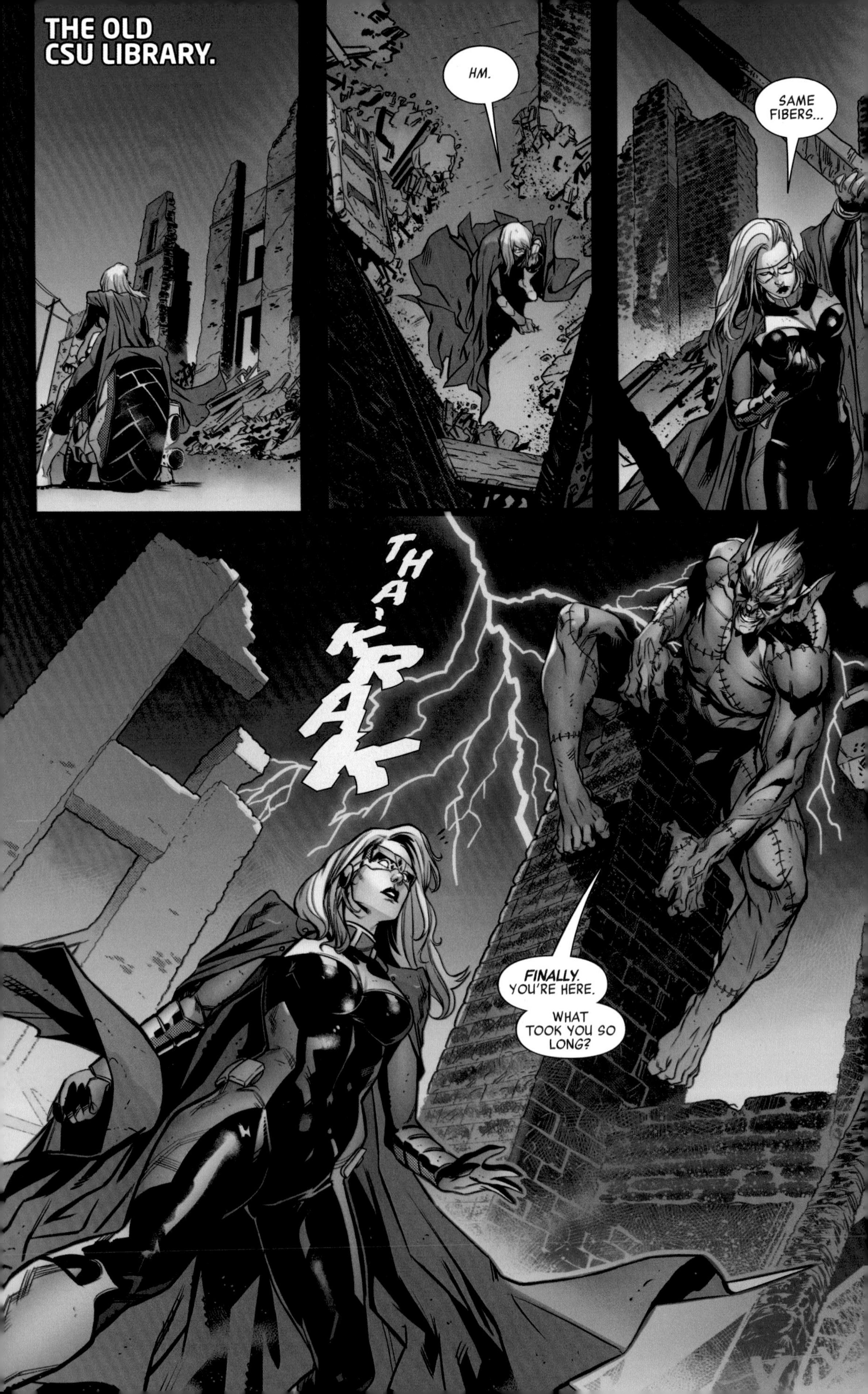
THE OLD CSU LIBRARY.
HM.
SAME FIBERS...
THA-KRAK
FINALLY. YOU'RE HERE.
WHAT TOOK YOU SO LONG?

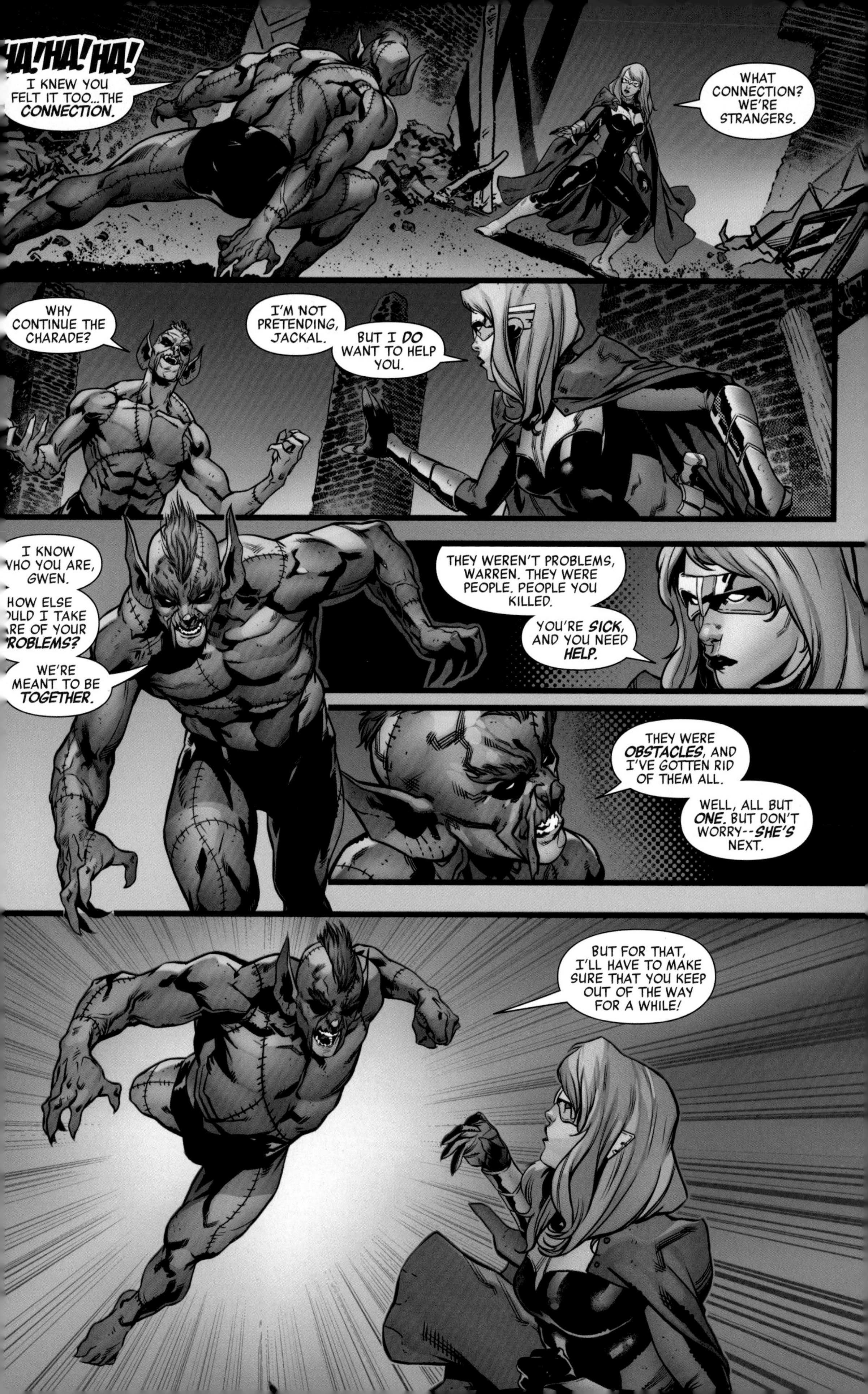
HA! HA! HA!
I KNEW YOU FELT IT TOO...THE CONNECTION.
WHAT CONNECTION? WE'RE STRANGERS.
WHY CONTINUE THE CHARADE?
I'M NOT PRETENDING, JACKAL.
BUT I DO WANT TO HELP YOU.
I KNOW WHO YOU ARE, GWEN.
HOW ELSE OULD I TAKE ARE OF YOUR PROBLEMS?
WE'RE MEANT TO BE TOGETHER.
THEY WEREN'T PROBLEMS, WARREN. THEY WERE PEOPLE. PEOPLE YOU KILLED.
YOU'RE SICK, AND YOU NEED HELP.
THEY WERE OBSTACLES, AND I'VE GOTTEN RID OF THEM ALL.
WELL, ALL BUT ONE. BUT DON'T WORRY--SHE'S NEXT.
BUT FOR THAT, I'LL HAVE TO MAKE SURE THAT YOU KEEP OUT OF THE WAY FOR A WHILE!

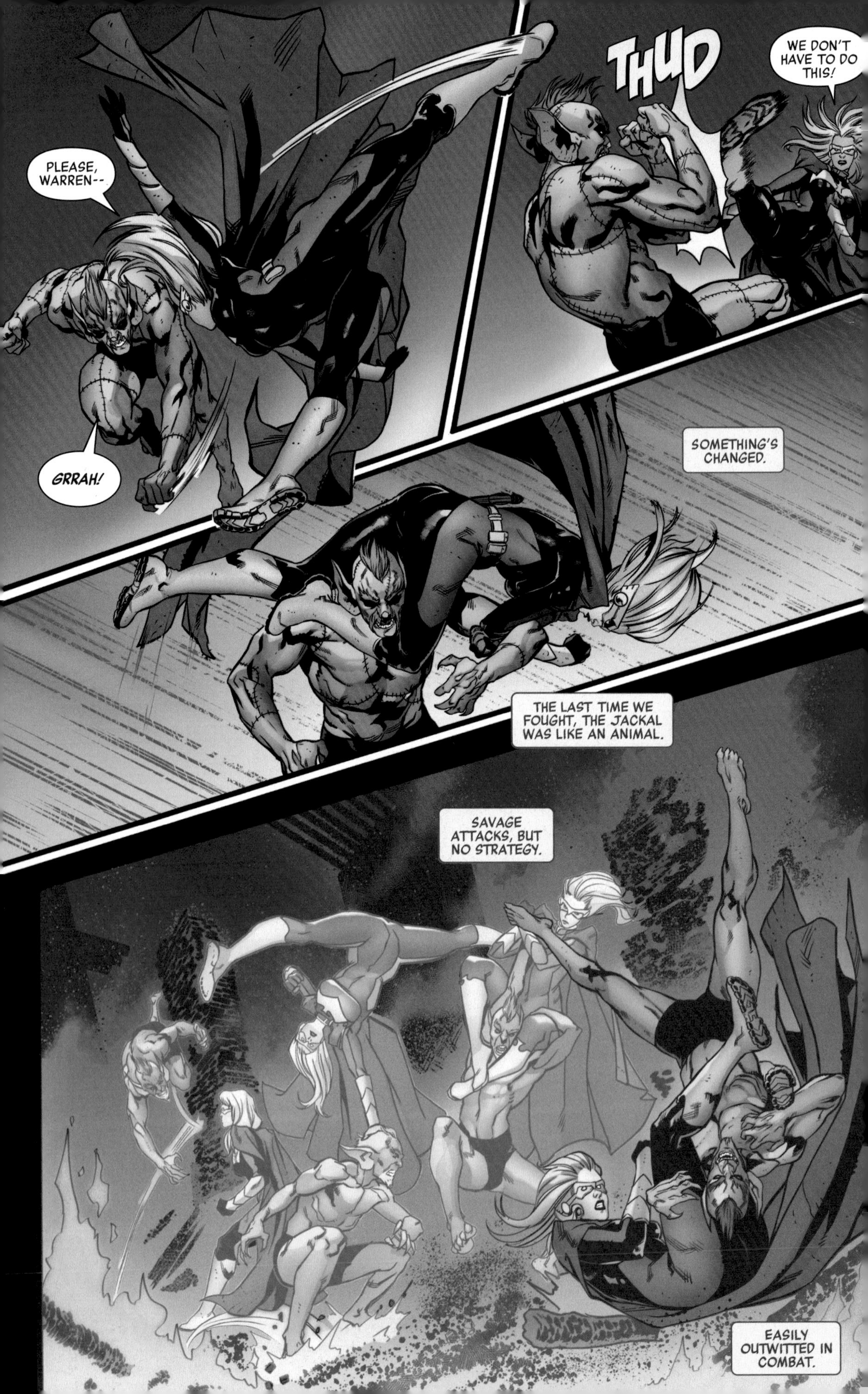
PLEASE, WARREN--
GRRAH!
THUD
WE DON'T HAVE TO DO THIS!
SOMETHING'S CHANGED.
THE LAST TIME WE FOUGHT, THE JACKAL WAS LIKE AN ANIMAL.
SAVAGE ATTACKS, BUT NO STRATEGY.
EASILY OUTWITTED IN COMBAT.

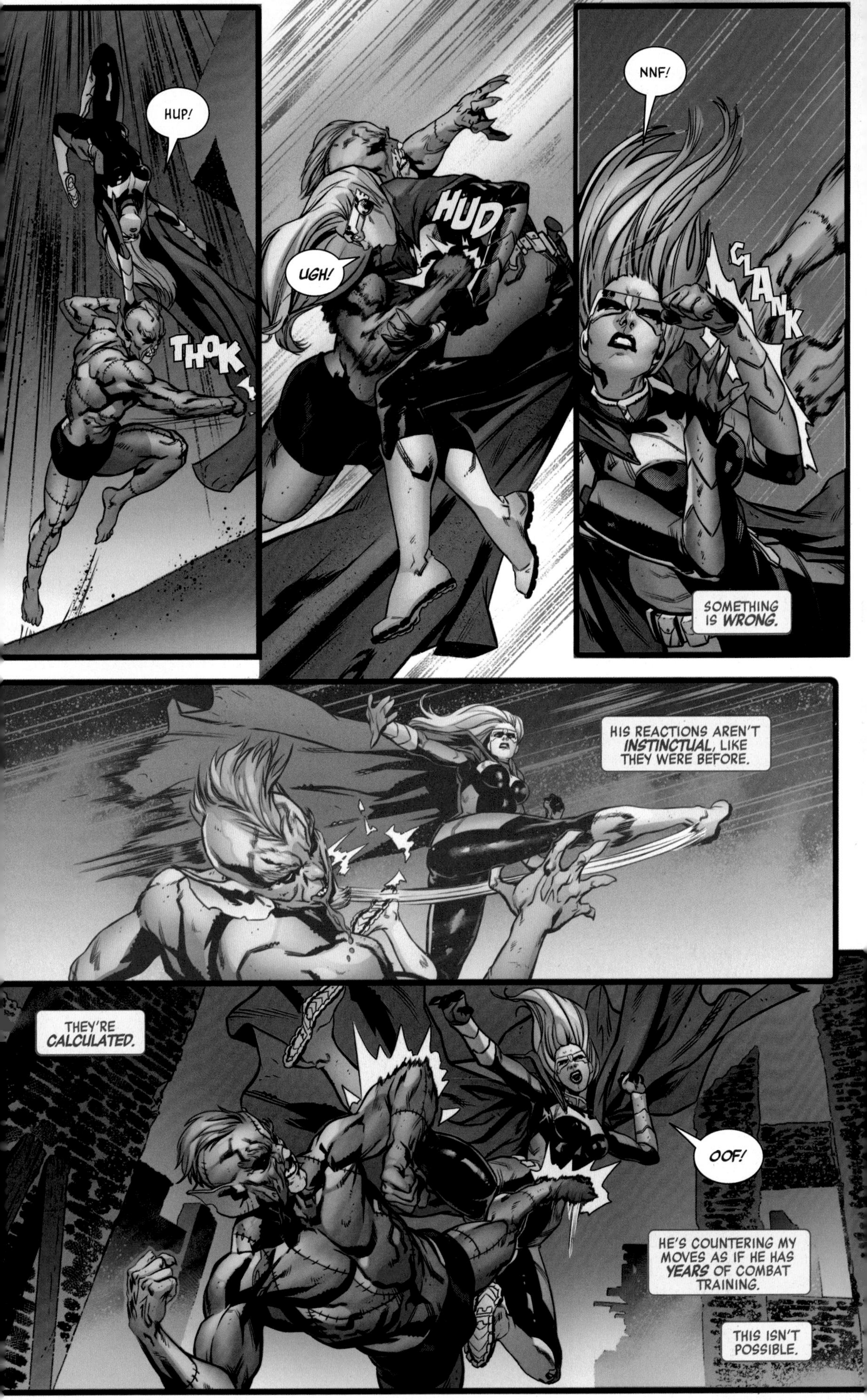
HUP!
THOK
UGH!
HUD
NNF!
CLANK
SOMETHING IS WRONG.
HIS REACTIONS AREN'T INSTINCTUAL, LIKE THEY WERE BEFORE.
THEY'RE CALCULATED.
OOF!
HE'S COUNTERING MY MOVES AS IF HE HAS YEARS OF COMBAT TRAINING.
THIS ISN'T POSSIBLE.

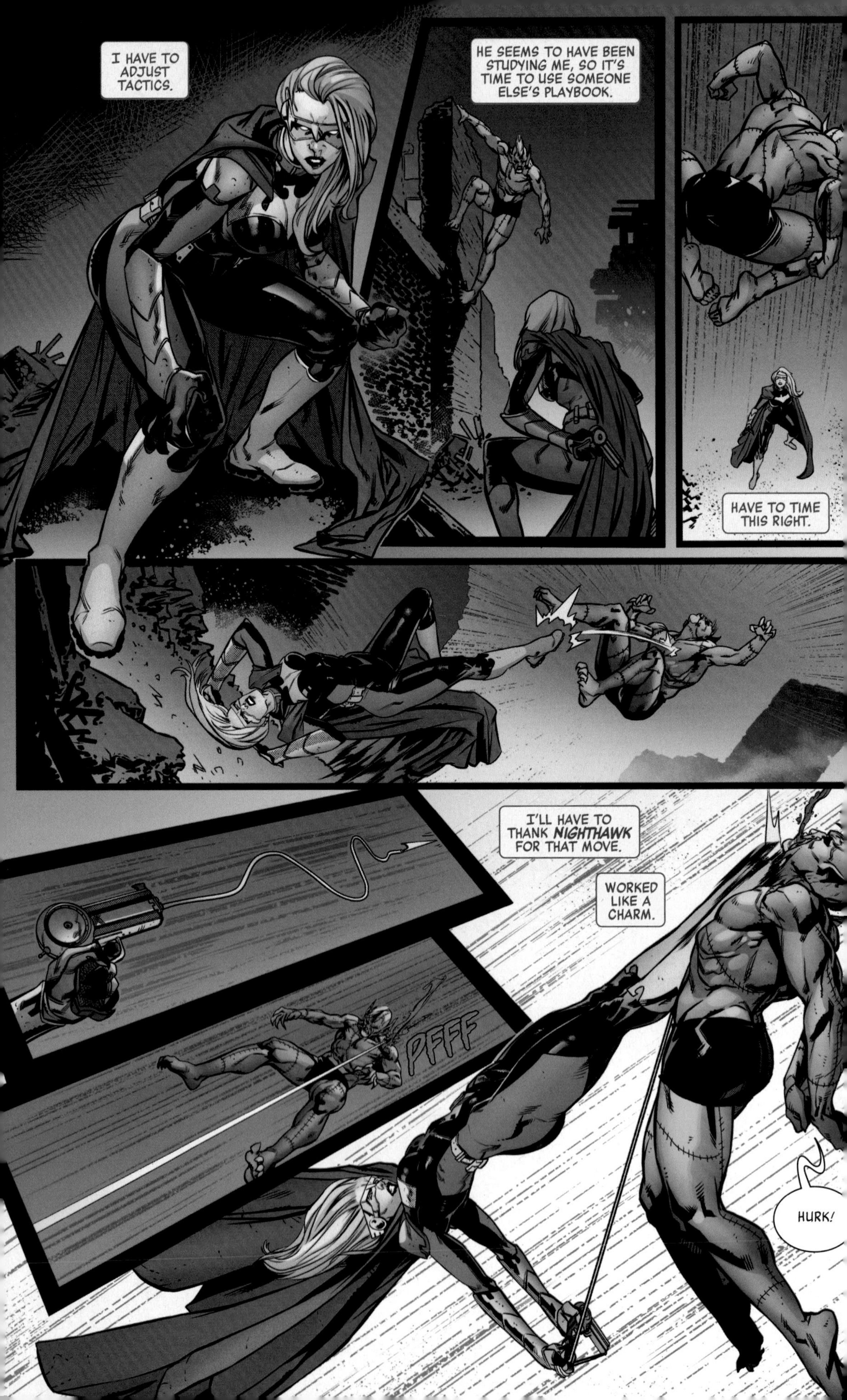
I HAVE TO ADJUST TACTICS.
HE SEEMS TO HAVE BEEN STUDYING ME, SO IT'S TIME TO USE SOMEONE ELSE'S PLAYBOOK.
HAVE TO TIME THIS RIGHT.
I'LL HAVE TO THANK NIGHTHAWK FOR THAT MOVE.
PFFF
WORKED LIKE A CHARM.
HURK!

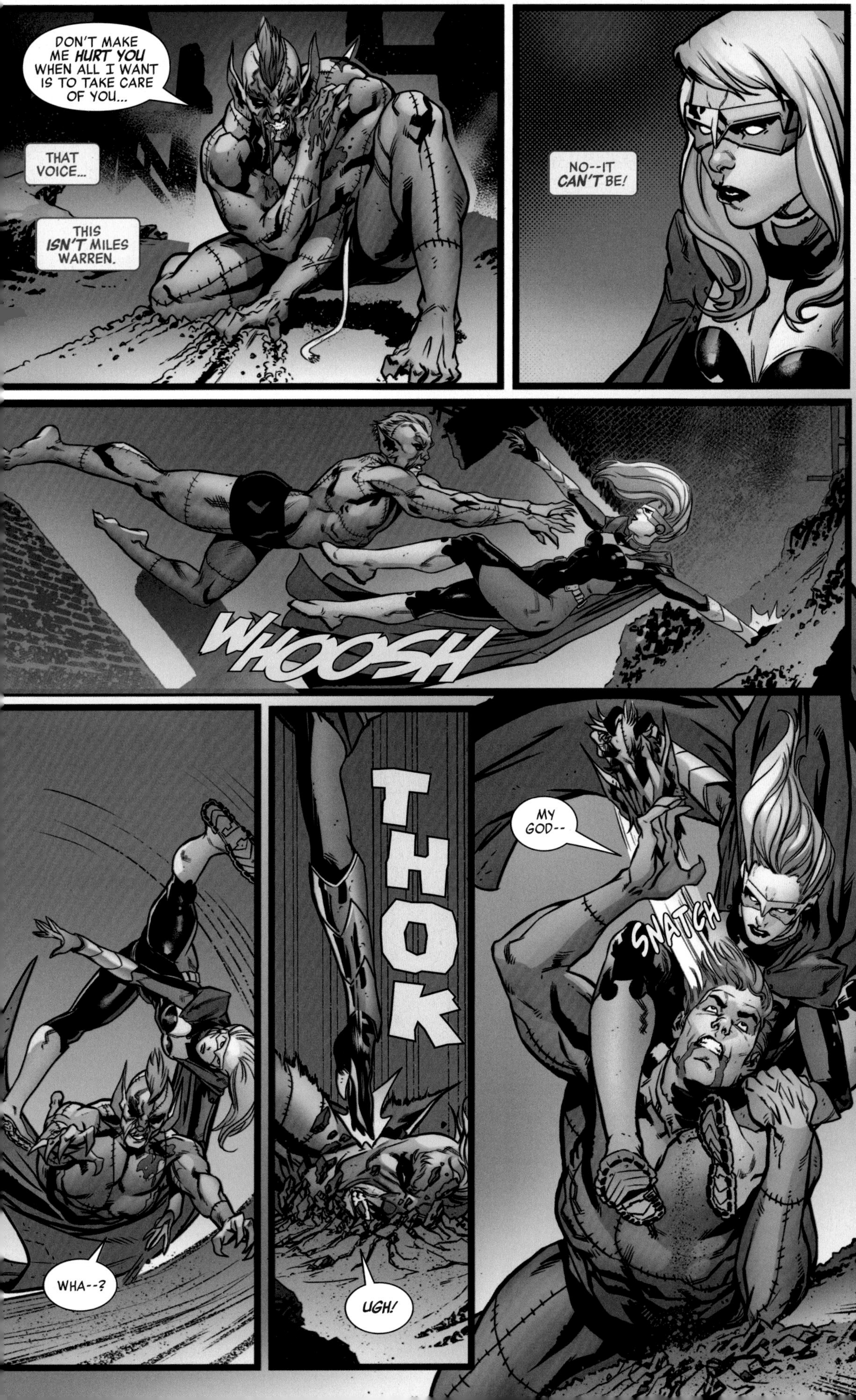
DON'T MAKE ME HURT YOU WHEN ALL I WANT IS TO TAKE CARE OF YOU...
THAT VOICE...
THIS ISN'T MILES WARREN.
NO--IT CAN'T BE!
WHOOSH
WHA--?
THOK
UGH!
MY GOD--
SNATCH

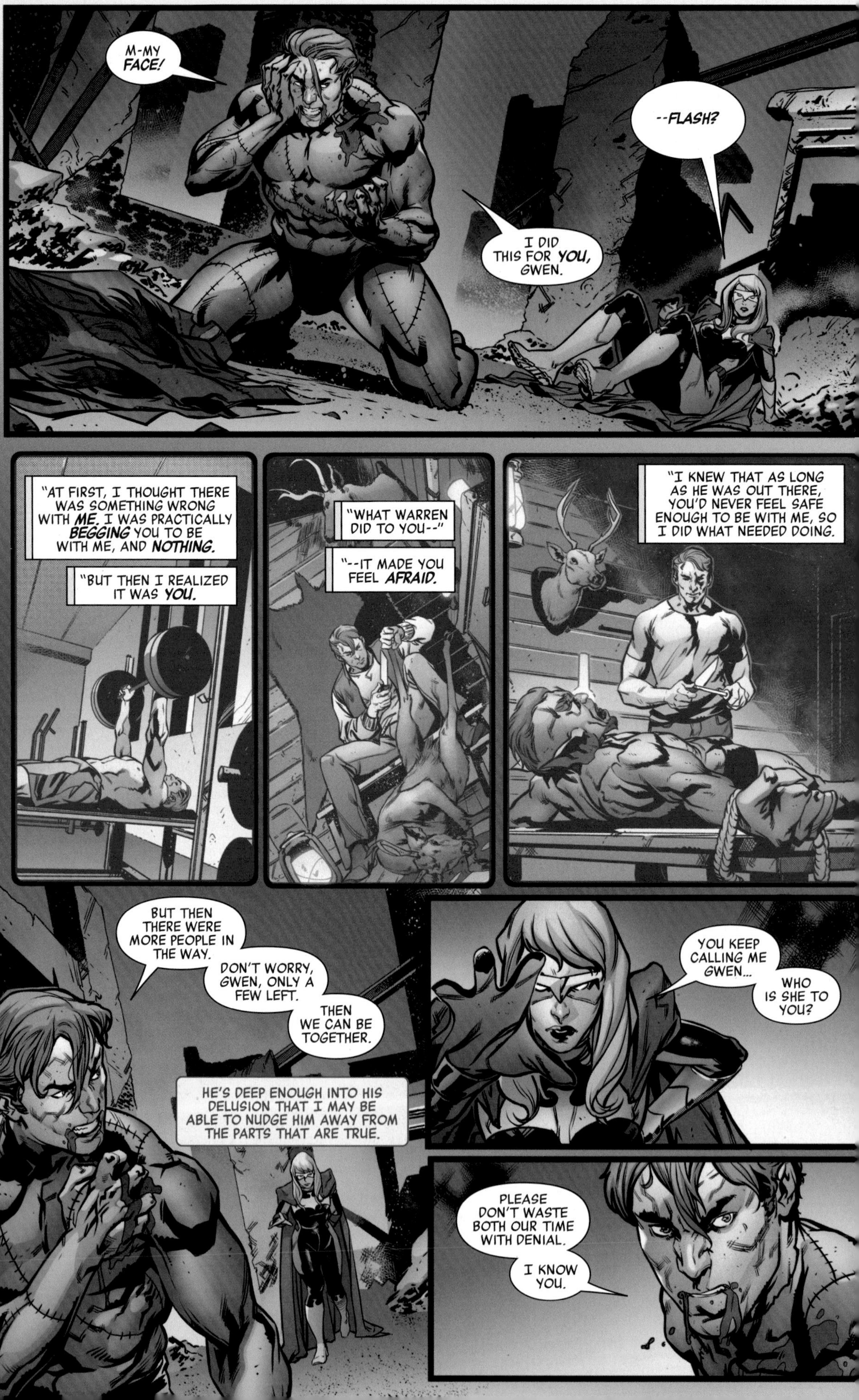
M-MY FACE!
--FLASH?
I DID THIS FOR YOU, GWEN.
"AT FIRST, I THOUGHT THERE WAS SOMETHING WRONG WITH ME. I WAS PRACTICALLY BEGGING YOU TO BE WITH ME, AND NOTHING.
"BUT THEN I REALIZED IT WAS YOU.
"WHAT WARREN DID TO YOU--"
"--IT MADE YOU FEEL AFRAID.
"I KNEW THAT AS LONG AS HE WAS OUT THERE, YOU'D NEVER FEEL SAFE ENOUGH TO BE WITH ME, SO I DID WHAT NEEDED DOING.
BUT THEN THERE WERE MORE PEOPLE IN THE WAY.
DON'T WORRY, GWEN, ONLY A FEW LEFT.
THEN WE CAN BE TOGETHER.
HE'S DEEP ENOUGH INTO HIS DELUSION THAT I MAY BE ABLE TO NUDGE HIM AWAY FROM THE PARTS THAT ARE TRUE.
YOU KEEP CALLING ME GWEN...
WHO IS SHE TO YOU?
PLEASE DON'T WASTE BOTH OUR TIME WITH DENIAL.
I KNOW YOU.

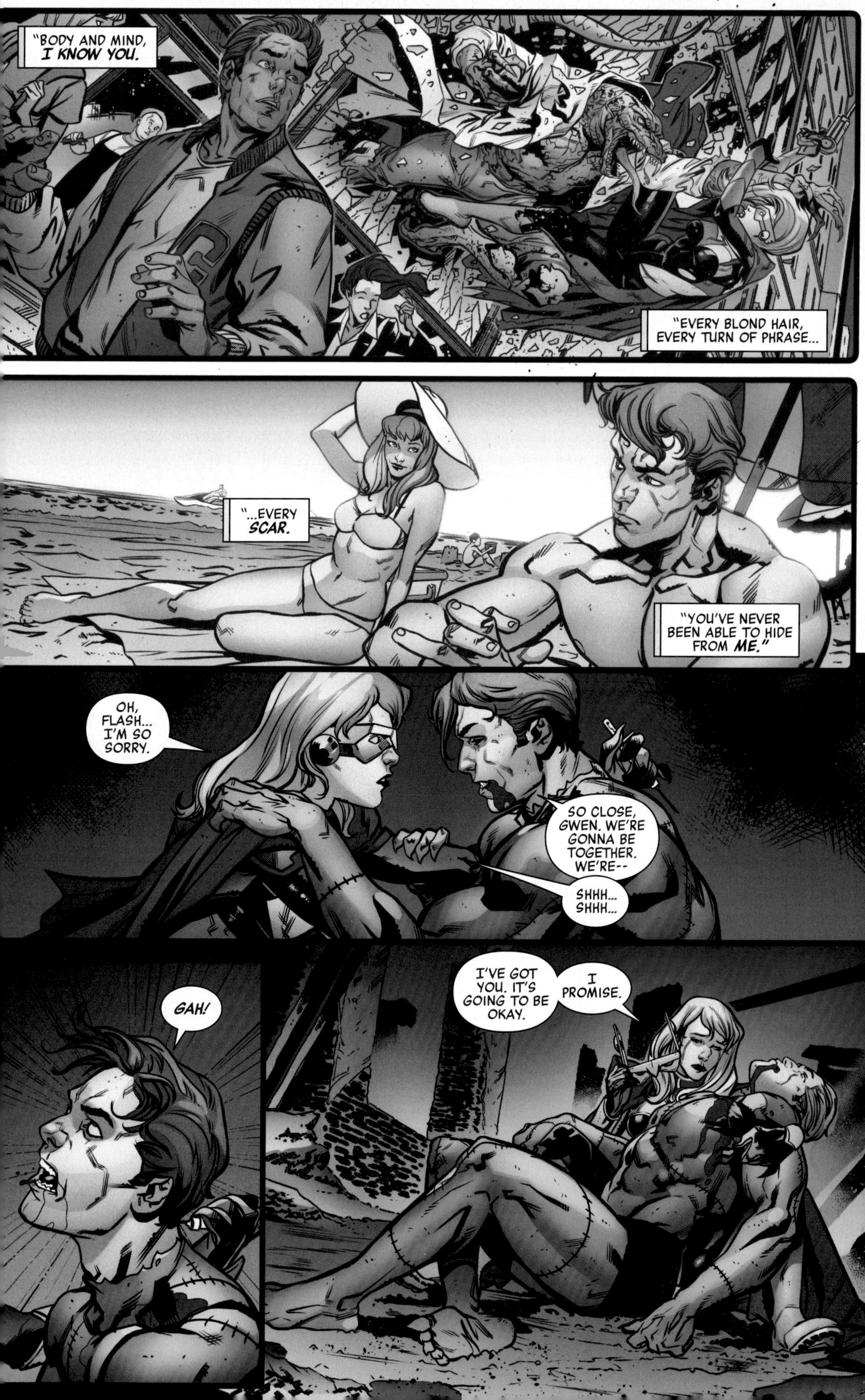
"BODY AND MIND, I KNOW YOU.
"EVERY BLOND HAIR, EVERY TURN OF PHRASE...
"...EVERY SCAR.
"YOU'VE NEVER BEEN ABLE TO HIDE FROM ME."
OH, FLASH... I'M SO SORRY.
SO CLOSE, GWEN. WE'RE GONNA BE TOGETHER. WE'RE--
SHHH... SHHH...
GAH!
I'VE GOT YOU. IT'S GOING TO BE OKAY.
I PROMISE.

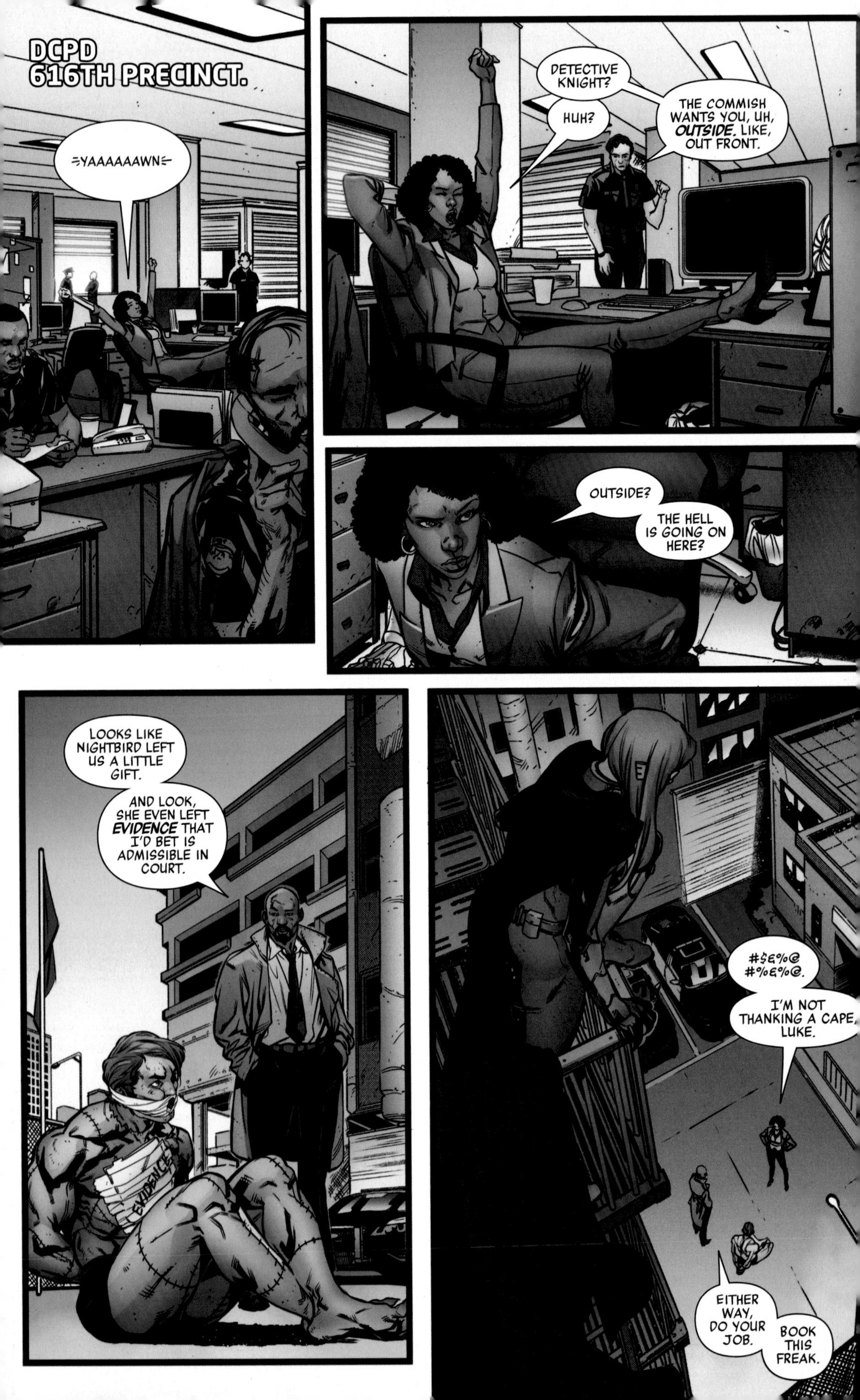
DCPD
616TH PRECINCT.
=YAAAAAAWN=
DETECTIVE KNIGHT?
HUH?
THE COMMISH WANTS YOU, UH, OUTSIDE. LIKE, OUT FRONT.
OUTSIDE?
THE HELL IS GOING ON HERE?
LOOKS LIKE NIGHTBIRD LEFT US A LITTLE GIFT.
AND LOOK, SHE EVEN LEFT EVIDENCE THAT I'D BET IS ADMISSIBLE IN COURT.
EVIDENCE
#$£%@
#%£%@.
I'M NOT THANKING A CAPE, LUKE.
EITHER WAY, DO YOUR JOB.
BOOK THIS FREAK.

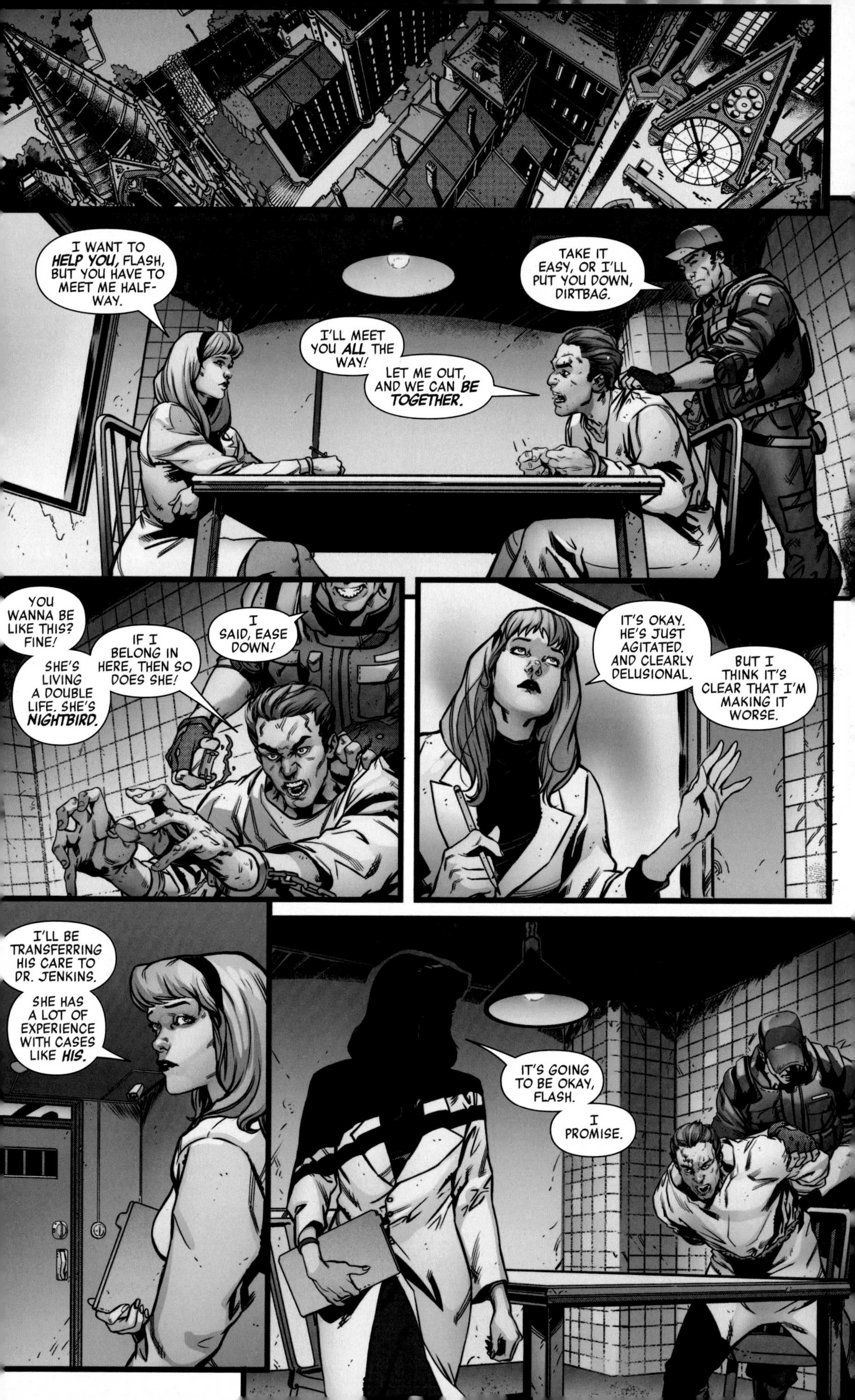
I WANT TO HELP YOU, FLASH, BUT YOU HAVE TO MEET ME HALF-WAY.
TAKE IT EASY, OR I'LL PUT YOU DOWN, DIRTBAG.
I'LL MEET YOU ALL THE WAY!
LET ME OUT, AND WE CAN BE TOGETHER.
YOU WANNA BE LIKE THIS? FINE!
SHE'S LIVING A DOUBLE LIFE. SHE'S NIGHTBIRD.
IF I BELONG IN HERE, THEN SO DOES SHE!
I SAID, EASE DOWN!
IT'S OKAY. HE'S JUST AGITATED. AND CLEARLY DELUSIONAL.
BUT I THINK IT'S CLEAR THAT I'M MAKING IT WORSE.
I'LL BE TRANSFERRING HIS CARE TO DR. JENKINS.
SHE HAS A LOT OF EXPERIENCE WITH CASES LIKE HIS.
IT'S GOING TO BE OKAY, FLASH.
I PROMISE.

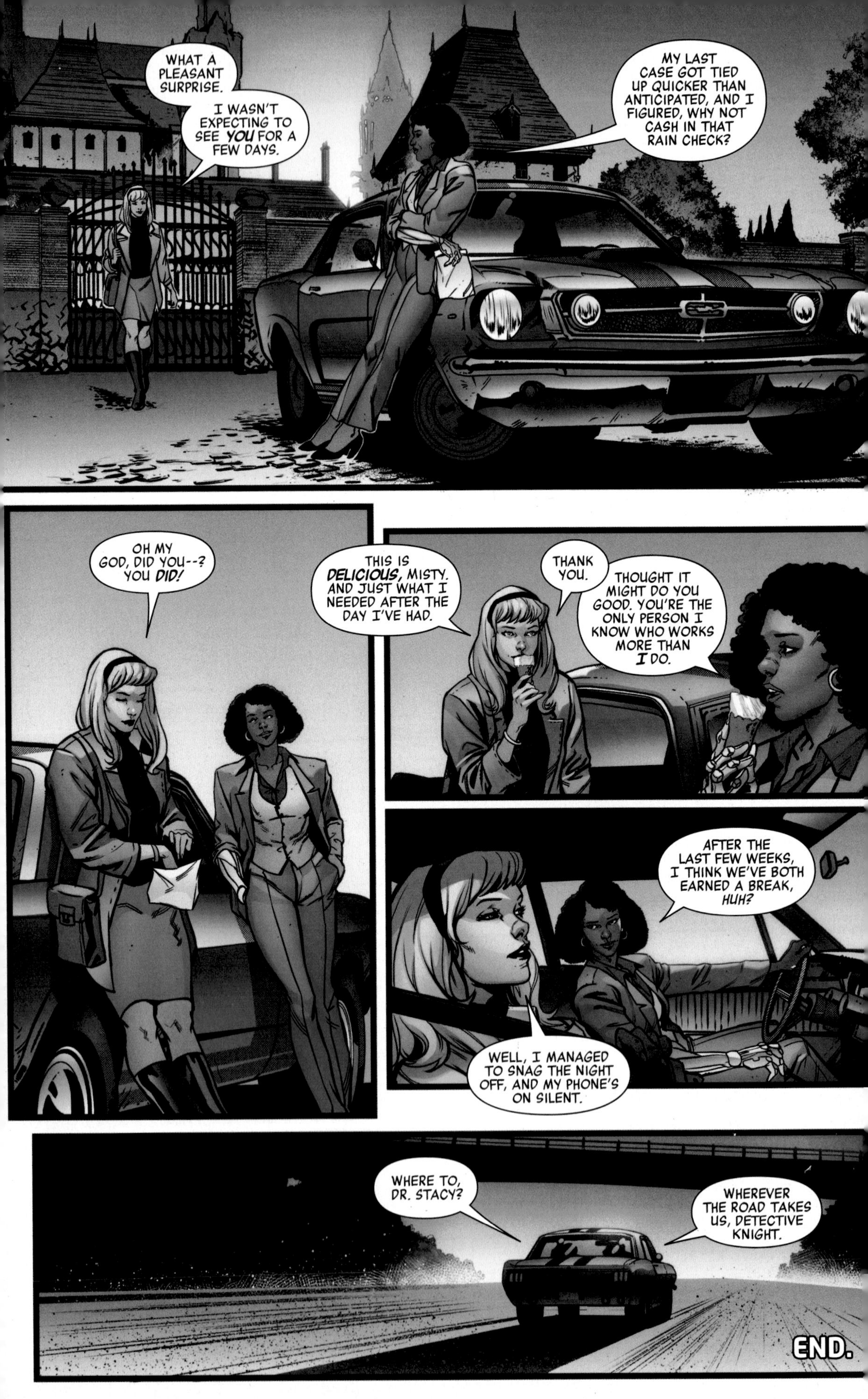
WHAT A PLEASANT SURPRISE.
I WASN'T EXPECTING TO SEE **YOU** FOR A FEW DAYS.
MY LAST CASE GOT TIED UP QUICKER THAN ANTICIPATED, AND I FIGURED, WHY NOT CASH IN THAT RAIN CHECK?
OH MY GOD, DID YOU--? YOU ***DID!***
THIS IS ***DELICIOUS,*** MISTY. AND JUST WHAT I NEEDED AFTER THE DAY I'VE HAD.
THANK YOU.
THOUGHT IT MIGHT DO YOU GOOD. YOU'RE THE ONLY PERSON I KNOW WHO WORKS MORE THAN ***I*** DO.
AFTER THE LAST FEW WEEKS, I THINK WE'VE BOTH EARNED A BREAK, *HUH?*
WELL, I MANAGED TO SNAG THE NIGHT OFF, AND MY PHONE'S ON SILENT.
WHERE TO, DR. STACY?
WHEREVER THE ROAD TAKES US, DETECTIVE KNIGHT.
END.

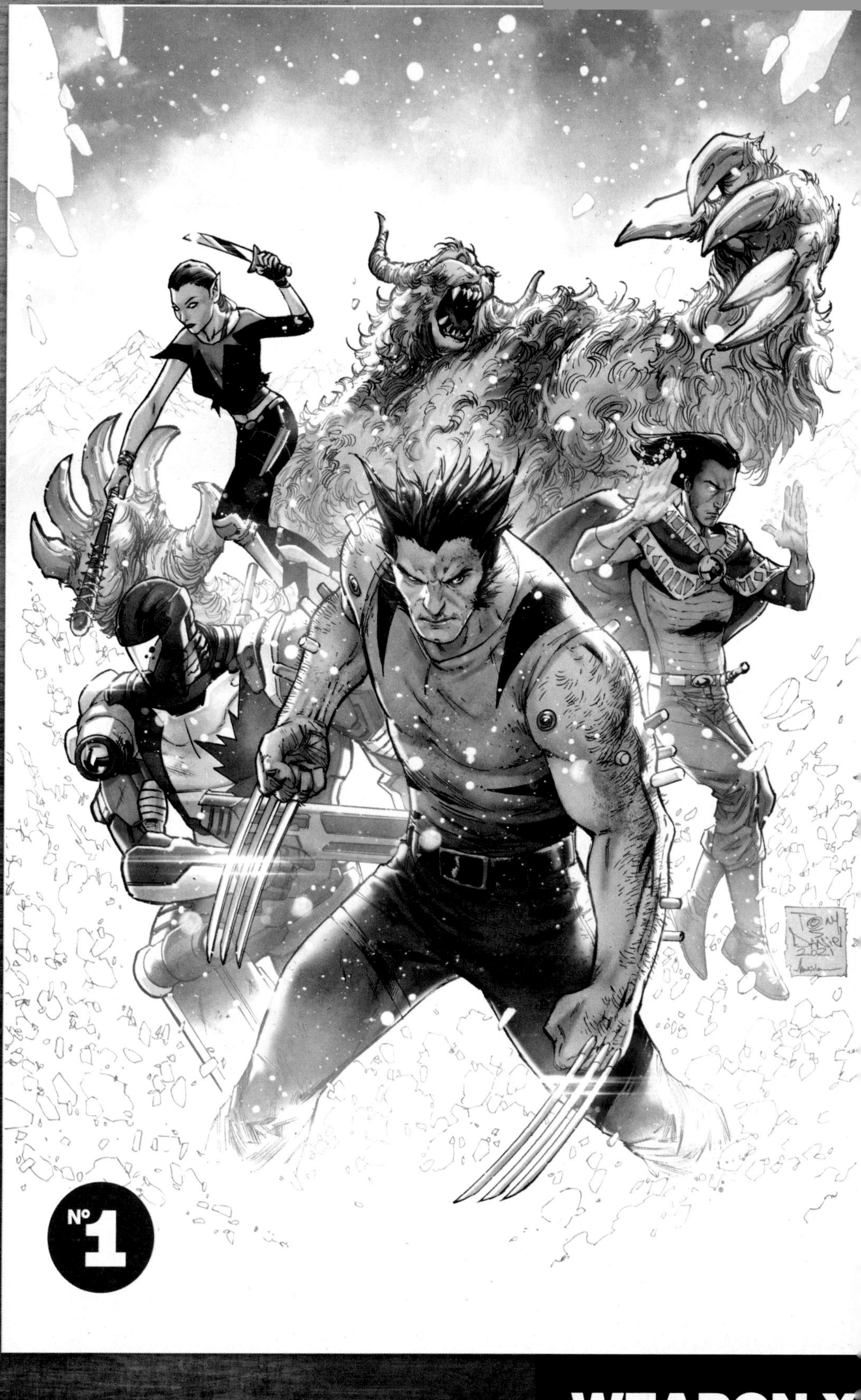

Nº 1
TONY DANIEL 2021

WEAPON X & FINAL FLIGHT

"FREEDOM OR DEATH"

In a world in which the Avengers never existed, the Squadron Supreme of America are and have always been Earth's Mightiest Heroes!

WEAPON X
& FINAL FLIGHT

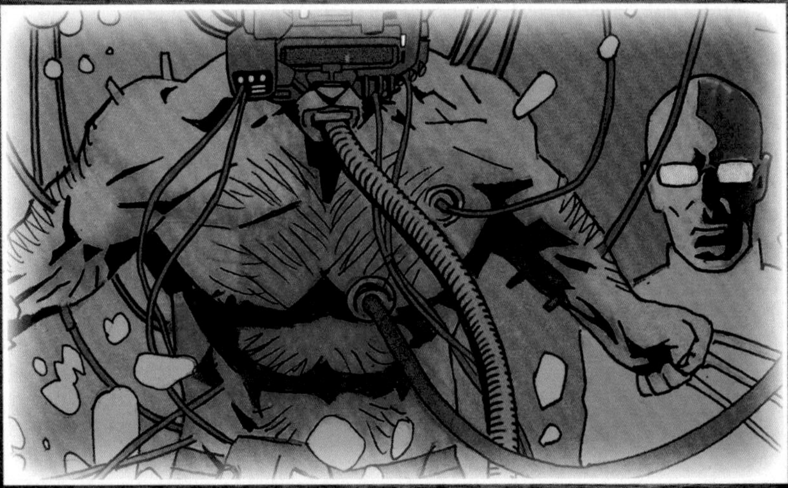

"FREEDOM OR DEATH"

ED **BRISSON** WRITER
ROLAND **BOSCHI** ARTIST
CHRIS **O'HALLORAN** COLORS
VC's CORY **PETIT** LETTERER
TONY **DANIEL** & MARCELO **MAIOLO** COVER ARTISTS
DAVID **YARDIN** VARIANT COVER ARTIST
JAY **BOWEN** GRAPHIC DESIGN
DARREN **SHAN** EDITOR
TOM **BREVOORT** EXECUTIVE EDITOR
C.B. **CEBULSKI** EDITOR IN CHIEF

HEROES REBORN

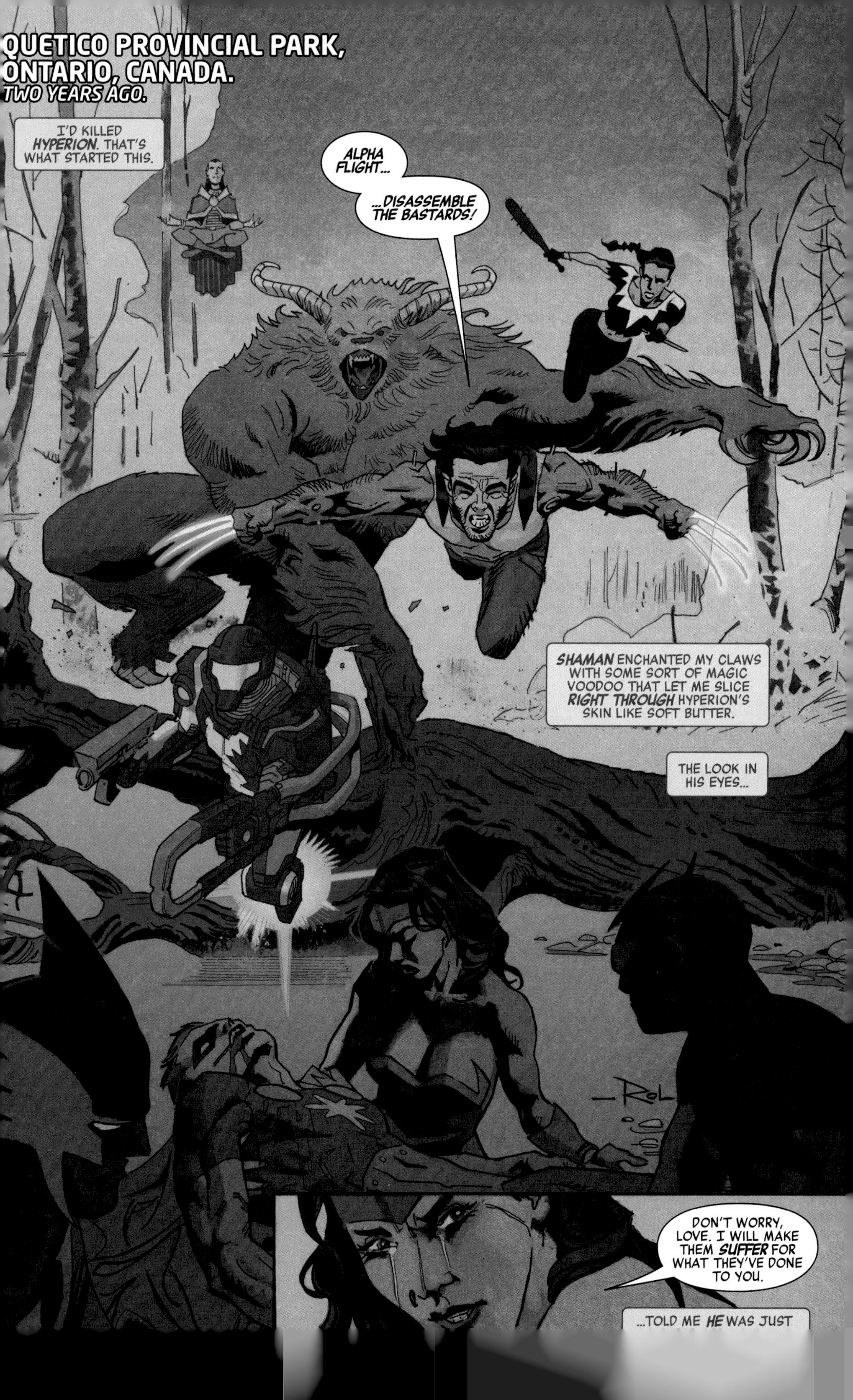
QUETICO PROVINCIAL PARK, ONTARIO, CANADA.
TWO YEARS AGO.
I'D KILLED HYPERION. THAT'S WHAT STARTED THIS.
ALPHA FLIGHT...
...DISASSEMBLE THE BASTARDS!
SHAMAN ENCHANTED MY CLAWS WITH SOME SORT OF MAGIC VOODOO THAT LET ME SLICE RIGHT THROUGH HYPERION'S SKIN LIKE SOFT BUTTER.
THE LOOK IN HIS EYES...
DON'T WORRY, LOVE. I WILL MAKE THEM SUFFER FOR WHAT THEY'VE DONE TO YOU.
...TOLD ME HE WAS JUST

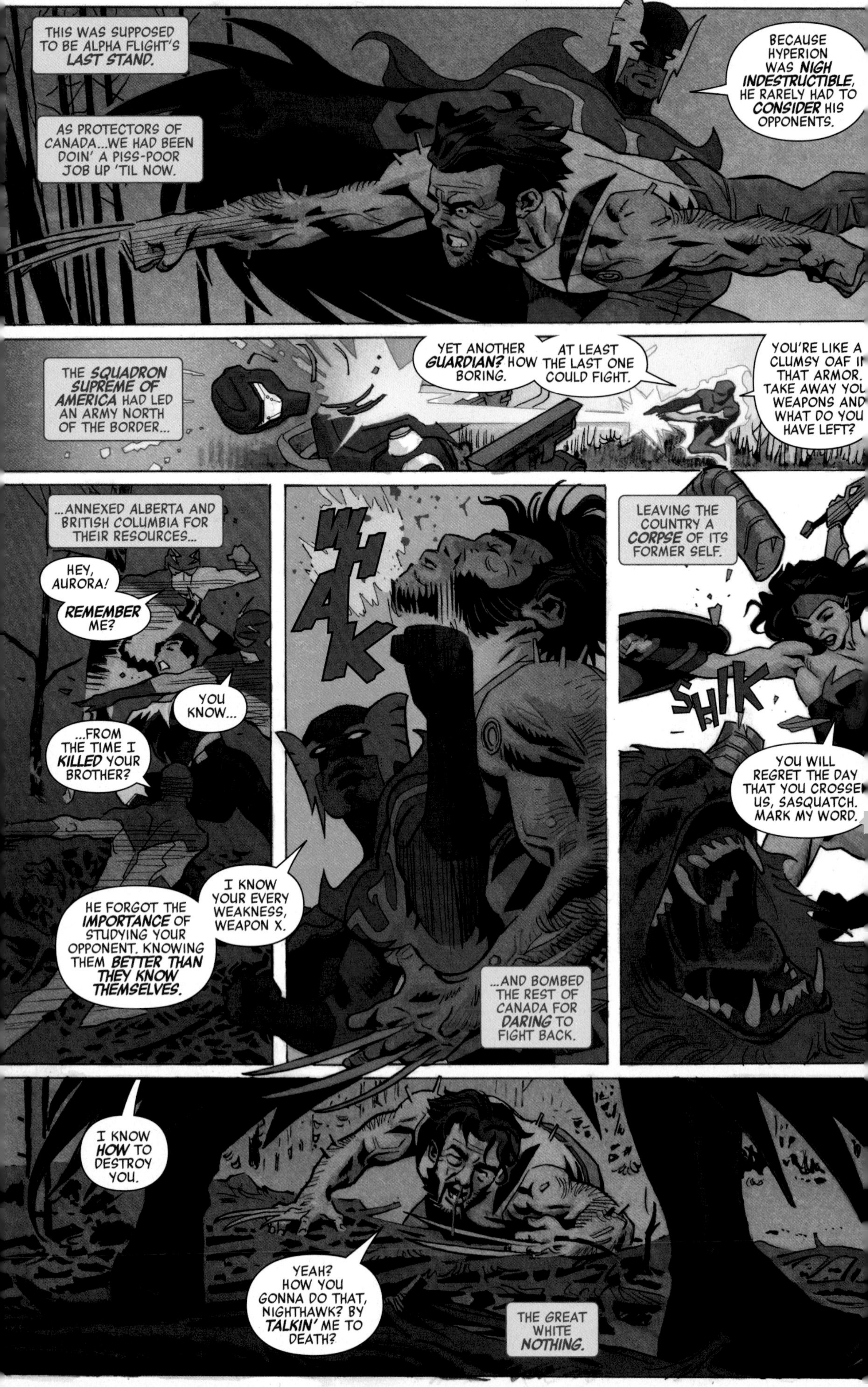
THIS WAS SUPPOSED TO BE ALPHA FLIGHT'S LAST STAND.
AS PROTECTORS OF CANADA...WE HAD BEEN DOIN' A PISS-POOR JOB UP 'TIL NOW.
BECAUSE HYPERION WAS NIGH INDESTRUCTIBLE, HE RARELY HAD TO CONSIDER HIS OPPONENTS.
THE SQUADRON SUPREME OF AMERICA HAD LED AN ARMY NORTH OF THE BORDER...
YET ANOTHER GUARDIAN? HOW BORING.
AT LEAST THE LAST ONE COULD FIGHT.
YOU'RE LIKE A CLUMSY OAF I THAT ARMOR. TAKE AWAY YO WEAPONS AND WHAT DO YOU HAVE LEFT?
...ANNEXED ALBERTA AND BRITISH COLUMBIA FOR THEIR RESOURCES...
HEY, AURORA! REMEMBER ME?
YOU KNOW...
...FROM THE TIME I KILLED YOUR BROTHER?
WHAK
LEAVING THE COUNTRY A CORPSE OF ITS FORMER SELF.
SHIK
YOU WILL REGRET THE DAY THAT YOU CROSSE US, SASQUATCH. MARK MY WORD.
HE FORGOT THE IMPORTANCE OF STUDYING YOUR OPPONENT. KNOWING THEM BETTER THAN THEY KNOW THEMSELVES.
I KNOW YOUR EVERY WEAKNESS, WEAPON X.
...AND BOMBED THE REST OF CANADA FOR DARING TO FIGHT BACK.
I KNOW HOW TO DESTROY YOU.
YEAH? HOW YOU GONNA DO THAT, NIGHTHAWK? BY TALKIN' ME TO DEATH?
THE GREAT WHITE NOTHING.

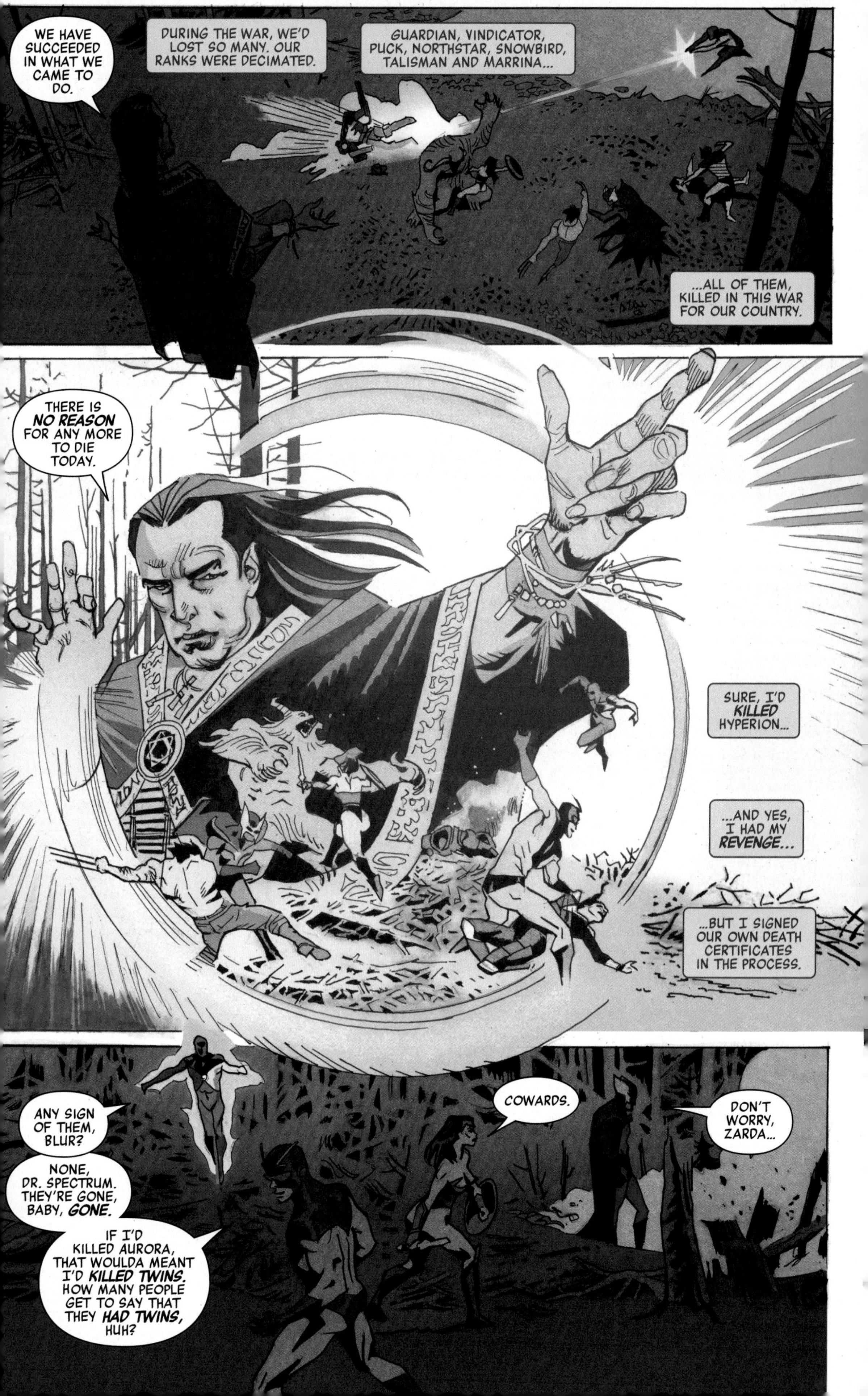
WE HAVE SUCCEEDED IN WHAT WE CAME TO DO.
DURING THE WAR, WE'D LOST SO MANY. OUR RANKS WERE DECIMATED.
GUARDIAN, VINDICATOR, PUCK, NORTHSTAR, SNOWBIRD, TALISMAN AND MARRINA...
...ALL OF THEM, KILLED IN THIS WAR FOR OUR COUNTRY.
THERE IS NO REASON FOR ANY MORE TO DIE TODAY.
SURE, I'D KILLED HYPERION...
...AND YES, I HAD MY REVENGE...
...BUT I SIGNED OUR OWN DEATH CERTIFICATES IN THE PROCESS.
ANY SIGN OF THEM, BLUR?
NONE, DR. SPECTRUM. THEY'RE GONE, BABY, GONE.
IF I'D KILLED AURORA, THAT WOULDA MEANT I'D KILLED TWINS. HOW MANY PEOPLE GET TO SAY THAT THEY HAD TWINS, HUH?
COWARDS.
DON'T WORRY, ZARDA...

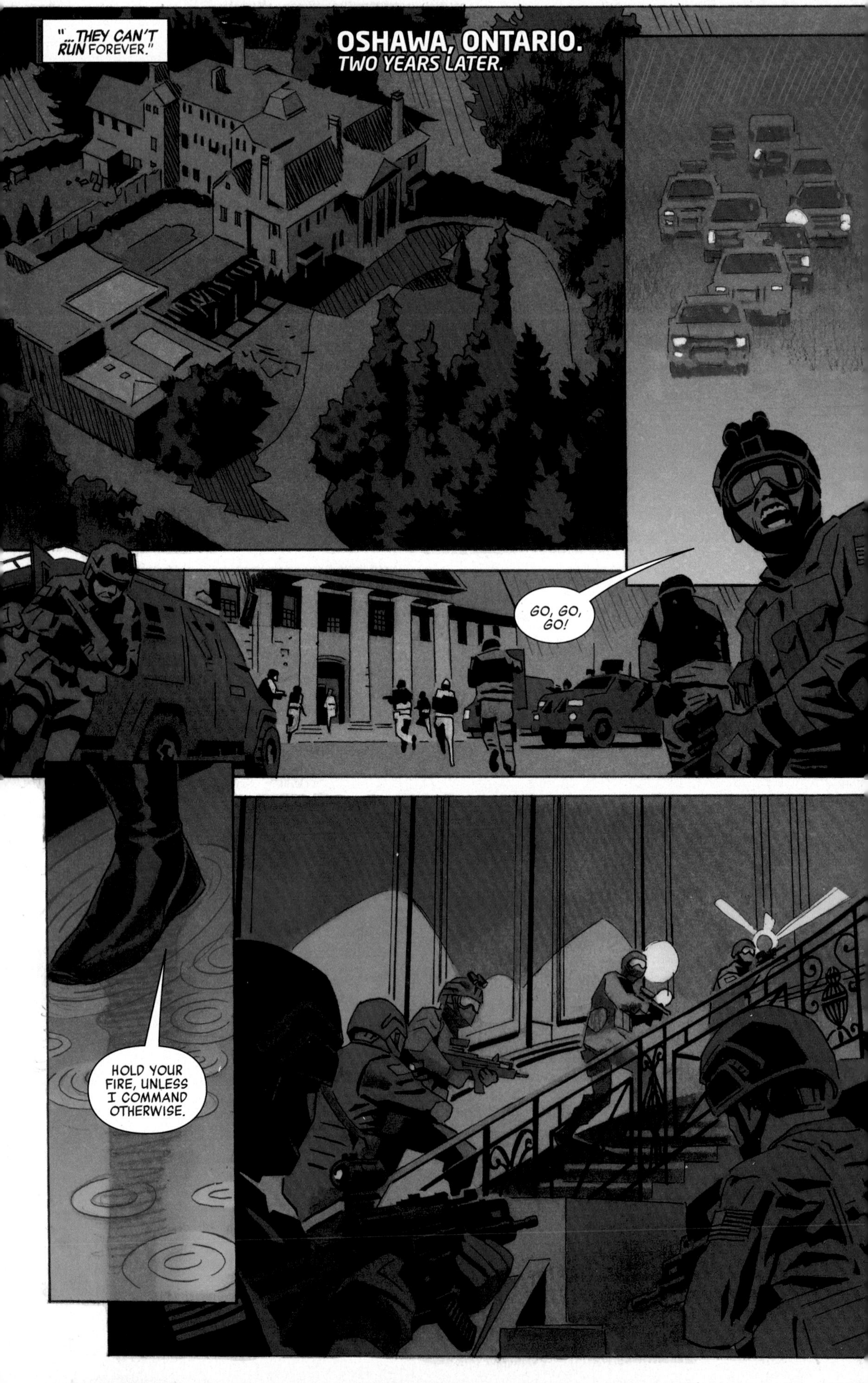
"...THEY CAN'T RUN FOREVER."
OSHAWA, ONTARIO.
TWO YEARS LATER.
GO, GO, GO!
HOLD YOUR FIRE, UNLESS I COMMAND OTHERWISE.

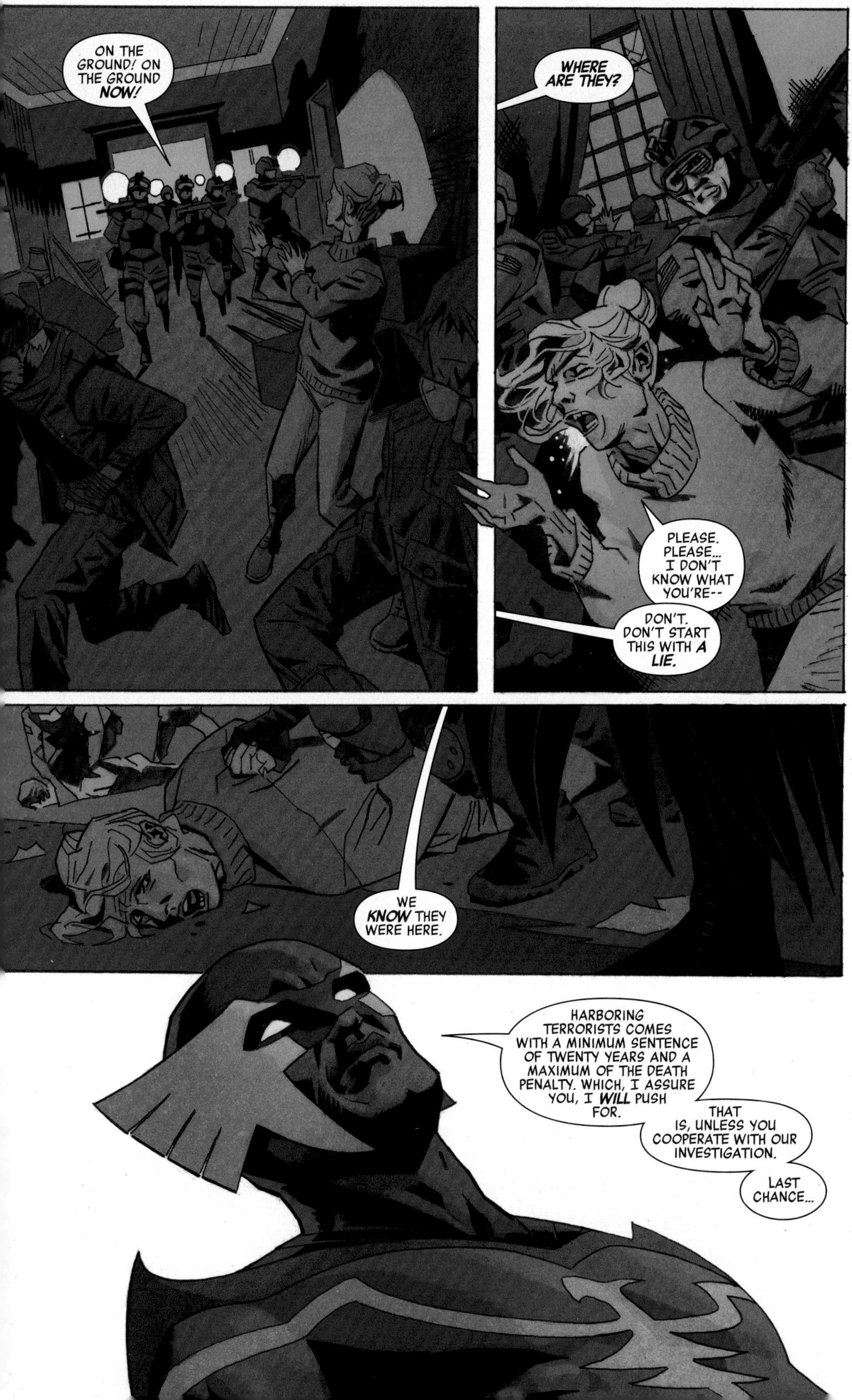
ON THE GROUND! ON THE GROUND NOW!
WHERE ARE THEY?
PLEASE. PLEASE... I DON'T KNOW WHAT YOU'RE--
DON'T. DON'T START THIS WITH A LIE.
WE KNOW THEY WERE HERE.
HARBORING TERRORISTS COMES WITH A MINIMUM SENTENCE OF TWENTY YEARS AND A MAXIMUM OF THE DEATH PENALTY. WHICH, I ASSURE YOU, I WILL PUSH FOR.
THAT IS, UNLESS YOU COOPERATE WITH OUR INVESTIGATION.
LAST CHANCE...

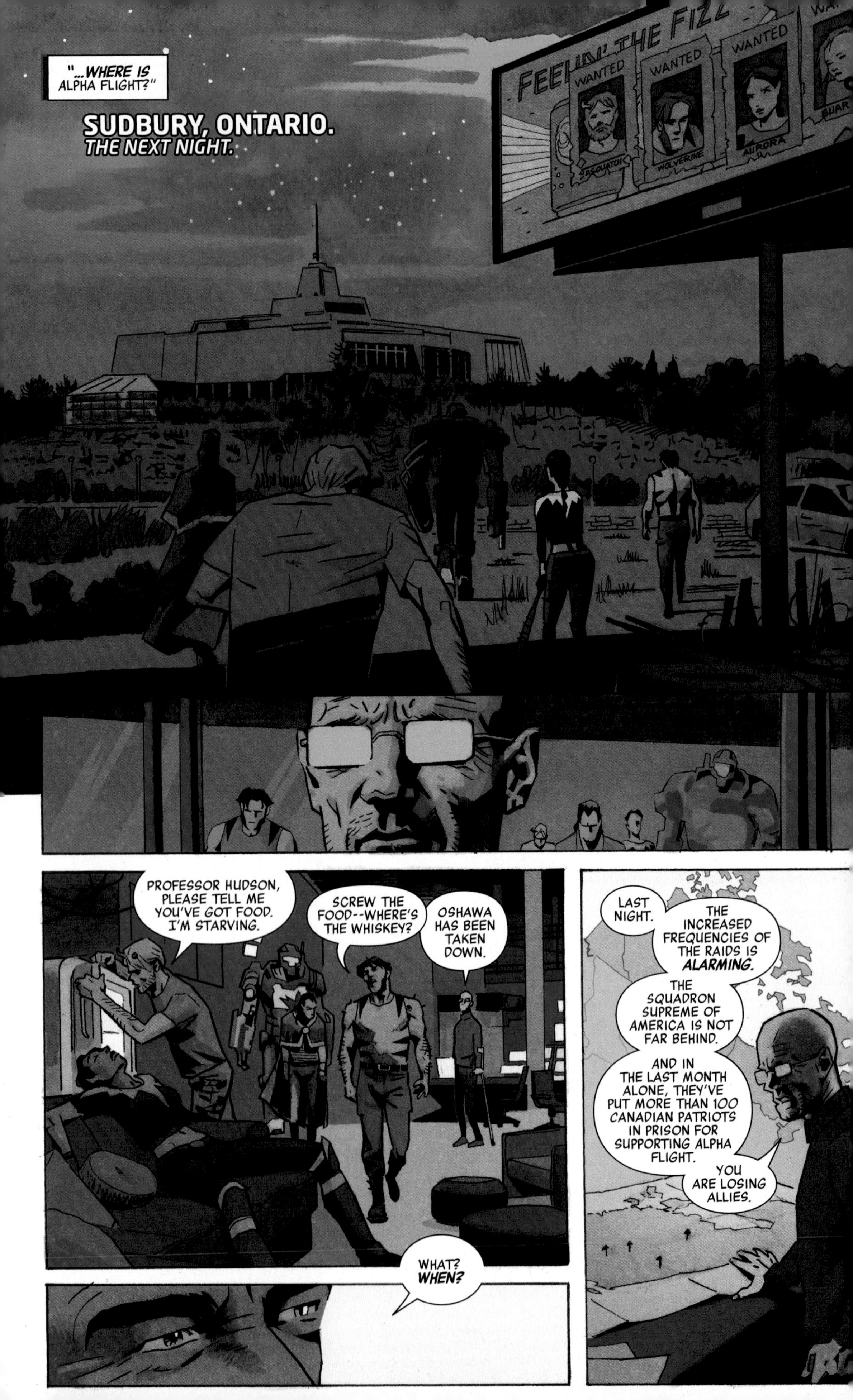
"...WHERE IS ALPHA FLIGHT?"
SUDBURY, ONTARIO.
THE NEXT NIGHT.
FEELIN' THE FIZZ
WANTED
WANTED
WANTED
SASQUATCH
WOLVERINE
AURORA
PROFESSOR HUDSON, PLEASE TELL ME YOU'VE GOT FOOD. I'M STARVING.
SCREW THE FOOD--WHERE'S THE WHISKEY?
OSHAWA HAS BEEN TAKEN DOWN.
WHAT? WHEN?
LAST NIGHT.
THE INCREASED FREQUENCIES OF THE RAIDS IS ALARMING.
THE SQUADRON SUPREME OF AMERICA IS NOT FAR BEHIND.
AND IN THE LAST MONTH ALONE, THEY'VE PUT MORE THAN 100 CANADIAN PATRIOTS IN PRISON FOR SUPPORTING ALPHA FLIGHT.
YOU ARE LOSING ALLIES.

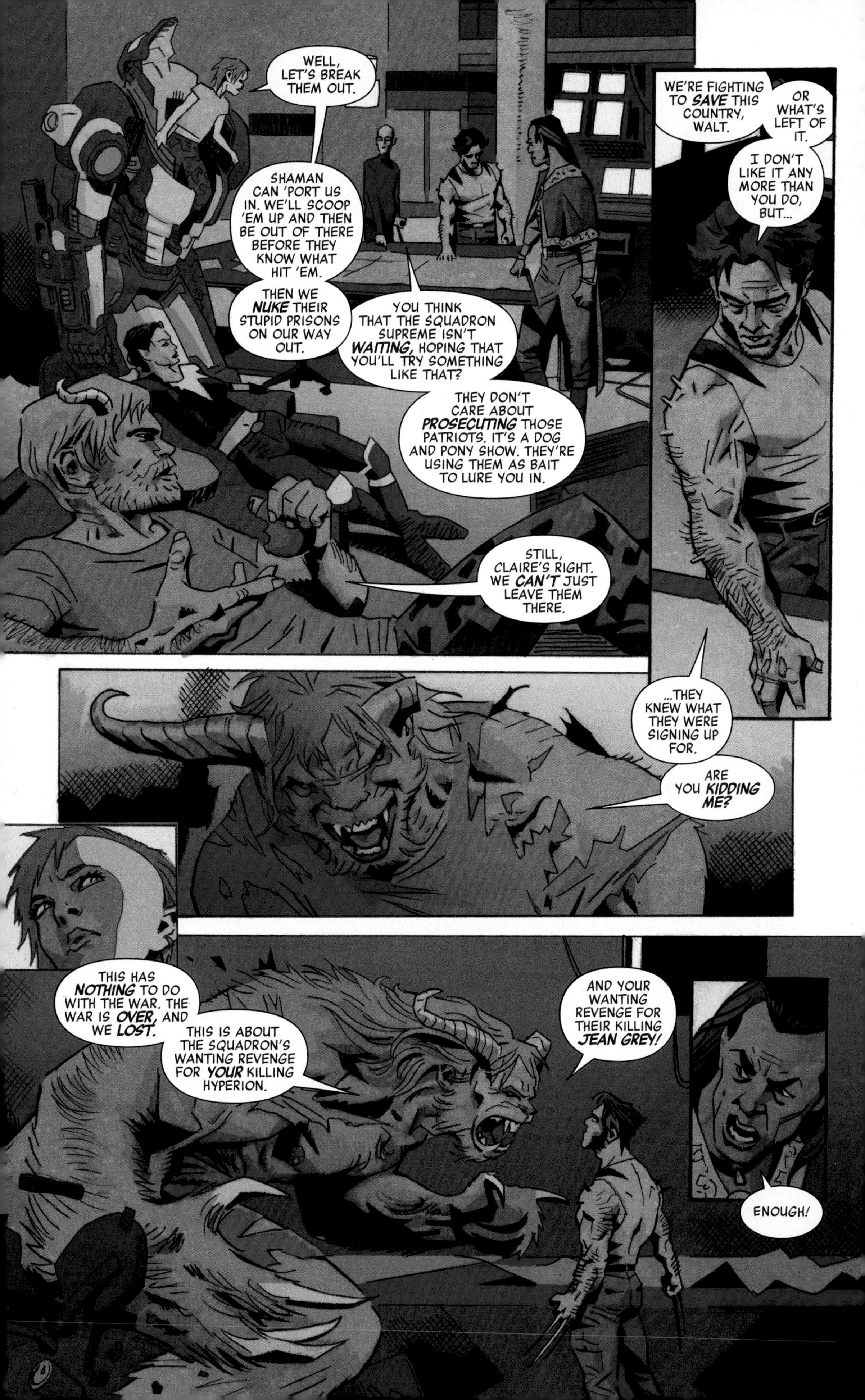
WELL, LET'S BREAK THEM OUT.
SHAMAN CAN 'PORT US IN. WE'LL SCOOP 'EM UP AND THEN BE OUT OF THERE BEFORE THEY KNOW WHAT HIT 'EM.
THEN WE NUKE THEIR STUPID PRISONS ON OUR WAY OUT.
YOU THINK THAT THE SQUADRON SUPREME ISN'T WAITING, HOPING THAT YOU'LL TRY SOMETHING LIKE THAT?
THEY DON'T CARE ABOUT PROSECUTING THOSE PATRIOTS. IT'S A DOG AND PONY SHOW. THEY'RE USING THEM AS BAIT TO LURE YOU IN.
STILL, CLAIRE'S RIGHT. WE CAN'T JUST LEAVE THEM THERE.
WE'RE FIGHTING TO SAVE THIS COUNTRY, WALT.
OR WHAT'S LEFT OF IT.
I DON'T LIKE IT ANY MORE THAN YOU DO, BUT...
...THEY KNEW WHAT THEY WERE SIGNING UP FOR.
ARE YOU KIDDING ME?
THIS HAS NOTHING TO DO WITH THE WAR. THE WAR IS OVER, AND WE LOST.
THIS IS ABOUT THE SQUADRON'S WANTING REVENGE FOR YOUR KILLING HYPERION.
AND YOUR WANTING REVENGE FOR THEIR KILLING JEAN GREY!
ENOUGH!

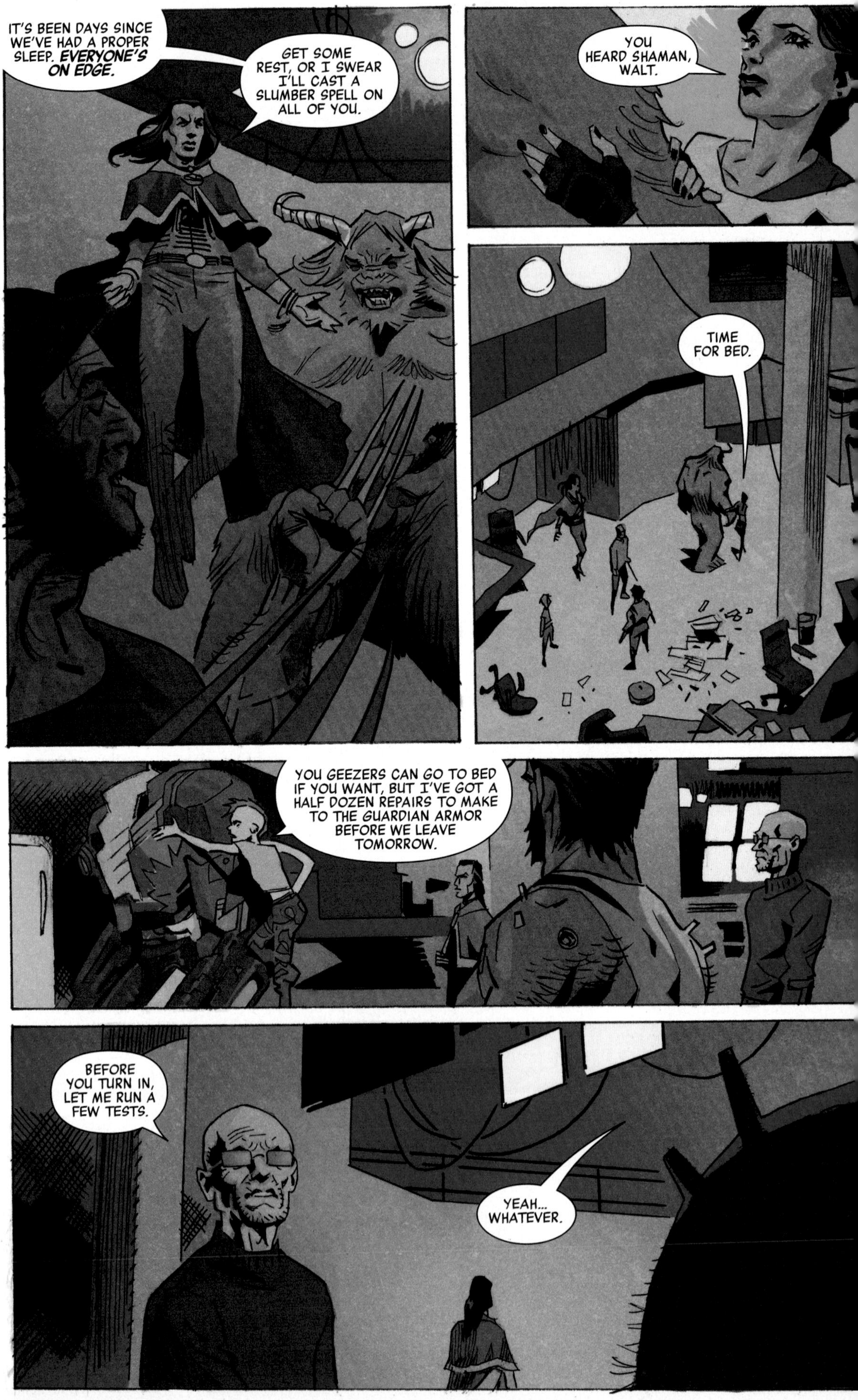
IT'S BEEN DAYS SINCE WE'VE HAD A PROPER SLEEP. **EVERYONE'S ON EDGE.**
GET SOME REST, OR I SWEAR I'LL CAST A SLUMBER SPELL ON ALL OF YOU.
YOU HEARD SHAMAN, WALT.
TIME FOR BED.
YOU GEEZERS CAN GO TO BED IF YOU WANT, BUT I'VE GOT A HALF DOZEN REPAIRS TO MAKE TO THE GUARDIAN ARMOR BEFORE WE LEAVE TOMORROW.
BEFORE YOU TURN IN, LET ME RUN A FEW TESTS.
YEAH... WHATEVER.

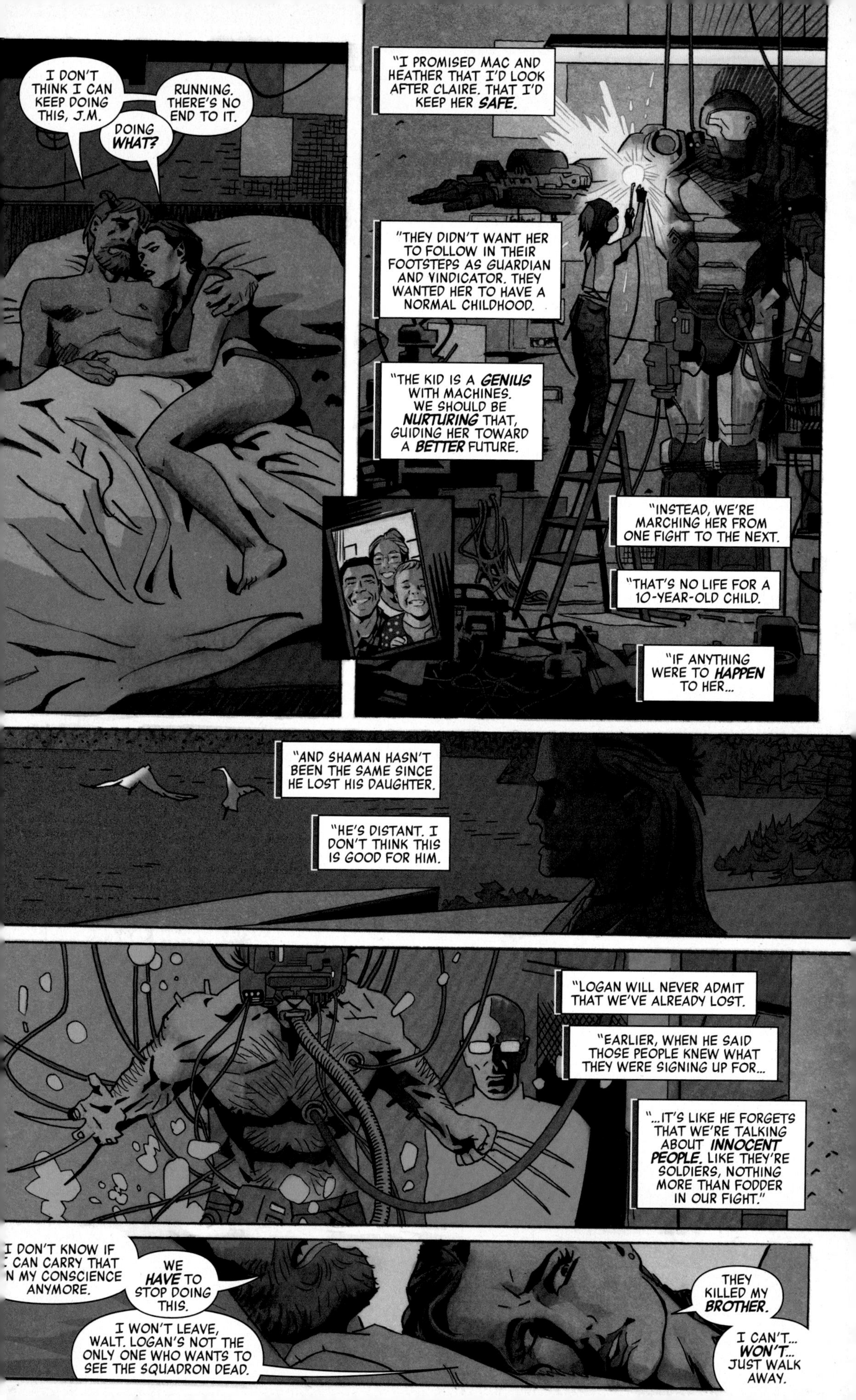
I DON'T THINK I CAN KEEP DOING THIS, J.M.
DOING WHAT?
RUNNING. THERE'S NO END TO IT.
"I PROMISED MAC AND HEATHER THAT I'D LOOK AFTER CLAIRE. THAT I'D KEEP HER SAFE.
"THEY DIDN'T WANT HER TO FOLLOW IN THEIR FOOTSTEPS AS GUARDIAN AND VINDICATOR. THEY WANTED HER TO HAVE A NORMAL CHILDHOOD.
"THE KID IS A GENIUS WITH MACHINES. WE SHOULD BE NURTURING THAT, GUIDING HER TOWARD A BETTER FUTURE.
"INSTEAD, WE'RE MARCHING HER FROM ONE FIGHT TO THE NEXT.
"THAT'S NO LIFE FOR A 10-YEAR-OLD CHILD.
"IF ANYTHING WERE TO HAPPEN TO HER...
"AND SHAMAN HASN'T BEEN THE SAME SINCE HE LOST HIS DAUGHTER.
"HE'S DISTANT. I DON'T THINK THIS IS GOOD FOR HIM.
"LOGAN WILL NEVER ADMIT THAT WE'VE ALREADY LOST.
"EARLIER, WHEN HE SAID THOSE PEOPLE KNEW WHAT THEY WERE SIGNING UP FOR...
"...IT'S LIKE HE FORGETS THAT WE'RE TALKING ABOUT INNOCENT PEOPLE. LIKE THEY'RE SOLDIERS, NOTHING MORE THAN FODDER IN OUR FIGHT."
I DON'T KNOW IF CAN CARRY THAT N MY CONSCIENCE ANYMORE.
WE HAVE TO STOP DOING THIS.
I WON'T LEAVE, WALT. LOGAN'S NOT THE ONLY ONE WHO WANTS TO SEE THE SQUADRON DEAD.
THEY KILLED MY BROTHER.
I CAN'T... WON'T... JUST WALK AWAY.

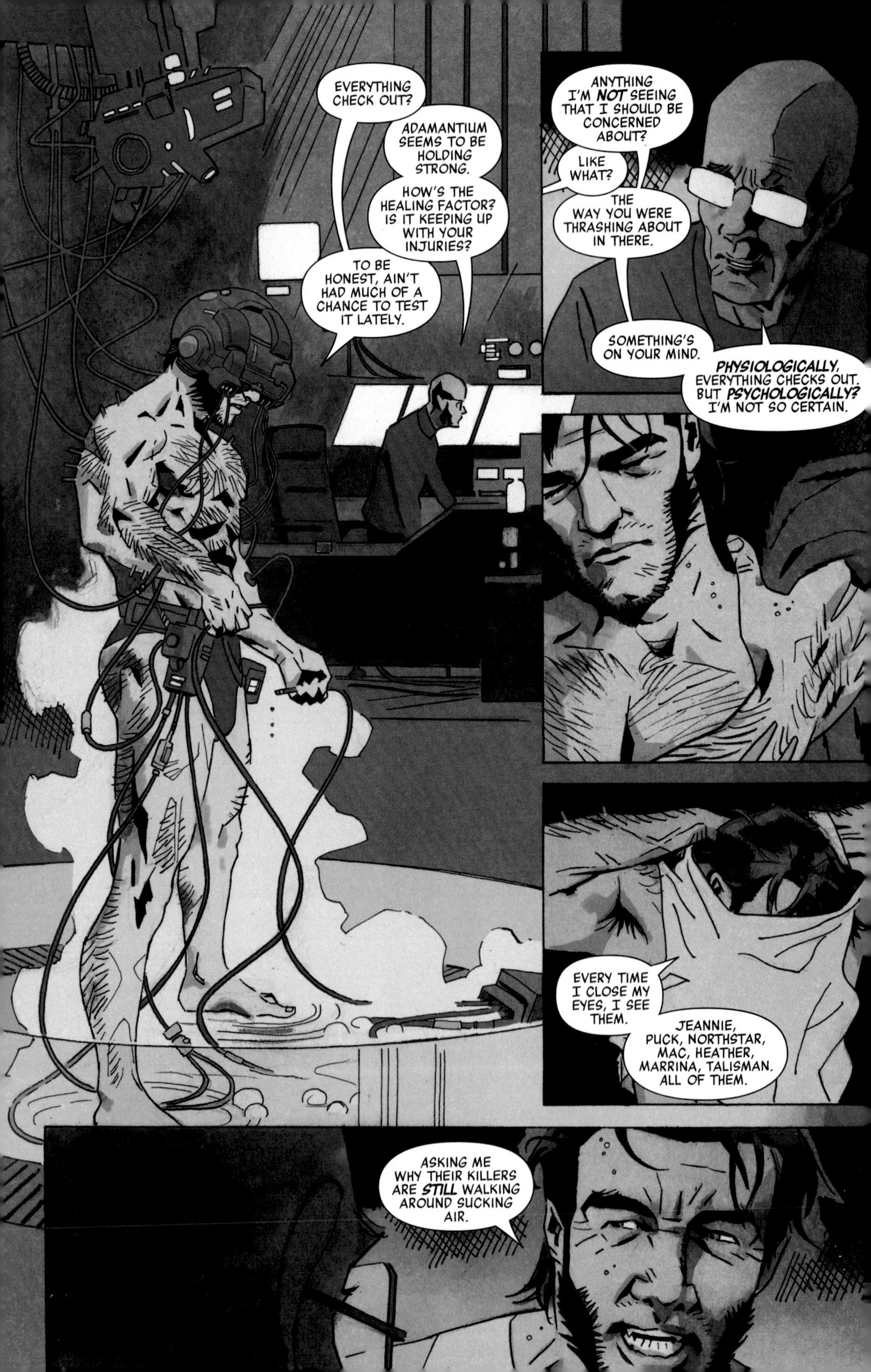
EVERYTHING CHECK OUT?
ADAMANTIUM SEEMS TO BE HOLDING STRONG.
HOW'S THE HEALING FACTOR? IS IT KEEPING UP WITH YOUR INJURIES?
TO BE HONEST, AIN'T HAD MUCH OF A CHANCE TO TEST IT LATELY.
ANYTHING I'M NOT SEEING THAT I SHOULD BE CONCERNED ABOUT?
LIKE WHAT?
THE WAY YOU WERE THRASHING ABOUT IN THERE.
SOMETHING'S ON YOUR MIND.
PHYSIOLOGICALLY, EVERYTHING CHECKS OUT. BUT PSYCHOLOGICALLY? I'M NOT SO CERTAIN.
EVERY TIME I CLOSE MY EYES, I SEE THEM.
JEANNIE, PUCK, NORTHSTAR, MAC, HEATHER, MARRINA, TALISMAN. ALL OF THEM.
ASKING ME WHY THEIR KILLERS ARE STILL WALKING AROUND SUCKING AIR.

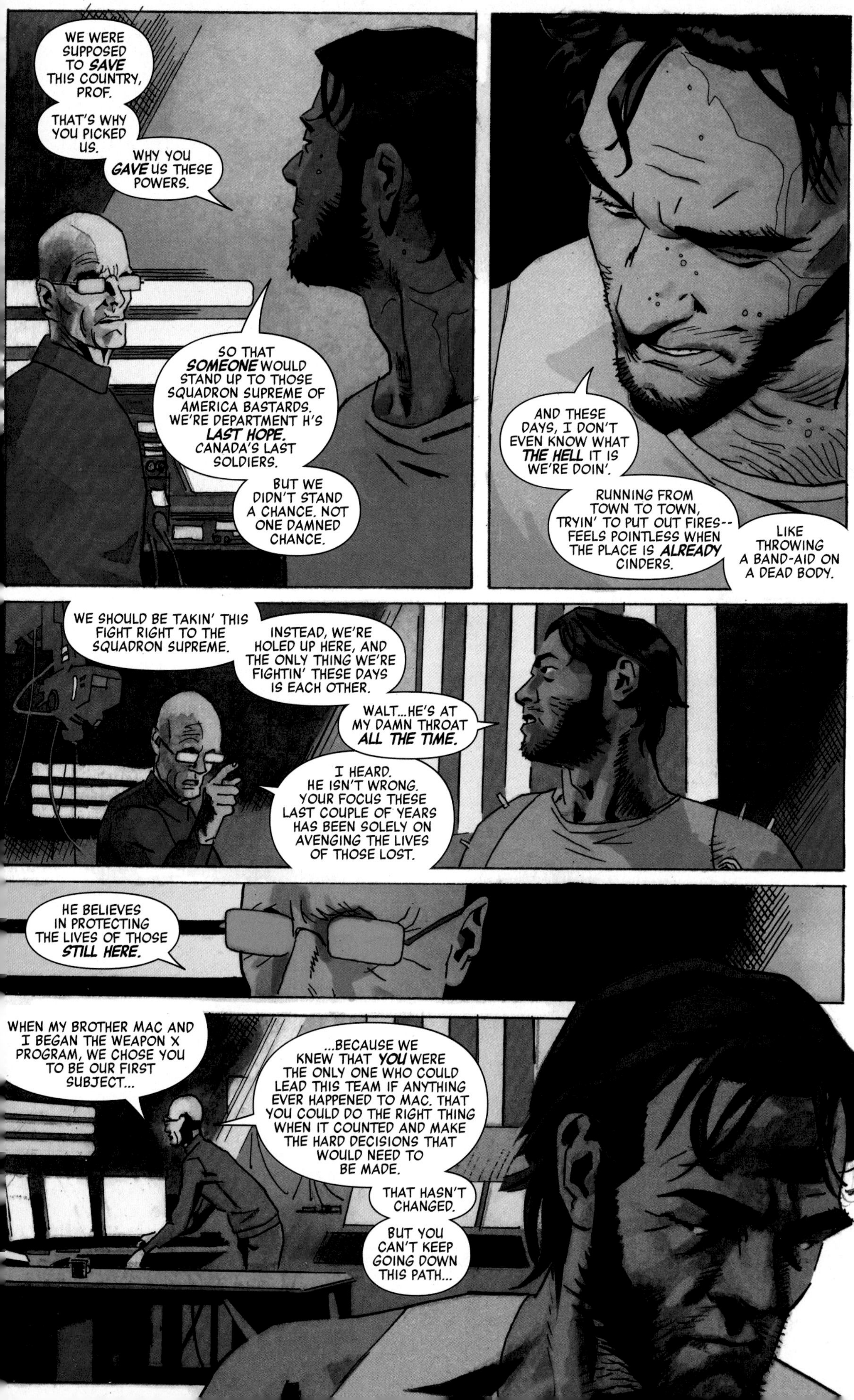

WE WERE SUPPOSED TO SAVE THIS COUNTRY, PROF.
THAT'S WHY YOU PICKED US.
WHY YOU GAVE US THESE POWERS.
SO THAT SOMEONE WOULD STAND UP TO THOSE SQUADRON SUPREME OF AMERICA BASTARDS. WE'RE DEPARTMENT H'S LAST HOPE. CANADA'S LAST SOLDIERS.
BUT WE DIDN'T STAND A CHANCE. NOT ONE DAMNED CHANCE.
AND THESE DAYS, I DON'T EVEN KNOW WHAT THE HELL IT IS WE'RE DOIN'.
RUNNING FROM TOWN TO TOWN, TRYIN' TO PUT OUT FIRES-- FEELS POINTLESS WHEN THE PLACE IS ALREADY CINDERS.
LIKE THROWING A BAND-AID ON A DEAD BODY.
WE SHOULD BE TAKIN' THIS FIGHT RIGHT TO THE SQUADRON SUPREME.
INSTEAD, WE'RE HOLED UP HERE, AND THE ONLY THING WE'RE FIGHTIN' THESE DAYS IS EACH OTHER.
WALT...HE'S AT MY DAMN THROAT ALL THE TIME.
I HEARD. HE ISN'T WRONG. YOUR FOCUS THESE LAST COUPLE OF YEARS HAS BEEN SOLELY ON AVENGING THE LIVES OF THOSE LOST.
HE BELIEVES IN PROTECTING THE LIVES OF THOSE STILL HERE.
WHEN MY BROTHER MAC AND I BEGAN THE WEAPON X PROGRAM, WE CHOSE YOU TO BE OUR FIRST SUBJECT...
...BECAUSE WE KNEW THAT YOU WERE THE ONLY ONE WHO COULD LEAD THIS TEAM IF ANYTHING EVER HAPPENED TO MAC. THAT YOU COULD DO THE RIGHT THING WHEN IT COUNTED AND MAKE THE HARD DECISIONS THAT WOULD NEED TO BE MADE.
THAT HASN'T CHANGED.
BUT YOU CAN'T KEEP GOING DOWN THIS PATH...

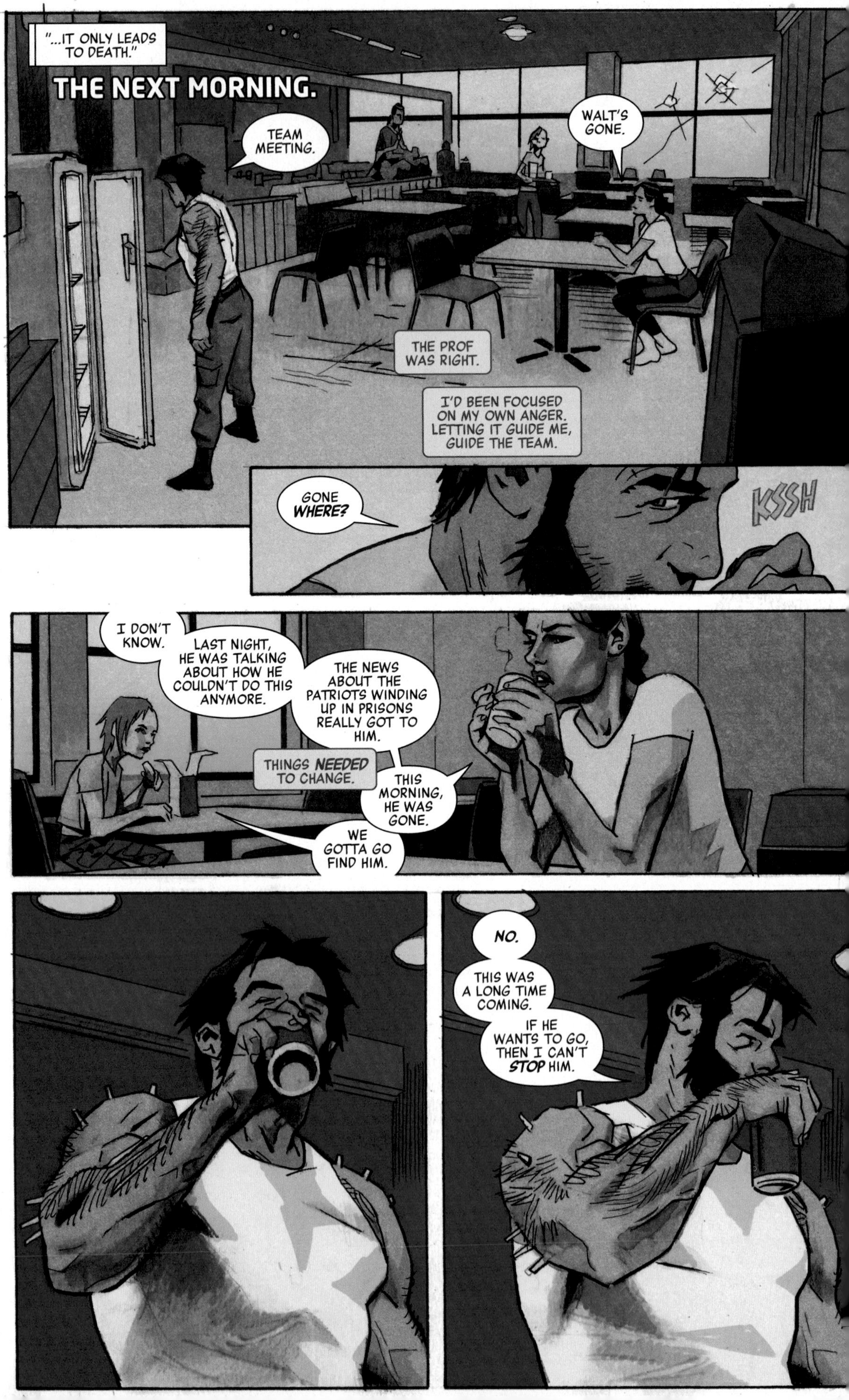
"...IT ONLY LEADS TO DEATH."
THE NEXT MORNING.
TEAM MEETING.
WALT'S GONE.
THE PROF WAS RIGHT.
I'D BEEN FOCUSED ON MY OWN ANGER. LETTING IT GUIDE ME, GUIDE THE TEAM.
GONE WHERE?
KSSH
I DON'T KNOW.
LAST NIGHT, HE WAS TALKING ABOUT HOW HE COULDN'T DO THIS ANYMORE.
THE NEWS ABOUT THE PATRIOTS WINDING UP IN PRISONS REALLY GOT TO HIM.
THINGS NEEDED TO CHANGE.
THIS MORNING, HE WAS GONE.
WE GOTTA GO FIND HIM.
NO.
THIS WAS A LONG TIME COMING.
IF HE WANTS TO GO, THEN I CAN'T STOP HIM.

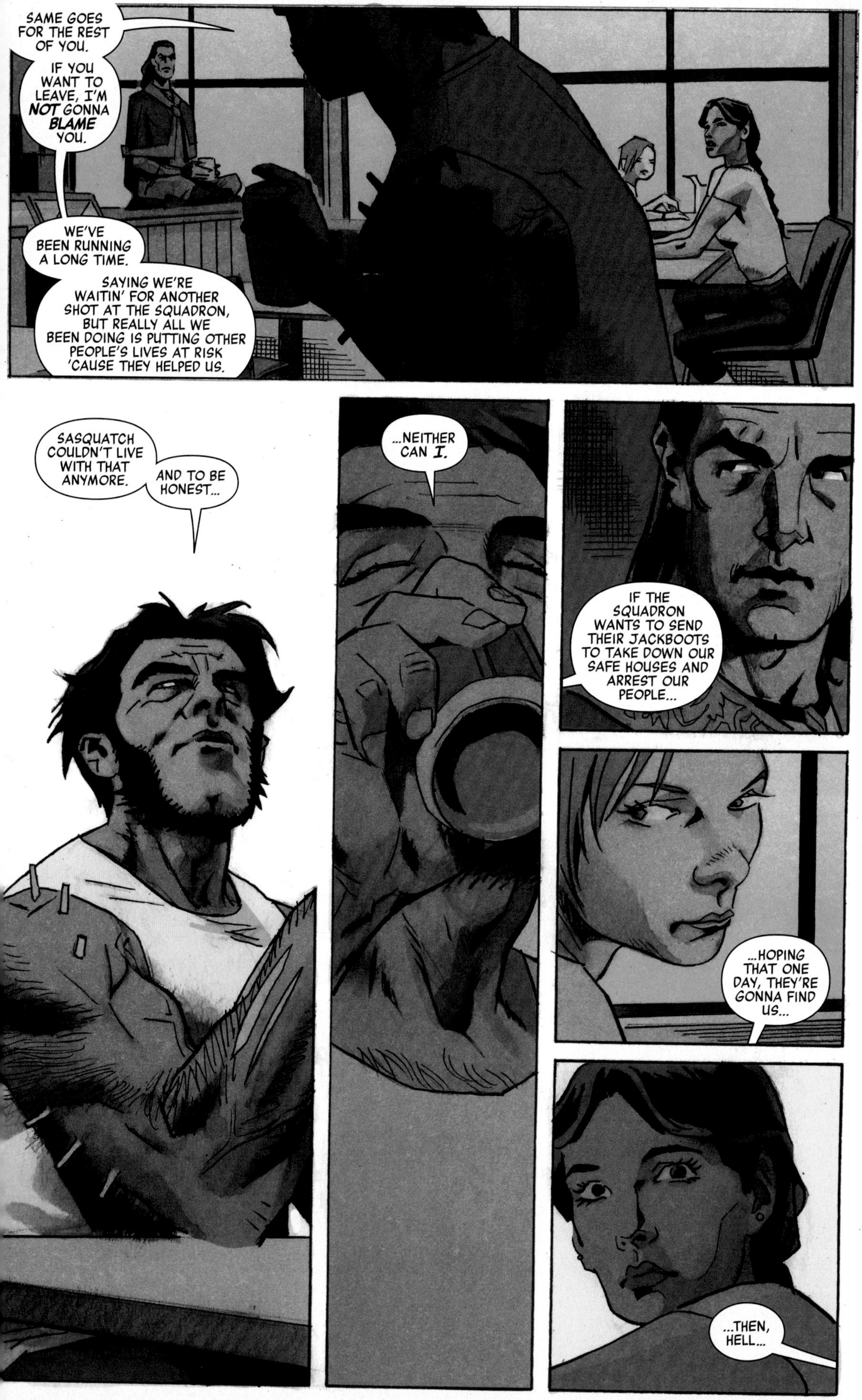
SAME GOES FOR THE REST OF YOU.
IF YOU WANT TO LEAVE, I'M NOT GONNA BLAME YOU.
WE'VE BEEN RUNNING A LONG TIME.
SAYING WE'RE WAITIN' FOR ANOTHER SHOT AT THE SQUADRON, BUT REALLY ALL WE BEEN DOING IS PUTTING OTHER PEOPLE'S LIVES AT RISK 'CAUSE THEY HELPED US.
SASQUATCH COULDN'T LIVE WITH THAT ANYMORE.
AND TO BE HONEST...
...NEITHER CAN I.
IF THE SQUADRON WANTS TO SEND THEIR JACKBOOTS TO TAKE DOWN OUR SAFE HOUSES AND ARREST OUR PEOPLE...
...HOPING THAT ONE DAY, THEY'RE GONNA FIND US...
...THEN, HELL...

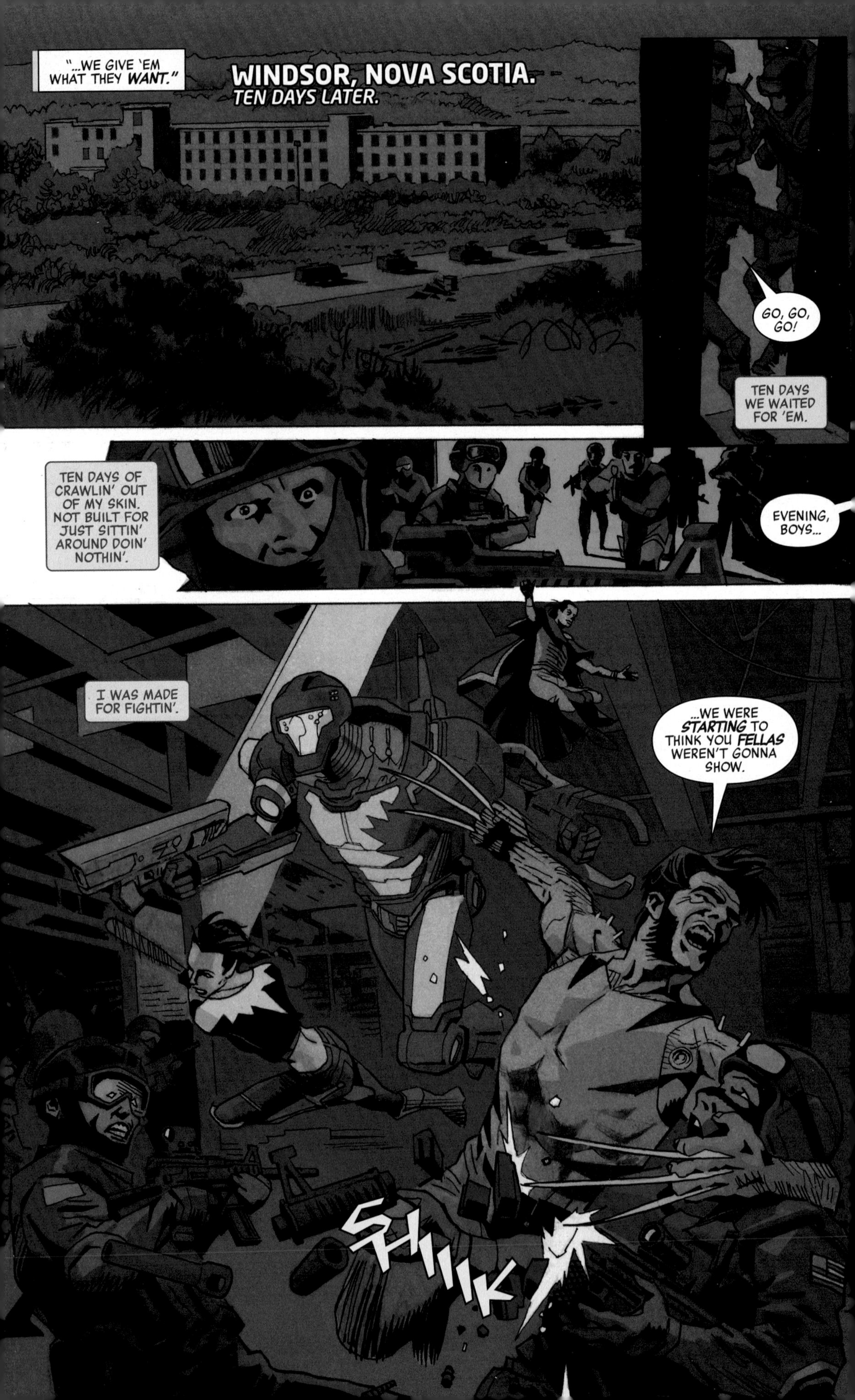
"...WE GIVE 'EM WHAT THEY WANT."
WINDSOR, NOVA SCOTIA.
TEN DAYS LATER.
GO, GO, GO!
TEN DAYS WE WAITED FOR 'EM.
TEN DAYS OF CRAWLIN' OUT OF MY SKIN. NOT BUILT FOR JUST SITTIN' AROUND DOIN' NOTHIN'.
EVENING, BOYS...
I WAS MADE FOR FIGHTIN'.
...WE WERE STARTING TO THINK YOU FELLAS WEREN'T GONNA SHOW.
SHIIIK

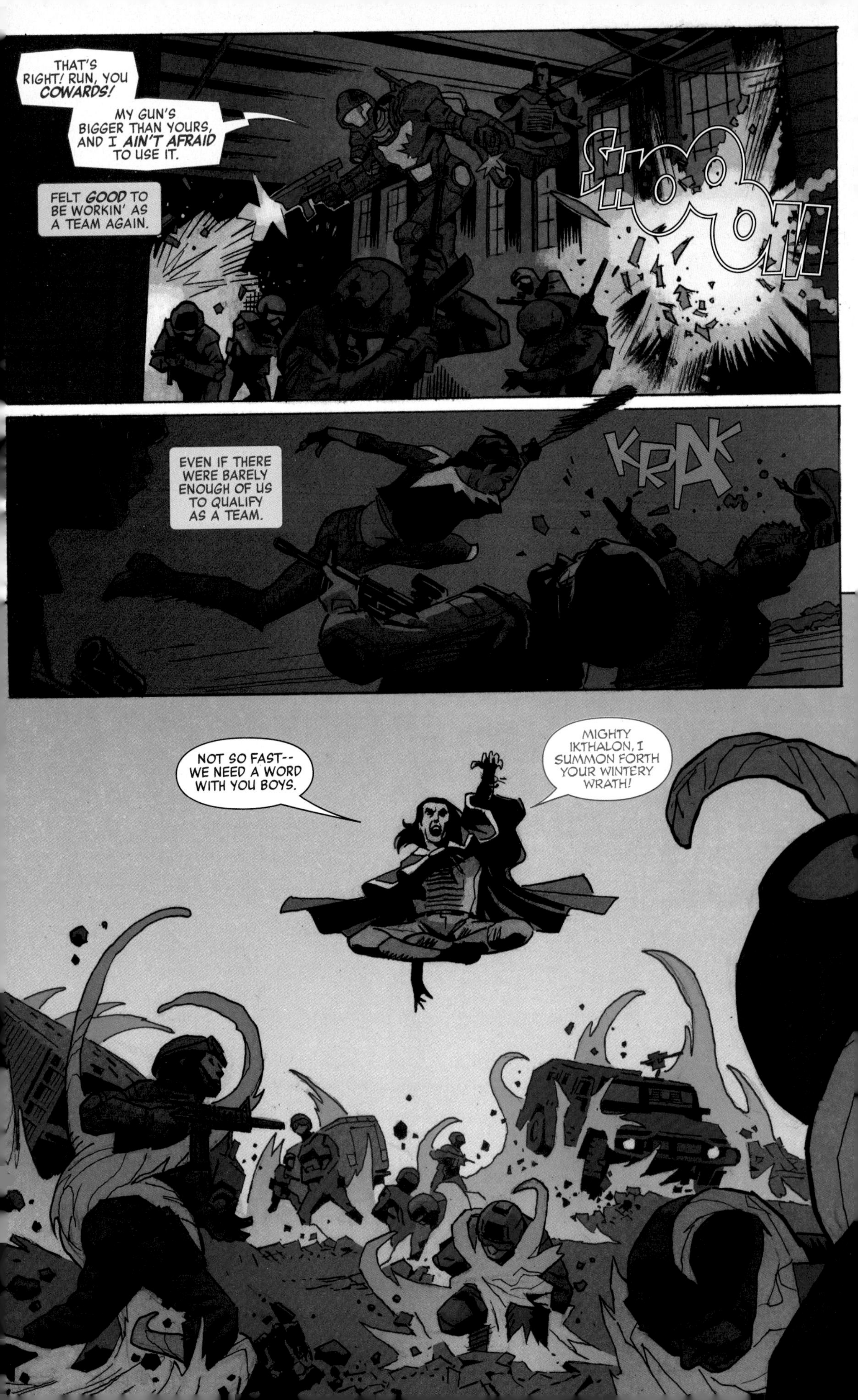
THAT'S RIGHT! RUN, YOU COWARDS!
MY GUN'S BIGGER THAN YOURS, AND I AIN'T AFRAID TO USE IT.
FELT GOOD TO BE WORKIN' AS A TEAM AGAIN.
SHOOOM!
EVEN IF THERE WERE BARELY ENOUGH OF US TO QUALIFY AS A TEAM.
KRAK
NOT SO FAST-- WE NEED A WORD WITH YOU BOYS.
MIGHTY IKTHALON, I SUMMON FORTH YOUR WINTERY WRATH!

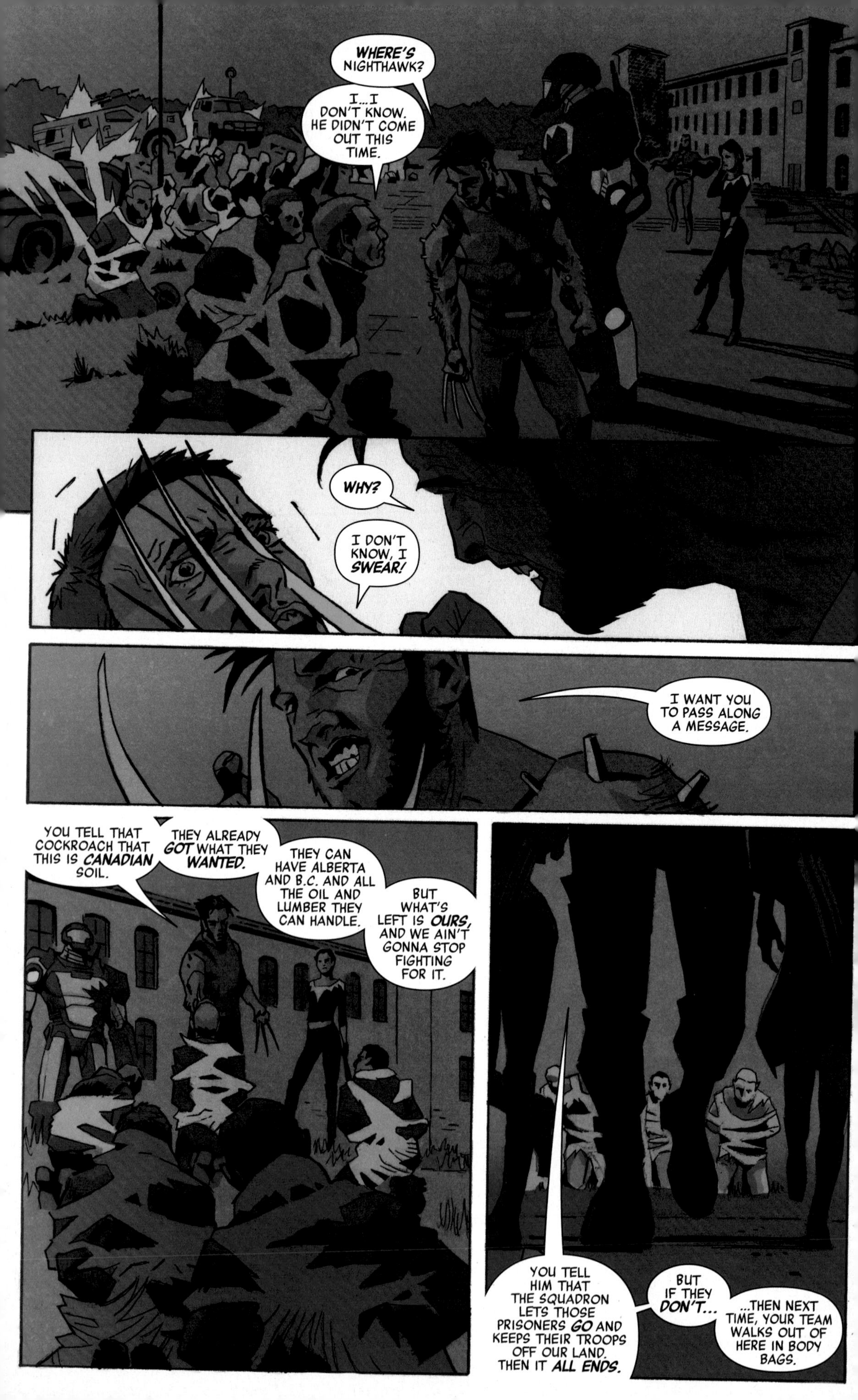
WHERE'S NIGHTHAWK?
I...I DON'T KNOW. HE DIDN'T COME OUT THIS TIME.
WHY?
I DON'T KNOW, I SWEAR!
I WANT YOU TO PASS ALONG A MESSAGE.
YOU TELL THAT COCKROACH THAT THIS IS CANADIAN SOIL.
THEY ALREADY GOT WHAT THEY WANTED.
THEY CAN HAVE ALBERTA AND B.C. AND ALL THE OIL AND LUMBER THEY CAN HANDLE.
BUT WHAT'S LEFT IS OURS, AND WE AIN'T GONNA STOP FIGHTING FOR IT.
YOU TELL HIM THAT THE SQUADRON LETS THOSE PRISONERS GO AND KEEPS THEIR TROOPS OFF OUR LAND. THEN IT ALL ENDS.
BUT IF THEY DON'T...
...THEN NEXT TIME, YOUR TEAM WALKS OUT OF HERE IN BODY BAGS.

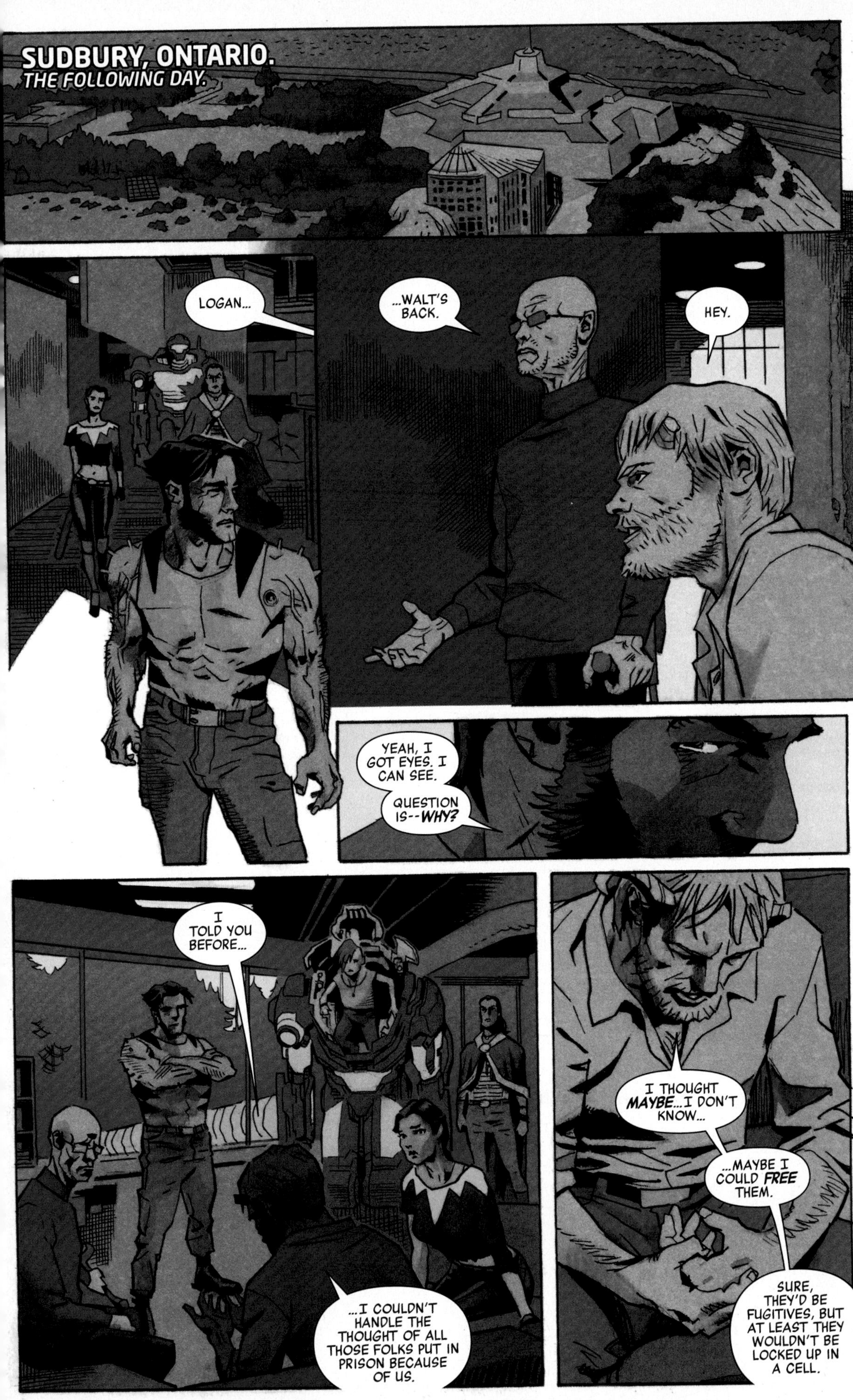

SUDBURY, ONTARIO.
THE FOLLOWING DAY.
LOGAN...
...WALT'S BACK.
HEY.
YEAH, I GOT EYES. I CAN SEE.
QUESTION IS--WHY?
I TOLD YOU BEFORE...
...I COULDN'T HANDLE THE THOUGHT OF ALL THOSE FOLKS PUT IN PRISON BECAUSE OF US.
I THOUGHT MAYBE...I DON'T KNOW...
...MAYBE I COULD FREE THEM.
SURE, THEY'D BE FUGITIVES, BUT AT LEAST THEY WOULDN'T BE LOCKED UP IN A CELL.

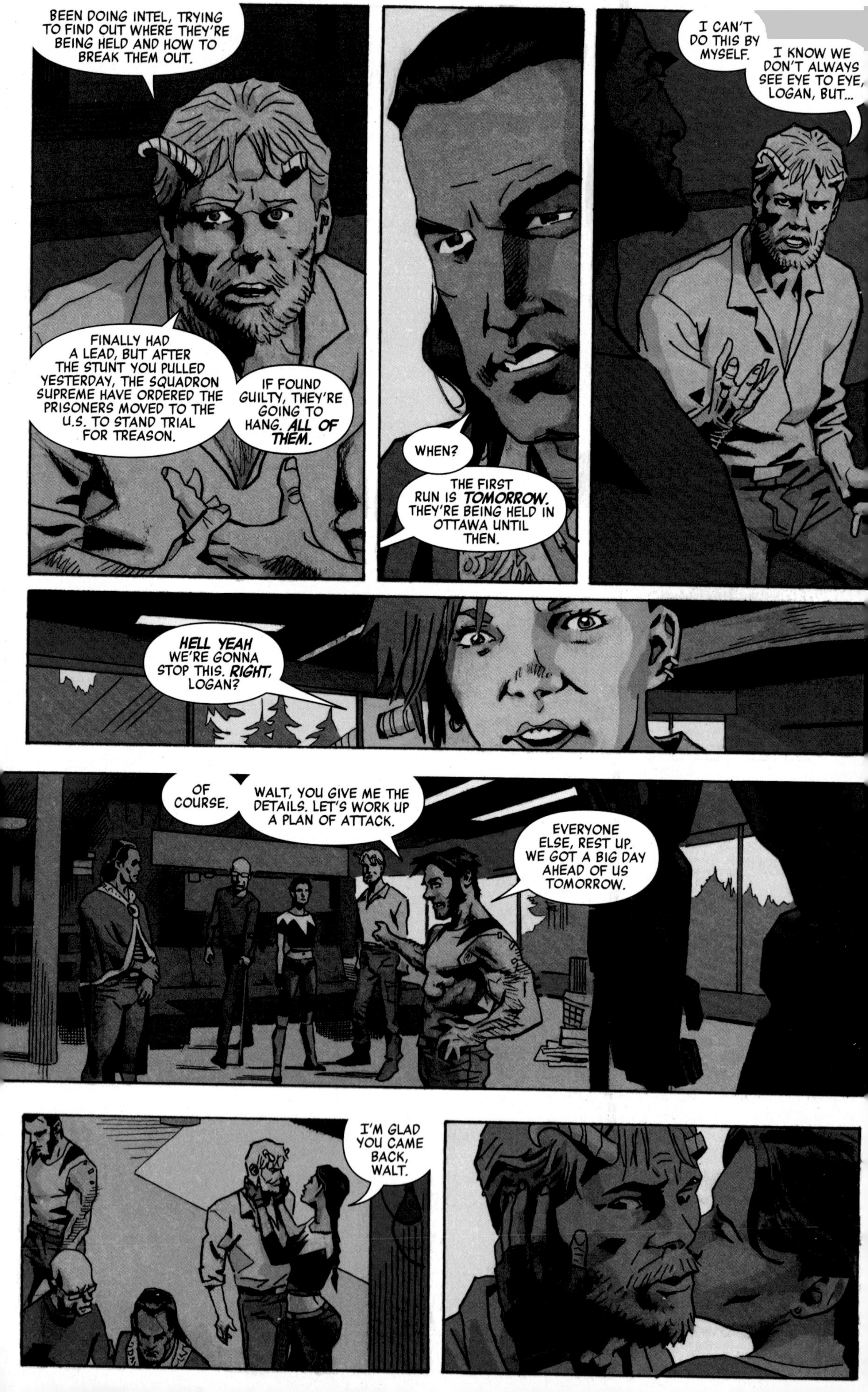
BEEN DOING INTEL, TRYING TO FIND OUT WHERE THEY'RE BEING HELD AND HOW TO BREAK THEM OUT.
FINALLY HAD A LEAD, BUT AFTER THE STUNT YOU PULLED YESTERDAY, THE SQUADRON SUPREME HAVE ORDERED THE PRISONERS MOVED TO THE U.S. TO STAND TRIAL FOR TREASON.
IF FOUND GUILTY, THEY'RE GOING TO HANG. ALL OF THEM.
WHEN?
THE FIRST RUN IS TOMORROW. THEY'RE BEING HELD IN OTTAWA UNTIL THEN.
I CAN'T DO THIS BY MYSELF.
I KNOW WE DON'T ALWAYS SEE EYE TO EYE, LOGAN, BUT...
HELL YEAH WE'RE GONNA STOP THIS. RIGHT, LOGAN?
OF COURSE.
WALT, YOU GIVE ME THE DETAILS. LET'S WORK UP A PLAN OF ATTACK.
EVERYONE ELSE, REST UP. WE GOT A BIG DAY AHEAD OF US TOMORROW.
I'M GLAD YOU CAME BACK, WALT.

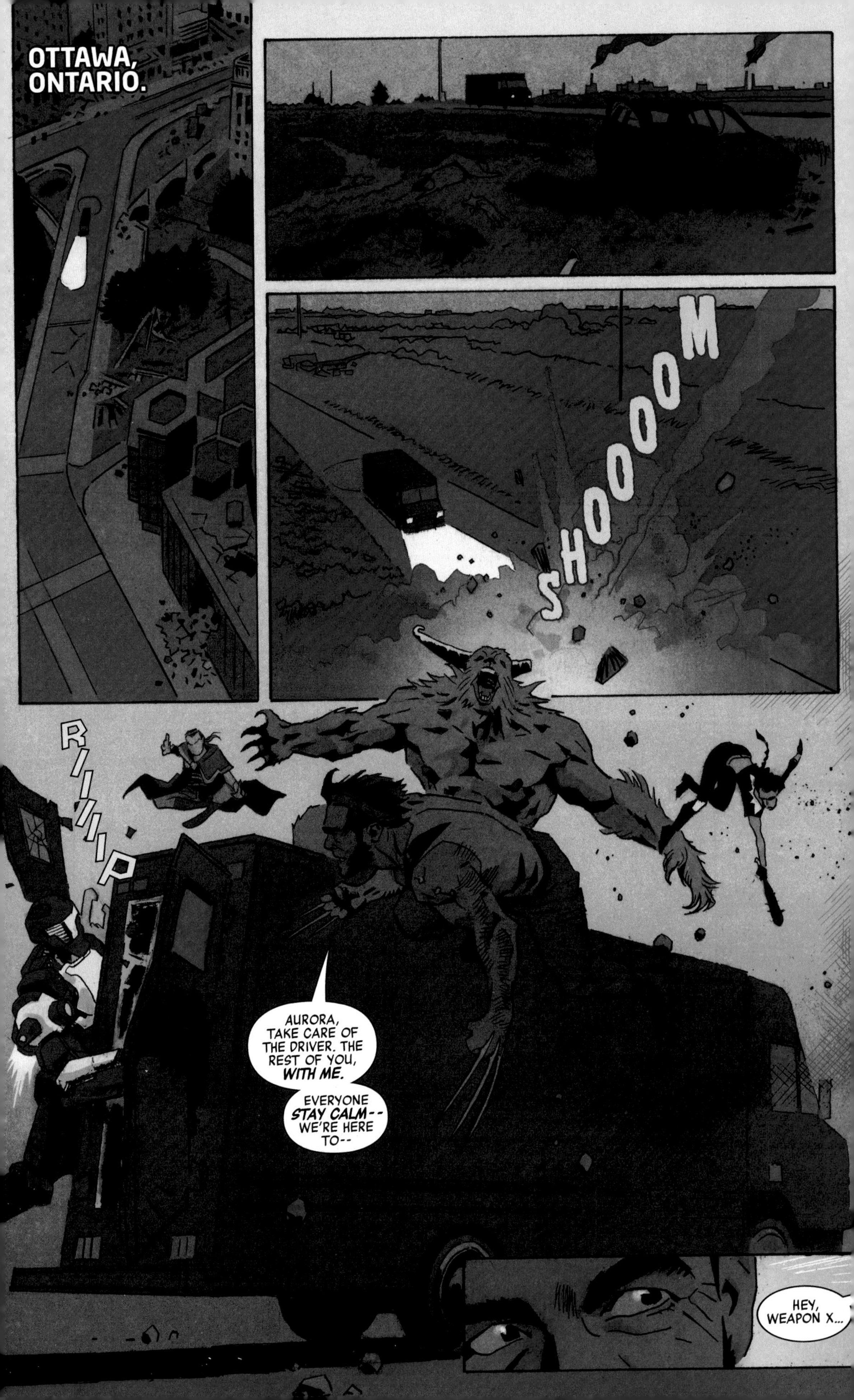
OTTAWA, ONTARIO.
SHOOOOM
RIIIIIP
AURORA, TAKE CARE OF THE DRIVER. THE REST OF YOU, WITH ME.
EVERYONE STAY CALM-- WE'RE HERE TO--
HEY, WEAPON X...

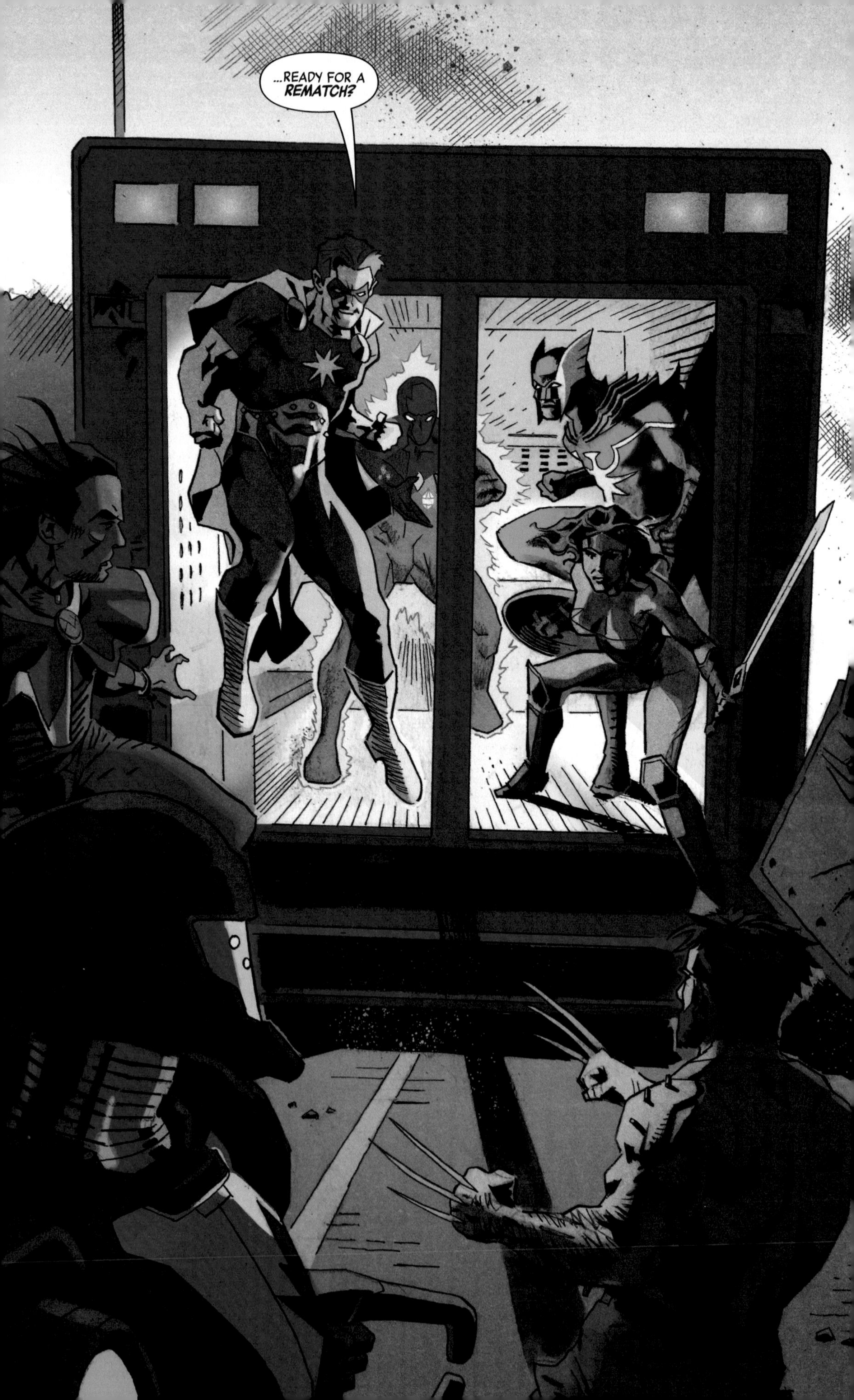
...READY FOR A REMATCH?

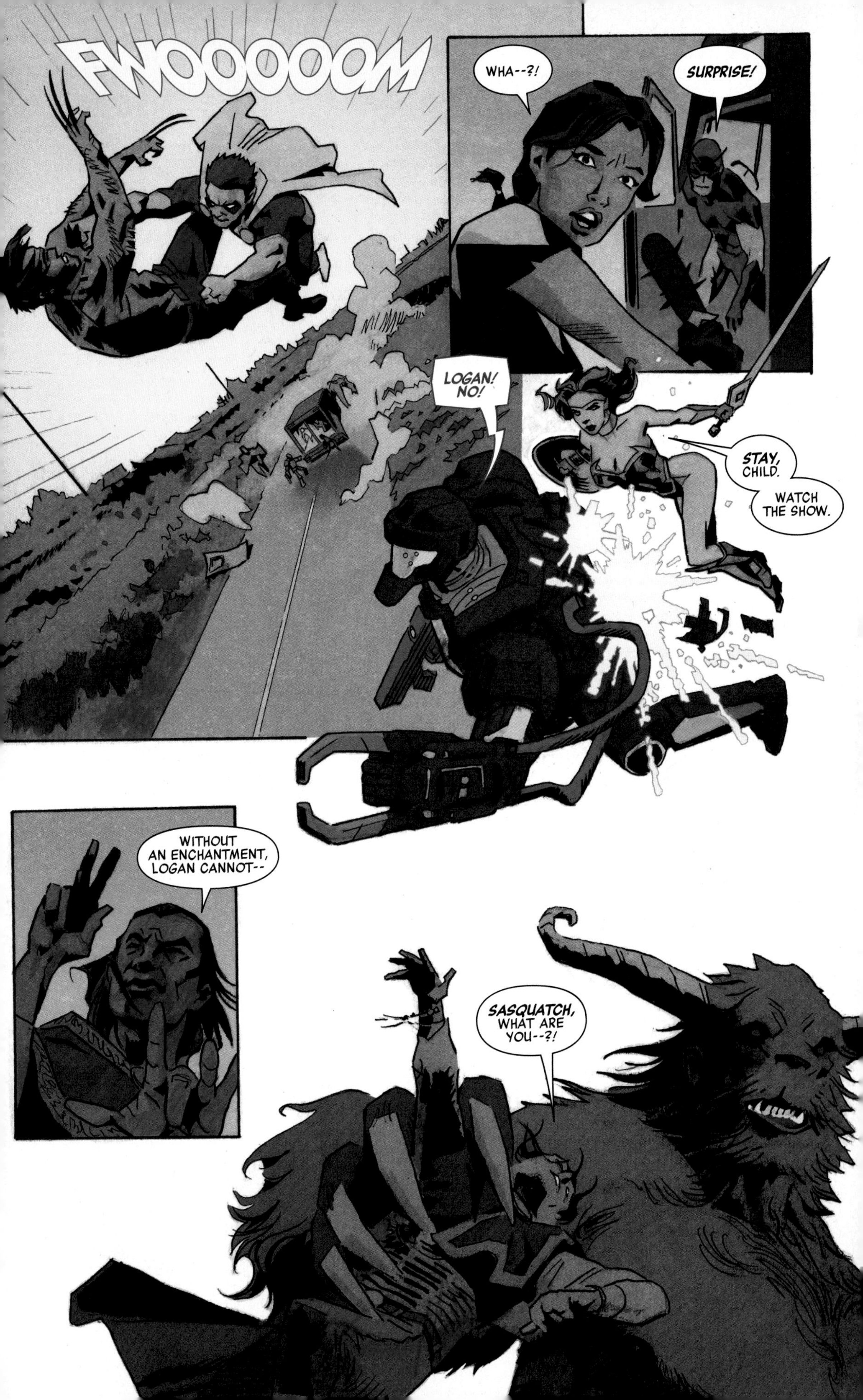
FWOOOOOM
WHA--?!
SURPRISE!
LOGAN! NO!
STAY, CHILD.
WATCH THE SHOW.
WITHOUT AN ENCHANTMENT, LOGAN CANNOT--
SASQUATCH, WHAT ARE YOU--?!

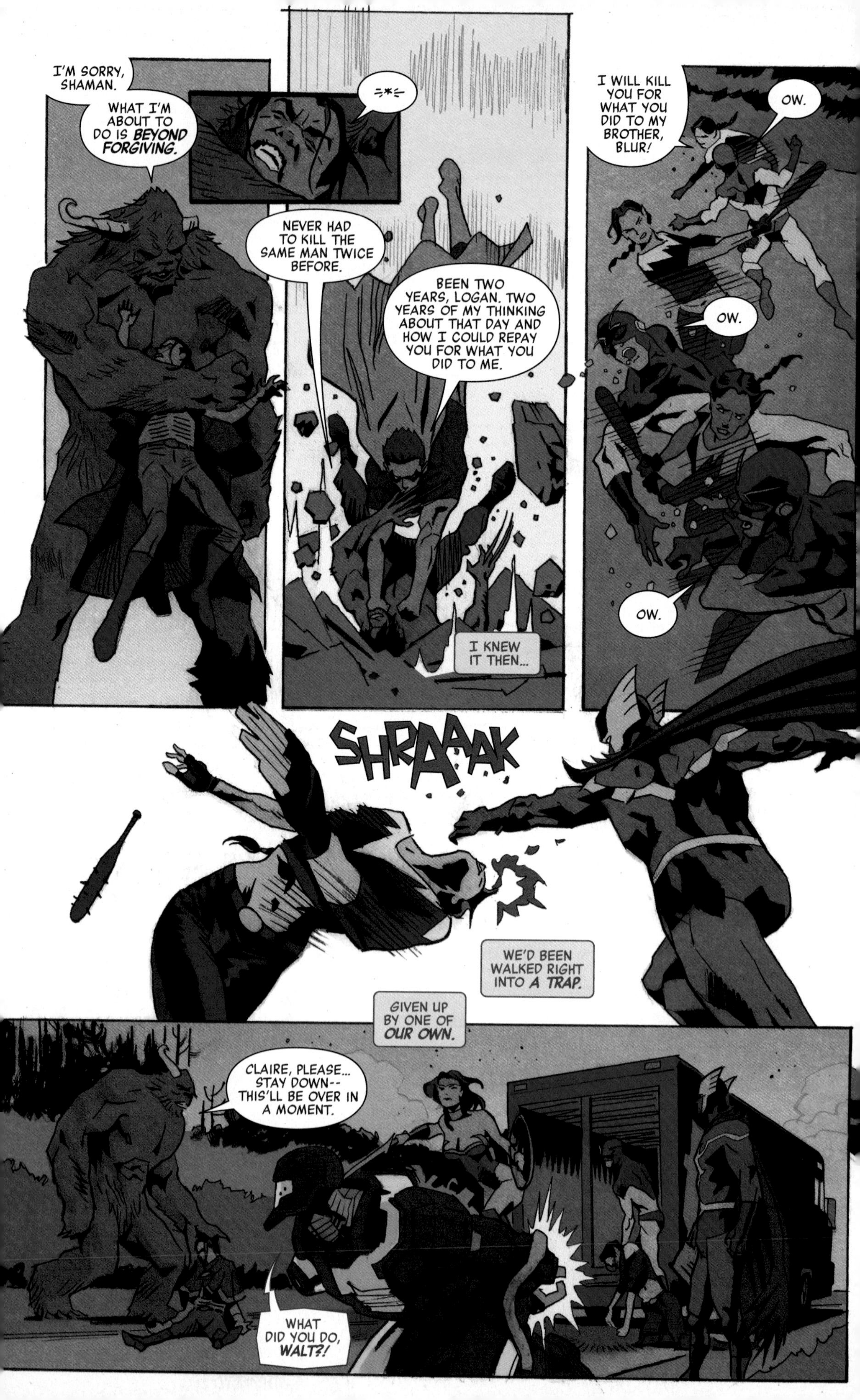
I'M SORRY, SHAMAN.
WHAT I'M ABOUT TO DO IS BEYOND FORGIVING.
=*=
NEVER HAD TO KILL THE SAME MAN TWICE BEFORE.
BEEN TWO YEARS, LOGAN. TWO YEARS OF MY THINKING ABOUT THAT DAY AND HOW I COULD REPAY YOU FOR WHAT YOU DID TO ME.
I KNEW IT THEN...
I WILL KILL YOU FOR WHAT YOU DID TO MY BROTHER, BLUR!
OW.
OW.
OW.
SHRAAAK
WE'D BEEN WALKED RIGHT INTO A TRAP.
GIVEN UP BY ONE OF OUR OWN.
CLAIRE, PLEASE... STAY DOWN-- THIS'LL BE OVER IN A MOMENT.
WHAT DID YOU DO, WALT?!

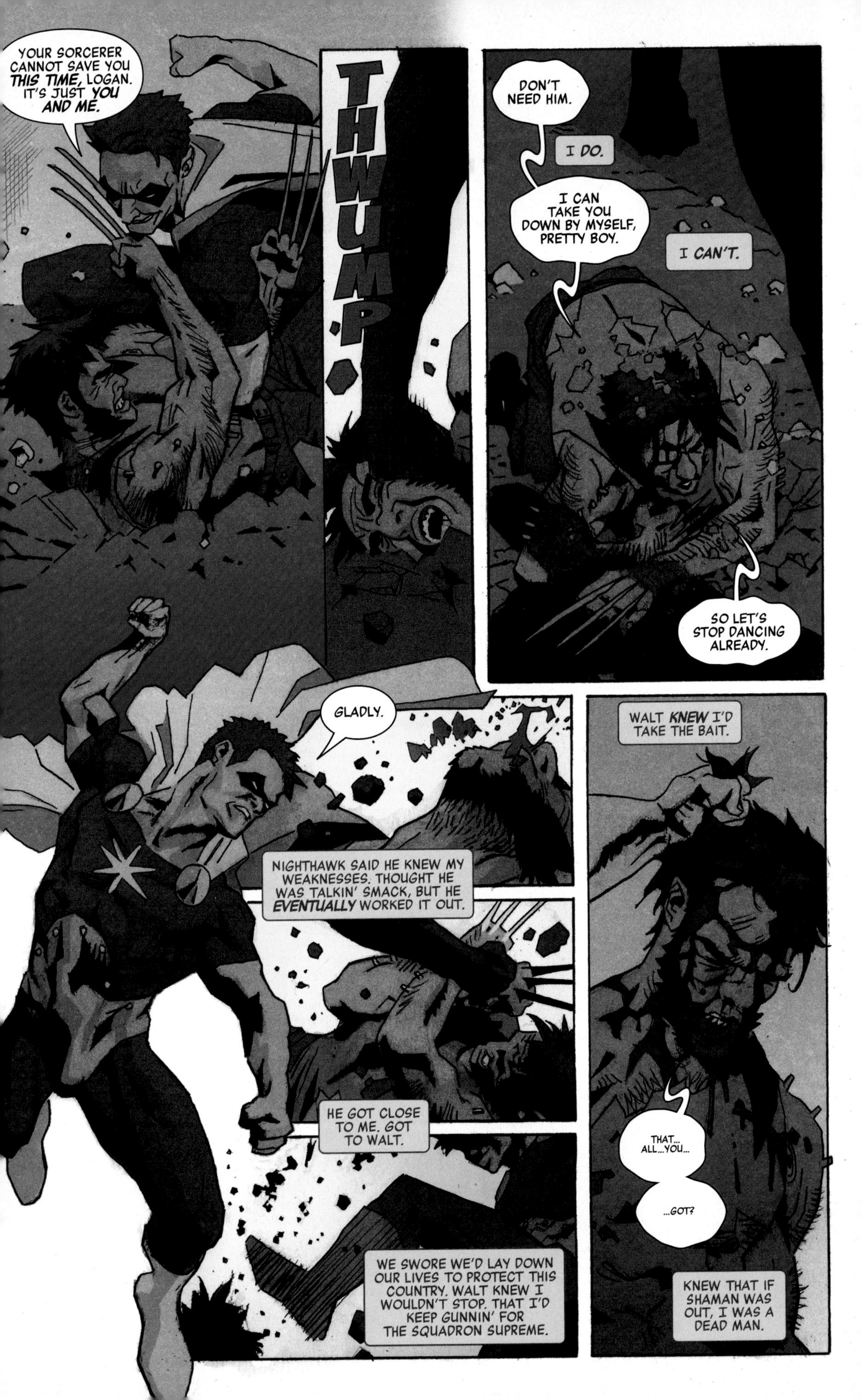
YOUR SORCERER CANNOT SAVE YOU THIS TIME, LOGAN. IT'S JUST YOU AND ME.
THWUMP
DON'T NEED HIM.
I DO.
I CAN TAKE YOU DOWN BY MYSELF, PRETTY BOY.
I CAN'T.
SO LET'S STOP DANCING ALREADY.
GLADLY.
NIGHTHAWK SAID HE KNEW MY WEAKNESSES. THOUGHT HE WAS TALKIN' SMACK, BUT HE EVENTUALLY WORKED IT OUT.
HE GOT CLOSE TO ME. GOT TO WALT.
WE SWORE WE'D LAY DOWN OUR LIVES TO PROTECT THIS COUNTRY. WALT KNEW I WOULDN'T STOP. THAT I'D KEEP GUNNIN' FOR THE SQUADRON SUPREME.
WALT KNEW I'D TAKE THE BAIT.
THAT... ALL...YOU...
...GOT?
KNEW THAT IF SHAMAN WAS OUT, I WAS A DEAD MAN.

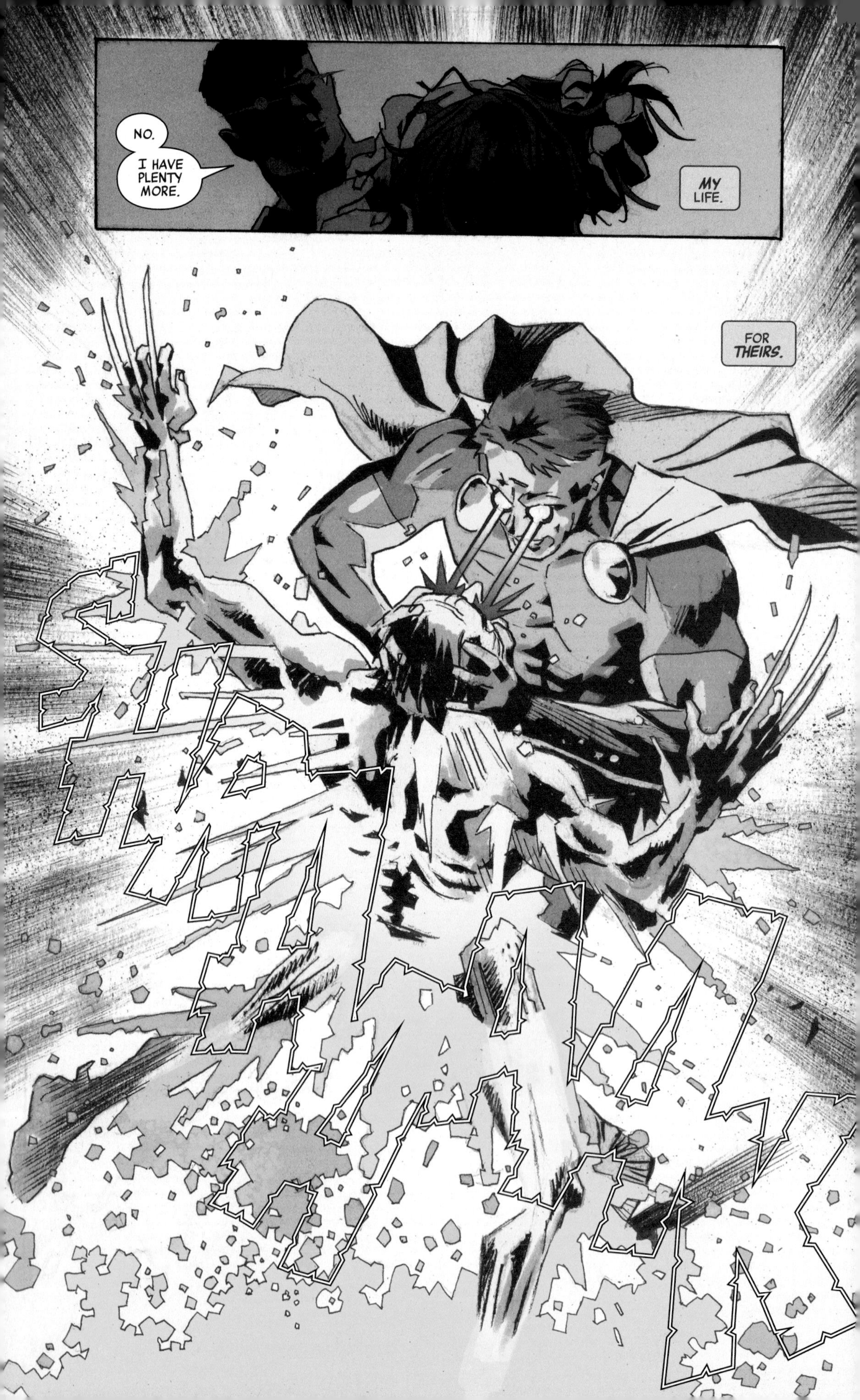
NO.
I HAVE PLENTY MORE.
MY LIFE.
FOR THEIRS.

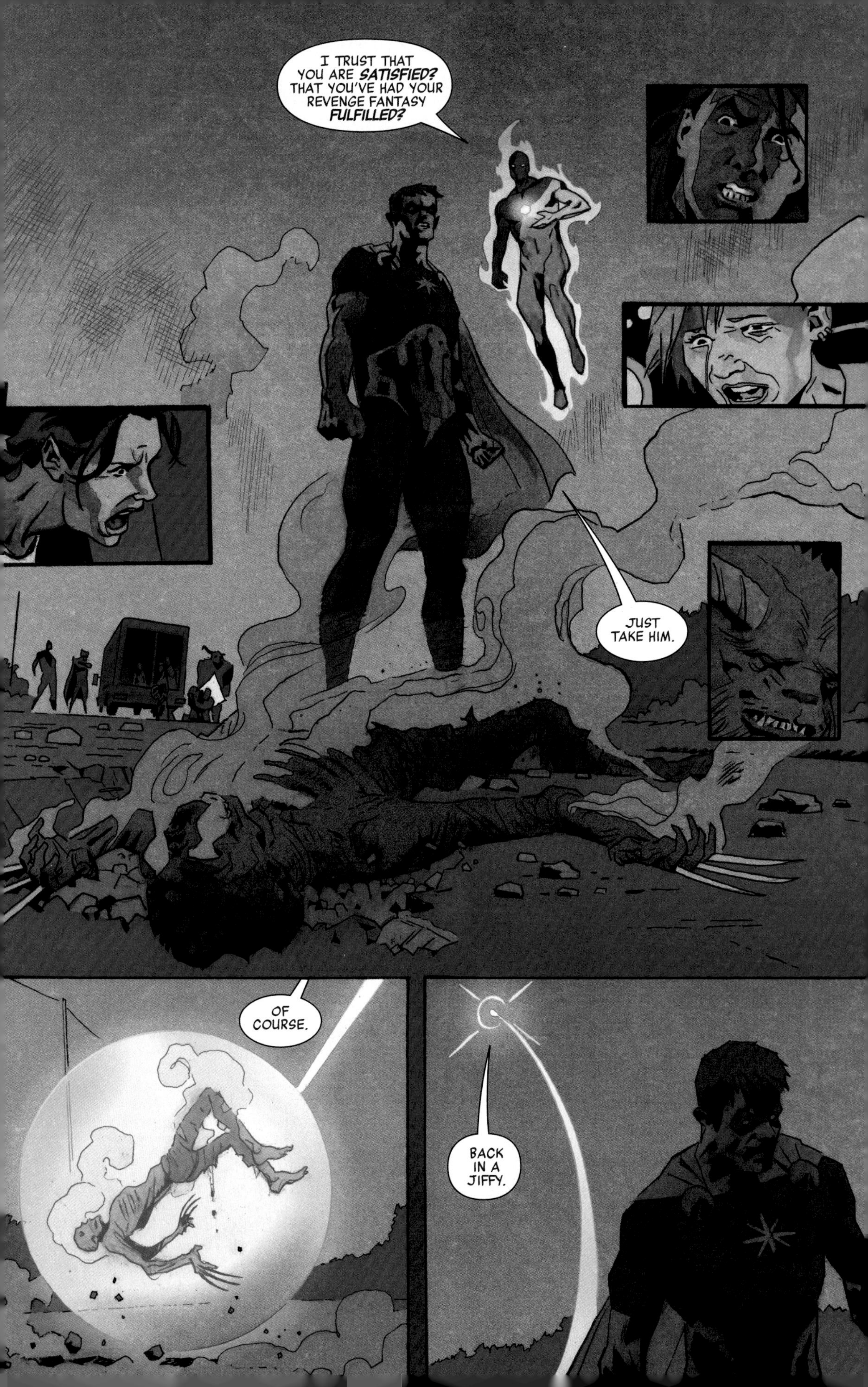
I TRUST THAT YOU ARE SATISFIED? THAT YOU'VE HAD YOUR REVENGE FANTASY FULFILLED?
JUST TAKE HIM.
OF COURSE.
BACK IN A JIFFY.

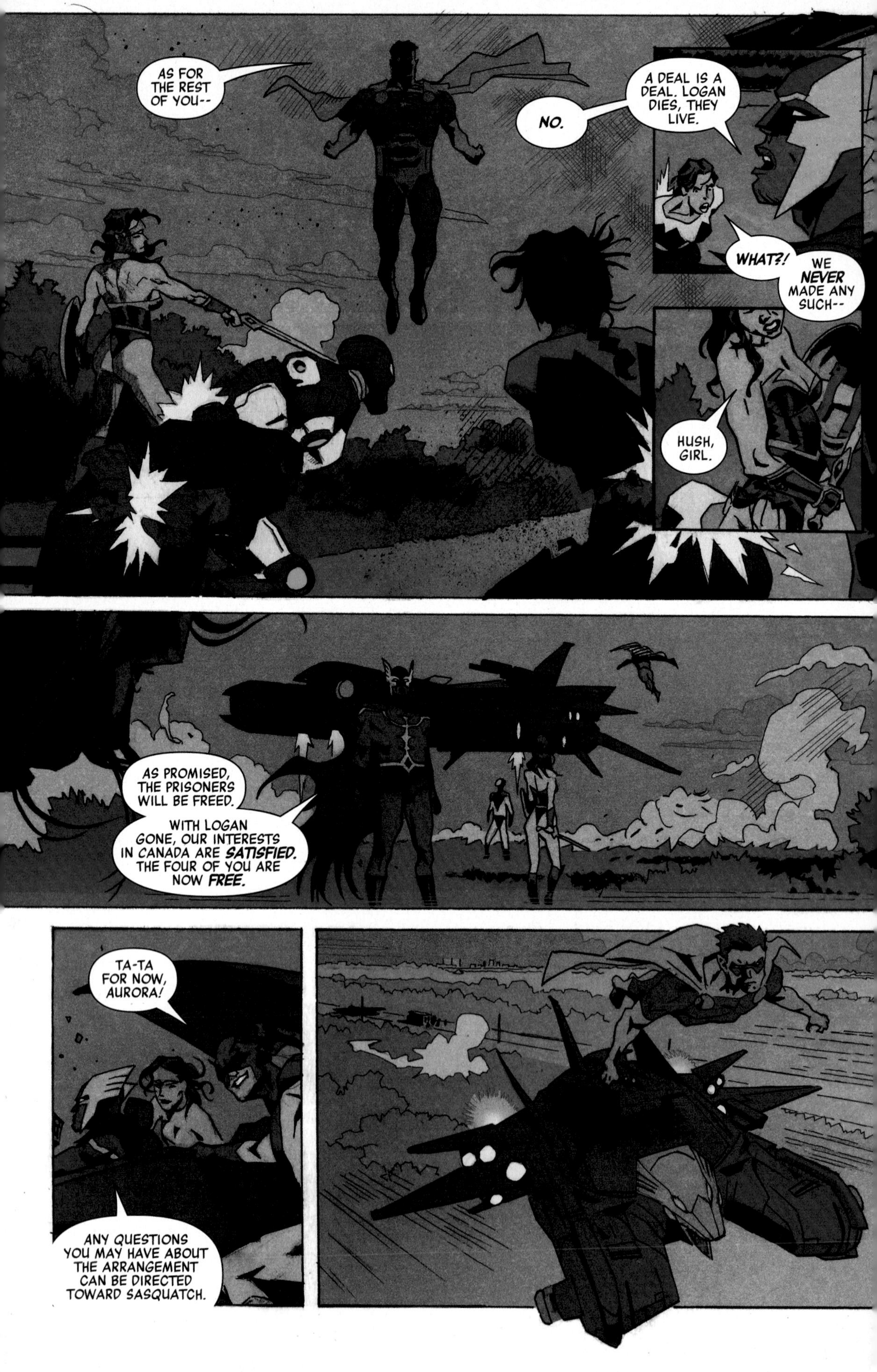
AS FOR THE REST OF YOU--
NO.
A DEAL IS A DEAL. LOGAN DIES, THEY LIVE.
WHAT?!
WE NEVER MADE ANY SUCH--
HUSH, GIRL.
AS PROMISED, THE PRISONERS WILL BE FREED.
WITH LOGAN GONE, OUR INTERESTS IN CANADA ARE SATISFIED. THE FOUR OF YOU ARE NOW FREE.
TA-TA FOR NOW, AURORA!
ANY QUESTIONS YOU MAY HAVE ABOUT THE ARRANGEMENT CAN BE DIRECTED TOWARD SASQUATCH.

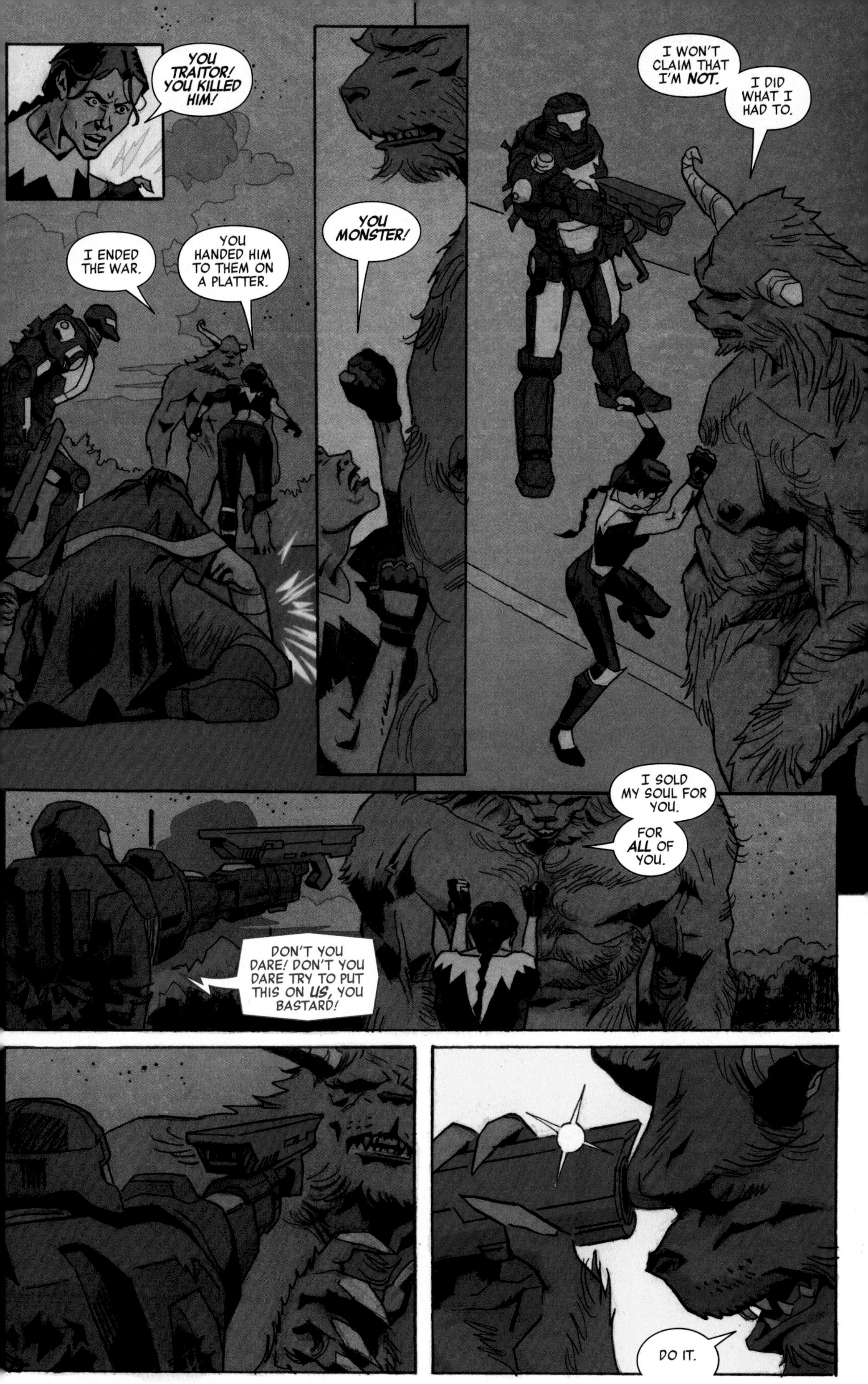
YOU TRAITOR! YOU KILLED HIM!
I ENDED THE WAR.
YOU HANDED HIM TO THEM ON A PLATTER.
YOU MONSTER!
I WON'T CLAIM THAT I'M NOT.
I DID WHAT I HAD TO.
I SOLD MY SOUL FOR YOU.
FOR ALL OF YOU.
DON'T YOU DARE! DON'T YOU DARE TRY TO PUT THIS ON US, YOU BASTARD!
DO IT.

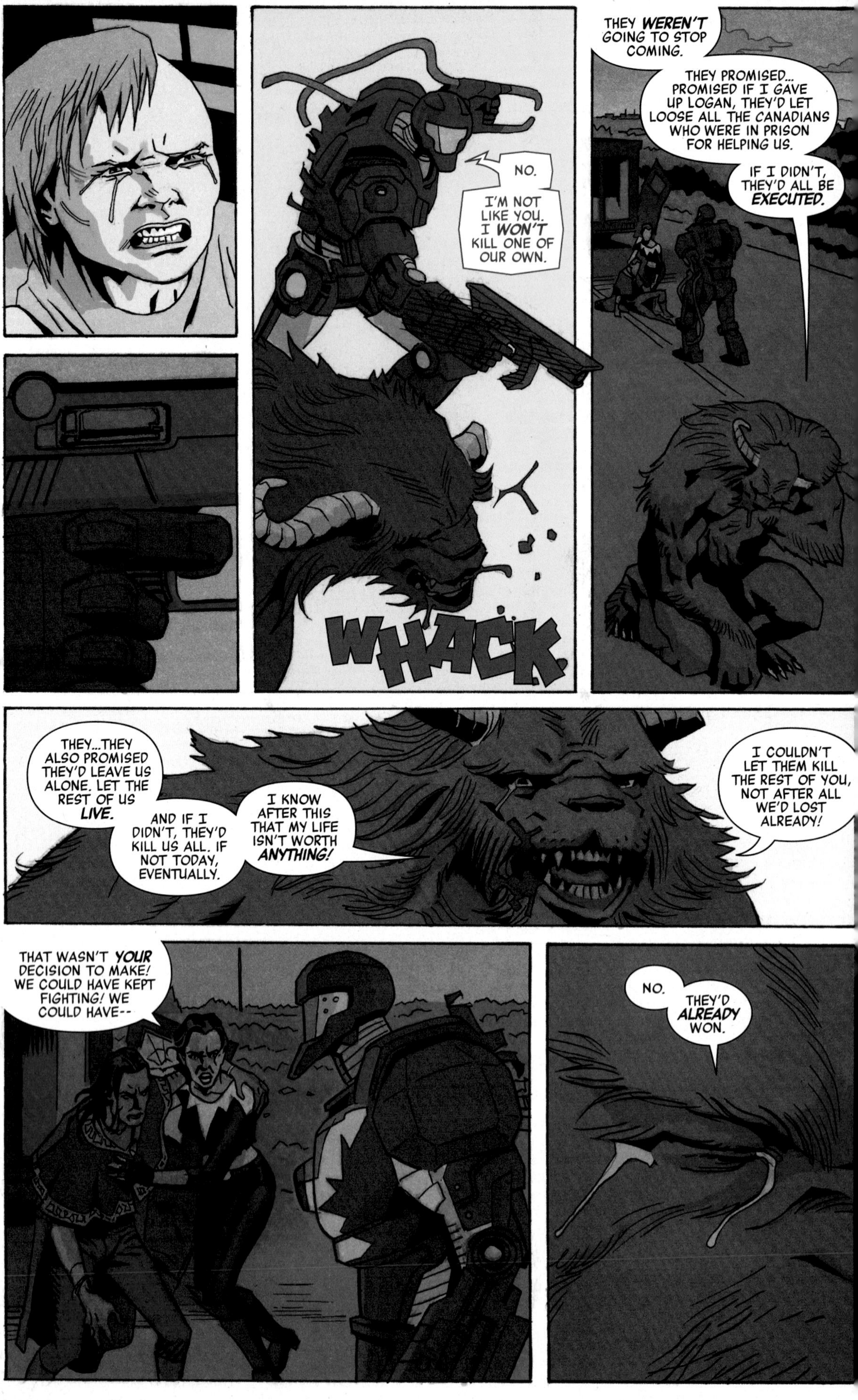
NO.
I'M NOT LIKE YOU. I WON'T KILL ONE OF OUR OWN.
WHACK
THEY WEREN'T GOING TO STOP COMING.
THEY PROMISED... PROMISED IF I GAVE UP LOGAN, THEY'D LET LOOSE ALL THE CANADIANS WHO WERE IN PRISON FOR HELPING US.
IF I DIDN'T, THEY'D ALL BE EXECUTED.
THEY...THEY ALSO PROMISED THEY'D LEAVE US ALONE. LET THE REST OF US LIVE.
AND IF I DIDN'T, THEY'D KILL US ALL. IF NOT TODAY, EVENTUALLY.
I KNOW AFTER THIS THAT MY LIFE ISN'T WORTH ANYTHING!
I COULDN'T LET THEM KILL THE REST OF YOU, NOT AFTER ALL WE'D LOST ALREADY!
THAT WASN'T YOUR DECISION TO MAKE! WE COULD HAVE KEPT FIGHTING! WE COULD HAVE--
NO.
THEY'D ALREADY WON.

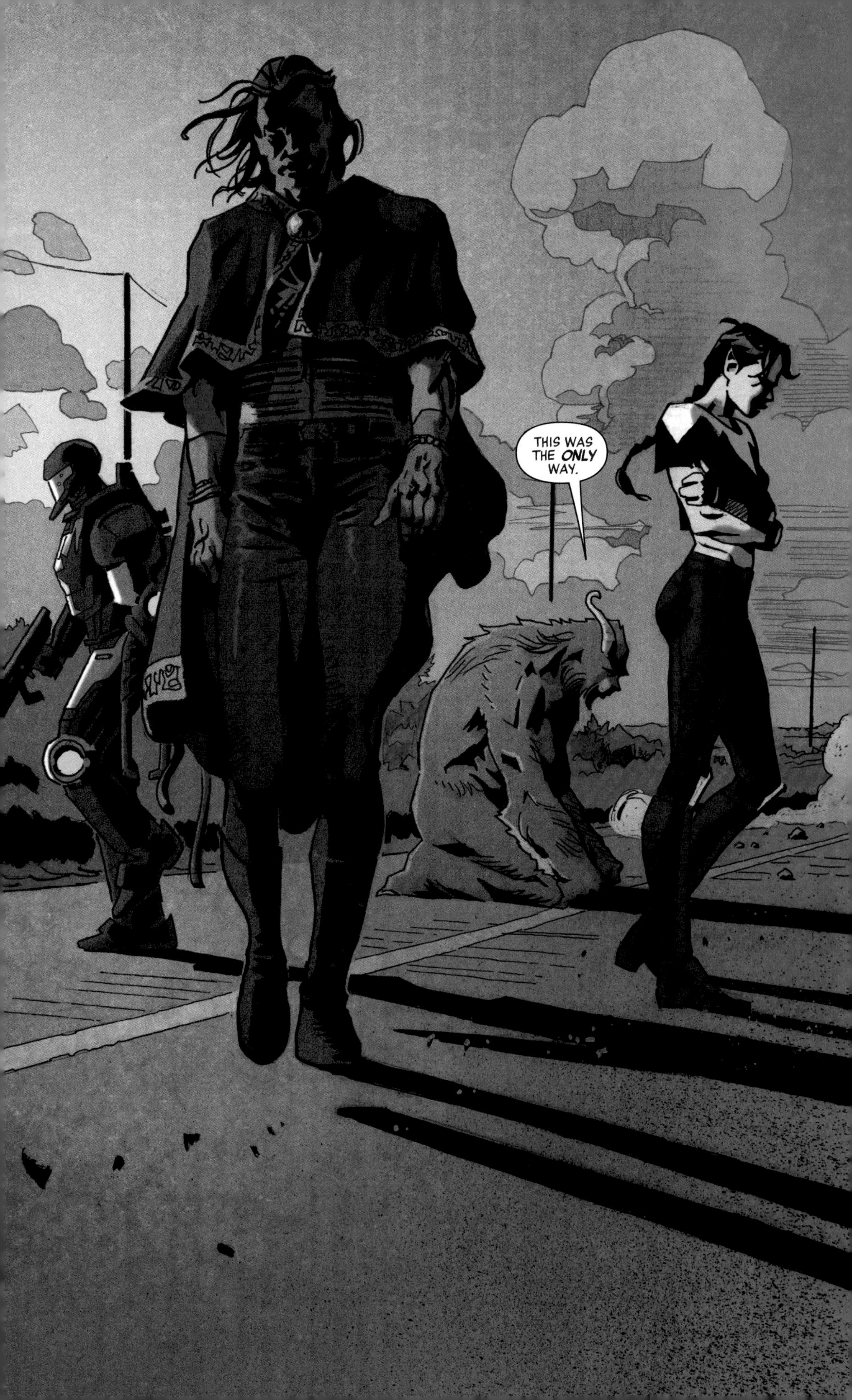
THIS WAS THE ONLY WAY.

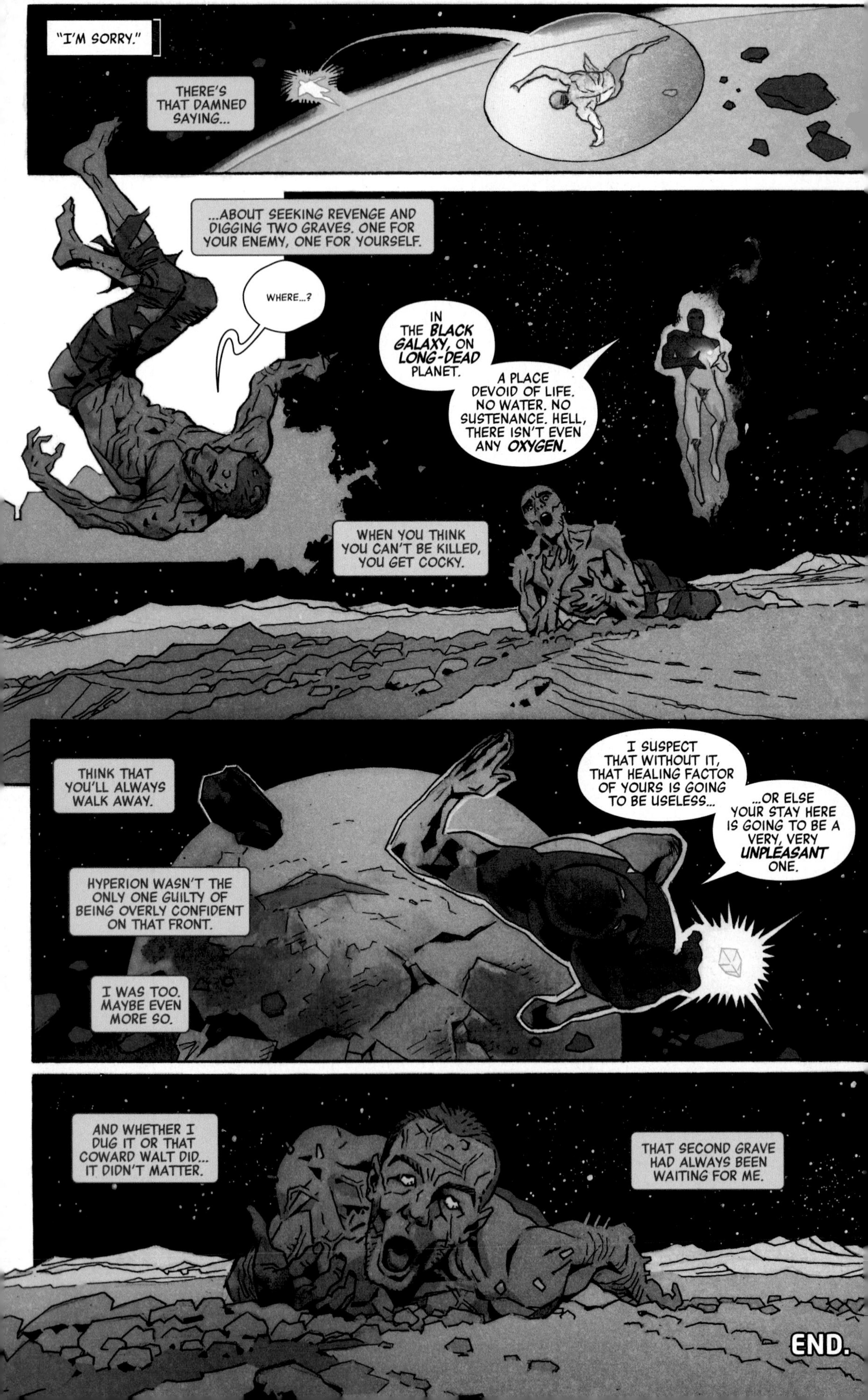

"I'M SORRY."
THERE'S THAT DAMNED SAYING...
...ABOUT SEEKING REVENGE AND DIGGING TWO GRAVES. ONE FOR YOUR ENEMY, ONE FOR YOURSELF.
WHERE...?
IN THE BLACK GALAXY, ON LONG-DEAD PLANET.
A PLACE DEVOID OF LIFE. NO WATER. NO SUSTENANCE. HELL, THERE ISN'T EVEN ANY OXYGEN.
WHEN YOU THINK YOU CAN'T BE KILLED, YOU GET COCKY.
THINK THAT YOU'LL ALWAYS WALK AWAY.
HYPERION WASN'T THE ONLY ONE GUILTY OF BEING OVERLY CONFIDENT ON THAT FRONT.
I WAS TOO. MAYBE EVEN MORE SO.
I SUSPECT THAT WITHOUT IT, THAT HEALING FACTOR OF YOURS IS GOING TO BE USELESS...
...OR ELSE YOUR STAY HERE IS GOING TO BE A VERY, VERY UNPLEASANT ONE.
AND WHETHER I DUG IT OR THAT COWARD WALT DID... IT DIDN'T MATTER.
THAT SECOND GRAVE HAD ALWAYS BEEN WAITING FOR ME.
END.

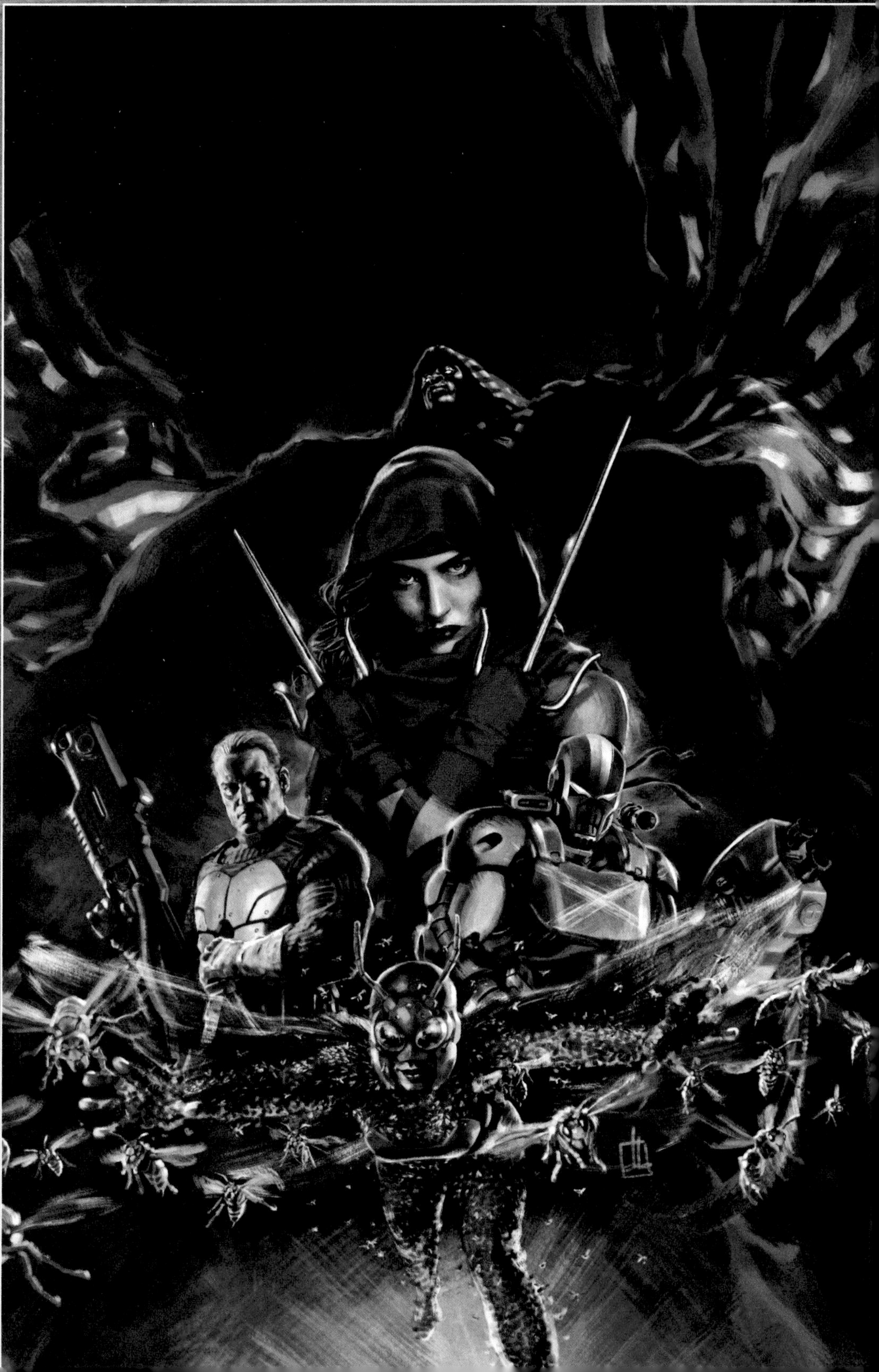

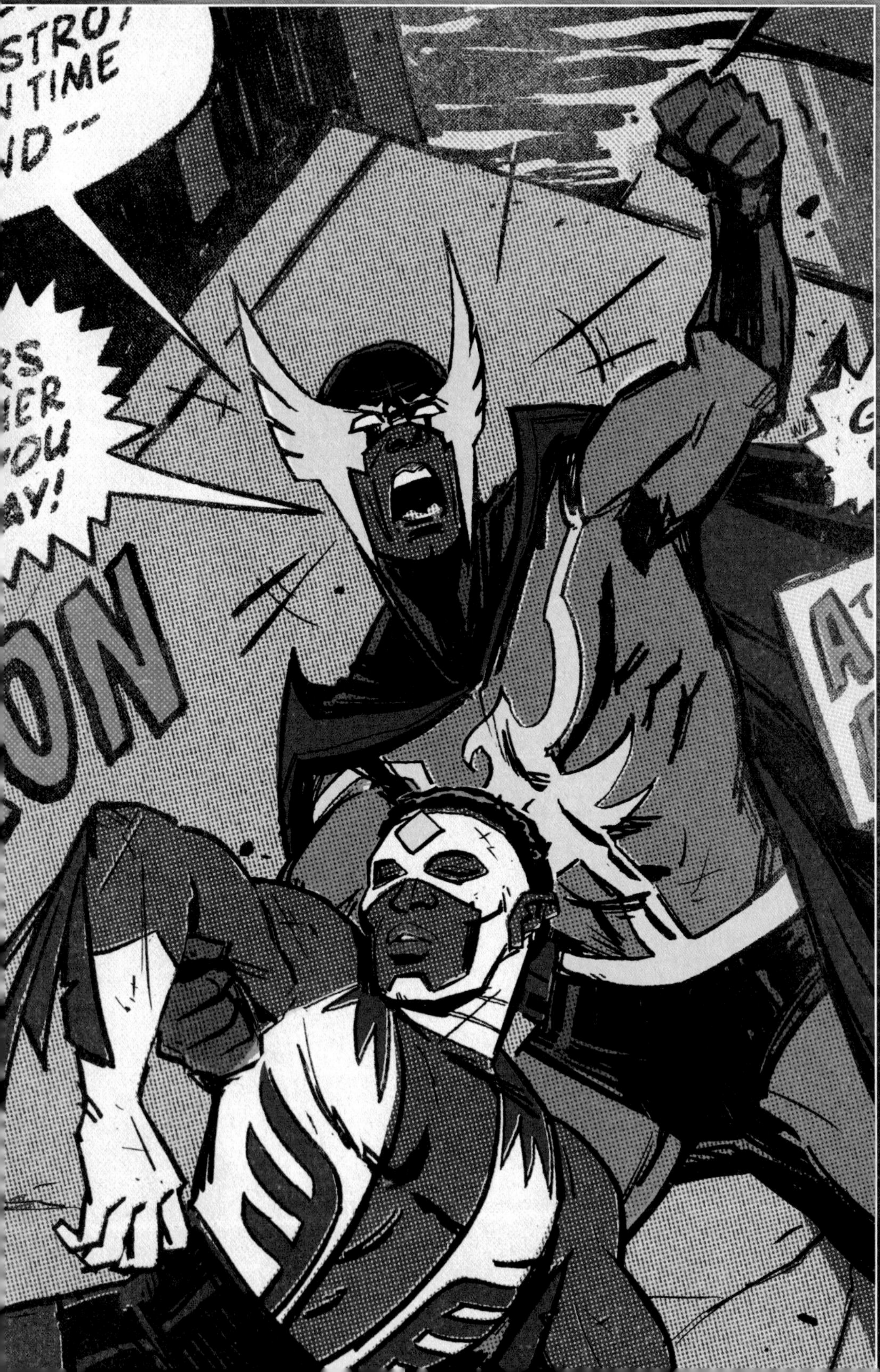

STRO!
N TIME
ND--
RS
HER
YOU
AY!
ON

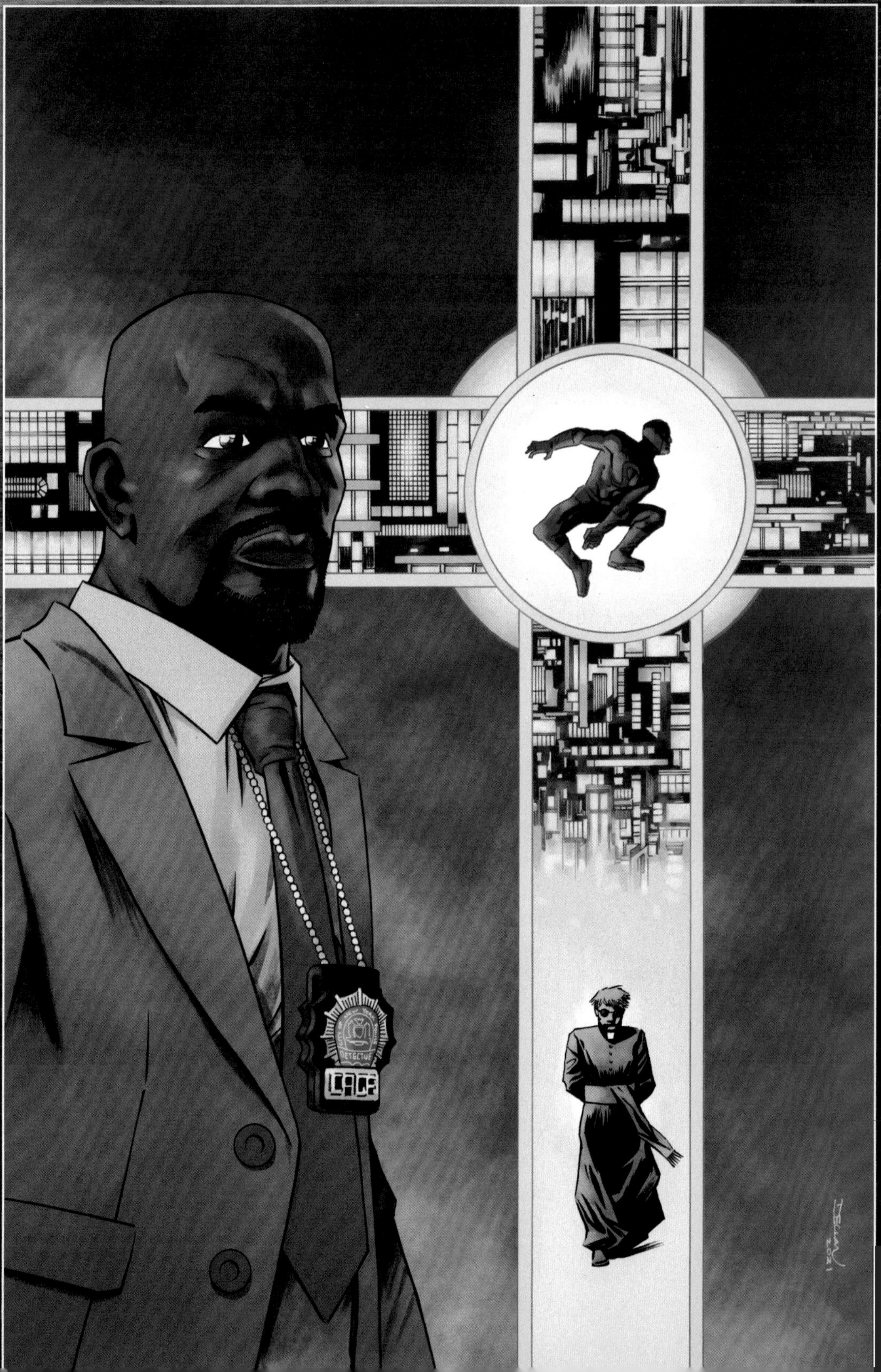
DETECTIVE
CAGE

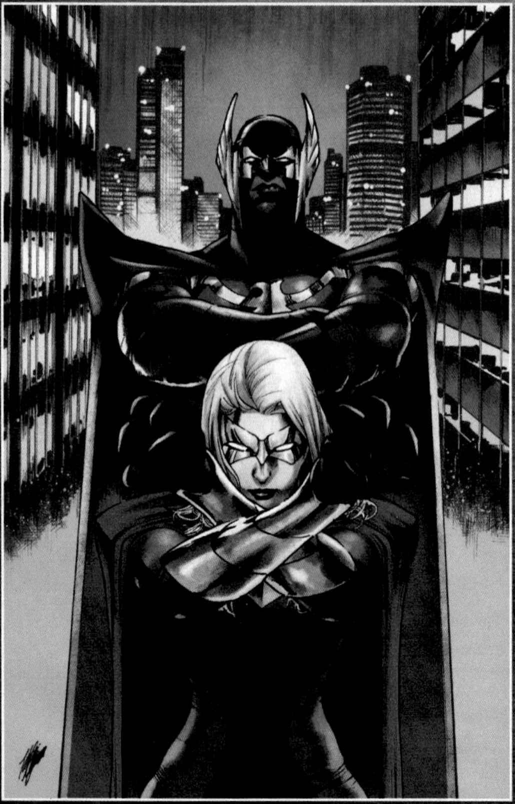

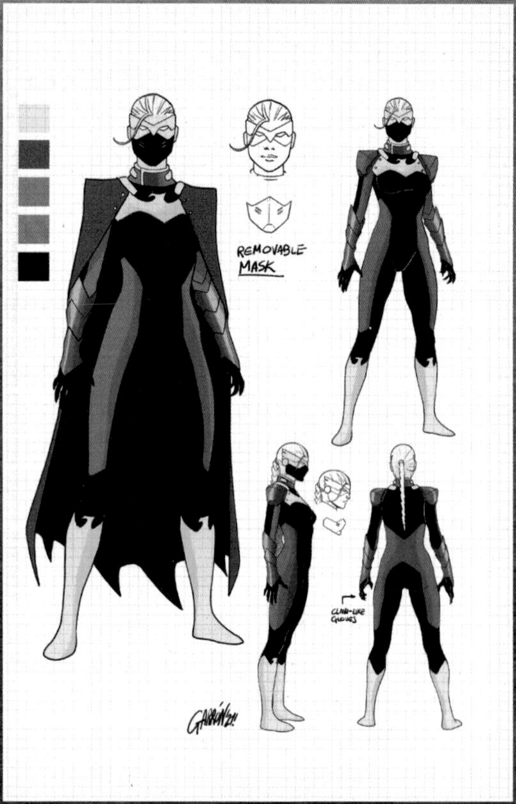
REMOVABLE MASK

TAKESHI **MIYAZAWA** & IAN **HERRING**
HEROES REBORN: NIGHT-GWEN Nº1 VARIANT

JAVIER **GARRÓN**
HEROES REBORN: NIGHT-GWEN Nº1 DESIGN VARIANT

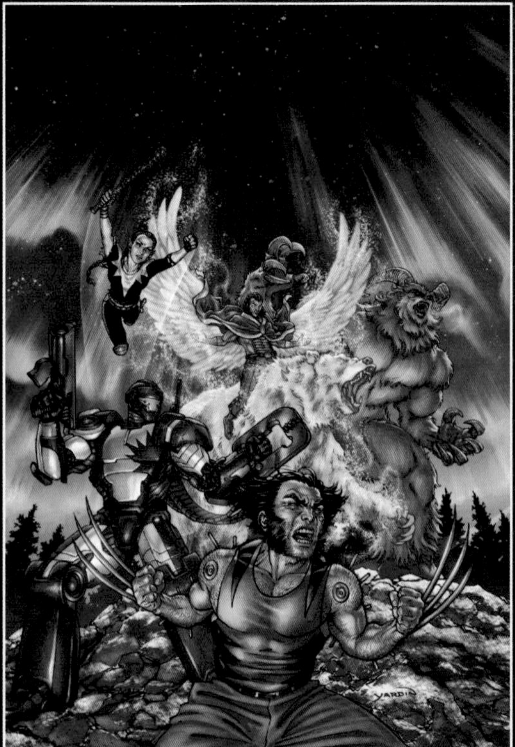